JOWETT'S
RAILWAY CENTRES
VOLUME I

JOWETT's

ATLAS OF RAILWAY CENTRES

of Great Britain showing their development from the
earliest times up to and including the 1990s

VOLUME I

Alan Jowett

Patrick Stephens Limited

First published in 1993

A catalogue record for this book is available from the British Library.

ISBN 1-85260-420-4

Patrick Stephens Limited is a member of the Haynes Publishing Group P.L.C., Sparkford, Nr Yeovil, Somerset, BA22 7JJ.

Lithographic Reproduction by Haynes Reprographics Limited
Printed by J.H. Haynes & Co. Ltd., Sparkford, Nr Yeovil, Somerset, BA22 7JJ.

10 9 8 7 6 5 4 3 2 1

CONTENTS

THE RAILWAY CENTRES   12

AUTHOR'S INTRODUCTION

My previous Railway Atlas published as Jowett's Railway Atlas of Great Britain + Ireland from pre-Grouping to the present day, did not have its title selected by me. My original choice of title was Pre-Grouping Railway Atlas of the British Isles, and if this had needed expansion it would have been more appropriate to add 'with the more up to date situation as at 1985'. It was not always possible to cover all developments from pre-grouping to the present day and there were two main reasons for that : First, available map information, since in most areas information was not availabe between 1928 and the late 1970s, so that if a station or a line both opened and closed within those dates it was not included. Secondly, and of more importance in the project, the inclusion of this information where it was available could obscure the prime purpose of the atlas which was to show clearly the pre-grouping position. This was particularly the case in complex and congested locations.

To show clearly the development of the railway network at complicated locations requires a series of maps. The maps also need to span a wider period of time to show the growth in the nineteenth century. Older maps have now been obtained covering both particular areas and the whole of Great Britain dating back to the beginnings of the railways to make production of this new atlas possible.

But one thing to remember about any map is this : A map is simply a snapshot and that in presenting in effect a series of snapshots it is still impossible to present a fully comprehensive cover of all events. There are other difficulties too in dating events from maps and some of these can be graphically illustrated by reference to a particular old map - Bradshaw's First Railway Map dated 1839. On this map, the railways are illustrated in three styles; constructed and under course of construction; authorised; and those projected. Historians are, of course, usually most interested in opening, but the map gives no information at all on this subject. In some cases it was several years before some of the railways shown as constructed (or in course of construction) were opened and in other cases they might never have reached that stage. But this type of difficulty is compounded by numerous other aspects of old maps: Quite often they are undated !. The reason for this was that with the dramatic expansion of the network in the early years a stock of maps was out of date in a few months and were added to at frequent intervals being issued to the public as completely up to date. This update process was often both inaccurate and contained omissions. Sometimes also to avoid frequent alterations anticipated routes and authorised routes were shown and inevitably some of these were not built or were built to an altered alignment. Even with the official Railway Clearing House the cartographers were dependent on the railways to keep the position up to date. This could result in information passed on being inexact or not passed on at all in addition to anticipated information often being included as noted above. Into this veritable minefield cartographers would at times inevitably misinterpret or mistranscribe correct information adding to the confusion besetting an historian, many years later, trying to ascertain a sequence of railway events.

Where possible, dates have been checked to other sources and where quoted, they are, unless stated otherwise, for opening to passengers. But even in this area diverse dates can occur as lines may have been in use both before and after official dates. Where then there is a conflict of dates a decision has had to be taken on which date to quote and it goes without saying that sometimes the decision taken will have been wrong.

Finally, in drawing the maps for the atlas, whilst every care will be taken, author errors are bound to occur either from some misunderstanding of the situation presented or through errors of transcription.

As I said in my previous atlas at the end of the Introduction: I hope you obtain as much enjoyment from this book as I am going to have in making it.

Alan Jowett
Bingley
March 1991

PREFACE

The primary objective of this work is to show in a series of maps how various Railway Centres developed from the earliest times to the present day.

Each Railway Centre is illustrated by a series of maps at a uniform scale, usually two miles to the inch. The number of maps used and the time interval between each map in the series varies dependent upon information available and also the times at which major development took place.

Within each series of maps there may also be one or more showing the area or the central part of the area at a larger scale. These maps usually show the area at its maximum development and sometimes include additional features including signal boxes and engineering features. Another innovation often incorporated into a selection of the maps in a series is the use of contours. This enables one to have a better understanding of route selection and helps to explain why some places enjoyed better facilities than others, due to local geographical features. Contours also highlight the location of viaducts and tunnels and explain why some lines took much longer to complete than others.

Accompanying each map on an adjoining page is a narrative commenting upon the events during the periods covered by the relative map or maps. The commentary will often include reference to proposed lines shown on the map including those schemes that were later abandoned. The railway network into the 1990's is entering a new phase. Following many years of rationalisation and obliteration, many major centres have seen, or proposals are being considered for, expansion of the local network with a series of Metro lines and the re-opening of suburban stations. Where possible information relative to these developments is sketched in on the map with indications of names and locations of projected new or re-opened previously closed stations.

The basic information contained in the maps is taken from Railway Clearing House maps and other railway maps of various ages and are all subject in some degree to the shortcomings outlined in the Author's Introduction. Where possible dates have been checked against other records. The Bibliography on page (ix) lists all the principal reference sources most of which are contained within the author's Railway Library.

It has been impossible to accommodate all railway centres suitable for this treatment within a single volume. This volume gives a wide geographical spread of centres and it is hoped that further volumes will follow. Selection of actual centres has also been governed by other factors. Most of the centres, as may be expected, are sizeable towns or cities, with a number of converging routes. But these two factors in themselves do not always qualify a centre for inclusion. For example, there are several places in Ireland with numerous lines radiating therefrom but connection between lines of different companies are few in Ireland which detracts from this type of presentation. For example, the development of a place such as Cork with a maze of lines to separate terminal stations could be adequately covered by one map showing opening and closing dates of lines and stations. In other areas where a railway grew to dominate an area this tended to stifle the wasteful duplication of routes where several companies were competing for the same traffic and this is often a factor in making these areas of less interest. Most of Scotland apart from the central waist is dominated by a single railway. Monoplies also existed throughout England's eastern counties. The most interesting centres therefore based on this criteria are mainly in the western half of England and in South Wales.

However, there are some country junctions served by a single railway that have interesting development histories and one such centre is included within this volume by way of contrast. There are also areas usually based on coalfields that have an interesting development in the competition to carry the coal traffic and that generated by associated industries. In some cases an extensive area can be covered by a network of lines lacking a single focal point. The atlas of Railway Centres includes therefore two areas within different coalfields illustrating the influence of coal in the development of the railway network.

The inclusion of London has also posed problems, not from an information point of view, but the complexities of continued development within a larger area necessitating the use of a larger scale. To cover everything would need an entire volume to itself. The solution, not entirely satisfactory, has been to include just a part of London within this volume. Further parts will follow in future volumes. Each part has been selected so far as is possible to make it so that it is self-contained, although some minor duplication particularly on the fringes of each area is inevitable.

Finally it is appropriate to briefly examine the entire railway network looking at the development periods, rationalisation and the Beeching report so that one can appreciate how closely the various centres represented the national pattern.

1776 – 1835 BIRTH PANGS The period opens with the incorporation of the Froghall Tramway and ends in a year in which London had no line carrying passengers yet open although construction of several lines was well under way.

1836 – 1851 THE MAIN LINE NETWORK IN PLACE. A surprisingly short period of just sixteen years saw this accomplished and the only areas of Great Britain outside the network were the North of Scotland and Central Wales. It is also worth noting the very great similarity of the network if all the Beeching proposals had been implemented and this development facet is often commented upon in looking at the individual centres.

1852 – 1914 INFILL TO A ZENITH During this period there was prodigous growth the chief part of which was concentrated in the 'mania' periods. But almost all this was infill of local and suburban lines whilst even lines described as trunk routes duplicated those already in place.

1915 – 1947 A STRUGGLE AGAINST COMPETITION This period saw the railways on a plateau in development. There were still new railways opening, together with many wayside unstaffed halts in competition with bus and tram services. But all these openings were balanced by closures to passengers of both country and suburban branches. A respite in the possibility of large-scale rationalisation came when the war and petrol shortages saw increased traffic using the railways. Following the end of the war and nationalisation there was a brief 'honeymoon period' due to continued petrol shortages lasting until 1950.

1948 – 1963 THE YEARS OF DECLINE This period of fifteen years saw a steady period of closures and concluded with the report by Dr. Beeching.

1964 – 1979 THE NADIR IN THE AFTERMATH OF BEECHING The start of this period saw implementation of a large proportion of the Beeching Report and it is worthwhile saying a few words about this. In spite of opinions to the contrary often expressed the report is well balanced and thoughtful with conclusions to fit the reasoning. It has one shortcoming in its failure to fully appreciate snowball effects and twenty years were to pass before taking action to redress that mistake. The report rightly calls attention to the heavy loss-makers being part wagon loads of short-haul freight and stopping passenger services. However, by the time the report was published the worst passenger loss-makers had gone, and as mentioned consideration on snowball effects was not considered in looking at the survivors. The situation can best be explained by looking at a suburban service between two large stations with five intermediate stations. The whole service is in profit, just, but two of the five stations make substantial losses, two make small profits and one a goodish profit. The Beeching proposal would be a modification of the service and closure of the two loss-makers. Now this is where the snowball effect comes into play. The two stations on marginal profits would loose the receipts coming from bookings to the stations now closed and they would become loss-makers resulting in closure which would then affect the surviving station, and the snowball does not stop there, it next affects the main stations not only in local traffic lost but in the greater proportion of track maintenance and the line signalling system carried by the main line service because quite often intermediate closures were not looked at on a marginal cost basis but share of total cost basis which could prove totally unrealistic. The correct solution in all these sort of cases was not even considered although used with some success by the Great Western between the wars; this was the use of unstaffed halts. In the above example it is quite clear that applying this solution would have cut costs whilst the receipts would be retained intact.

1980 onwards A MODEST REVIVAL During this last period there has been a steady policy of opening unstaffed halts usually jointly with local authority schemes to reduce their subsidy by increased receipts. But this solution is not always possible in cases where BR have sold the old station site and alternative sites available are not always convenient. Metro systems have been opened and Light Rapid Transit systems and the success of these in use has spawned a host of similar proposals elsewhere. Looking to other future developments: There are several schemes in London, both LT and main line, and further possibilities with cross-city links and the Channel Tunnel. Prospects for the future look hopeful.

BIBLIOGRAPHY

1. MAPS - RAILWAY CLEARING HOUSE + PREDECESSORS:
in the list which follows c before date shows map is undated
(A) after date indicates AIREY, (B) indicates BRADSHAW and (M) indicates
MACAULAY. No letter shows RCH own maps:
- GREAT BRITAIN: 1839(B), 1842 (Walker), 1854(M), c1860(M with additions), c1876(M).
- SCOTLAND: 1849(M), 1879(A), 1891(A), 1907, 1927.
- ENGLAND + WALES: 1884(A), 1899, 1915, 1917, 1926, 1940.
- SOUTH: ?(B - additions make map impossible to date).
- EDINBURGH + GLASGOW: 1898
- CUMBERLAND + WESTMORLAND: 1912.
- DURHAM + DISTRICT: 1914
- LANCASHIRE + DISTRICT: 1879(A), 1901.
- MANCHESTER DISTRICT: 1881(A), 1911.
- YORKSHIRE DISTRICT: 1885(A), North -1921, South -1923.
- STAFFORDSHIRE DISTRICT: 1898, 1918.
- DERBY + NOTTINGHAM DISTRICT: 1889(A).
- SOUTH WALES: 1899, 1926.
- GLOUCESTERSHIRE + OXFORDSHIRE DISTRICT: 1911.
- EAST OF ENGLAND: 1917.
- WEST OF ENGLAND: 1889(A), 1918, 1924.
- LONDON + ENVIRONS: 1891(A), 1910, 1927.
- SOUTH OF ENGLAND: 1906.
- JUNCTION DIAGRAMS: 1914, 1915, 1928.

2. OTHER MAP SOURCES:
GWR and connections in the British Isles 1910
MIDLAND - DISTANCE DIAGRAMS c 1922
RAIL ATLAS - BRITAIN (+ IRELAND) 1977, 1984, 1988, 1990 - Baker (published by OPC).
BRITISH RAILWAYS PREGROUPING 1922 (Ian Allan).
SECTIONAL MAPS OF BRITISH RAILWAYS 1947 (Ian Allan).
ATLAS OF GWR - RA Cooke 1947 (WSP published 1988)
BARTHOLOMEWS SURVEY ATLAS - England + Wales 1938.
MASTER ATLAS OF GREATER LONDON - 1990 (Geographer).
MODERN HOME ATLAS (George Philip).
L+Y DIAGRAM showing WIDENINGS AUTHORISED + CONSTRUCTED -1914.
VILLAGE ATLAS SERIES (2" to mile OS maps of 19th c) (published by Alderman Press):
- DERBYSHIRE, NOTTINGHAMSHIRE, LEICESTERSHIRE.
- LONDON
- MANCHESTER, LANCASHIRE + NORTH CHESHIRE.
- NORTH + WEST YORKSHIRE.
- BIRMINGHAM + WEST MIDLANDS.

3. SPECIALIST REFERENCE PUBLICATIONS:
RCH HANDBOOK OF STATIONS: 1904, 1908
GWR ROUTES, STATUTES, OPENING DATES + OTHER PARTICULARS (reprint by Avon-Anglia Publications).
MIDLAND RAILWAY - A CHRONOLOGY - John Gough (Gough)
LNER - LISTS OF LINES WITH ACTS + DATES OF OPENING (Avon-Anglia Publications)
RAILWAYS OF WEST MIDLANDS - A CHRONOLOGY 1808-1954 (published by The Stephenson Locomotive Society).
CHRONOLOGICAL LIST OF RAILWAYS OF LANCASHIRE 1828-1939. M D Greville (Historical Society of Lancashire).
RAILWAY HISTORICAL SOURCES - Clinker (Avon-Anglia).
LNER - ROUTES, RUNNING POWERS, WORKING ARRANGEMENTS + JOINT RAILWAYS (Avon-Anglia).
A LONDON CHRONOLOGY - H V Borley (Canal and Railway Historical Society)
A CHRONOLOGY OF THE CONSTRUCTION OF BRITAINS RAILWAYS 1778 -1855 - Leslie James (Ian Allan).
CLINKERS REGISTER OF CLOSED STATIONS - Clinker (Avon-Anglia)
GWR DOCKS 1939.
THE RE-SHAPING OF BRITISH RAILWAYS -1963- BEECHING REPORT (HMSO)
ENCYCLOPAEDIA OF BRITISH RAILWAY COMPANIES - C Awdry (PSL)
TIMETABLES: Various company timetables and working timetables,
- BRADSHAWS from 1840 (available at NRM YORK).
- BRITISH RAILWAYS 1984 - 1991

4. REGIONAL HISTORY OF RAILWAYS OF GREAT BRITAIN (David + Charles)

Vol	Region	Author
1	THE WEST COUNTRY	St. John Thomas
2	SOUTHERN ENGLAND	White
3	GREATER LONDON	White
4	THE NORTH EAST	Hoole
5	THE EASTERN COUNTIES	Gordon
6	SCOTLAND - THE LOWLANDS + BORDERS	Thomas
7	THE WEST MIDLANDS	Christiansen
8	SOUTH + WEST YORKSHIRE	Joy
9	THE EAST MIDLANDS	Leleux
10	THE NORTH WEST	Holt
11	NORTH + MID WALES	Baughan
12	SOUTH WALES	Barrie
13	THAMES + SEVERN	Christiansen
14	THE LAKE COUNTIES	Joy

5. FORGOTTEN RAILWAYS: (David + Charles)

2	EAST MIDLANDS	Anderson
6	SOUTH-EAST ENGLAND	White
7	EAST ANGLIA	Joby
8	SOUTH WALES	Page
10	WEST MIDLANDS	Christiansen
11	SEVERN VALLEY + WELSH BORDER	Christiansen

6. COMPANY HISTORIES:
GREAT WESTERN (Reprint - Ian Allan)

Vol 1	1833 - 1863	MacDermot + Clinker
Vol 2	1863 - 1921	MacDermot + Clinker
Vol 3	1923 - 1947	Nock

SOUTHERN — Marshall + Kidner (Ian Allan)
METROPOLITAN — Jackson (David + Charles)
MIDLAND NORTH OF LEEDS — Baughan (David + Charles)
NORTH EASTERN — Tomlinson + Hoole (David + Charles)
GREAT CENTRAL — Dow (Ian Allan)

Vol 1	1813 - 1863	THE PROGENITORS
Vol 2	1864 - 1899	DOMINION OF WATKIN
Vol 3	1900 - 1922	FAY SETS THE PACE

LONDON'S UNDERGROUND — Howson (Ian Allan)
THE METROPOLITAN DISTRICT — Lee (Oakwood Press)
THE CITY + SOUTH LONDON — Lascelles (Oakwood Press)
WEST LONDON + WL EXTENSION — Borley + Kidner (Oakwood Press)

7. ENGINE SHEDS:
GREAT WESTERN
- 1947 — Lyons (OPC)
- 1837 -1947 — Lyons + Mountford (OPC)
- London Division — Hawkins + Reeve (WSP)
SOUTHERN — Hawkins + Reeve (OPC)
LONDON MIDLAND + SCOTTISH — Hawkins + Reeve (WSP)
- Vol 1 LNW
- Vol 2 Midland
- Vol 3 L+Y
- Vol 4 Smaller English Constituents
- Vol 5 Caledonian
LONDON + NORTH EASTERN
- Great Eastern Part I — Hawkins + Reeve (WSP)
- Great Eastern Part II — Hawkins + Reeve (WSP)
- Great Northern Vol — Griffiths + Hooper (IP)

8. OTHERS:
PSL FIELD GUIDES — Body (PSL)
- WESTERN REGION, SOUTHERN REGION, EASTERN REGION VOLS 1 + 2 (Eastern Region 1 includes the new ANGLIA region).
THE RAILWAY HISTORY OF LINCOLN — Ruddock + Pearson (Ruddock).
PICTORIAL RECORD OF LNWR SIGNALLING — Foster (OPC)
LONDON'S TERMINI — Jackson (David + Charles)
LONDON + ITS RAILWAYS — Davies + Grant (David + Charles).
THE EXE VALLEY RAILWAY — Owen (Kingfisher)
GWR THE BADMINTON LINE — Robertson + Abbot (Alan Sutton)
CANALS OF THE WELSH VALLEYS — Gladwin + Gladwin (Oakwood)
INLAND WATERWAYS OF GT BRITAIN — Edward (Imray).

KEY TO SYMBOLS USED ON MAPS

 **LINE** with passenger **STATION** Lines are normally shown in black outline, but, RED or GREEN is sometimes used to distinguish BR Goods lines, to highlight specific development, to show LT lines or Metro systems.

HALT/UNSTAFFED STATION Only distinguished on maps prior to nationalisation.

 **GOODS ONLY STATION** Ex passenger station changed to goods only station since previous map. The blue and red underlining shows station open for goods, but line all traffic, a double blue underline shows line goods only

NEW LINES PROJECTED On post nationalisation maps this style also used for completed new lines

CLOSED LINES

 **ENGINE SHED** (if symbol not used the exact site is unclear); **JUNCTION** ; **FLAT CROSSINGS**

CANAL

TUNNEL (length if shown is in yards); **VIADUCT** ; **BRIDGE**

SIDING (side of line indicated); **SIDING** (side of line not known); **SIGNAL BOX**

DALKEITH — **OPEN STATION**

(PORTOBELLO 1846) **STATION OPENED SINCE PREVIOUS MAP** – Date of opening, if known, included bracketed

Canonmills (SCOTLAND STREET) **NAME CHANGE** - the later name is in brackets (IF LATER NAME IN CAPITALS STATION STILL OPEN AT MAP DATE)

St Leonards 1860 Station closed to passengers from date shown. Now Goods station. Just one blue underline indicates line reduced to goods only + station **may** have continued to handle goods

(Jock's Lodge) 1848 Station opened + Closed during map period – date is closure date – opening date if certain would be included within brackets. The red underlining indicates line remained open for all traffic

● Corstorphine 1967 Closed all traffic – closure date shown

○ Craiglockhart 1962 Closed to passengers on date shown - line retained for goods traffic

FEATURES ON MAPS ARE USUALLY COLOUR CODED. THE LIST FOLLOWING INDICATES THE NORMAL RELATIONSHIP OF COLOURS TO FEATURES

BLACK	LINES, PASSENGER STATIONS
RED	SIGNAL BOXES, LT + METRO STATIONS, HIGHLIGHTING NEW FEATURES as alternative to normal colour
DARK BLUE	GOODS ONLY STATION NAMES
PALE BLUE	CANALS, WATER FEATURES
GREEN	JUNCTION NAMES
VIOLET	TUNNELS, VIADUCTS ETC
PINK	NAMES OF RAILWAYS
BROWN	SIDINGS

Other symbols used occasionally are explained on the individual maps

SCALE: 1:4M

CARLISLE

CARLISLE as a railway centre is one of the most complicated of all locations outside London. Although it did not have a complex structure of branch and suburban lines as did such places as Edinburgh, Glasgow, Newcastle, Liverpool and similar other centres of large population, it was nevertheless the meeting place of no less than seven main lines and each line was owned by an entirely independant company. In fact the only amalgamations related to the absorption or construction of branch lines, all strangely enough affecting only one company, the North British. This network was completely in place by 1862 with the sole exception of the Midland's Settle-Carlisle line which did not open for passenger traffic until 1876. The main line network was intact until 1969 although all the branch lines had already closed before that date.

But this is only the smaller part of the story. The complication resulting from seven companies plus three joint undertakings tells its own story with each company having its own engine shed and one or more goods depôts. Grouping did result in some rationalisation of locomotive facilities but all that happened on the goods side was some name changes to avoid confusion between depôts now under the same management. It is recorded that during the war a goods train working from one Carlisle Depôt to another did 2 miles in 7½ hours. Nationalisation initially had if anything a negative effect since two grouping companies became three regions and it was into the 'sixties before common sense prevailed but by then it was almost too late. Even in the 1990's and inspite of the new KINGMOOR yard wagon loads are still dealt with at London Road, one can only suppose because it serves another region.

To illustrate the development of this unique location two series of maps are used. The first series follows the general way centres are illustrated at the standard scale of 2 miles to the inch; these maps show the growth and rationalisation of the area, its trunk lines, branches and wayside stations. The second series shows the step-by-step development of the centre forming a fascinating kaleidoscope of enterprise, frustration, sharp practice, waste, manipulation and apathy.
There is also a maximum development map of the central area showing engine sheds and signal Boxes. Two other special maps are also included, one showing the signalling rationalisation with the commissioning of the Carlisle Power Box in 1973 with one box covering the entire general map area, and beyond it. In fact an interesting question to ask about present day signalling might be — how many signal boxes are there between Motherwell and Preston? The answer, just one at Carlisle. The other special map is a strip map of the Settle-Carlisle line showing Tunnels, Sidings, Viaducts, Signal Boxes besides all stations and connections with other railways.

A brief commentary relates to each map, but with some of the central area maps it appeared appropriate to give dates and events in chronological order to give clarity to the series of events highlighting the development from one map to the next. Also included on the narrative pages are charts: highlighting company history with regard to formation, opening, take overs and name changes; and showing development of both goods and locomotive facilities. However, in the two latter cases early details are not always available or fully accurate.

In compiling this chapter on Carlisle some forty-five different reference sources have been consulted mainly to check on dates; most of these are general works or maps which have also been used with other centres and are included in the Bibliography. The following supplementary items however relate to Carlisle alone:

Title	Author	Publisher
Two-way Guide to the SETTLE LINE	James R Wood	White Frog Productions
Carlisle at Night	Robert H Foster	Railway World June 1981
Rail Centres CARLISLE	Peter W Robinson	Ian Allan
CARLISLE (CITADEL) Railway Scene	G G Dorman	George Allen + Unwin
The Midland Railway North of Leeds	Peter E Baughan	David + Charles
Stations + Structures of the SETTLE + CARLISLE RAILWAY	V R Anderson + G K Fox	OPC
The Midland Railway Settle to Carlisle (Folding Map)	Alan Jowett	not published

Researching Carlisle has been a fascinating and interesting experience and sometimes surprising also. The greatest suprise awaiting was to discover that most of the early chaos and bad relationships resulted from a brief foray into the Carlisle scene by the infamous 'railway king' George Hudson and for the only time in the border city's history until the grouping Carlisle had a through line in the sole management of one company, even though this was the York Newcastle + Berwick!

LINES TO CARLISLE

This may in some respects appear a strange subheading for the general maps relating to Carlisle but with quite minor exceptions Carlisle in its formative years was an objective in railway terms rather than a starting point. A glance at the names of the early companies serves to confirm this; the Newcastle + Carlisle, Maryport + Carlisle and Lancaster + Carlisle were the first three railways to reach the border town. Carlisle of course was in fact a natural meeting point of the English + Scottish companies in establishing through routes and it was also a limit of penetration. In fact no English Company reached Scotland except through joint lines and although both the North British + Caledonian established lines into England (apart from Carlisle) these were unremunerative branches and never paid their way.

UP TO 1845

The first event of significance was the opening in 1823 of the CARLISLE CANAL from a basin on the northwest side of the city to Fisher Cross (later renamed Port Carlisle). Although this seems a strange opening to a railway saga, it was an event that was to have a profound effect on the railway development which would follow and in due course it was later to be converted to a railway. The canal was purely a local venture to enable produce from Carlisle and district to reach the sea as at that time coastwise shipping gave the most rapid transport.

Following this there was a desire to connect Carlisle + Newcastle by canal or railway thus enabling coal from the area near Brampton to reach Carlisle for onward transmission to the coast via the Carlisle Canal to the benefit of the latter's revenues. The link was surveyed in 1824 for both canal and railway, the estimated cost of the railway being about £250,000 whilst a canal would have cost three times as much. In spite of this early activity the NEWCASTLE-UPON-TYNE + CARLISLE RAILWAY (usually — Newcastle + Carlisle) was not incorporated until 1829. The Carlisle portion opened in 1836 and it was opened throughout in 1838. Connection with the canal increased the latter's revenues and profitability. The opening of the wayside stations in the area closest to Carlisle all appear to have opened with the Carlisle terminal station in 1836. One final oddity was that the N+C trains used the right hand road and continued to do so until conversion to the left in the early 1960's !

The final development in this early period was the arrival of the Maryport + Carlisle. The company in view of its comparitively short length took a long time to make any progress. It was incorporated in 1837 and it was three years before the section Maryport to Aspatria was opened; a further three years passed before the next section Wigton to Carlisle was opened and even then it was only a single line. It was not in fact until 1845 that it was opened throughout and a further ten years would pass before the line was doubled over its full course. With the opening throughout of this railway the death knell was sounded for the Carlisle Canal but the interesting but futile results of this took place during the next period.

1846 TO 1855

The next railway to reach Carlisle was the LANCASTER and CARLISLE. This company incorporated in June 1844 and reached Carlisle in 1846. Originally the Newcastle + Carlisle station was used but Citadel station was brought into use the following year. A wayside station was opened at Brisco but closed in 1852 and was replaced the following year by a station at Wreay just beyond the southern limits of the map.

The CALEDONIAN was the next railway to open. This was authorised in 1845 and the section Beattock to Carlisle was open coincidentally with the opening of Citadel station in September 1847. It was opened to both Glasgow + Edinburgh in 1848, its rapid development contrasting sharply with the lethargic Maryport + Carlisle noted above. Wayside stations were opened at Gretna, Floriston and Rockcliffe in the area covered by the map.

Both 1846 and 1847 had seen a new railway reach Carlisle and 1848 continued that pattern. The Glasgow Dumfries + Carlisle Railway had been incorporated in 1846 and opened between Dumfries + Gretna where it made a junction with the Caledonian There was an intermediate station at Gretna Green. This railway amalgamated with the Glasgow, Paisley, Kilmarnock + Ayr in 1850 to become GLASGOW + SOUTH WESTERN. Running powers over the Caledonian Railway into Citadel became effective from 1851. Being dissatisfied, and seeking an independant route into England, in 1853 powers were sought for a branch to Brampton on the Newcastle + Carlisle but these failed.

The final railway development during this period concerns the Carlisle Canal. As mentioned earlier the opening of the Maryport + Carlisle Railway had sounded the death knell of this locally inspired concern. With the local support of the town it was decided a railway was needed and so in the summer of 1853 the PORT CARLISLE RAILWAY was incorporated with the purpose of converting the canal to a railway. The canal was closed and drained and the resultant railway then constructed following the old canal. There was a deviation at Kirkandrews but this was probably not far so long a stretch as the map shows. The line was level but with short steep grades, the site of former locks, and had many sharp curves. It proved a failure to tranship goods; the superior Maryport facilities ensured its continued demise. On opening intermediate stations at Drumburgh + Burgh were opened, stations at Kirkandrews + Glasson being opened soon afterwards. The whole line was opened in just over nine months from authorisation.

So by the end of 1855 there were trains of six different companies running into Carlisle; meanwhile the NORTH BRITISH were looking to extend their line from Hawick to reach Carlisle but this was a difficult territory for the construction of a railway with little prospect of intermediate traffic, not to mention the obstruction tactics of the 'Caley'.

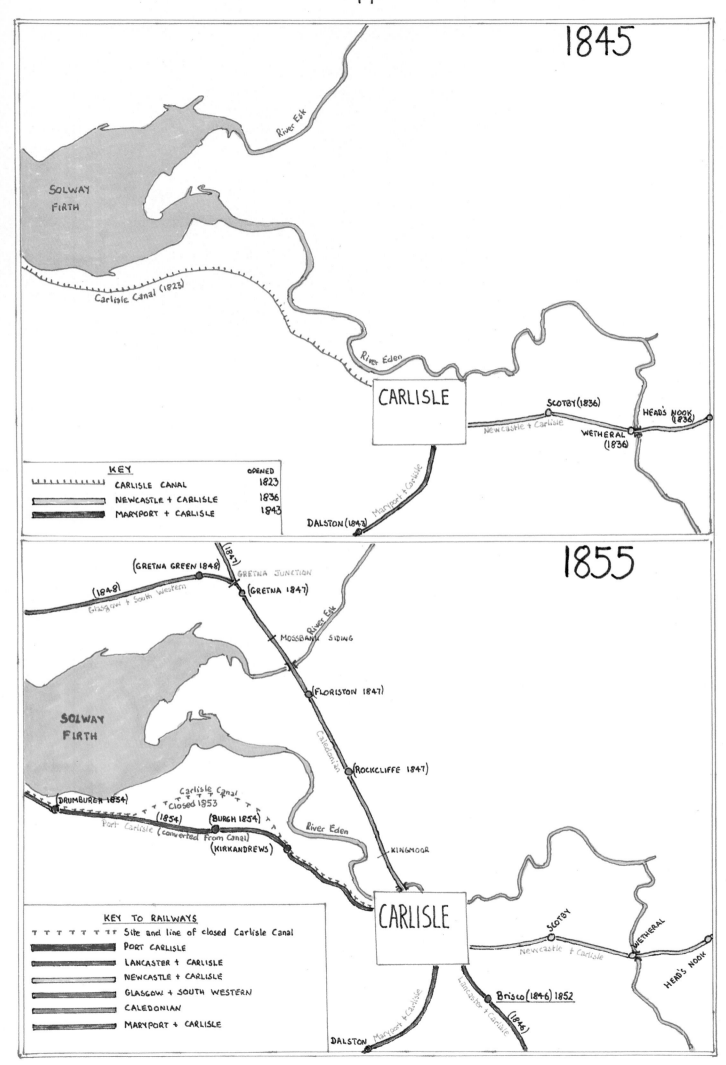

1845

SOLWAY FIRTH

River Esk

Carlisle Canal (1823)

River Eden

CARLISLE

SCOTBY (1836)

Newcastle + Carlisle

WETHERAL (1836)

HEAD'S NOOK (1836)

Maryport + Carlisle

DALSTON (1843)

KEY   OPENED
CARLISLE CANAL   1823
NEWCASTLE + CARLISLE   1836
MARYPORT + CARLISLE   1843

1855

(1847)

(GRETNA GREEN 1848)   Gretna Junction

(1848)   (GRETNA 1847)
Glasgow + South Western

River Esk

MOSSBAND SIDING

SOLWAY FIRTH

FLORISTON 1847)

Caledonian

ROCKCLIFFE 1847)

Carlisle Canal
Closed 1853

DRUMBURGH 1854)

(1854)   (BURGH 1854)

Port Carlisle (converted from Canal)   River Eden

(KIRKANDREWS)

KINGMOOR

CARLISLE

SCOTBY

Newcastle + Carlisle

WETHERAL

HEAD'S NOOK

KEY TO RAILWAYS
T T T T T T T T Site and line of closed Carlisle Canal
PORT CARLISLE
LANCASTER + CARLISLE
NEWCASTLE + CARLISLE
GLASGOW + SOUTH WESTERN
CALEDONIAN
MARYPORT + CARLISLE

Maryport + Carlisle

Lancaster + Carlisle

Brisco (1846) 1852

(1846)

DALSTON

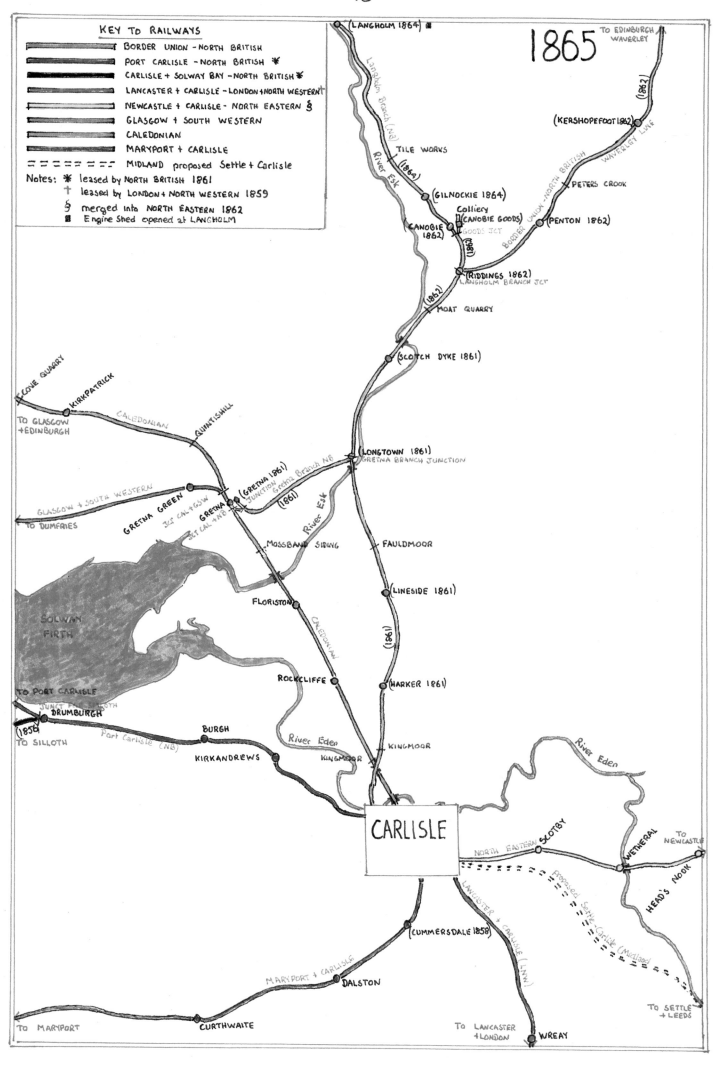

1865

KEY TO RAILWAYS

BORDER UNION - NORTH BRITISH
PORT CARLISLE - NORTH BRITISH ✳
CARLISLE + SOLWAY BAY - NORTH BRITISH ✳
LANCASTER + CARLISLE - LONDON + NORTH WESTERN †
NEWCASTLE + CARLISLE - NORTH EASTERN §
GLASGOW + SOUTH WESTERN
CALEDONIAN
MARYPORT + CARLISLE
MIDLAND proposed Settle + Carlisle

Notes: ✳ leased by NORTH BRITISH 1861
† leased by LONDON + NORTH WESTERN 1859
§ merged into NORTH EASTERN 1862
▪ Engine Shed opened at LANGHOLM

LINES TO CARLISLE

1856 TO 1865 Most of the railway development within this period was related to the NORTH BRITISH or to lines that it would ultimately absorb. In chronological order the first event was the opening of the CARLISLE + SILLOTH BAY RAILWAY on 28th of August 1856. This railway had obtained its Act in July 1855 in spite of strong opposition from the Maryport + Carlisle. It was promoted by similar interest and parties involved in the Port Carlisle Railway and though nominally independant the two concerns were soon to be run by a joint committee. With little traffic finding its way into the Port Carlisle backwater it was thought that Silloth could develop into a convenient outlet, being more accessible to shipping than Port Carlisle and closer to Carlisle than Maryport by land. Realising that coastwise traffic, which in any case was declining, might not be lured from Maryport, the site at Silloth was developed as a holiday resort. Although it saw modest traffic it never realised its expectations and in the meantime the Port Carlisle Railway became a branch of its junior partner.

North British ambitions to reach Carlisle have already been noted. In 1857 and 1858 both the Caledonian + North British presented proposals for links between Hawick and Carlisle. Both failed. But in 1859 the Border Union NORTH BRITISH scheme was authorised. Scotch Dyke to both Carlisle and Gretna opened in 1861 and the full 'Waverley' route completed the following year. Stations at Harker, Lineside, Longtown, Scotch Dyke and Gretna (where a junction facing North was made with the Caledonian by the branch from Longtown) were all opened in 1861. With full opening in 1862 stations were opened at Riddings, Penton, Kershopefoot and Canobie. This last station was the first on a proposed branch to Langholm and its early opening was no doubt clue to the hope of colliery traffic. The rest of the branch opened in 1864 with stations at Gilnockie and Langholm. In the meantime in 1862 the North British leased the Port Carlisle and Carlisle + Silloth Bay railways which both in effect became part of the North British. These were fully absorbed but not until 1880.

Two other development events can be noted, first the opening of Cummersdale station on the Maryport + Carlisle. The other event was promotion of the Settle - Carlisle line by the MIDLAND. This would obtain its Act in 1866 but would not open to passengers until '76.

A FAMILY TREE OF CARLISLE'S RAILWAYS

Note: Companies which were ultimately to become grouped are 'boxed' thus ⌷NORTH BRITISH⌷ including name changes by leasing, absorbing or merging. ACT shows incorporation, and line construction ACT when different. Opening is for passengers and refers to lines only in the map area. Opening is ALL lines unless specified (but only those portions in the map area).

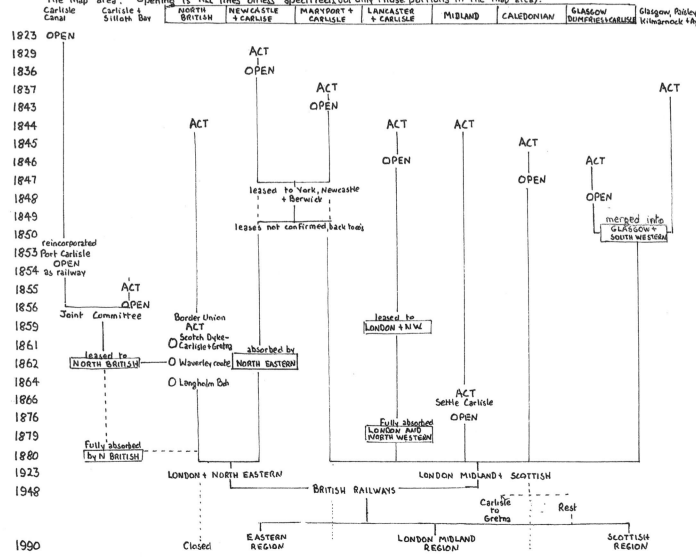

LINES TO CARLISLE

1866 TO 1880 The only addition to the network of lines to Carlisle during this period was the opening of the MIDLAND Settle-Carlisle line which opened throughout to all traffic in 1876 having already opened to goods services during the previous year. In the map area two intermediate stations were opened co-incidentally with the opening of the line, these being located at Scotby and Cumwhinton.

The only other events of any note related to the full absorption of leased lines etc. Before this period began an absorption can be noted. The Newcastle + Carlisle had been merged into the North Eastern in 1862. In 1879 Lancaster + Carlisle was fully absorbed into the London + North Western having been leased and under the effective control of the latter company for twenty years. Then in 1880 North British fully absorbed the two Cumbrian companies Port Carlisle and Carlisle and Silloth Bay having leased these since 1862.

The almost continual development at Carlisle had now come to an end and from 1876 right up to 1969, a period of almost one hundred years, there was to be no change in the main line network. There were changes however with some branch rationalisation both before and after grouping. So over the next sixty-five years the changes are looked at in three periods: First the 42 years to grouping, next from grouping to 1938, and finally the war years.

1881 TO 1922 During this long period there was but one station opening and one closure. The opening was Rigg, a small intermediate station near Gretna on the Glasgow + South Western. The precise opening date is unclear but it is not on a map of 1880 but appears in the RCH Station Handbook of 1904.

The closure was Gretna North British in 1915 but the branch from Longtown remained in use for goods for a further 55 years and remains partly in use in the Admiralty Sidings complex into the 1990's. The reason for this very early closure is worth pursuing and in fact dates back to opening of the line. At that time the North British had designs on running through services to the Ayr coast, and obtained, running powers to Gretna Green with hopes of extending these to reach the west coast but the Glasgow + South Western took action in blocking any such move, the North British being left with a branch service to nowhere calling at one station en route requiring reversal. The situation became even more bizarre when shortly before closure it is understood the passenger service used the Caledonian Gretna station. This meant that a train from Longtown started at a North British station, called at a Caledonian station and finished its journey at a Glasgow + South Western Station. By 1910 the service was two trains in each direction. The war economy measures resulted then in putting the final nail in this unique service's coffin. It was not re-instated after the war.

1923 TO 1938. The only development arising directly from grouping was Burgh (ex North British) which became Burgh-by-Sands to distinguish it from Burgh in Lincolnshire, both stations having come into the LNER.

The next occurrence was closure to passengers of Lyneside (previously Lineside) and Harker on the Waverley route.

The final event in this period was closure of the Port Carlisle branch to all traffic. Once again there is a bizarre story underlying closure. As recalled earlier this line was a converted canal which with the competitive outlets at both Silloth and Maryport never carried but paltry goods traffic and insignificant numbers of passengers. The strange tale starts in 1857 when the joint committee decided to add to the locomotive stock by purchase of a horse to haul passenger trains; goods trains continued to be locomotive hauled. In due course during World War I there was a measure of progress when steam was reintroduced but before this it is recorded that the track had deteriorated to such an extent in 1899 that the spasmodic goods service was withdrawn. However, goods traffic re-started only five months later but by horse traction! The line closed in the 1932-3 period for all traffic.

1939 TO 1945 Following the strange stories behind closures in the last two periods the wartime closures are quite mundane. There were two closures, no doubt for economy purposes; these were Rigg on the ex-Glasgow + South Western and Scotby on the Settle-Carlisle. Scotby was however still served by the more convenient LNER station. Both stations closed in 1942.

To partly balance a new halt was opened on the Waverley line just south of the old Harker station; it was called Park-house Halt and its precise opening date is unclear. It would appear to have been used to convey work people.

As mentioned elsewhere rationalisation is often associated with the Beeching report but that can often be unfair, as these maps disclose rationalisation did occur after grouping, and in the case of Carlisle area we even have a pre-grouping example. The next maps do in fact show that pre-Beeching closures of stations were more than those closed under the 'Good Doctor's' report. It is also known that some of the Beeching proposed closures were in fact under consideration before the publication of the report.

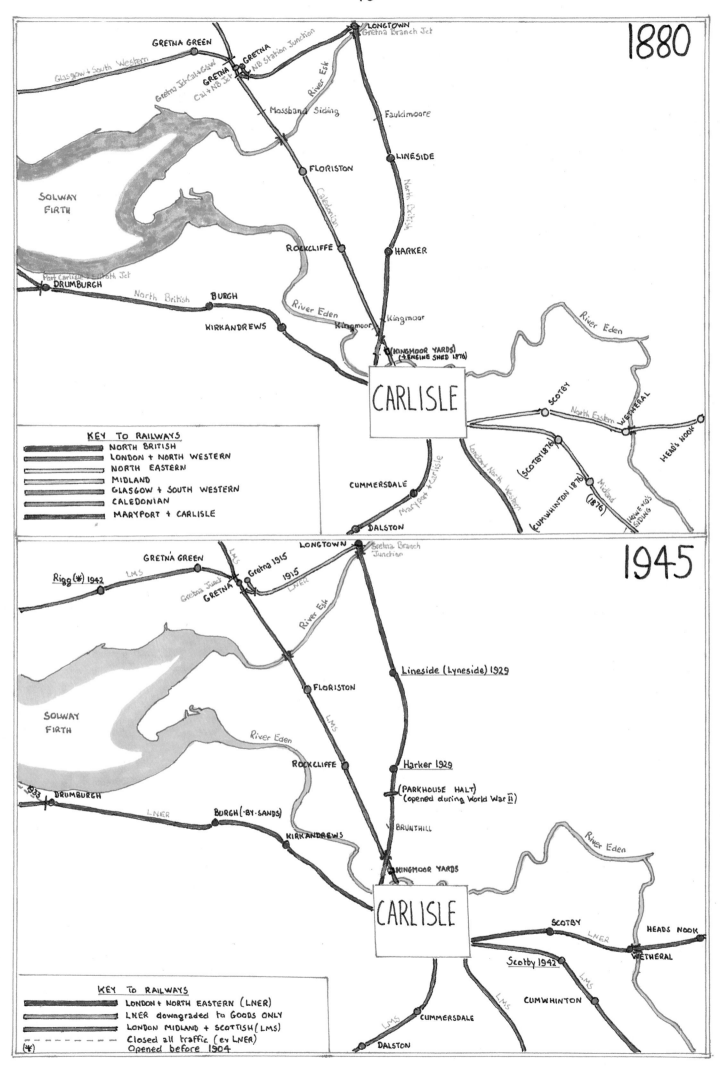

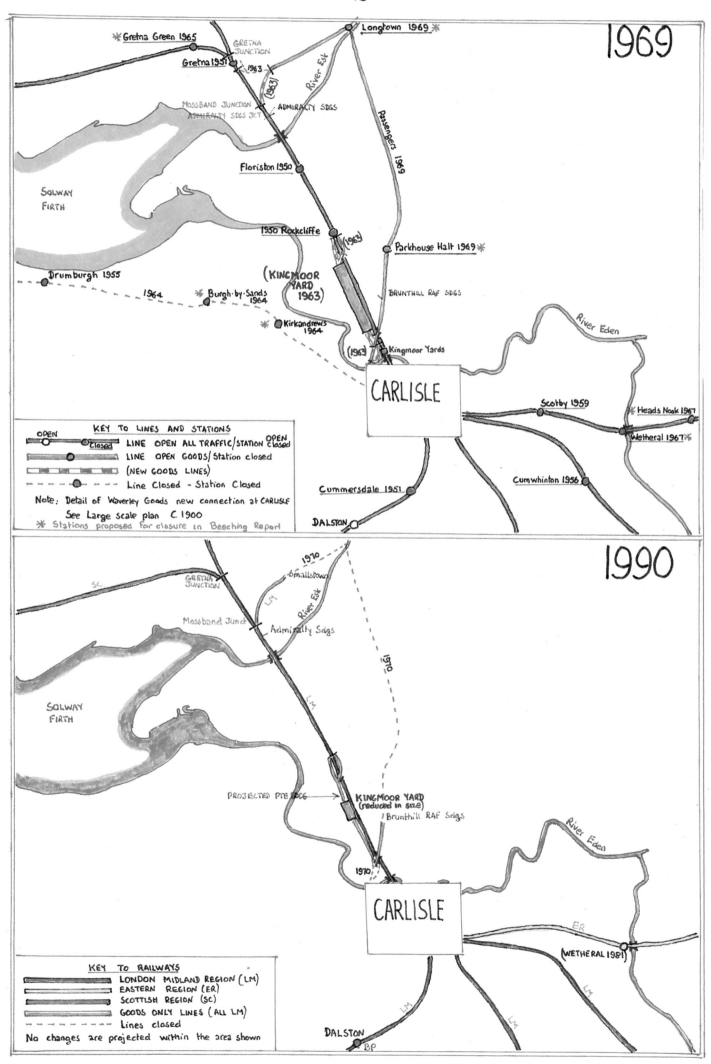

1969

Gretna Green 1965 *
GRETNA JUNCTION
Longtown 1969 *
Gretna 1951
1963
(1963)
River Esk
MOSSBAND JUNCTION
ADMIRALTY SDGS JCT
ADMIRALTY SDGS
Passengers 1969
SOLWAY FIRTH
Floriston 1950
1950 Rockcliffe
(1963)
Parkhouse Halt 1969 *
Drumburgh 1955
(KINGMOOR YARD 1963)
1964
Burgh-by-Sands 1964
BRUNTHILL RAF SDGS
River Eden
Kirkandrews 1964
(1963)
Kingmoor Yards
CARLISLE
Scotby 1959
Heads Nook 1967
Wetheral 1967 *

KEY TO LINES AND STATIONS
OPEN ○━━━━━●Closed   LINE OPEN ALL TRAFFIC/STATION OPEN/OPEN CLOSED
━━━━━●   LINE OPEN GOODS/Station closed
(NEW GOODS LINES)
- - - -●- - - -   Line Closed - Station Closed
Note: Detail of Waverley Goods new connection at CARLISLE
See Large scale plan C.1900
* Stations proposed for closure in Beeching Report

Cummersdale 1951
Cumwhinton 1956
DALSTON

1990

SC
GRETNA JUNCTION
1970
Smallstown
River Esk
LM
Mossband Junct
Admiralty Sdgs
1970
LM
SOLWAY FIRTH
PROJECTED PTE SDGS
KINGMOOR YARD (reduced in size)
Brunthill RAF Sdgs
1970
River Eden
CARLISLE
ER
(WETHERAL 1981)

KEY TO RAILWAYS
━━━━━   LONDON MIDLAND REGION (LM)
━━━━━   EASTERN REGION (ER)
━━━━━   SCOTTISH REGION (SC)
━━━━━   GOODS ONLY LINES (ALL LM)
- - - -   Lines closed
No changes are projected within the area shown

DALSTON
BP
LM
LM

LINES TO CARLISLE

The next map takes the development story up to 1969 and is conveniently looked at in two unequal periods, the Beeching report of 1963 making a logical and natural break.

1946 TO 1963 In this period, following nationalisation, the closure of intermediate stations started in the '20s continued. On the ex-Caledonian line all the intermediate stations within the map area closed, Floriston and Rockcliffe closing 1950 and Gretna the following year. Most other lines also lost an intermediate station in this period. The first in point of time was Cummersdale on the Maryport line in 1951. This was followed by Drumburgh (Silloth line) in 1955 and Cumwhinton on the Settle and Carlisle the following year. The final closure in this period was Scotby (North Eastern) in 1959.

However, this period also saw development. In 1956 British Railways purchased land alongside the ex-Caledonian main line between Kingmoor + Rockcliffe. Three years later construction started on one of the largest and most ambitious plans of the modernisation programme. This was Kingmoor New Yard to eliminate the interyard movements which had caused chaos to goods traffic for over one hundred years. Associated new connections for the Waverley line were built at the same time and brought into use with the opening of the yard in 1963. Up traffic was routed from Longtown along the old Gretna branch but diverted southwards to a new junction at Mossband joining the up goods running line which then crossed the passenger lines by a flyover at the entrance to the new yard. In the down direction a double track chord line was constructed from just to the north of Canal junction to make a trailing connection into the down goods line just south of KINGMOOR new yard. (This latter connection has been sketched in on the extended central area map of 1900).

1963 TO 1969 The Beeching proposals relative to Carlisle's line network are simply described as closure of every line opened after 1850, the stations to close being those marked on the map. As can be seen, by 1969 all station closures had been implemented, but with line closures it was a different story influenced by many different factors. The first of the line closures was the Silloth branch and this was done amidst quite massive public demonstrations with the last train from Silloth. BR were so alarmed, and faced with the possibility of having to reopen, that track removal commenced the very next day. Nothing further happened until 1969 except for the closure of intermediate stations; Gretna Green closed in 1965 when local services on the line were pruned but this did not affect the express services which under the Doctor's report were to continue. The remaining Newcastle line stations were closed in the vicinity of Carlisle two years later in implementation of the proposals to modify the service on the line.

The other closures threatened in the report had mixed fortunes. The Waverley route for a time appeared as though it might survive since BR themselves showed some resistance to the closure proposal since not only had links to the new Kingmoor Yard been opened from the Waverley line a few weeks before publication of the report but another new yard actually on the route had been built at the Edinburgh end. However, it was still a duplicate route passing through desolate and unpopulated countryside and one is bound to say that ultimately common sense prevailed. It closed throughout to all traffic in 1969 although the lines from Longtown to Mossband + Carlisle were retained for a further few months. The Settle and Carlisle closure threat has had a happier outcome and is more fully related elsewhere. Suffice it to say that during this period it was retained initially at any rate until increased line utilisation of the Shap route was able to cope with traffic demands.

1970 TO 1990 This period, as already noted, commenced with the closure to all traffic of the remnant of the North British lines. Throughout the period the Kingmoor Marshalling Yard has been progressively reduced in size and although still in use the hump closed in the earlier part of the 80's reflecting a similar pattern nationwide.

But there have been positive aspects during this period illustrated on the final map. Spurs of the ex North British are retained at Mossband + Kingmoor giving access to siding complexes. The need for the continued existance of goods facilities on a reduced scale appears secure as Carlisle is still a focal point of six routes. Also it would appear that retention of the Settle to Carlisle route is at last secure. Finally there has been a station reopening, WETHERAL re-opening to passenger trains in 1981.

1991 INTO THE FUTURE. What of the future? At Carlisle the remaining network and all other facilities appear secure and there has been some increase in rail-served industries in the vicinity and others are planned. A visit to Carlisle is still a fascinating railway experience particularly if one reaches it via the Settle and Carlisle.

One unique feature of Carlisle under British Rail is that it is served by trains from three regions as the 1990 map shows and this can result in an Eastern Region departure connection refusing to await a late London Midland Region arrival with the result that passengers continue their journey to Newcastle by taxi and at the expense of British Rail. Inter-regional lack of co-operation has continued the intercompany rivalries of the Victorian age!

LINES IN CARLISLE

The development of the Railway Network is illustrated by a series of maps showing the position at each phase of the very complicated development. In the early period development was a continuous process and the interval between maps is short; in fact the first four maps cover a period of ten years only. The various events are listed in chronological order and only expanded where explanation is necessary to illustrate their importance upon the overall development pattern.

DATE

12.3.1823 CARLISLE CANAL opened. Though not a railway it did eventually become one and had a profound influence on development since the first railway built connected to it, and north-south lines then had to cross this railway; thus the growth in the dangerous flat crossings at Carlisle, the cause of chaos, difficulties and frustration

21.7.1824 CARLISLE - NEWCASTLE link proposed - Canal or Railway?

22.5.1829 NEWCASTLE-UPON-TYNE + CARLISLE Railway Authorised (usually known as NEWCASTLE + CARLISLE).

19.7.1836 LONDON ROAD opened by NEWCASTLE + CARLISLE (middle section still under construction).

9.3.1837 CANAL BRANCH opened to Goods sidings for loading at canal basin.

12.7.1837 MARYPORT + CARLISLE - Authorised.

18.6.1838 NEWCASTLE - CARLISLE - Opened throughout.

10.5.1843 MARY PORT + CARLISLE opened between Wigton + Carlisle; Junction with N+C at Bog Junction; Station Water Lane; also used London Rd.

6.6.1844 LANCASTER + CARLISLE Railway Authorised.

30.12.1844 Water Lane or Bog Field - Closed. New temporary station opened at CROWN STREET. M+C prohibited from making flat crossing over the in course of construction line from Lancaster. Negotiations commenced for joint station. Some M+C trains continue to use LONDON ROAD involving three changes of direction. M+C use London Road for Goods + Shed facilities.

10.2.1845 MARYPORT + CARLISLE opened throughout.

31.7.1845 CALEDONIAN RAILWAY - Incorporated.

27.7.1846 CITADEL STATION ACT (Caledonian and Lancaster + Carlisle); other companies could not agree terms to become partners also.

13.8.1846 GLASGOW, DUMFRIES + CARLISLE Railway incorporated.

17.12.1846 LANCASTER + CARLISLE opened to LONDON ROAD; M+C refuse to give up land; ST NICHOLAS GOODS (L+C) opened?

9.1847 CITADEL STATION brought into use.

9.9.1847 CALEDONIAN opened from Carlisle to Beattock - Goods at West Walls - Locomotive facilities nearby.

1.8.1848 YORK, NEWCASTLE + BERWICK lease the NEWCASTLE + CARLISLE

15.9.1848 M+C on verge of agreement with Citadel station partners re compensation for Crown Street land and use of Citadel station.

1.10.1848 YORK, NEWCASTLE + BERWICK lease the MARYPORT + CARLISLE. Hudson as chairman of leasing company takes up negotiations in connection with Crown Street Land. Demands £100,000; in the meantime M+C trains were crossing the L+C on the level up to six times in running into Carlisle, twice each time entering and leaving Crown Street and twice more for trains terminating at London Road. The L+C went to court who awarded just over £7000, a similar figure to that which M+C had previously been on verge of agreeing.

3.1849 L+C pay agreed sum for Crown Street but Hudson refuses to vacate.

17.3.1849 Sheriff takes possession of Crown Street on behalf of L+C. Followed by 200 L+C men who dismantle and take up tracks. M+C trains approaching diverted directly to London Road.

1.1.1850 Leases of N+C and M+C not confirmed; both companies revert to their original managements.

28.10.1850 GLASGOW + SOUTH WESTERN incorporated - a merger of Glasgow, Paisley, Kilmarnock + Ayr with Glasgow Dumfries and Carlisle (see 13.8.46 above); the latter company line had been opened to Junction at Gretna with the Caledonian on 23.8.1848.

1.3.1851 GLASGOW + SOUTH WESTERN authorised to run into Citadel station. Shed facilities to be shared with Caledonian.

2.4.1851 MARYPORT + CARLISLE agree to become permanent tenant of CITADEL station.

1.6.1851 M+C start to use CITADEL following opening of new North to East spur.

1.1.1852 M+C open CROWN STREET GOODS later to be known as Bog. Not to be confused with earlier passenger station of the same name or later LNW Goods which became Crown Street after grouping.

8.8.1852 M+C Forks Junction to CITADEL brought into use. At last the M+C reached Carlisle without the need for reversal! But only at the 4th attempt. Goods station also now using the FORKS JUNCTION connection.

1852 Brisco station on L+C Closed. It had opened with the line in 1846. It was to be replaced the following year by a new station at WREAY. This latter station was outside the confines of the area covered by the maps

Although at the end of this period the development was far from complete, the seeds of the dangerous flat crossings and their increased useage leading to the chaotic traffic congestion were firmly in place germinated from two factors - the Carlisle Canal and the greed of the dishonest Hudson in stifling a truly joint passenger/goods station(s) at Carlisle.

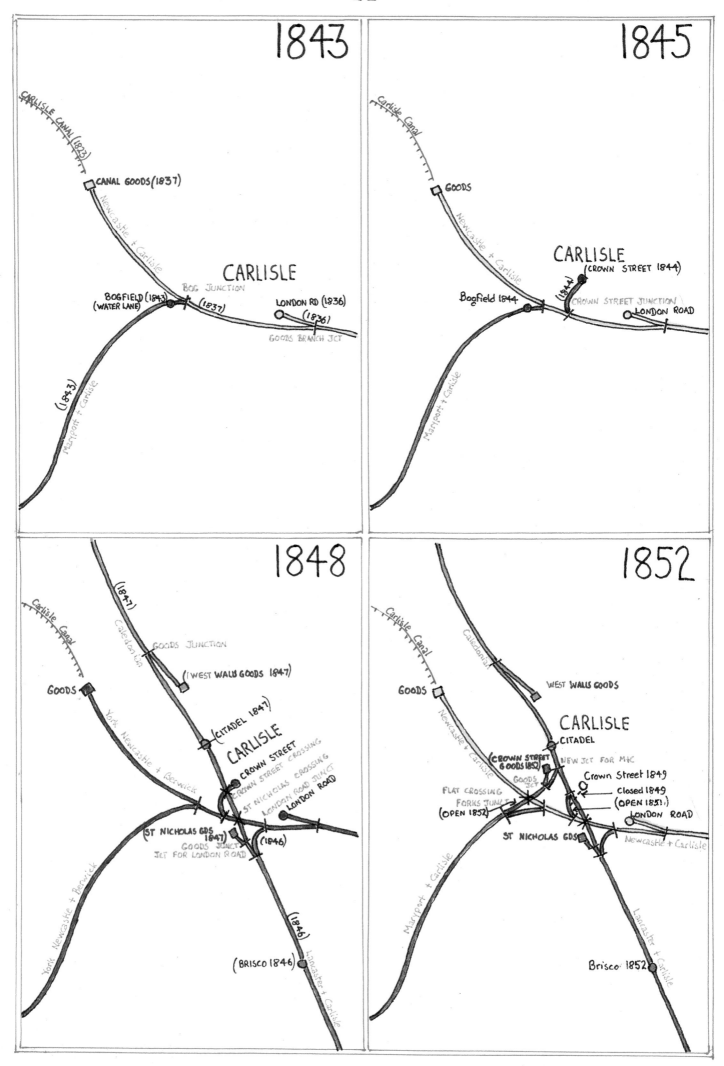

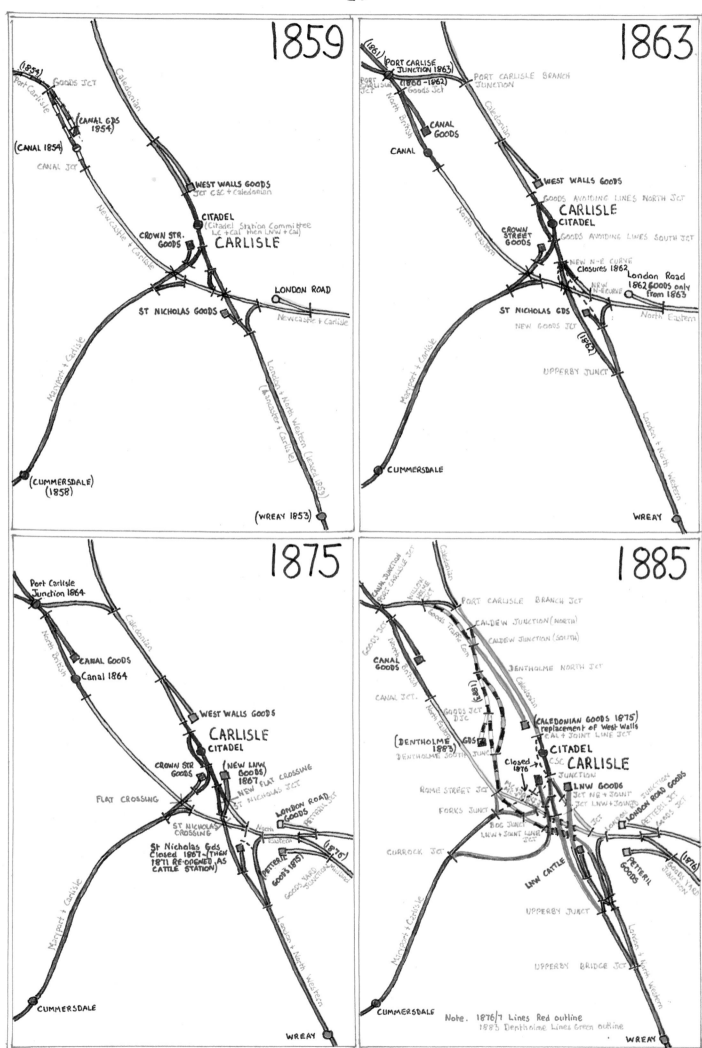

LINES IN CARLISLE

DATE

4. 8.1853 CARLISLE CANAL re-incorporated as PORT CARLISLE RAILWAY (PCR) to convert canal to a railway.

22. 5.1854 PORT CARLISLE RAILWAY opened for goods, CANAL GOODS opened on site of Canal basin. End on Junction with NEWCASTLE+CARLISLE (N+C), N+C Goods on their goods branch became sidings, exchange traffic used PCR Canal Goods from this date.

22. 6.1854 PCR opened to passengers, passenger station (CANAL) opened just north of end on junction with N+C.

1855 MARYPORT + CARLISLE (M+C) now double track throughout.

16. 7.1855 CARLISLE + SILLOTH BAY incorporated after abortive attempt the previous year.

28. 8.1856 CARLISLE + SILLOTH BAY opened; closely associated with PCR; a joint committee operated the two locally inspired lines

10. 5.1857 CITADEL STATION COMMITTEE formed (Caledonian and L+C) station and approaches became joint property.

1857-8 schemes (abortive) by both NORTH BRITISH (NB) and CALEDONIAN (Cal) to connect Hawick to Carlisle

1858 Cummersdale station opened (M+C).

1859 LONDON + NORTH WESTERN (LNW) lease L+C.

21. 7.1859 Border Union Railway (NB) to junction with PCR authorised.

13. 8.1859 New alignment of L+C/LNW authorised from Upperby Junction to Citadel station.

30. 6.1860 Port Carlisle Junction to Port Carlisle Branch Junction opened by Caledonian (had been authorised in 1858).

22. 7.1861 Goods relief lines to pass to west of Citadel station are authorised.

15.10.1861 Border Union ready for opening from Scotch Dyke but cannot use Caledonian spur until undertaking to double line is given.

29.10.1861 Border Union passenger services – connecting service (possibly to begin with run by Caledonian).

24. 1.1862 Upperby Junction to Citadel on new alignment to the west brought into use; New St Nicholas crossing. New goods connection

30. 4.1862 New North to East spur from N+C to Citadel station – used for goods only, old connecting spur (laid for M+C) closed.

1862 Goods avoiding lines brought into use.

3. 6.1862 NORTH BRITISH lease Port Carlisle Railway and Carlisle + Silloth Bay Railway.

?1. 7.1862 Edinburgh – Carlisle NB service commenced using the 'Waverley' route.

17. 7.1862 NORTH EASTERN fully absorbed the Newcastle + Carlisle.

1. 1.1863 NORTH EASTERN (NE) passenger services use Citadel via North to East spur later doubled, London Rd closed for passengers.

7.1863 Port Carlisle Junction station opened to enable traffic exchange between Waverley line and Silloth as Silloth trains not yet authorised to run into Citadel.

13. 6.1864 Doubling N to E spur authorised and brought into use shortly afterwards.

1. 7.1864 Silloth trains run into Citadel. Canal + Port Carlisle Junction both closed to passengers. Canal goods retained.

16. 7.1866 MIDLAND Settle to Carlisle authorised.

25.11.1867 New LNW Goods opened on old M+C site involving yet another flat crossing over NE line to Citadel. St Nicholas Gds closed.

circa 1871 LNW CATTLE opened on site of St Nicholas, still often referred to by its old name.

21. 7.1873 Citadel Station Act – Goods + passenger traffic to be segregated, flat crossings replaced by bridges + to take account of Mid line.

3. 8.1875 Settle Carlisle line opened for goods traffic. GLASGOW + SOUTH WESTERN (GSW) start to use Midland shed facilities.

1. 5.1876 Settle Carlisle line opened throughout for passenger traffic

1876~1877 New lines authorised 1873 as detailed below brought into use. New Goods only lines in new GOODS TRAFFIC COMMITTEE (Cal, GSW, LNW+Mid)

1883 Dentholme Lines brought into use administered by new railway, DENTHOLME JOINT COMMITTEE (GSW, Mid +NB)

1879-1880 LNW fully absorb L+C; 12/8/80 NB fully absorb PCR and Carlisle + Silloth Bay railways

DETAILS OF LINES BUILT 1876-7

RAILWAY NO	line details	OWNERSHIP
1	UPPERBY JUNCTION (possibly Upperby Bridge Jct) to CITADEL bridges over railways 4+5, to W existing line	LNW
2	CALDEW JUNCTION to CITADEL to East existing line, Goods resited to west, shed moved to Kingmoor	Cal
3	WILLOWHOLME JCT - CALDEW JCT - BOG JUNCTION new goods avoiding line	GOODS TRAFFIC COM.
4	LONDON ROAD JCT - ROME STREET JCT realigned and lowered to pass under other lines	NE
5	UPPERBY JCT - BOG JCT New Goods lines	LNW + GTC
6	CITADEL STATION - LONDON ROAD JCT new alignment passing under LNW new goods line	NE (+CSC)
7	UPPERBY JCT - To LNW GOODS new connection passing over 4, 5+6	LNW
8	CURROCK JCT - CITADEL new approach line passing over 4+5	M+C
9	M+C NEW GOODS BRANCH (from 8)	M+C
10	FORKS JCT - BOG JCT (old spur to Gds + Citadel from M+C closed)	M+C
11	FORKS JCT - ROME STREET JCT	M+C
12	CANAL BRANCH partly realigned with new bridge over Caldew	NE

MAXIMUM DEVELOPMENT- CARLISLE-1900

This map although c.1900 could well have been dated at any time between 1883 and 1923. However, 1900 happens to be the year when signal box details are available to enable this information to be incorporated. All boxes however are not shown but the inner area is comprehensively covered.

The map has also been extended North to include the Kingmoor area and the line of 1963 goods connection is shown as its exact alignment is difficult to show on the general maps on which the Kingmoor area appears. A selection of sidings has also been shown; the two shown with their own line are distinguished from the rest in that the owners had their own locomotive to work these sidings. The final additional feature shown is engine sheds and these have their own development story. This is told below. It must remembered in studying this that many of the early details are shrouded in mystery and exact dates are sometimes doubtful:

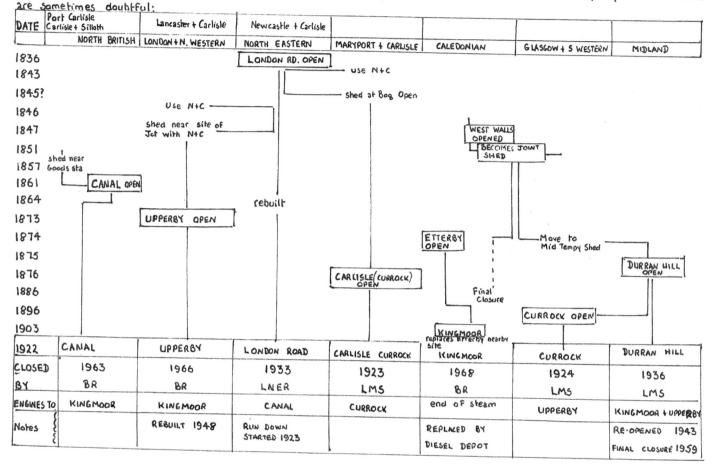

DATE	Port Carlisle Carlisle + Silloth — NORTH BRITISH	Lancaster + Carlisle — LONDON + N. WESTERN	Newcastle + Carlisle — NORTH EASTERN	MARYPORT + CARLISLE	CALEDONIAN	GLASGOW + S WESTERN	MIDLAND
1836			LONDON RD. OPEN				
1843			use N+C				
1845?			shed at Bog Open				
1846		Use N+C					
1847		Shed near site of Jct with N+C			WEST WALLS OPENED		
1851	shed near Goods sta				BECOMES JOINT SHED		
1857							
1861	CANAL OPEN						
1864			rebuilt				
1873		UPPERBY OPEN					
1874				ETTERBY OPEN	Move to Mid Tempy Shed		
1875							
1876				CARLISLE(CURROCK) OPEN			DURRAN HILL OPEN
1886					Final Closure		
1896					CURROCK OPEN		
1903				KINGMOOR replaces Etterby nearby site			
1922	CANAL	UPPERBY	LONDON ROAD	CARLISLE CURROCK	KINGMOOR	CURROCK	DURRAN HILL
CLOSED	1963	1966	1933	1923	1968	1924	1936
BY	BR	BR	LNER	LMS	BR	LMS	LMS
ENGINES TO	KINGMOOR	KINGMOOR	CANAL	CURROCK	end of steam	UPPERBY	KINGMOOR + UPPERBY
Notes {		REBUILT 1948	RUN DOWN STARTED 1923		REPLACED BY DIESEL DEPOT		RE-OPENED 1943 FINAL CLOSURE 1959

The table below gives a brief History of the various Goods Depots and also some sidings which were extensively used.

Originating Company 1922 OWNING COMPANY	Abbreviation	OPEN	DEVELOPMENTS	CLOSED
Newcastle + Carlisle NORTH EASTERN	N+C NE	1836	LONDON ROAD in early years was used by MC + LC	STILL OPEN
Lancaster + Carlisle LONDON + NORTH WESTERN	LC LNW	1846?	ST NICHOLAS Closed 1867 reopened 1871 as CATTLE station but often called by old name	1970
LONDON + NORTH WESTERN		1867	renamed CROWN STREET at grouping	1966
CALEDONIAN	Cal	1847	WEST WALLS repositioned in 1874/7 following realignment of main line	1877
		1874	CARLISLE replacement of West Walls known as VIADUCT after grouping	1965
		1875	Land bought at Kingmoor in 1859 to block NB, sidings in place soon afterwards but no use made until Engine Shed move to nearby site. Facilities gradually increased over years at both sides of line became known as KINGMOOR UP + DOWN. Down became Diesel Depot	} 1960
MARYPORT + CARLISLE	MC	1852	CROWN STREET. Temporary facilities before this, also use made of N+C at London Rd BOG from 1923	1970
GLASGOW + SOUTH WESTERN	GSW		from 1851 and entry to Citadel used West Walls, then in 1874 to Petteril and Durran Hill	}
DENTHOLME JOINT COMMITTEE		1883	DENTHOLME although joint property of GSW, NB + Mid became effectively GSW Goods	} 1935
Port Carlisle Carlisle + Silloth Bay }	PCR	1854	CANAL on site of Canal Basin. Used by NB from time they reached Carlisle	1963
NORTH BRITISH	NB			?
MIDLAND	Mid	1874	DURRAN HILL later described as Sidings, thought to have been used by GSW	}
		1875	PETTERIL possibly used also by GSW. Renamed PETTERIL BRIDGE at Grouping possibly to make a distinction between LNW Petteril Sidings	} 1963
BRITISH RAILWAYS	BR	1963	KINGMOOR New Yard brought into use. 1973 Down Yard Closed. 1981 Hump shunting ceased. Although some further rationalisation is possible its future on this reduced scale appears to be secure.	STILL OPEN

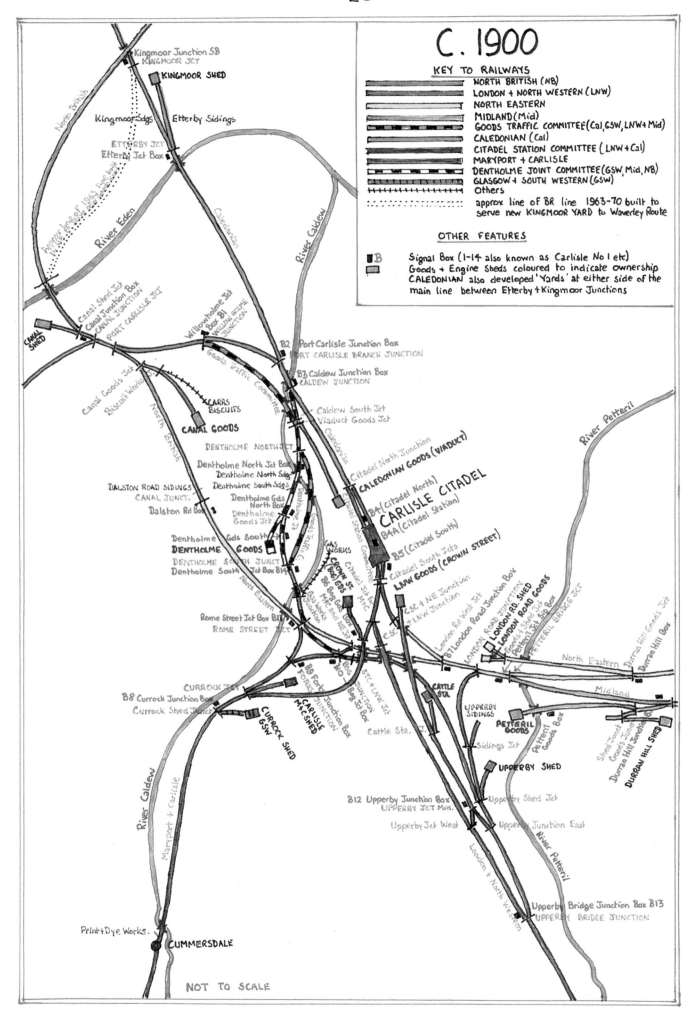

C. 1900

KEY TO RAILWAYS

NORTH BRITISH (NB)
LONDON + NORTH WESTERN (LNW)
NORTH EASTERN
MIDLAND (Mid)
GOODS TRAFFIC COMMITTEE (Cal, GSW, LNW + Mid)
CALEDONIAN (Cal)
CITADEL STATION COMMITTEE (LNW + Cal)
MARYPORT + CARLISLE
DENTHOLME JOINT COMMITTEE (GSW, Mid, NB)
GLASGOW + SOUTH WESTERN (GSW)
Others
approx line of BR line 1963-70 built to serve new KINGMOOR YARD to Waverley Route

OTHER FEATURES

■B   Signal Box (1-14 also known as Carlisle No 1 etc)
□□   Goods + Engine Sheds coloured to indicate ownership
CALEDONIAN also developed 'Yards' at either side of the main line between Etterby + Kingmoor Junctions

Kingmoor Junction SB
KINGMOOR JCT
KINGMOOR SHED
Kingmoor Sdgs   Etterby Sidings
ETTERBY JCT
Etterby Jct Box
Approx line of 1963 line built

River Eden
North British
Caledonian
River Caldew

Canal Shed Jct
Canal Junction Box
CANAL JUNCTION
PORT CARLISLE JCT
CANAL SHED
Willowholme Jct
Box B11
WILLOWHOLME JUNCTION

B2 Port Carlisle Junction Box
PORT CARLISLE BRANCH JUNCTION
Canal Goods Jct
Goods Traffic Committee
B3 Caldew Junction Box
CALDEW JUNCTION
Biscuit Works
CARRS BISCUITS
Caldew South Jct
Viaduct Goods Jct
CANAL GOODS
North British
Caledonian
DENTHOLME NORTH JCT
Dentholme North Jct Box
Dentholme North Sdgs
DALSTON ROAD SIDINGS   Dentholme South Sdgs
CANAL JUNCT.
Dentholme Gds North Box
Dalston Rd Box
DALSTON ROAD SIDINGS
Dentholme Goods Jct
Citadel North Junction
CALEDONIAN GOODS (VIADUCT)
CARLISLE CITADEL
B4 (Citadel North)
B4A (Citadel Station)
B5 (Citadel South)
Dentholme Gds South Box
DENTHOLME GOODS
DENTHOLME SOUTH JUNCT
Dentholme South Jct Box B14
GAS WORKS
Citadel Station Committee
Citadel South Jcts
LNW GOODS (CROWN STREET)
CSC + NE Junction
CSC + LNW Junction
Rome Street Jct Box B10
ROME STREET JCT
CROWN ST (Good) GDS
B6 Goods Box GDS
M&C and NE Jcts
GTC + LNW Jct
London Rd West Jct
B7 London Road Junction Box
LONDON ROAD JUNCTION
LONDON RD. SHED
LONDON ROAD GOODS
Goods Shed Jct
Petteril Jct Sig Box
PETTERIL BRIDGE JCT
North Eastern   Durran Hill Goods Jct
Durran Hill Box
River Petteril

CURROCK JCT
B8 Currock Junction Box
Currock Shed Junct
CURROCK SHED GSW
CURROCK SHED
B9 Forks Junction Box
CARLISLE M&C SHED
M&C Forks Junction Box
CATTLE STA.
Cattle Sta. Jct
GTC + LNW Jct
UPPERBY SIDINGS
PETTERIL GOODS
Petteril Goods Box
Midland
Shed Junct
Goods Junction
DURRAN HILL SHED
Durran Hill Junction Box
UPPERBY SHED
B12 Upperby Junction Box
UPPERBY JCT Mid.
Sidings Jct
Upperby Shed Jct
Upperby Jct West
Upperby Junction East
River Petteril

River Caldew
Maryport + Carlisle
North British
London + North Western

Upperby Bridge Junction Box B13
UPPERBY BRIDGE JUNCTION

Print + Dye Works.
CUMMERSDALE

NOT TO SCALE

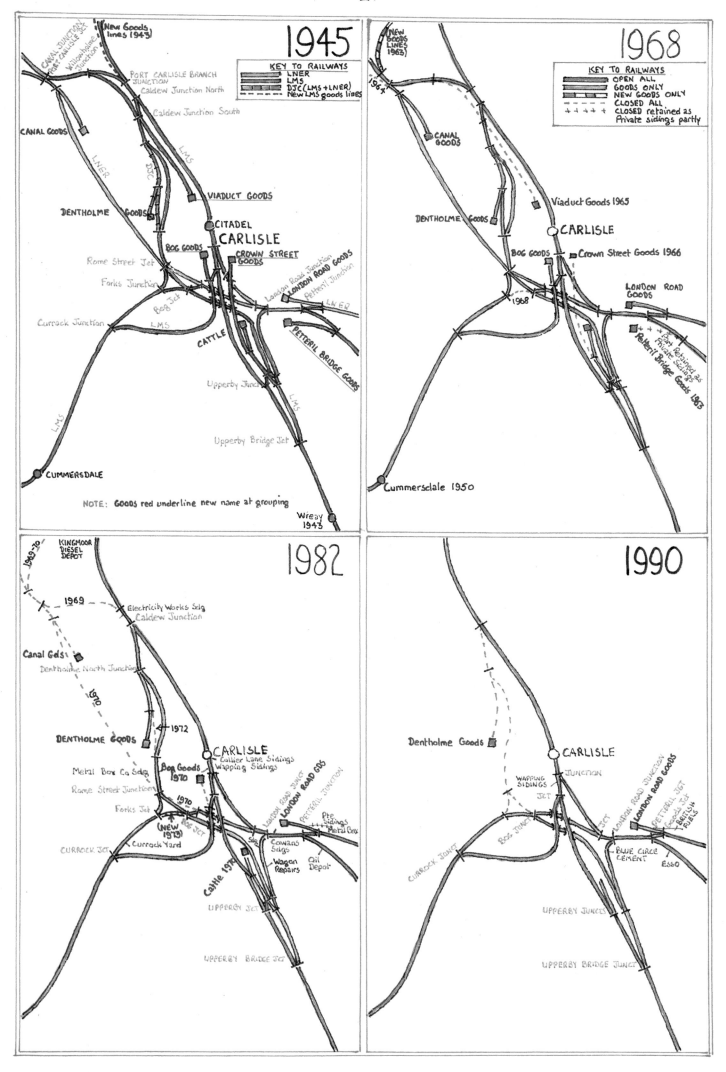

1945

KEY TO RAILWAYS
- LNER
- LMS
- DJC (LMS + LNER)
- New LMS goods lines

(New Goods lines (1943)

CANAL JUNCTION
Port Carlisle Jct
Willowholme Junction
PORT CARLISLE BRANCH JUNCTION
Caldew Junction North
Caldew Junction South

CANAL GOODS

LNER

DJC

LMS

VIADUCT GOODS

DENTHOLME GOODS

CITADEL
CARLISLE

BOG GOODS

CROWN STREET GOODS

Rome Street Jct

Forks Junction

London Road Junction
Petteril Junction
LONDON ROAD GOODS

Bog Jct

LNER

Currock Junction

LMS

CATTLE

PETTERIL BRIDGE GOODS

LMS

Upperby Junction

LMS

Upperby Bridge Jct

CUMMERSDALE

NOTE: GOODS red underline new name at grouping

Wreay 1943

1968

KEY TO RAILWAYS
- OPEN ALL
- GOODS ONLY
- NEW GOODS ONLY
- CLOSED ALL
- + + + CLOSED retained as Private sidings partly

(New Goods Lines (1963)

1964

CANAL GOODS

DENTHOLME GOODS

Viaduct Goods 1965

CARLISLE

BOG GOODS

Crown Street Goods 1966

1968

LONDON ROAD GOODS

Part retained as Private sidings
Petteril Bridge Goods 1863

Cummerscdale 1950

1982

KINGMOOR DIESEL DEPOT

1969-70

1969

Electricity Works Sdg
Caldew Junction

Canal Gds

Dentholme North Junction

1970

DENTHOLME GOODS

1972

CARLISLE

Collier Lane Sidings
Wapping Sidings

Metal Box Co Sdg

Bog Goods 1970

Rome Street Junction

London Road Junct
Petteril Junction
LONDON ROAD GDS

Forks Jct

1970

Bog Jct

(NEW 1970)

Currock Yard

Pte Sidings Metal Box

Currock Jct

Sdg

Cowans Sdgs

Wagon Repairs

Oil Depot

Cattle 1970

UPPERBY JCT

UPPERBY BRIDGE JCT

1990

Dentholme Goods

CARLISLE

Junction

London Road Junction
Petteril Jct
LONDON ROAD Goods
Goods Jct
BRITISH FUELS

Wapping Sidings

Jct

Jct

Bog Junct

Currock Junct

Blue Circle Cement

Esso

UPPERBY JUNCT

UPPERBY BRIDGE JUNCT

CARLISLE 1881 TO 1990

After the active development noted in Carlisle from 1843 to 1885, a period of just 43 years illustrated by eight maps, there follows the contrast of 110 years covered by only 4 maps.

The period of 65 years 1881 to 1945 was a period of inertia and apathy so far as Carlisle was concerned. The alterations of 1876/7 had swept away the dangerous flat crossings and effectively segregated goods and passenger traffic. To begin with it appeared that a simplified goods exchange system would develop when DENTHOLME had been completed in 1883 which would enable the Midland to exchange traffic with its Scottish associates the GLASGOW + SOUTH WESTERN and NORTH BRITISH. But logic did not prevail and Dentholme became in fact in the main a GSW depot, the other partners using their own established yards.

At grouping with lines becoming LMS and/or LNER an obvious opportunity to rationalise goods traffic presented itself but was simply ignored, the only effect being the name changes of some goods stations of the LMS so a distinguishing identity could be preserved when ownership alone was now insufficient. Two other minor changes in the period up to the end of the war remain to be recorded; both strangely enough were in 1943 when the ex LNWR intermediate station of Wreay closed and when the lines northward from Port Carlisle Branch Junction were quadrupled by the insertion of a pair of goods running lines to the west of the main line.

The map for 1945 does however form an essential snapshot of Carlisle in showing the make-up of the grouping companies, and also highlights the continued use of all pre-grouping goods facilities. This latter point is stressed by the new goods lines built to deal with the heavy increases from wartime circumstances. But the sensible solution available from the 1870's was not to be used for almost a further two decades!

The remaining story of the lines in Carlisle, and covered by the final three maps in this series, are the results of just two factors. Both strangely enough occurred in 1963. The first was the commissioning of the new KINGMOOR YARD which though outside the confines of the area covered by the maps nevertheless had a profound effect on lines within the city. In the chronological tables which follow all events stemming from this, are written in lower case. The second event of 1963 was issue of the Beeching Report and the events stemming from this are shown in CAPITALS. Where precise year is unclear it is followed by a (?) thus. Non-connected events are in italics.

1950 *Cummersdale station closed*
1963 Kingmoor New Yard brought into use
1963 THE BEECHING REPORT - THE RESHAPING OF BRITISH RAILWAYS
1963 New Goods line from near Canal Junction to enable down traffic to reach Kingmoor (new) Yard from the Waverley route
1963 Petteril Bridge Goods Closed - part retained as private sidings
1964 SILLOTH BRANCH CLOSED TO ALL TRAFFIC
1965 Viaduct Goods (ex Caledonian) Closed
1966 Crown Street Goods Closed
1968 Forks Junction to Bog Junction Closed

1969 WAVERLEY LINE CLOSED to passengers, map portion retained a further year for Goods
1969 CANAL JUNCTION TO PORT CARLISLE BRANCH JUNCTION CLOSED
1970 1963 NEW CONNECTION CLOSED, Canal Branch Closed, Bog Goods Closed, Ex LNW Cattle Closed
1970 WAVERLEY LINE CLOSED COMPLETELY
1972 Dentholme Goods Junction to Dentholme South Junction closed
1973 Forks Junction to Bog Junction re-opened

There now followed a period of relative inaction with the last two goods depots lingering on, BUT WITH THE BEECHING SWORD STILL POISED OVER THE SETTLE-CARLISLE LINE.

1985? Caldew Junction to Dentholme Goods Closed, Dentholme Goods Junction - Rome Street Junction - Bog Junction closed, Rome Street Jct to Forks Junction Closed
1989 THREAT OF CLOSURE ON SETTLE-CARLISLE LINE lifted.
It is interesting to note that if the Settle-Carlisle closure had been implemented the lines from Carlisle remaining would have been precisely those in existence in 1850.

Looking to the future the remaining main line network appears secure and any future developments are likely to be with freight. The remaining goods only network could well become redundant together with London Road Goods but it appears that these would still be needed for such purposes as wagon repairs, railcar servicing, carriage depot and engineering services. On the positive side Carlisle's position as a focal point of trunk routes has attracted and continues to attract industry seeking the advantages of rail distribution for its products. Meanwhile although the hump yards at Kingmoor have gone and the yard has been reduced in size it appears certain it will remain in use due again to its location at a focal point.

THE SETTLE-CARLISLE LINE

Of all the lines reaching Carlisle the Settle-Carlisle is the best known not only because of its magificent scenery and the wild and desolate Pennine uplands of its route, but the dramatic engineering feats accomplished in its construction. No narrative relative to Carlisle as a railway centre can ignore the final line to arrive and at least it gives the excuse to include a strip map of the line showing not only its passenger stations but also a full selection of its engineering features, line-side industries and signal boxes.

The credit for building the line is usually and naturally given to the expansionist Midland management of the time. But this is not entirely accurate and perhaps the prime credit to its conception at any rate lay at Euston rather than Derby. It is certain that the goad to construction was applied by the London & North Western Railway in its treatment of both goods and passengers from the Midland to Carlisle and Scotland. At one stage a reasonable compromise appeared to have been reached with a joint leasing of the Lancaster and Carlisle by the LNW & Midland but this was only a delaying tactic all very typical of the LNW policy at that time. When after opposition the Midland received authorisation for the line in 1866 the LNW became alarmed and agreed terms with the Midland with regard to the latter's traffic to Scotland. In view of this and tightened financial position of the Midland Railway and the difficulty in seeking fresh capital, abandonment was sought but was rejected. It was 1875 before the line opened to goods traffic and passenger opening had to be deferred a further year. The long period that elapsed between authorisation and opening can be attributed to two factors. The first of these delaying the start of construction has already been mentioned, the attempted abandonment. The second factor is usually associated to the difficulty of the terrain; but is this really the case? Undoubtedly it is a very difficult territory but not more so than had been traversed in early days. Thinking solely of the earlier lines into Carlisle, the first railway to reach Carlisle across the Pennines took seven years from its Act to the opening of a terminal station into Carlisle although as noted earlier a further two years elapsed before the line was opened throughout. But both the Lancaster & Carlisle and the Caledonian, traversing equally difficult terrain, were open to traffic within three years of obtaining their Acts. In the case of the Caledonian, lines were opened from Carlisle to reach both Glasgow and Edinburgh. In addition to all this, experience had been gained by the time of the construction of the Settle-Carlisle, so one needs to look elsewhere for the reason of this slow progress. The answer of course does partly rely on the terrain but more particularly in the way it was crossed. The Midland had two requirements for the route; these were no sharp curves and no steep gradients. It was these two requirements which lead to the heavy engineering works, viaduct succeeding tunnel to ensure the ruling gradient of 1 in 100 was never exceeded and resulted in fifteen miles of continual climb from Settle at this gradient to be known as the 'Long Drag'. But it would mean the achievement of express schedules and ensure the Midland line would be truly seen as an alternative to the well established east and west coast routes to Scotland. A glance at the railways mentioned above bears out this reasoning and the total length of tunnels for example on the three of them together is but a modest fraction of those on the Settle & Carlisle. One final oddity about the construction of the line remains to be noted; that is there were no facing connections between Settle Junction and Petteril Junction. This meant that trains from Bradford and Leeds routed on the Hawes branch had to draw past the station then reverse along the up line before drawing forward again into the branch platform.

Following its opening the line settled into its place within the Midland system as an important trunk route. A local all-stations service was inaugurated but this was never of much moment and in fact Appleby was the only station along the whole line which developed a substantial traffic both goods and passengers, no doubt helped by many of the through expresses calling there. This background explains the change in the situation following grouping. The rival main lines were no longer in competition, so far as London - Glasgow services were concerned the longer established more direct route of LNW and Caledonian rather than the longer Midland & GSW route. But at this point in time closure was not contemplated; the line was still important for through traffic from Nottingham, Sheffield & Leeds.

From the nationalisation of the railways the scenario changed but not until the Beeching report. Up to that time there had been closure of intermediate stations as already noted, but this pattern was reflected on Carlisle's other main lines, but the threatened closure brought a storm of protest and an implementation of closure by stealth was pursued. First goods facilities were withdrawn from most intermediate stations, then followed downgrading of all stations still open except Settle and Appleby to unstaffed halts, followed by withdrawal of the local passenger services. In the meantime, on the main line front, trains were terminated at Nottingham and later Leeds to the south and eventually at Carlisle to the north. So we now had the postion of a branch line without stations. Coupled with this was a lack of proper maintenance leading to a crumbling Ribblehead viaduct.

Happily closure has now been averted and the future looks secure; many of the stations have been re--opened and British Rail are committed to improving the service on what has become a major tourist attraction.

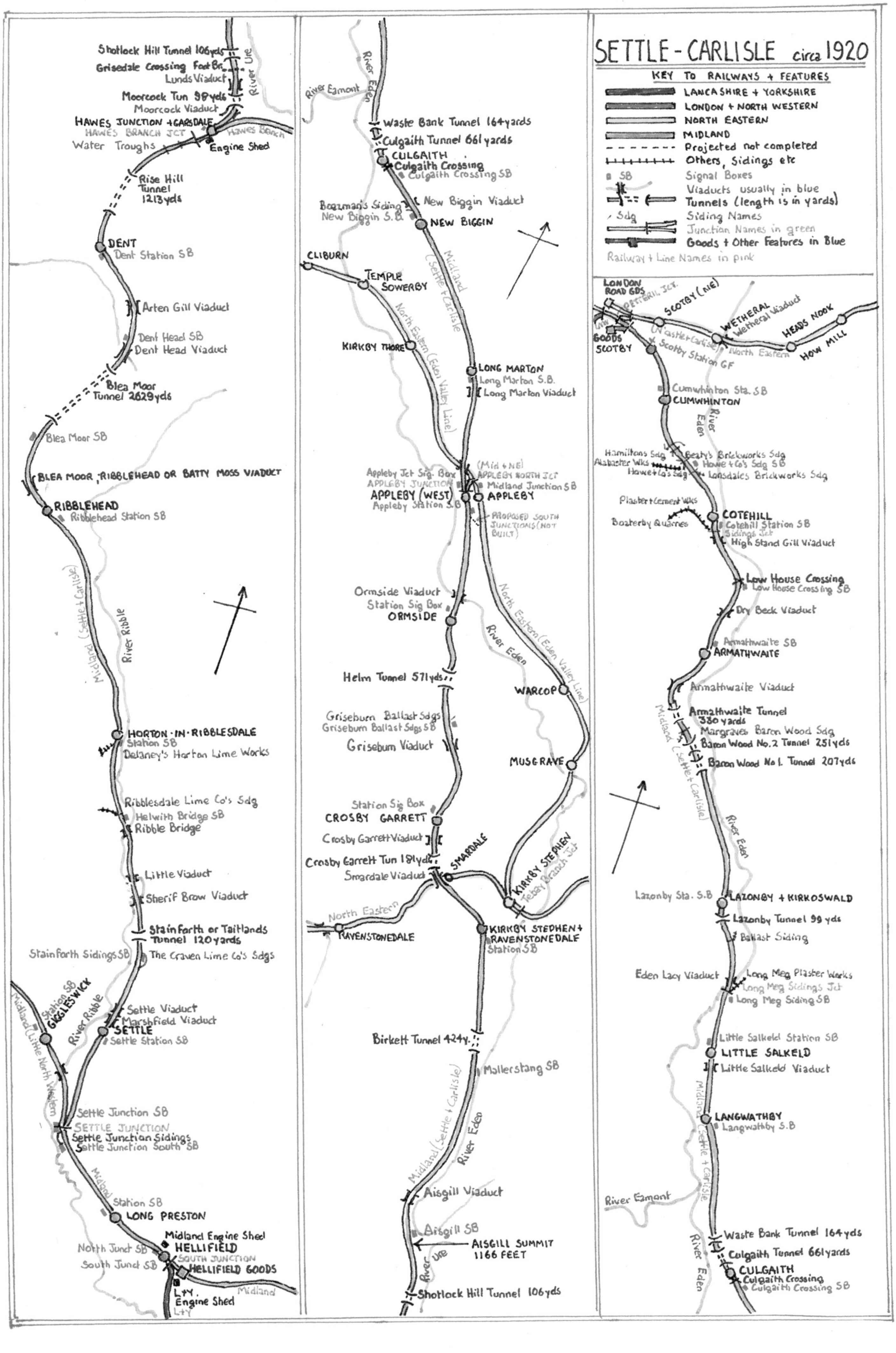
SETTLE - CARLISLE circa 1920
KEY TO RAILWAYS + FEATURES
LANCASHIRE + YORKSHIRE
LONDON + NORTH WESTERN
NORTH EASTERN
MIDLAND
Projected not completed
Others, Sidings etc
SB Signal Boxes
Viaducts usually in blue
Tunnels (length is in yards)
Sdg Siding Names
Junction Names in green
Goods + Other Features in Blue
Railway + Line Names in pink
Shotlock Hill Tunnel 106yds
Grisedale Crossing Foot Br.
Lunds Viaduct
River Ure
Moorcock Tun 98yds
Moorcock Viaduct
HAWES JUNCTION + GARSDALE
HAWES BRANCH JCT
Hawes Branch
Water Troughs
Engine Shed
Rise Hill Tunnel 1213yds
DENT
Dent Station SB
Arten Gill Viaduct
Dent Head SB
Dent Head Viaduct
Blea Moor Tunnel 2629yds
Blea Moor SB
BLEA MOOR, RIBBLEHEAD OR BATTY MOSS VIADUCT
RIBBLEHEAD
Ribblehead Station SB
Midland (Settle + Carlisle)
River Ribble
HORTON-IN-RIBBLESDALE
Station SB
Delaney's Horton Lime Works
Ribblesdale Lime Co's Sdg
Helwith Bridge SB
Ribble Bridge
Little Viaduct
Sherif Brow Viaduct
Stainforth or Taitlands Tunnel 120 yards
Stainforth Sidings SB
The Craven Lime Co's Sdgs
Station SB
GIGGLESWICK
River Ribble
Settle Viaduct
Marshfield Viaduct
SETTLE
Settle Station SB
Midland (Little North Western)
Settle Junction SB
SETTLE JUNCTION
Settle Junction Sidings
Settle Junction South SB
Midland
Station SB
LONG PRESTON
Midland Engine Shed
HELLIFIELD
North Junct SB
SOUTH JUNCTION
South Junct SB
HELLIFIELD GOODS
L+Y Engine Shed
L+Y
Midland
River Eden
River Eamont
Waste Bank Tunnel 164yards
Culgaith Tunnel 661yards
CULGAITH
Culgaith Crossing
Culgaith Crossing SB
Bozman's Siding
New Biggin S.B.
New Biggin Viaduct
NEW BIGGIN
CLIBURN
TEMPLE SOWERBY
Midland (Settle + Carlisle)
North Eastern (Eden Valley Line)
KIRKBY THORE
LONG MARTON
Long Marton S.B.
Long Marton Viaduct
(Mid + NE)
APPLEBY NORTH JCT
Midland Junction SB
Appleby Jct Sig. Box
APPLEBY JUNCTION
APPLEBY (WEST)
Appleby Station S.B.
APPLEBY
PROPOSED SOUTH JUNCTIONS (NOT BUILT)
Ormside Viaduct
Station Sig Box
ORMSIDE
North Eastern (Eden Valley Line)
River Eden
Helm Tunnel 571yds
WARCOP
Griseburn Ballast Sdgs
Griseburn Ballast Sdgs SB
Griseburn Viaduct
MUSGRAVE
Station Sig Box
CROSBY GARRETT
Crosby Garrett Viaduct
Crosby Garrett Tun 181yds
SMARDALE
Smardale Viaduct
KIRKBY STEPHEN
Tebay Branch Jct
North Eastern
RAVENSTONEDALE
KIRKBY STEPHEN + RAVENSTONEDALE
Station SB
Birkett Tunnel 424y.
Mallerstang SB
Midland (Settle + Carlisle)
River Eden
Aisgill Viaduct
Aisgill SB
AISGILL SUMMIT 1166 FEET
River Ure
Shotlock Hill Tunnel 106yds
LONDON ROAD GDS
PETTERIL JCT.
GOODS
SCOTBY
SCOTBY (NE)
N'castle+Carlisle
Scotby Station GF
WETHERAL
Wetheral Viaduct
North Eastern
HEADS NOOK
HOW MILL
Cumwhinton Sta. SB
CUMWHINTON
River Eden
Hamiltons Sdg
Alabaster Wks
Beaty's Brickworks Sdg
Howe + Co's Sdg SB
Howe + Co's Sdg
Lonsdales Brickworks Sdg
Plaster + Cement Wks
Boazerby Quarries
COTEHILL
Cotehill Station SB
Sidings Jct
High Stand Gill Viaduct
Low House Crossing
Low House Crossing SB
Dry Beck Viaduct
Armathwaite SB
ARMATHWAITE
Armathwaite Viaduct
Armathwaite Tunnel 330 yards
Margraves Baron Wood Sdg
Baron Wood No.2 Tunnel 251yds
Baron Wood No.1 Tunnel 207yds
Midland (Settle + Carlisle)
River Eden
Lazonby Sta. S.B
LAZONBY + KIRKOSWALD
Lazonby Tunnel 99 yds
Ballast Siding
Eden Lacy Viaduct
Long Meg Plaster Works
Long Meg Sidings Jct
Long Meg Siding SB
Little Salkeld Station SB
LITTLE SALKELD
Little Salkeld Viaduct
LANGWATHBY
Langwathby S.B
Midland (Settle + Carlisle)
River Eamont
Waste Bank Tunnel 164yds
Culgaith Tunnel 661yards
CULGAITH
Culgaith Crossing
Culgaith Crossing SB
River Eden

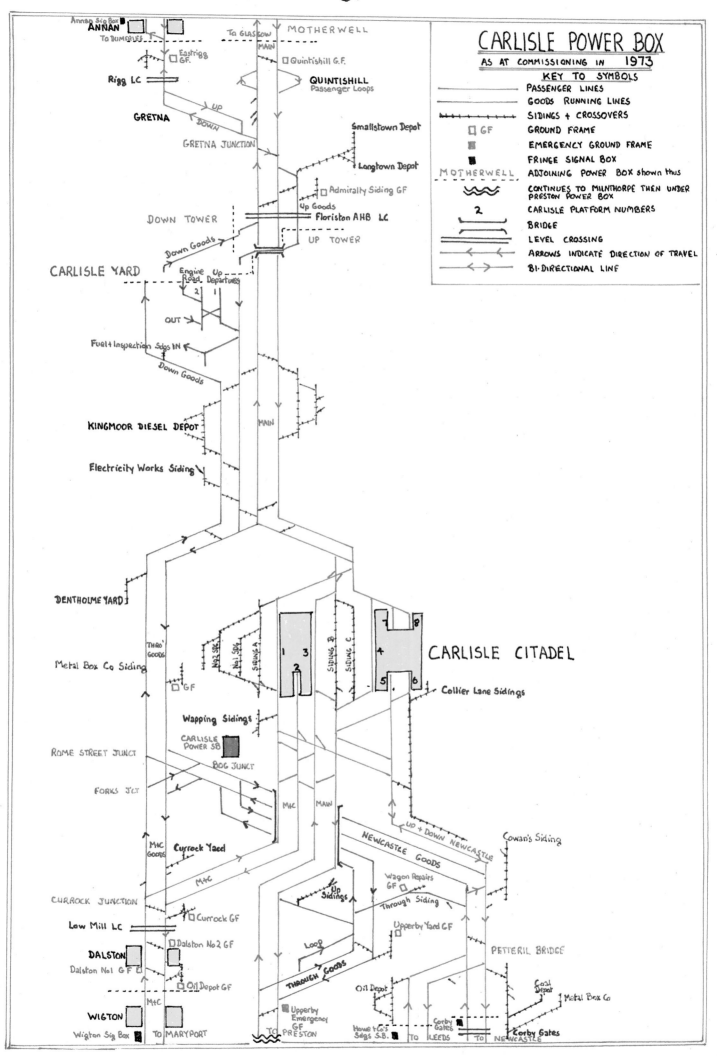

CARLISLE POWER BOX
AS AT COMMISSIONING IN 1973
KEY TO SYMBOLS

PASSENGER LINES
GOODS RUNNING LINES
SIDINGS + CROSSOVERS
GF   GROUND FRAME
EMERGENCY GROUND FRAME
FRINGE SIGNAL BOX
MOTHERWELL   ADJOINING POWER BOX shown thus
CONTINUES TO MILNTHORPE THEN UNDER PRESTON POWER BOX
2   CARLISLE PLATFORM NUMBERS
BRIDGE
LEVEL CROSSING
ARROWS INDICATE DIRECTION OF TRAVEL
BI-DIRECTIONAL LINE

CARLISLE POWER BOX 1973

A glance at the map of Central Carlisle circa 1900 does show graphically the complexities of the signalling. The small area covered includes no less than 26 signal boxes many of which were not only extremely busy but were open continuously. Added to this some fringe boxes and goods yard boxes are not shown since their exact location is not clear. The complexities of the system and the curtailment on line occupancy was undoubtedly the single greatest influence in saving the Settle-Carlisle line from closure, since until line occupancy could be increased the Settle-Carlisle was needed to absorb goods traffic peaks, and by the time power signalling was installed there was a sufficiently strong lobby to delay closure and ultimately to save the line.

To understand how the modern system achieves greater line occupancy apart from its obvious labour savings it is appropriate to look briefly at some of the difficulties inherent in conventional semaphore signalling. There were two principal difficulties and the first of these tended to affect closely spaced junction boxes in an area such as Carlisle and was the lack of overall view. Of course signalmen were aware of the working timetable but it was not always so easy to be aware of late trains and the snowball effect... This difficulty was accentuated at Carlisle with its seven different companies and three joint under-takings in the city. Some effort was made to partly overcome this in 1896 when fifteen central Carlisle boxes were placed under control of the London + North Western irrespective of which company line they controlled. Although this worked up to a point with passenger trains it was not so successful with goods traffic where delay could be chronic and with even greater snowball effect. Consider a train approaching Rome Street Junction on time and scheduled to travel on the line to Upperby and then join the LNW main line to the south; at the same time another train is approaching Rome Street from the M+C line due to go via Caldew Junction onto the Caledonian main line and on to Scotland. Which train is given priority can only be decided on the principle of how the two trains are running but this is likely to be wrong half the time. In practice priority needs to be given to path availability when the train will reach the main line but this information · is not available to the signalman and seeking it will in itself cause further delays. Grouping did nothing to eliminate this; and as mentioned earlier it is recorded a goods train at Carlisle ran only two miles in seven and a half hours. The other difficulty arises on plain track at intermediate boxes which can be unequally spaced, thus increasing the distance between trains to the length of the longest section. This difficulty too can be further accentuated at night when some intermediate boxes are switched out with the consequent curtailment of line occupancy. In addition to this further delays must always result from a signalman's need to record occurrences and communicate with his colleagues and others. A further facet to possible delay though not anything to do with signalling is the difference between goods and passenger train speeds.

Looking at the Carlisle Power Box it is immediately obvious that an excellent overall picture is available so that possible bottlenecks and giving mistaken priorities can be avoided. Keeping the traffic moving obviously increases line occupancy but this is enhanced by the colour light signals being equally spaced. Also the four aspect colour light signals are normally, in areas of plain track, at green and only change to red behind a train; the caution aspect then follows as soon as a train has passed the clearing point beyond the next signal. This latter aspect also greatly reduces work-load aspects, all that is needed is to set up the route and the rest is automatically taken care of. At the same time most of the needs of communicating and recording are entirely eliminated or greatly reduced.

A few facts about the box with a note of its enhancements and flexibity will be of interest, also its shortcomings that might have been avoided. First the good news: The box on commissioning controlled 114 route miles and 221 track miles; There were 135 points and 356 signals on the control panel. The full layout is shown in the diagram except for the plain track to the south; also shown are the adjoining boxes distinguishing between power boxes and convential boxes. The diagram also codifies goods only and all traffic lines besides distinguishing sidings. The diagram also shows numerous ground frames usually controlling sidings, yards, or similar and this obviously increases flexibility since to decide on movements in these areas needs to be decided by the man on the spot, the power signal box only becoming interested in finding a path when the running line needs to be regained. There are also emergency ground frames usually with facing crossovers between up and down lines which enable single line working if this is needed for track maintenance or other reasons. Turning to the not-so-good, the first shortcomings to note are the apparently pointless single track sections; some delays as a result of these sections would appear inevitable, made worse that both are close to the fringe of the area. One example will suffice relative to the single track section near Annan. To understand the argument one needs to appreciate that the double track Gretna Junction to Gretna is only a few hundred yards in length and its purpose is to enable a train to be held clear of the main line if the single track section is occupied. Gretna to Annan is about eight miles. Now if a train to Dumfries has been given priority over another train into Carlisle and when it turns onto its line at Gretna Junction there is a train at Annan one of the two must needs be delayed and whatever decision is reached there will have been two delays. Although double track would have eliminated the delay, greater knowledge of the line between Annan + Dumfries could have enabled the Dumfries-bound train to not have had priority at Carlisle and the delay caused by the single track section at Gretna to have been avoided. On this line of reasoning it is clear that Newcastle line single track problems will be even greater.

EDINBURGH

Edinburgh has both an unusual and a fascinating development history. The first unusual facet was that unlike most of the centres it did not have lines radiating outwards from it, but, particularly in early days, lines inwards towards it. This factor which arose from a combination of accidental reasons may appear an irrelevance in the growth of a focal point and so far as trunk routes were concerned this was undoubtedly true. But local and suburban lines and branches were affected by this as we shall see. On the first two maps every railway was either planned to bring traffic to Scotland's capital or constructed with entry to Edinburgh as the final stage.

The railway history of Edinburgh starts as early as 1817 when a group of promoters sought to construct a railway to convey coal from the Lothian coalfield to Edinburgh. The scheme though abortive was revived seven years later. With the support of the colliery owners it was successful at the second attempt, the result being the incorporation of the Edinburgh and Dalkeith Railway in 1826. The railway was constructed to a gauge of 4'6" and was horse drawn. The main line was from Dalhousie to St Leonards (via Niddrie which became the focal point). Ultimately branches radiated from Niddrie to Fisherrow and Leith. In addition branches to South Esk and Dalkeith reached other collieries. Passenger traffic was soon introduced and was very successful carrying more passengers per mile than both the Liverpool & Manchester and the Stockton & Darlington, that in spite of the latter companies both enjoying the advantage of steam haulage. The Edinburgh & Dalkeith was purchased by the North British in 1845 and in late 1846 the work of conversion of gauge was commenced. The line was re-opened for both goods and passengers in 1847, but St Leonard's soon lost its passenger service due to its inconvenient location. The Edinburgh & Glasgow Railway had in the meantime opened to Haymarket in 1842 whilst the North British trunk route was opened throughout to North Bridge in June 1846. In some ways this railway could be regarded as starting from Edinburgh, since as yet there was no railway connection into England. But the influence from the south was in English capital which had earlier declined to support a more local scheme. The final line shown on the first map was that proposed by the Edinburgh Leith & Newhaven which was intended to start from Edinburgh and link the points of its title. But fate again intervened to obstruct this objective due to geographical difficulties and a long litigation battle where owners of new prestige properties sought to prevent the railway going under their properties. Eventually the title was changed to Edinburgh Leith & Granton, as it was realised that Granton would become important with its connecting ferry to enable a trunk route from Edinburgh and England to continue rail journeys to the north. As the first map shows, the connection to Edinburgh was as yet incomplete. All these railways would in due course be absorbed by the North British.

The last nine months of 1846 saw a great deal of railway development in Edinburgh. The line to Granton mentioned above had in fact become the main line of Edinburgh, Leith & Granton. In May 1846 a branch opened from Bonnington Junction, later known as Warriston Junction, to Leith. In June, as noted above, the North British opened to North Bridge, whilst at the same time work was in hand in converting the Edinburgh & Dalkeith. The final event of 1846 saw the Edinburgh & Glasgow open from Haymarket to North Bridge where connection was made with the North British.

Development continued unabated during the following eighteen months. In chronological order the first event was in May 1847 when at last the Edinburgh Leith & Granton reached its cramped Canal Street terminus adjoining the North British North Bridge terminus but set at right angles to it. In June Portobello to Niddrie was re-opened following gauge change. Then in July most of the remaining Edinburgh & Dalkeith system opened to passengers and goods. Other openings by the North British included New Hailes to Musselburgh and Newton Grange to Gorebridge (this latter line being a portion of the route of a company, the Edinburgh & Hawick, which had been absorbed by the North British in 1846). 1847 also witnessed some rationalisation in November with the closure of St Leonards for passengers. It did enjoy a brief further period as a passenger station for a few weeks in 1860. Obviously the station suffered in attracting passenger traffic due to its very inconvenient site compared to central location of North Bridge, Canal and Haymarket. It was, however, to remain for goods traffic for well over another hundred years. 1848 also saw a closure on the North British main line. This was the station at Jock's Lodge. But the main event of 1848 was the arrival of the Caledonian railway at its Lothian Road terminus with intermediate stations within the map area at Slateford, Kingsknowe and Currie.

Following this intense development activity in the late 1840's a much quieter period followed. In fact over the next 13 years only two new lines appeared. The first of these promoted by the Peebles Railway ran from Hardengreen Junction to Peebles and this opened in 1855. It was leased by the North British in 1857 but not fully absorbed by that company until 1876. The final development shown was in 1861 when the Caledonian opened a branch from a junction near Slateford to Granton Dock, but this was, and destined to remain Goods only.

The available information covering this period is confusing and it has not always been possible to show station dates of opening and in particular intermediate stations. The exact track layout and junctions in the Niddrie area is also unclear.

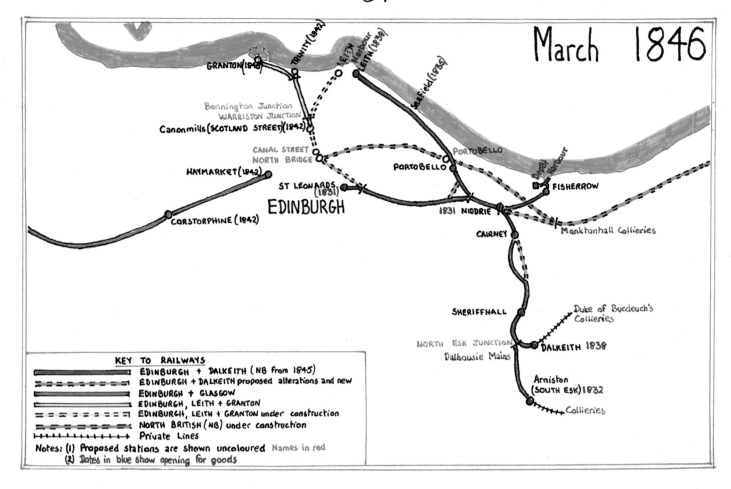

March 1846

KEY TO RAILWAYS

EDINBURGH + DALKEITH (NB from 1845)
EDINBURGH + DALKEITH proposed alterations and new
EDINBURGH + GLASGOW
EDINBURGH, LEITH + GRANTON
EDINBURGH, LEITH + GRANTON under construction
NORTH BRITISH (NB) under construction
Private Lines

Notes: (1) Proposed stations are shown uncoloured Names in red
(2) Dates in blue show opening for goods

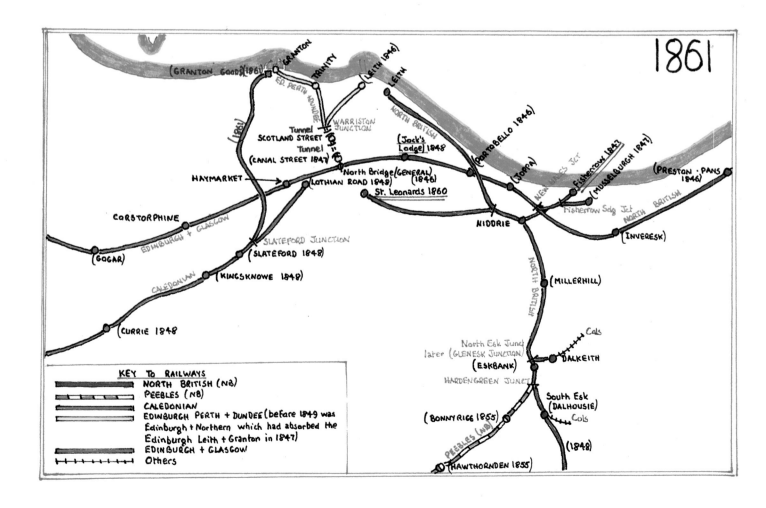

1861

KEY TO RAILWAYS

NORTH BRITISH (NB)
PEEBLES (NB)
CALEDONIAN
EDINBURGH PERTH + DUNDEE (before 1849 was
Edinburgh + Northern which had absorbed the
Edinburgh Leith + Granton in 1847)
EDINBURGH + GLASGOW
Others

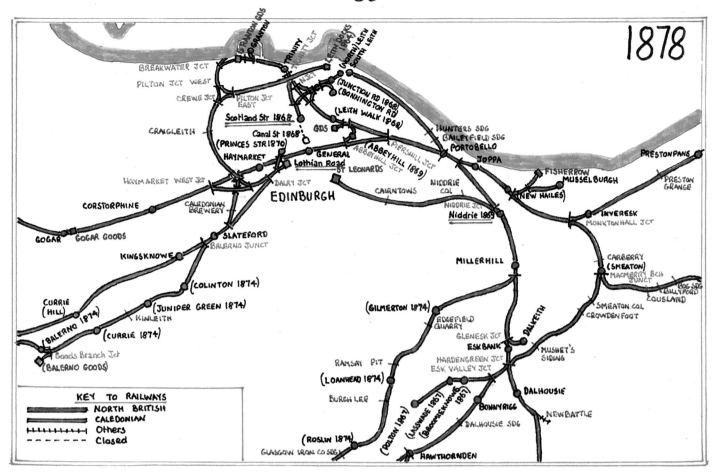

1878

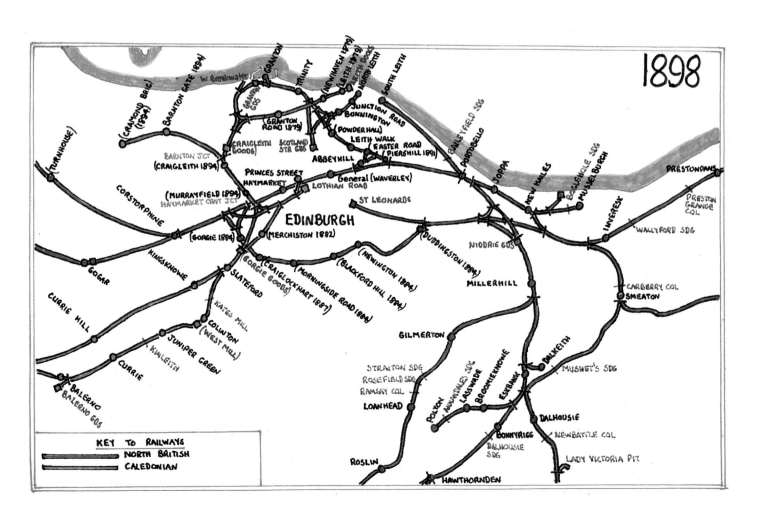

1898

The next period up to 1878 saw no new mainline development but a host of branch lines, concerned chiefly in tapping the freight traffic, serving associated industries and conveying merchandise, manufactured products and minerals to the Lothian coast at Leith. The passenger traffic associated with these developments was normally of secondary consideration.

Looking first at the Caledonian - The Leith Goods-only branch from Crewe Junction on the Granton goods line was opened in 1864 and a triangular junction of lines was added to give a direct connection between Leith and Granton. Fifteen years were to pass before this new line carried a passenger service and the Caledonian Granton station never enjoyed a passenger service. This was because the Caledonian preferred to get its passengers, mainly from the west, to north of the Forth by way of Stirling and Alloa. Even the North British were using the crossing less by making use of the much shorter Queensferry crossing. The other Caledonian developments during this period were: Princes Street was opened in 1870 and the original Lothian Road terminus was reduced to a goods station; the Balerno branch opened in 1874 primarily to serve lineside industries but in this case it also carried a passenger service. Finally 1876 saw the opening of connecting spurs to give Lothian Road Goods station direct connection with Leith and Granton, and also to the North British line at Haymarket West.

By contrast with the Caledonian who themselves built all the above lines, the North British, although building some lines, continued to expand by acquisition. The North British family tree below shows all the railways within the map area which came ultimately to be part of that company.

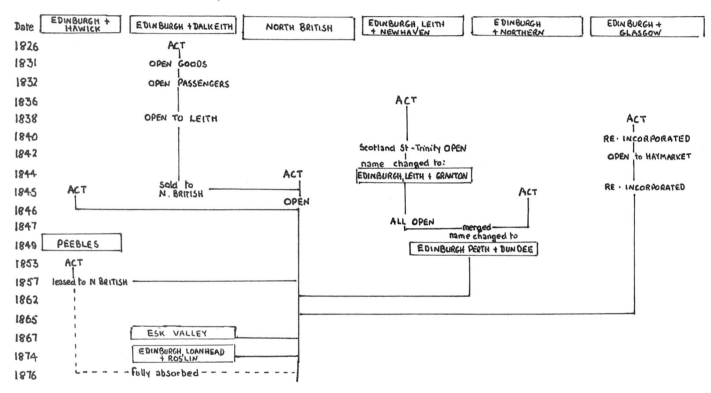

The other North British openings were from Abbeyhill to Trinity (after Edinburgh, Perth + Dundee had been absorbed) in 1868. The cramped Canal Street terminus together with the tunnel to Scotland Street were closed to all traffic. Trinity to Scotland Street was kept open but for goods only. The other opening by the North British was the Smeaton lines opened for goods in 1872, but it then opened for passengers shortly afterwards.

The next twenty years showed a continuation of this type of development. The Caledonian opened a passenger service on a new branch to Cramond Brig in 1894, having in the meantime introduced a passenger service on the Leith branch in 1879. The North British also turned its attention to passenger traffic. On the line eastwards from Smeaton, passenger workings had been introduced in 1872. Now a light railway was promoted to reach Gifford, which, however, did not open until 1901. But during this period the North British were involved in two through routes. The first of these was a direct connection from a junction Corstorphine to Queensferry in preparation for the opening of the Forth Bridge. This magnificent structure opened for traffic in early 1890. The result was that the roundabout connection to Granton ceased to be a main line and became so far as passengers were concerned an inconvenient and little-used branch line. The connecting ferry service continued but was little used. The other through line was the Edinburgh Suburban + Southside Junction Railway. From its title this might be regarded as a suburban traffic development line, and so it was, and with the associated new connections at Niddrie and Gorgie a suburban passenger circular service was inaugurated. But the more important aspects of this line was that of a goods avoiding line to keep goods traffic away from the congestion of Waverley station. It is not without significance that although the suburban passenger service has long been withdrawn, new connections were added in BR times so that it would more effectively serve its goods function.

The next map which is at a larger scale covers two periods showing the position at 1905 and shows the new lines added up to 1928. The first date is but seven years later than the previous map but included suburban development on a large scale and in fact completed Edinburgh's maximum railway development. There were later additions of both lines and stations of course, but these were balanced by closures from the period of grouping onwards. In addition all the new lines were, as the map shows, lines to assist goods traffic flows at Leith and Niddrie.

In trying to develop the suburban network the North British had two difficulties to contend with. The first of these was geographical resulting in the local network following roundabout routes. The direct distances to places such as Granton, North Leith, Duddingston and Newington from the central stations of Waverley and Haymarket compared to the rail distances only need a casual glance to appreciate the difficulties faced. The second difficulty only serves to accentuate the first in that it is a legacy from the old Edinburgh + Dalkeith. That railway was not centred on Edinburgh at all, but Niddrie. This was the place coal reached from the pits to the south whence it was sent forward to Edinburgh, Leith or Fisherrow. Routes to all these places from Niddrie are direct routes but they become inappropriate in particular in reaching to Leith and Granton where to travel in effect via Niddrie is well out of one's way. But of course Niddrie had already closed to passenger traffic although retaining its importance as a freight centre.
These two factors explain the North British developments around the turn of the century. The branch to Corstorphine was opened in 1902 and was followed in 1903 by the new direct link to Leith Central. The Caledonian had very similar aims to the North British with its two promotions during the same period. But they were not so successful. The first of these was a scheme to reach both Central and South Leith by a branch from a junction at Newhaven calling at Bonnington, Leith Walk and Restalrig before turning north to reach the Docks at South Leith. Although the platforms were built, they were never used, and a glance at the map and the roundabout route to Leith shows why there were second thoughts. The line, however, was used for goods traffic. The other Caledonian scheme was even less successful than the first; this was to have been an extension of the Barnton branch to form a circular route not unlike the existing North British southern circle. But the scheme failed to get off the ground.

In spite of these difficulties, however, the Edinburgh local services proved financially more rewarding to the North British than its Glasgow suburban counterpart. This appears strange bearing in mind the disadvantages inherent in Edinburgh's round about routes and geographical difficulties. Also of course the greater size of Glasgow would, one would have thought, made a suburban network easier to support. But at this stage there were several compensating factors: In Glasgow there were three main line railways competing for suburban traffic to which in due course would be added the subway line. The second factor was that in Glasgow an excellent tramway system creamed off much short-haul traffic, whilst in Edinburgh the inefficient counterpart had a very limited orbit. Added to this, many of the remoter branches radiating from Edinburgh were patronised by a very high proportion of first class passengers.

Grouping had little effect upon Edinburgh as the two pre-grouping railways remained independant of each other and continued in competition. The North British became part of the LONDON + NORTH EASTERN whilst the Caledonian became part of the LONDON, MIDLAND + SCOTTISH.

The most noticeable event in the post-grouping scenario was in the suburban network. Although there is little to show on the map, road competition was putting pressures on the railways in filching suburban traffic. The seeds of obliteration were sown in the developments of road transport. The tramway system was electrified and extended having immediate effect on the short-haul services. In the meantime cars and buses were gradually winning the longer-distance traffic. Thus the road transport system had overcome its shortcomings and the inherent weakness of the railway system was unable to make any adequate counter-measures. No-one was going to use one of the roundabout routes with no regular service and face the stairs at Waverley when a tram at street level offered door-to-door services at a cheaper price.

The railways made strenuous efforts to retain some of the traffic and the next period shows opening of halts on the more competitive routes, but this only available countermeasure had little effect. In contrast the Glasgow local services, which had experienced much fiercer road competition at an earlier date now showed a great resilience in retaining more of their suburban traffic.

Finally three closures remain to be noted. The first was South Leith in 1903, effectively replaced by the more direct Leith Central line. The other two were Trinity and Granton. Following the opening of the Forth Bridge this route had lost its main line status and remained only as a little-used circuitous branch. All stations were North British and all remained in use for goods traffic.

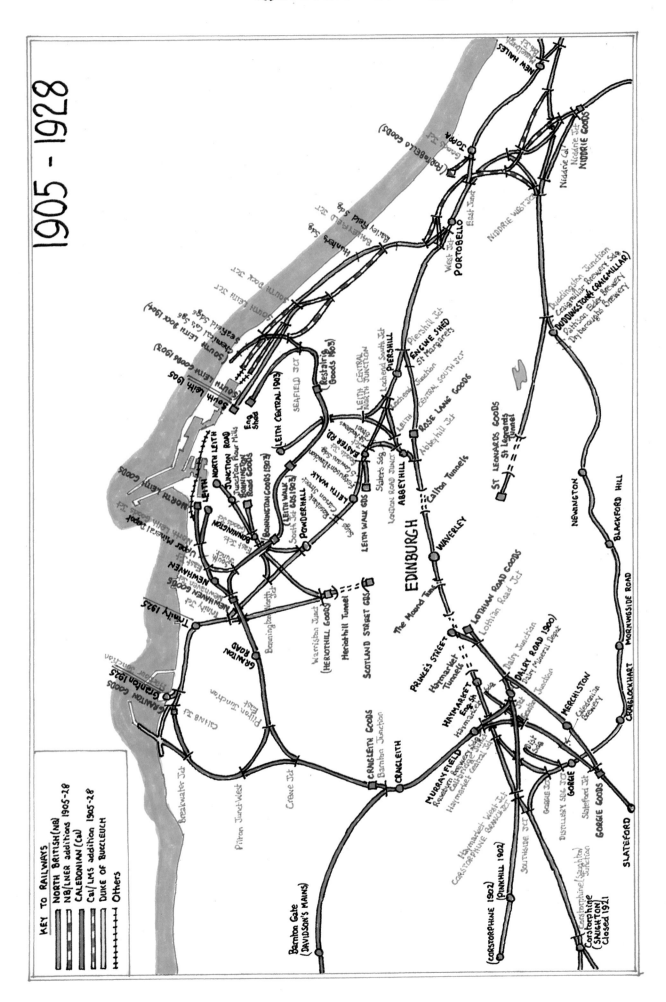

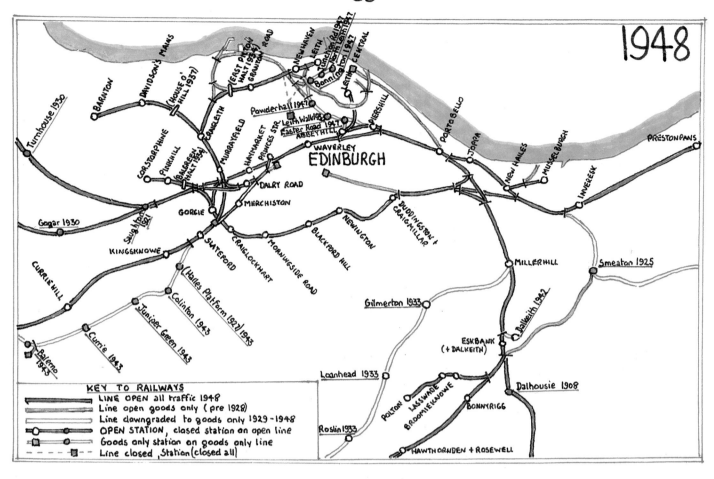

1948

KEY TO RAILWAYS
LINE OPEN all traffic 1948
Line open goods only (pre 1928)
Line downgraded to goods only 1929-1948
OPEN STATION, closed station on open line
Goods only station on goods only line
Line closed , Station(closed all)

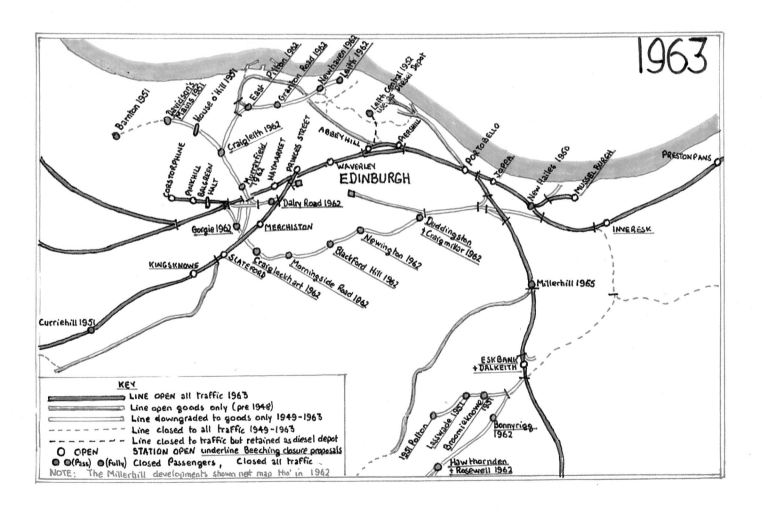

1963

KEY
LINE OPEN all traffic 1963
Line open goods only (pre 1948)
Line downgraded to goods only 1949-1963
Line closed to all traffic 1949-1963
Line closed to traffic but retained as diesel depot
O OPEN   STATION OPEN underline Beeching closure proposals
O(Pass) O(Fully) Closed Passengers,   Closed all traffic
NOTE: The Millerhill developments shown not map tho' in 1962

The next two maps show the commencement of the decimation process of Edinburgh's local services. Two dates have been chosen to illustrate; the closures prior to nationalisation, and those closed by British Rail before production of the Beeching report. As is also seen elsewhere it is nevertheless interesting to note that the closures in each of these periods are greater by some margin as compared with the closure proposals recommended in the Good Doctor's publication. The closures fall into two categories. First, on the main lines there was a steady reduction in the number of intermediate stations. The second category comprises entire branches downgraded to goods only to be followed later by total closure. Before looking in detail at the two periods them-selves it is appropriate to look at some earlier events affecting lines on the outer fringes not included on the 1905-29 map. Dalhousie closed as early as 1908 and Smeaton closed in 1925 at the same time as Granton and Trinity (already noted). But to the periods themselves:

It has already been told how, with the upsurge of road transport in the early 'twenties, traffic dwindled alarmingly. In a vain effort to stem this loss, new intermediate stations and halts were opened in an effort to cater for what were visualised as particular needs. But this policy appears to have been restricted to LMS (ex Caledonian) lines, although a halt at Balgreen on the Corstorphine branch opened in 1934. LMS halts were opened at Hailes Platform (to serve a golf course) in 1927, followed by East Pilton in 1934 and House o' Hill in 1937. On the other side of the coin the earliest closures were the two branches eastwards from Smeaton downgraded to goods only by 1925 as noted above. A similar fate awaited the Glencorse line with a death sentence in 1933. The next branch closures were war-time economy measures and these were the downgrading to goods only of the Balerno branch; there was a similar fate awaiting the North Leith branch just before nationalisation in 1947. The Scotland Street Goods-only connections appear to have closed about this time. So far as intermediate stations are concerned the closures of Dalhousie and Saughton were in the pre-grouping period. 1930 saw the closure of Gogar and Turnhouse stations. The final closure to be noted with some nostalgia was Dalkeith in 1942, the last surviving passenger station of Edinburgh's first railway, the Edinburgh + Dalkeith. The town, however, continued to be rail-served by Eskbank station on the main line. In most of the closures noted above goods services continued for some time, but closure dates for goods traffic are both unclear and unmeaningful. In many cases traffic can have ceased and track lifted before official date of closure whilst less frequently the reverse can occur. On the maps goods closure dates are not therefore shown unless clear cut.

The nationalisation of railways brought one immediate benefit to Scotland, a united regional management. This possibility had been considered at grouping but was surprisingly rejected. Elsewhere regional boundaries followed grouping boundaries and in England and Wales many years would pass before some commonsense adjustment of regional boundaries would ensue. The united management approach enabled a more realistic view of rationalisation to prevail and accelerated the closure of suburban and country branches. To begin with petrol rationing gave a short respite but increased car ownership would soon bring this fleeting honeymoon period to an end.

Most of the network previously reduced to goods only closed entirely during this period, the main exception being Millerhill to Roslin. The connection from Piershill and Abbeyhill through Granton to East Pilton also survived the period in theory but in practice the branch was little used if at all after 1962.

The programme of closures commenced in 1950 with the closure of New Hailes on the East Coast Main line (ECML). The following year, 1951, saw closure of two branches to passenger traffic; Craigleith to Barnton (Barnton to goods also) and the Polton branch. Currichill also closed (on the LMS Glasgow line). Then in 1952 the short-haul Leith Central closed, but loop connections enabled some ECML trains to be diverted to call at Piershill and Abbeyhill and there was even an intermediate halt in use for a time. Following this period of closure activity only one further closure remains to be noted, Millerhill in 1955.

The last eight years of the period were dominated by two events. The first was BR's Modernisation plan which was to concentrate freight marshalling throughout Great Britain at just twenty-five locations. An Edinburgh yard at Millerhill was planned between Millerhill and the junction location of Niddrie. This yard together with its associated new lines was actually opened in 1962 but all these new developments have been shown slightly out of context on the post 1963 map so that the 1963 map could show clearly both pre-Beeching closures together with those recommended in the report for closure. The closures of 1962 involved most of the remaining branch and suburban network and included the Peebles line; the ex-Caledonian line to Leith together with the connecting spurs in the Dalry area; and finally the Edinburgh Southside line which was, however, to be retained as essential goods running lines, in the Millerhill development. Just two branches remained, the short Musselburgh and Corstorphine branches. With all these closures effected there was little more for Beeching to recommend. The proposed closures are indicated on the map by underline in red of open stations. The Musselburgh branch was to go, but that to Corstorphine was to survive; the longer-term results here were almost diametrically opposite. The Waverley line was to close, and the remaining closures were further intermediate main line stations. The final proposal to note was Princes Street which was under consideration for closure at the time of the report but which would need upgrading of a siding and goods connection so that trains from the ex LMS main line from Glasgow could run directly into Haymarket and Waverley. The final maps show the results of the Beeching Report and the development of 1962 from the Modernisation plan.

The further development story up to 1994 must begin with the opening of the MILLERHILL YARD in 1962. As mentioned earlier it has been deliberately omitted from the map to 1963 so that the results of the Modernisation plan and the Beeching report can be looked at together clear of all earlier events.

The Millerhill was intended to rationalise all Edinburgh Goods facilities basing the new yard at a convenient site that would assist goods traffic flows. It was astride the Waverley route to Carlisle and with direct access to the Docks at South Leith. To improve matters new goods lines were built: The first of these gave a facing connection for down traffic from the ECML at a new Monktonhall Junction giving up and down connections to the Waverley route and the new yard. At the same time a chord line from Slateford to Craiglockhart gave direct access to the yard to and from the ex-Caledonian Glasgow main-line. The Haymarket West and Gorgie Junction existing line already gave access to the old Edinburgh & Glasgow line and also via the Forth Bridge to the North. Furthermore all goods traffic could entirely avoid the city centre. Following this all other goods facilities were closed with the exception of South Leith, but even here reduction in use was planned and implemented. One final point regarding location of the yard is worth noting — that it makes use of the focal point of the first railway, the Edinburgh & Dalkeith, which of course had been centred on Niddrie. The yard never worked to its full capacity reflecting the position elsewhere. It was of course affected by closure of the Waverley route. It has been in a state of progressive rationalisation ever since. In the early 80's closure was a possibility; however, it appears secure in its present form due to two factors: First, despite the Waverley line closure it is sited in an excellent position; secondly, the ECML electrification proposals have resulted in its adaption as a Speedlink centre.

Turning to the results of the Beeching proposals, these had a mixed fate. First the branches - Musselburgh closed in 1964 but it would in due course gain compensation in a station on the ECML. Corstorphine branch on the other hand, although not scheduled for closure in the report, was closed to all traffic in 1967. The only other line closure was the Waverley line which closed in 1969. It would doubtless have gone sooner but for the Millerhill Yard and its position astride the route coupled with KINGMOOR NEW YARD at Carlisle, the other end of the route. Intermediate stations had a mixed fate and the following chart lists the fate of all Edinburgh stations either closed or threatened with closure during this period:

BEECHING PROPOSED CLOSURES	Implemented	Abbeyhill, Inveresk, Joppa, Musselburgh + Piershill all in 1964. Merchiston and Princes St in 1965. Eskbank + Dalkeith (the remaining Waverley station in the map area) in 1969.
	Not Implemented	SLATEFORD
	Closed + Re-opened	KINGSKNOWE Closed 1964 (RE-OPENED 1971)
OTHER CLOSURES		Portobello 1964; Corstorphine 1967; Pinkhill 1967; Balgreen Halt 1967.

With the closure of the Waverley line in 1969 the passenger stations in the area reached a nadir, and although as noted above KINGSKNOWE re-opened in 1971, it would be the mid 80's before any further positive development was seen.

The final period has seen a mild upsurge in traffic and the use of unstaffed stations has led to some re-openings and some entirely new stations. New stations opened during the period have been at MUSSELBURGH (MONKTONHALL) to replace the closed branch station but located on the ECML; also opened in new locations have been WESTER HAILES and SOUTH GYLE. The final opening has been CURRIEHILL. This may appear rather as a re-opening, but it is some distance south-west of the old closed station of that name which had closed in 1951. Also as noted above the future of MILLERHILL, albeit in modified form, appears secure. Goods traffic also continues to be handled at Leith and as the map shows there has been some upsurge in industries seeking rail connections.

The future shows proposals for two further stations: One at WALLYFORD on the ECML and a further one at EDINBURGH AIRPORT on the approximate site of the old Turnhouse station closed in 1930. In connection with this latter station, a new chord line is also proposed to give direct access to the Glasgow line without the need of reversal. This will be just off the edge of the map north of the station making a facing connection with the down line.

One final point which merits comment is that it is quite uncanny to note the close resemblance of the 1990 map to that extant in 1850 (between the first two maps); the differences are small and virtually all can be accounted for. First, although the Musselburgh branch has gone it has been replaced by in effect a more convenient station on the ECML. Next although the Granton line has long gone its substitute as main line to Queensferry and the Forth Bridge is very much in evidence. The focal point for goods remains and the only enhancement the 1990 map shows is the south side goods line now giving through running. This odd state of affairs will be found repeated at many other centres.

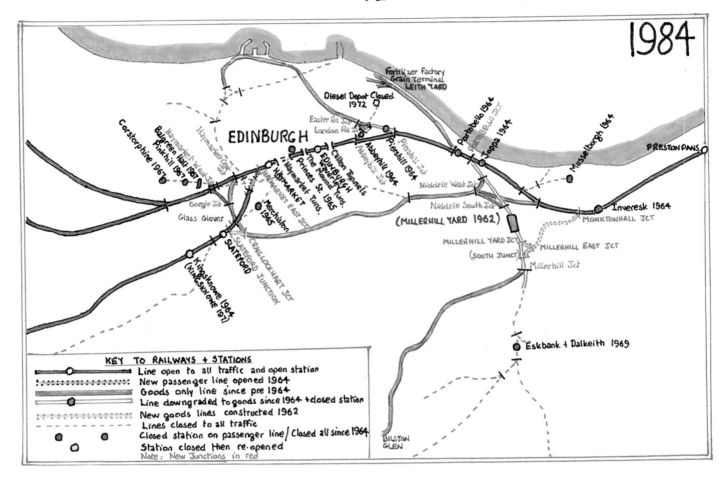

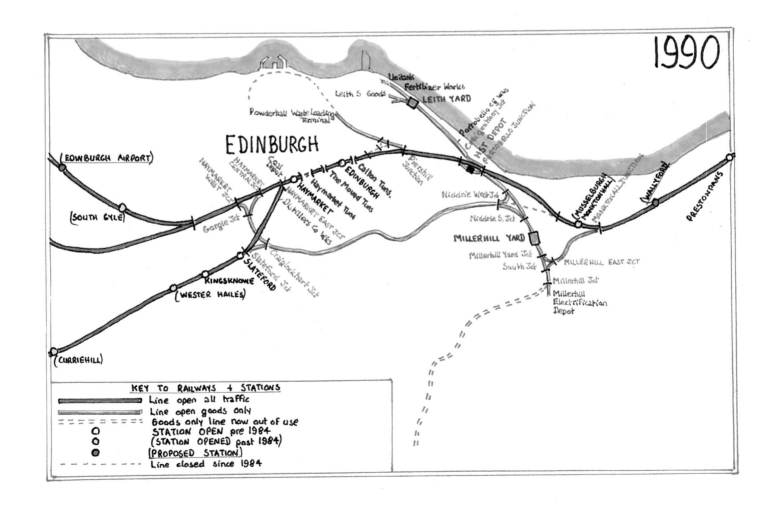

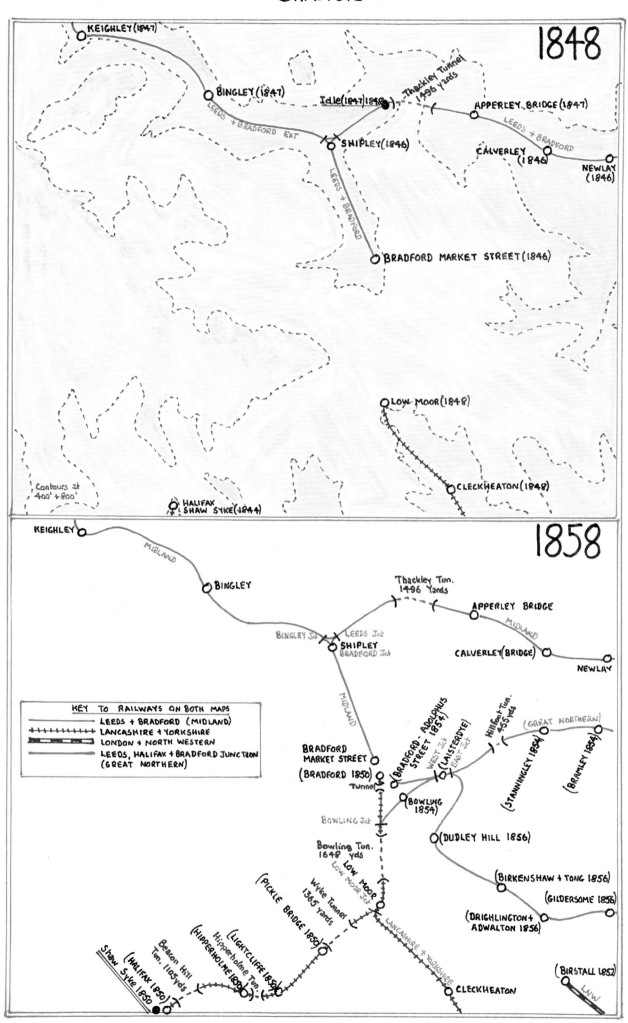

1848

KEIGHLEY (1847)

BINGLEY (1847)

Idle (1847/1848)

Thackley Tunnel
1496 yards

APPERLEY BRIDGE (1847)

LEEDS + BRADFORD

LEEDS + BRADFORD EXT

SHIPLEY (1846)

CALVERLEY
(1846)

NEWLAY
(1846)

LEEDS + BRADFORD

BRADFORD MARKET STREET (1846)

LOW MOOR (1848)

Contours at
400' + 800'

HALIFAX
SHAW SYKE (1844)

CLECKHEATON (1848)

1858

KEIGHLEY

MIDLAND

BINGLEY

Thackley Tun.
1496 Yards

APPERLEY BRIDGE

MIDLAND

Bingley Jct
Leeds Jct

SHIPLEY
BRADFORD Jct

CALVERLEY (BRIDGE)

NEWLAY

MIDLAND

KEY TO RAILWAYS ON BOTH MAPS

⎯⎯⎯ LEEDS + BRADFORD (MIDLAND)
+++++ LANCASHIRE + YORKSHIRE
▓▓▓▓▓ LONDON + NORTH WESTERN
⎯⎯⎯ LEEDS, HALIFAX + BRADFORD JUNCTION
(GREAT NORTHERN)

BRADFORD
MARKET STREET
(BRADFORD 1850)

BRADFORD-ADOLPHUS STREET (1854)

WEST Jct
(LAISTERDYKE)
EAST Jct

Hillfoot Tun.
455 yds

(GREAT NORTHERN)

(STANNINGLEY 1854)

(BRAMLEY 1854)

Tunnel

BOWLING
(1854)

Bowling Jct

(DUDLEY HILL 1856)

Bowling Tun.
1648 yds

Low Moor Jct

(BIRKENSHAW + TONG 1856)

(GILDERSOME 1856)

(PICKLE BRIDGE 1850)

Wyke Tunnel
1365 yards

LOW MOOR

LANCASHIRE + YORKSHIRE

(DRIGHLINGTON +
ADWALTON 1856)

(LIGHTCLIFFE 1850)

Beacon Hill
Tun. 1105yds

(HIPPERHOLME 1850)

Shaw Syke (HALIFAX 1850)

(BIRSTALL 1852)

CLECKHEATON

LNW

BRADFORD

To describe BRADFORD as a railway centre is something of a misnomer. It has always been, and remains, a backwater, albeit at times it has been a very busy one. It is also the largest inland place, by some considerable margin, never to have had a through station.

These facts and the comparatively late arrival of the first railway in Bradford may appear strange but a glance at the geographical location provides the answer. Bradford is situated in a bowl in the hills and there is only one possibility of a level route into the city. This is by using the tributary valley of the Aire, known locally as the Mucky Beck which joins the main valley at Shipley. However, this tributary was not able to provide the basis of a through route because after reaching the centre of Bradford it turns sharply west towards high ground effectively barring any simple way forward. In addition to this there is an additional geographical oddity, in that the smaller settlements in the area surrounding the city which would later be incorporated into Bradford as suburbs were not situated is such valleys as existed but on the ridges. When therefore railways reached these suburbs the stations tended to be somewhat remote from the population they intended to serve and became vulnerable to road competition.

The first railway to reach Bradford was the LEEDS + BRADFORD. This line reached its Market Street terminus in 1846 with just one intermediate station at Shipley. This was by the easy graded Aire valley route adding four miles to the direct distance between the two places of nine miles. The extra distance could have been greater if the engineers had not bored the 1496 yard Thackley Tunnel through the north projecting spur of land on the approach to Shipley. Intermediate stations at Calverley and at Newlay were opened later in the year and at Apperley Bridge and Idle in the following year. 1847 also saw the Leeds and Bradford Extension Railway opened to Bingley, Keighley and beyond. Already the Shipley to Bradford portion had become a branch. The final event relative to the Leeds and Bradford during this period saw a closure! Idle closed after only one year due to its awkward approach and the fact that is was over a mile from the hill top village it was supposed to serve. The station site is still rural in character and difficult of access.

In the meantime railway development was taking place to the south. The MANCHESTER + LEEDS, which in due course was to become one of the main constituents of the LANCASHIRE + YORKSHIRE, had penetrated the Bradford area by two branches. The first of these had reached HALIFAX Shaw Syke in 1844 from a junction at Greetland and work was in progress on a further branch from Mirfield to Bradford, but by the end of 1848 this had only reached a station at Low Moor, the final entry to Bradford experiencing engineering difficulties. The Manchester + Leeds had refused to build a direct route from Halifax to Bradford pointing out that once this line was completed there would be a rail link between the two places. This would involve 21 rail miles between places seven miles apart and possibly two changes of train!

The first map, which shows relief, is interesting in so far as it is significant that only one appreciable breach of the 'too' contour occurs, that being Thackley Tunnel. It is obvious that engineering difficulties, steep gradients, and the extra costs associated were all factors stemming from the geography of the location deferring network growth.

Ten years later the network had grown to include most of what remains open on the 1991 map. In chronolgical order: the line from Low Moor reached Bradford in early 1850. The difficulties here were the 1648 yards long Bowling Tunnel and another shorter tunnel later opened out. The line was also handicapped by being steeply graded. Later the same year the Halifax to Low Moor route was opened; this too had been beset by heavy engineering works, since the line runs against the grain of the land with tunnel following viaduct, through spurs and across valleys.

The next development was the opening of the LONDON + NORTH WESTERN branch to Birstall in 1852. This was planned as a line to reach Bradford, but the engineering difficulties in completing the project, together with the shortage of cash and the opposition of other railway companies, meant it was destined to remain an unremunerative branch to nowhere. The remaining additions to the local network were all constructed by the LEEDS, BRADFORD + HALIFAX JUNCTION Railway. This company was later absorbed by the Great Northern. The direct Leeds to Bradford route opened in 1854, with, as its title implied, a connection from Laisterdyke to Bowling Junction and connection with the Lancashire + Yorkshire route to Halifax. This resulted in a third Bradford terminus at Adolphus Street designed and located to avoid gradients steeper than 1:100. But due to its location remote from the commercial centre it was to last only thirteen years before a new link was built to connect with the Lancashire + Yorkshire terminal. The final line to be constructed during this period was also part of the Great Northern system. This was the line from Laisterdyke to Ardsley to provide connection with Wakefield. Heavy gradients and long tunnels were avoided but at the expense of a tortuous route, as the map shows. From Adolphus Street to Dudley Hill is about 1½ miles but the rail distance was four miles!

One final interesting feature of note on the first two maps is the absence of any intermediate stations between the Market Street, Midland terminus and Shipley. As mentioned above this was due to the settlements in the area surrounding Bradford tending to be located on the hillsides and ridges and away from the valleys. Even up to the present time the valleys are comparatively lacking in residential development.

The next map shows the further developments over the next thirty years and charts development up to the end of 1885. All the new lines opened during this period were confined to companies already operating in the area. Sometimes a nominally independant company was authorised to construct a line but this was inevitably with financial support of one of the major companies, and such companies were quickly absorbed. Most of the lines built during this period took a very long time to progress from authorisation to opening for passengers. This was due to two closely associated factors. First was the heavy engineering works which made the line costly to construct. Secondly the works needed always tended to cost more than the original estimate, necessitating raising further finance which was not always easily obtained and this could bring construction to a halt.

During this period the Midland opened three new intermediate stations between Bradford and Bingley. These were: Saltaire in 1859 to serve Salts mill and its associated model village; Manningham in 1868 following the residential development round the mills, although most of it was somewhat remote from the station; and finally Frizinghall (1875) which was developing as a commuter area for both Leeds and Shipley. Turning to new lines opened by the Midland during this period, in 1867 the Worth Valley line, a single track branch to Oxenhope, was opened. Then in 1876 the Shipley to Guiseley line opened to give Bradford access to the Leeds-Ilkley line. The Leeds connection had opened eleven years earlier. A glance at the 1905 map gives partly the explanation of the wide difference in opening dates, because whilst the Leeds line has a natural line of approach up a side valley, the approach line from Bradford crosses the grain of the country with three tunnels and three substantial viaducts.

The Lancashire + Yorkshire opened only one line during this period but it was quite an important one being from Wyke to connect with the LNW at Bradley Wood to enable a direct service to be run between Bradford and Huddersfield. The Lancashire + Yorkshire did, however, own jointly with the Great Northern the Halifax + Ovenden Joint which was a part of the Queensbury lines.

The most active railway, however, in new promotions during this period was the Great Northern. In 1866 the line from Adwalton Junction gave the GN direct connection to the heavy woollen district at Batley. The following year, 1867, saw closure of the remote Adolphus Street terminal as a passenger station and a new line joining the LY at Mill Lane Junction enabling the GN to use the more conveniently sited EXCHANGE station. The next line to open was Laisterdyke to Shipley which comprised two nominally independant lines, the Bradford, Eccleshill + Idle and the Idle + Shipley. There were no heavy engineering works involved but there was a 1:50 climb from Shipley. The line provided a commuter service of sorts at its two ends, but it is doubtful if much use was made of the route for its Bradford to Shipley connection. Then in 1878 a short branch was opened from a junction east of Stanningley to Pudsey Greenside with an intermediate station at Lowtown. Finally the Queensbury lines were opened throughout by 1879, having taken fourteen years to complete at a cost of over £1,000,000. A glance at the 1905 map with the contours and a selection of the engineering features gives a graphic explanation of the time and money involved.

The map of 1905 shows the network at its maximum extent. The Pudsey branch has been extended to Laisterdyke, and the old connection at Stanningley has been abandoned in favour of a connection from Bramley facing the opposite way enabling a train between Leeds and Bradford to use either the direct route or the route via Pudsey (1893). A short goods-only branch from Rawdon Junction to Yeadon opened in 1894. This was to have reached Leeds via Headingley but after absorption by the MIDLAND this plan was abandoned. Although regular use was goods, passenger trains did use the station for many years in the local holiday week. In the meantime another grandiose scheme had been put forward to link Bradford, Halifax and Huddersfield with Hull, but only three miles of this scheme got beyond the drawing board to become the HALIFAX HIGH LEVEL between Holm Field and St. Pauls, opened in 1890. In 1893 a line was opened from Dudley Hill to Low Moor which did not appear to serve any useful purpose although a circular service was run from Leeds Central, but even this if it was viable could have been routed through Laisterdyke and Bowling Junction rather than Dudley Hill probably to better effect. South Curves were added by the GN at Dudley Hill and by the LY at Low Moor. That at Dudley Hill does not ever appear to have been used, but the Low Moor curve was used by both goods and passenger traffic. There was only one other line opened in the area that remains to be mentioned and this had no effect on Bradford but is included to give a complete picture. This was a new LNW line from Huddersfield to Leeds to enable LNW trains from Leeds to reach Huddersfield without encroaching on LY metals.

It remains to record station openings on existing lines, and one closure. In chronolgical order: WILSDEN opened in 1886, set amidst fields at some distance from its village; in 1892 Thwaites (Midland) opened - again inconveniently sited for its village; Bowling GN closed in 1896 (retaining goods traffic) to be replaced in 1902 by the better sited BOWLING JUNCTION which served both GN and LY lines.

The map showing relief and tunnels does illustrate at least in part the reasons for Bradford's backwater status; lines had been costly to construct, were difficult to work, and inconveniently sited stations were inconducive to attracting passengers even before the advent of trams, trolley-buses and motor-buses. But the struggle with these factors belongs to the next instalment of the story.

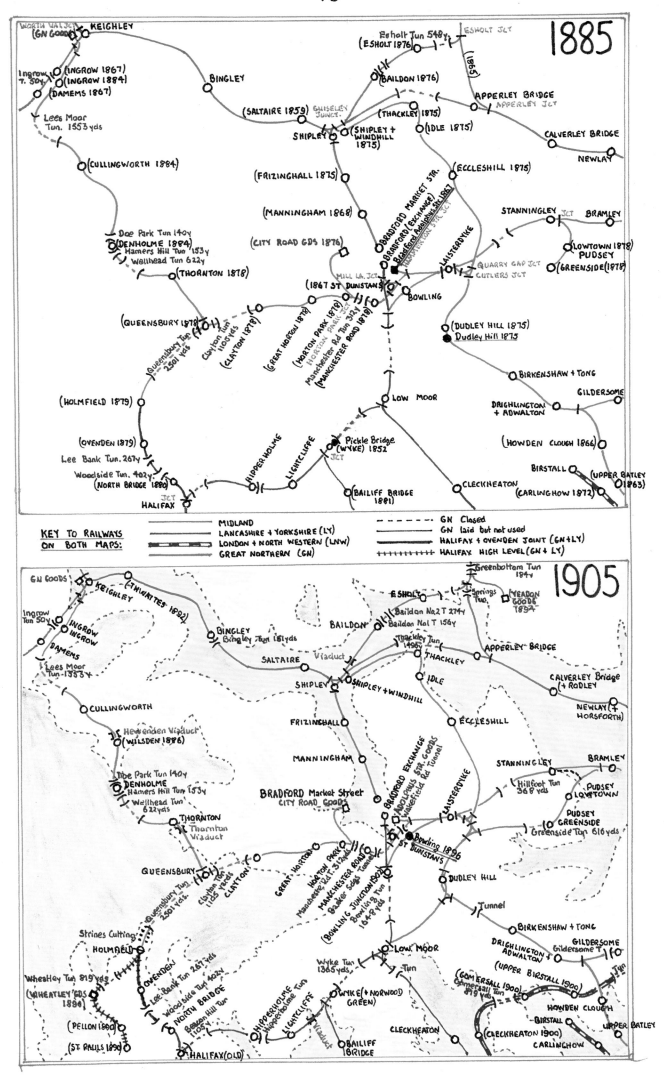

KEY TO RAILWAYS ON BOTH MAPS:
MIDLAND
LANCASHIRE + YORKSHIRE (LY)
LONDON + NORTH WESTERN (LNW)
GREAT NORTHERN (GN)
GN Closed
GN laid but not used
HALIFAX + OVENDEN JOINT (GN+LY)
HALIFAX HIGH LEVEL (GN + LY)

1885
1905

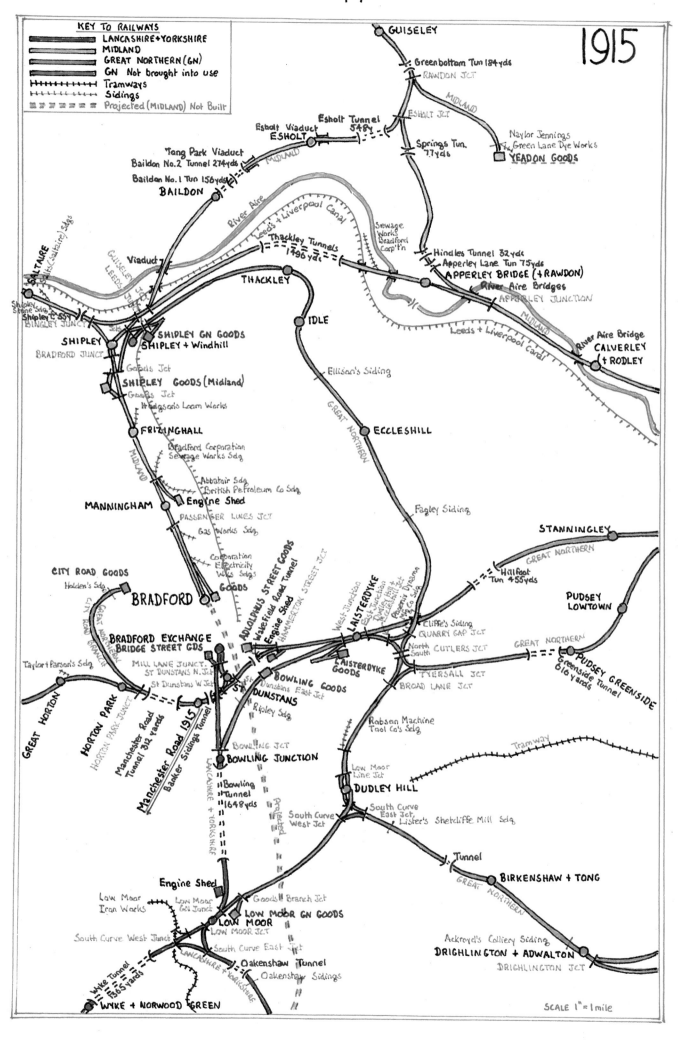

1915

KEY TO RAILWAYS
LANCASHIRE+YORKSHIRE
MIDLAND
GREAT NORTHERN (GN)
GN Not brought into use
Tramways
Sidings
Projected (MIDLAND) Not Built

GUISELEY

Greenbottom Tun 184 yds
RAWDON JCT
MIDLAND
ESHOLT JCT
Esholt Tunnel 548y
Springs Tun. 77 yds
Naylor Jennings
& Green Lane Dye Works
YEADON GOODS

Esholt Viaduct
ESHOLT

Tang Park Viaduct
Baildon No.2 Tunnel 274 yds
Baildon No.1 Tun 156 yds
BAILDON

River Aire
Leeds + Liverpool Canal

Thackley Tunnels 1496 yds

Sewage Works Bradford Corp'tn

Hindles Tunnel 32 yds
Apperley Lane Tun 75 yds
APPERLEY BRIDGE (+RAWDON)
River Aire Bridges
APPERLEY JUNCTION
MIDLAND

Viaduct

THACKLEY

IDLE

River Aire Bridge
CALVERLEY + RODLEY

Leeds + Liverpool Canal

SALTAIRE
Shsl Saltaire Sdgs
Shipley Stone Sdg
Shipley C.Sstn
BINGLEY JUNCT
SHIPLEY
BRADFORD JUNCT.

SHIPLEY GN GOODS
SHIPLEY + Windhill
Goods Jct
SHIPLEY GOODS (Midland)
Goods Jct
Ht Sdgsario Loam Works

Ellison's Siding
GREAT NORTHERN

ECCLESHILL

FRIZINGHALL
Bradford Corporation Sewage Works Sdg

Abbatoir Sdg
British Petroleum Co Sdg

MANNINGHAM
Engine Shed
PASSENGER LINES JCT
Gas Works Sdg

Fagley Siding

STANNINGLEY
GREAT NORTHERN

Hillfoot Tun 455 yds

PUDSEY LOWTOWN

CITY ROAD GOODS
Holden's Sdg
BRADFORD
Corporation Electricity Wks Sdgs
GOODS

ADOLPHUS STREET GOODS
Wakefield Road Tunnel
Engine Shed
HAMMERTON STREET JCT

West Junction
LAISTERDYKE
East Junction
Pudsey Hill + Chdlesthill
Phoenix Dynamo
Wd Co Sdg
Cliffe's Siding
QUARRY GAP JCT
North
South CUTLERS JCT

GREAT NORTHERN
Greenside Tunnel 616 yards
PUDSEY GREENSIDE

BRADFORD EXCHANGE
BRIDGE STREET GDS
MILL LANE JUNCT.
ST DUNSTANS N.JCT
St Dunstans W Jct
Taylor+Parson's Sdg
GREAT HORTON
HORTON PARK
HORTON PARK JUNCT
Manchester Road Tunnel 312 yards
Manchester Road 1915
Banker Sidings Tunnel

Bowling East Jct
BOWLING GOODS
St Dunstans
DUNSTANS
Ripley Sdg
LAISTERDYKE
LAISTERDYKE GOODS

TYERSALL JCT
BROAD LANE JCT

Robson Machine Tool Co's Sdg

LANCASHIRE + YORKSHIRE

BOWLING JCT
BOWLING JUNCTION
Bowling Tunnel 1648 yds
Projected

Low Moor Line Jct
DUDLEY HILL

South Curve West Jct
South Curve East Jct,
Lister's Shelcliffe Mill Sdg

Tramway

Tunnel
BIRKENSHAW + TONG
GREAT NORTHERN

Engine Shed
Low Moor Iron Works
Low Moor Gds Junct
South Curve West Junct.
LANCASHIRE + YORKSHIRE
South Curve East Jct
Goods + Branch Jct
LOW MOOR GN GOODS
LOW MOOR JCT
LOW MOOR
Oakenshaw Tunnel
Oakenshaw Sidings

Wyke Tunnel 1305 yards
WYKE + NORWOOD GREEN

Ackroyd's Colliery Siding
DRIGHLINGTON + ADWALTON
DRIGHLINGTON JCT

SCALE 1" = 1 mile

The map of 1915 shows only one material change compared to that of 1905. That was the down-grading of Manchester Road to Goods only as a wartime economy measure. In fact its closure to passengers was permanent.

The map shows the central area at a larger scale enabling extra detail to be shown including separate Goods Depots, Engine Sheds, Junctions and Tunnels. Also shown are a selection of Viaducts and Private sidings. One aspect that is highlighted, emphasising Bradford's backwater status, is the development by the three companies serving Bradford of an individual railway centre in the vicinity of the city. The Midland route focal point was firmly established at Shipley, with the Lancashire + Yorkshire at Low Moor; both these centres also had a Great Northern route from it leading to the Great Northern Centre at Laisterdyke from which a veritable maze of routes radiated.

The one additional feature shown on the map comparing it with that of 1905 is of great interest, the proposed Midland line. This was to have made a triangular junction with the LANCASHIRE + YORKSHIRE between Low Moor and Cleckheaton and then to have run by way of tunnels to reach the Midland station at Bradford. Its purpose was to provide the Midland with a shorter through route to Carlisle. The Scottish expresses would then have avoided Leeds. The steepest gradient was to have been 1:100. The line had been supported by Bradford Corporation who had not only cleared a path for the line through central Bradford but had offered rating concessions to the railway as a positive inducement in view of estimated heavy financial costs of construction. The outbreak of war resulted in postponement, and in the post-war period the back log of essential maintenance and the anticipated grouping of the railways caused further deferment. Once grouping took place the necessity of a competitive shorter route no longer existed since through traffic from London to Scotland was concentrated on the ex LNW route and the Midland route was used to pick up traffic from intermediate centres; it thus became more important to pass through Leeds rather than avoid it.

Although it was stated in the comment about the 1848 map that geographical aspects were responsible for the city not having a through route, this was only a part of the story. To understand the position fully one needs to go back in time to the opening of the first railway to reach Bradford, the LEEDS + BRADFORD. In obtaining its Act it had only been able to overcome opposition by promising to build a number of extension lines. These extensions were lines to Sowerby Bridge via Halifax and from Low Moor to Dewsbury and Mirfield in addition to the Aire valley route actually built. The MANCHESTER + LEEDS having reached Halifax in 1844 categorically refused to extend this line to Bradford, but in view of the projected invasion of their territory put forward their own scheme of identical lines on the reasonable assumption that parliament faced with identical proposals would reject them both. Just to make certain that neither scheme would go ahead there was a rigged public meeting in favour of the Manchester + Leeds' quite ludicrous proposals which included a section of atmospheric railway (know to have failed elsewhere) and 1:25 rope inclines since tunnels were dangerous, this latter assertion from a company having just built a two mile tunnel. How much manipulative malpractice in this unsavoury story was instigated by George Hudson is not known. But the next stage is pure Hudson. He proposed that the two companies should merge. In the meantime Hudson offered large share options to various cronies in the Leeds and Bradford to such an extent that demands for shares by the general public were unsatisfied. He then got the Leeds and Bradford to offer itself to the Midland and in the lease proposed 10% interest would be guaranteed. This was the incentive the Leeds and Bradford needed to opt out of the merger which they duly did on various trumped up charges. However, something was salvaged by Robert Stephenson who advised the merger of the constructing companies, as the WEST RIDING UNION. This enabled the Midland to abandon the cross city link. Although the new company was forced into a merger with the Manchester + Leeds and various other companies to form a new company, the LANCASHIRE + YORKSHIRE, which undertook to build the agreed lines, it too wriggled off the hook. Most of the lines were built but not the cross-city line; this was possibly due to two factors. First the LANCASHIRE + YORKSHIRE became firmly Lancashire based with the city of Bradford at the edge of its operating area and thus of little interest. The other reason was that it was felt that any such line would be of more benefit to competitors rather than the constructing company and this may well have been the case.

One gains the impression in retrospect that but for the dishonest manipulations of the 'Railway King' Bradford would have been on a through route prior to 1850. Also of course there was a general policy pursued by very many railways who did not wish to risk capital in building a new line but wished to safeguard existing revenues by insuring that another company didn't. This strategic plan was highly successful and carried out in such a way that it has lasted for a further 140 years. There were at later dates various proposals for a link across the city but these all came to nothing and in fact the one that came nearest to implementation was that of the Midland shown on the 1915 map. In recent years there has again been talk about closing the new Bradford Interchange and making a through circular route from Leeds based on a revamped Forster Square but it doesn't really appear likely.

The policy of railway closures is inevitably associated in people's minds with the Beeching report. However, it is true on a national basis that pre-Beeching closures exceeded those recommended for closure in the report. The reason for this is two-fold; First the Beeching report looked at the whole of Great Britain and therefore it made national news, whilst earlier closures were purely local affairs not always even getting a mention locally let alone in the national papers. The other reason was of course that the earlier closures were spread over a considerable period of time commencing in most places during the First World War. Bradford was no exception to this general pattern with regard to pre-Beeching closures but there was a surprising twist in that Bradford's post-report closures also exceeded those of the report.

The first closure was Thwaites in 1909. This station served a community a mile away up a steep hill and was unable to compete with the bus service. Following this there was a spate of war-time closures due to staff shortages, although in most cases goods traffic survived for another thirty to forty years. First to go during the war, was Manchester Road, as already mentioned. Then 1917 saw passenger services withdrawn from three branches. The LNW branch to Birstall, having failed to reach Bradford, had never carried much passenger traffic; and the same could be said of the Halifax High Level route; but both these branches retained a goods service. This was not the case, however, with the final branch closure, that between Dudley Hill and Low Moor, where all services were discontinued and for further help in the war effort the track was lifted to turn rails into tanks.

Following the war and grouping there was a period of inaction on the closure front except that the war-time closures, which had been expressed to be a temporary measure, became permament. The reason for this of course was there was no possibity of the inconveniently sited stations taking back from the road even the meagre number of passengers they had previously carried. The hopeless situation is illustrated by a not untypical story of a service offered from St Pauls to Sowerby Bridge at the turn of the century. The distance by road was only a mile but the rail journey took 55 minutes and involved two changes. Even a baby crawling at one mile per hour could beat the train if the connection was late!

The only other closure of the pre-war period was in 1931 when the Laisterdyke-Shipley service to passengers was withdrawn. There was some public outcry and some sort of service may have been introduced at a later date since I do have a memory as a very small boy of a train journey from Eccleshill to Great Horton and a long wait on the way, obviously at St. Dunstans.

The next thirty years to 1967 saw many further closures but only those underlined in red on the map were included in the Beeching report. The First further closures were wartime economy measures as happened during the previous war although only Esholt (1940) was actually closed during the period of hostilities, but Bailiff Bridge also comes effectively into this category although not closing until 1948. But in this case the entire branch closed to passenger traffic, and to goods four years later.

The remaining closures prior to the Beeching report fall into two categories: entire branches and intermediate stations. In the former category the Queensbury lines had passenger traffic withdrawn in 1955 and this was followed by the progressive closure to goods traffic so that by 1967 only two short spurs to Great Horton and City Road remained. Then in 1961 the Worth Valley line closed to passengers with goods traffic being withdrawn just six months later. Intermediate station closures were Damems (1949), Bowling Junction (1951), St Dunstans (1952), then in 1953 there were three closures: Baildon, Hipperholme and Wyke & Norwood Green.

Turning now to the Beeching report, so far as its implementation was concerned only the Pudsey loop line was lost; the other recommendations were intermediate stations on lines that were to be retained albeit with local services modified or abolished. One aspect of the Beeching proposals is not shown on the map, closure of the Ilkley lines, since the stations in the map area had already closed. In the event this closure was not carried out due to the intervention of the local authority.

The post-Beeching closures as mentioned above outnumbered those of the report so that ultimateley only 5 passenger stations in the entire map area remained. In date order Gildersome, Howden Clough and Upper Batley were closed in 1964; Newlay & Horsford, Cleckheaton (Spen), Gomersall and Birstall Town followed in 1965; and Bramley, Dudley Hill, Laisterdyke and Birkenshaw & Tong in 1966. Only one station closed in 1967 - Stanningley - but this was re--placed by an opening at New Pudsey (a Beeching opening). This opening was to serve long-distance travellers who were provided with ample car parking and good road access. But the station did not cater for the local commuter unless he or she had a car.

The decimation of Bradford's network having been completed it is sad to record that the use of unstaffed halts was not considered. These could have cut costs but retained revenue. But this type of mistake was often made irreversible by sale of station sites for other purposes even when the line remained open. But BR policy of trying to wipe Bradford off the railway map was to continue, as we shall see.

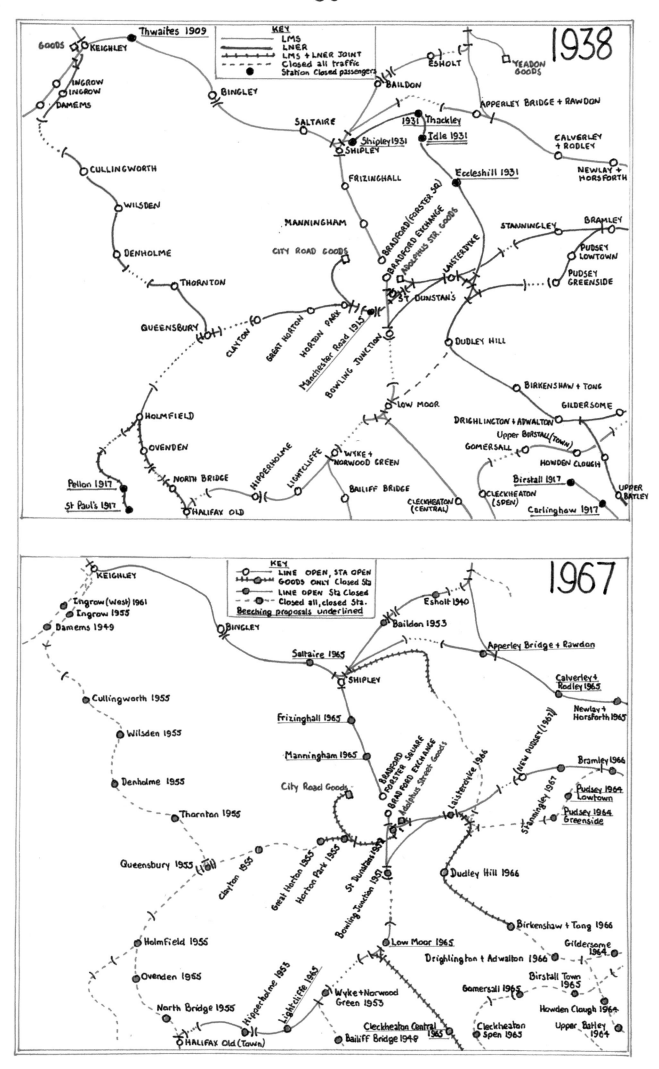

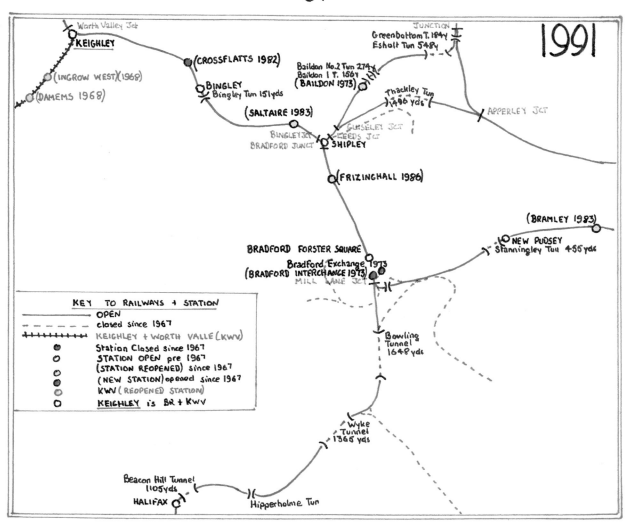

SHIPLEY

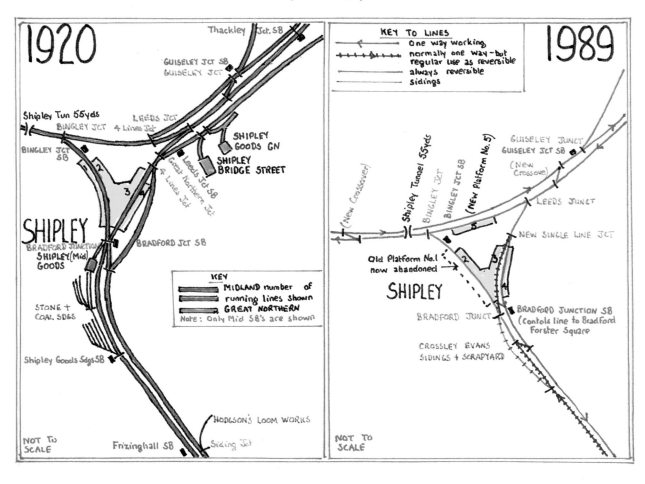

The final map shows the position in 1991 and all the goods-only lines have long since vanished and in fact very little goods traffic operates within the area covered by the map. A further closure was the line from Laisterdyke to Bowling Junction, this being closed to passengers in 1969. Goods traffic lingered for a further fifteen years but during the later part of this period it had been operated as a siding only.

In looking at subsequent developments it is easier to consider events as they affected each terminal station in turn. First Exchange: It has already been noted that New Pudsey had opened in 1967 to give a convenient access to Bradford-London trains which would use the Wortley curve, to avoid Leeds and consequent reversal, after closure of the Bradford to Wakefield line. This appeared to work well and patronage of the early morning express was such that even with six first class coaches included on the train one had to book in advance to be sure of a seat. This train was producing a revenue, at 1990 prices, of millions per year. In the light of these facts BR's subsequent actions defy all rational explanation. The first move was to run return workings via Leeds adding to the time of the journey and increasing operating costs. The next move was to run the up early morning train via Leeds, and to ensure that this was an irreversible action the points were lifted at Wortley South Junction. Despite public outcry services over the curve have never been renewed. Meanwhile 1973 had seen the replacement of Bradford Exchange by an intergrated Bradford Interchange to link with buses and having nearby excellent car parking facilities. These excellent facilities were ignored in BR's next move which was to withdraw the London service from Interchange and re-route it to run from Forster Square, with poor parking, and calling at Shipley with inadequate platforms. Further comments about this new service are noted under Forster Square; suffice it to say with regard to the Interchange this decision made New Pudsey redundant for its stated purpose and so far as local traffic is concerned it is convenient only if one arrives by car. Two final factors regarding the Interchange station remain to be noted, the removal of all quadruple track and the re-opening of Bramley as an unstaffed halt. Most long-distance services have been withdrawn and all that remains is a basic regular Leeds-Bradford service with some Bradford trains continuing to Manchester and a few of the trains to Leeds continuing to York or even beyond!

At Forster Square the entire Midland network remains intact in spite of strenuous efforts by BR to close the system. As noted, intermediate stations had been closed, seriously affecting the viability of local services; this was coupled with the progressive withdrawal of every single long-distance service. Strange when pre-war statistics show 50% more passengers from Bradford compared to Leeds using the Midland network over the same lines. Closure of the Ilkley lines was proposed but these were rescued by local authority subsidy together with the Keighley line now also under threat. In the meantime the Worth Valley line was reopened under private ownership together with all stations and sharing at Keighley with BR. But the policy of trying to wipe Bradford off the railway map continued. All quadruple track and sidings were lifted except for part of the goods depot at Shipley; Guiseley to Shipley and to Apperley Junction were singled and Bradford Forster Square was reduced to two half platforms. On the apparent positive side, to avoid reversals for Leeds-Bingley workings a new platform 5 was put on the down line and reversible working introduced (the 1989 Shipley plan shows all the new features). The result of conflicting movements over this revised layout effectively ensures that peak period trains are delayed and to make this certain impossible movements are incorporated into the timetables. One example of this from the BR 1989 timetable shows a 9.40 departure from Shipley to Guiseley and a 9.44 arrival from Guiseley at Shipley (ie two trains meet on a single line!). Turning to the newly introduced London service, when introduced the platforms at both Forster Sq. and Shipley were of inadequate length. The train cannot be stored at Bradford thus needlessly increasing operating costs, and its length fouls the crossing points causing effective disruption of local services. Excluding the new London service the normal limit of travel is to Ilkley and Keighley from Bradford, and to get to Keighley a change is often necessary at Shipley. Longer distances are limited to three trains daily to Skipton and one per week (in summer only) to Morecambe. Added to all this there is a mis-use of resources in various ways. For example, at the morning peak period most passengers are travelling towards Leeds and Bradford and these are normally the shorter trains, whilst trains in the other direction can have 50% more accommodation available, and it can be two or three times as much. Also services are provided inversely proportionate to demand. For example, the greatest utilisation of the Ilkley service is between Bradford and Guiseley but there are twice as many Guiseley-Ilkley trains compared to the trains between Bradford and Guiseley; the situation with the Keighley service is similar. The only really positive moves in this sad story have been the opening or re-opening of intermediate stations as unstaffed halts. These have been at BAILDON (1973), CROSSFLATTS (an entirely new station in 1982), SALTAIRE (1983), and finally FRIZINGHALL (1986).

Looking to the future, the London service is under threat, but there is again the possibility on a through line for Bradford, but with what hopes of success remains to be seen.

As a postscript to the situation at Bradford Forster Square the station is being rebuilt further from the centre of the city making it less convenient. The old site is planned for development as a shopping centre and this will effectively block any possibility of a through route based on the station. The new station is even more remote from convenient parking and although ample land is available, presently derelict, there is no sign that any of this spare land will become parking space.

HULL

Hull, in common with most railway centres, had a unique set of circumstances affecting its growth and decline. The individual factors were not in themselves unique, it was the combination of them all together that resulted in the way Hull's railway network developed. There were three principal factors which combined to have this effect. First, and of most importance, was Hull's position on the Humber and its development as the third port of the UK, having particular shipping links with the Scandinavian countries. The Humber also formed an effective barrier to the south and has of course only been bridged in recent times, whilst a railway journey southwards from Hull involves initial travel westwards and this factor has tended to isolate Hull. This relative isolation has been accentuated by the second factor which is the hinterland of Hull is mainly agricultural and there were, and still are, few nearby centres of large population, thus making Hull the end of the line. The final factor influencing development was that from the start of railway development the network was under effective control of one company. This had its effect on the situation together with the continued efforts of Hull Corporation to break this monopoly. Whilst monopoly avoids wasteful duplication of routes, the absence of competition can stifle development that competition might have encouraged. Hull Corporation, aware of this, spent years to promote a rival line by making development difficult for the North Eastern by placing obstacles in the way of improvements, and this had ultimately the

1850

The first railway to reach Hull should have been the LEEDS + HULL formed in 1824, but this company became the LEEDS + SELBY and with the potential loss of dock traffic to the port of Goole the HULL + SELBY was incorporated in 1836. It took four years to construct the level line between Hull and Selby which opened 1840. It became part of the YORK + NORTH MIDLAND in 1845. The latter company opened the Bridlington branch in 1846. Branches to Hornsea (1846) and to Market Weighton (1849) were authorised. The former was not built, and it was 1865 before the latter connection was made.

1851-1865

This period saw most of the network completed. In 1854 the YORK + N. MIDLAND became part of the NORTH EASTERN. The same year also saw the opening of the HULL + HOLDERNESS. This line was to be worked by the NORTH EASTERN from 1860 and absorbed by that company two years later. In 1864 the HULL + HORNSEA opened worked by the NORTH EASTERN from the outset and fully absorbed in 1866. In 1865 the NORTH EASTERN finally completed the Hull-York link with the opening of the line from Beverley to Market Weighton.

1866-1915

The only additions to the network during this period were those resulting from the docks development and the desire of Hull Corporation to break the monopoly of the NORTH EASTERN. The HULL + BARNSLEY opened from Cudworth to Cannon Street and the new ALEXANDRA DOCK in 1885, with further goods lines opened the following year. In 1914 a further new dock KING GEORGE opened and was served by both NE and HB. There was one closure during the period being Ellerby in 1902, closed due to its close proximity to adjoining stations.

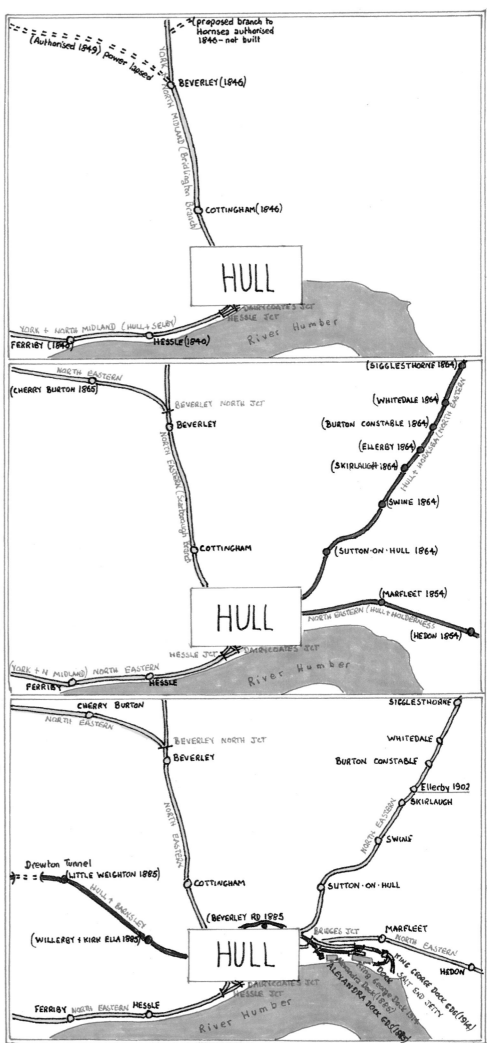

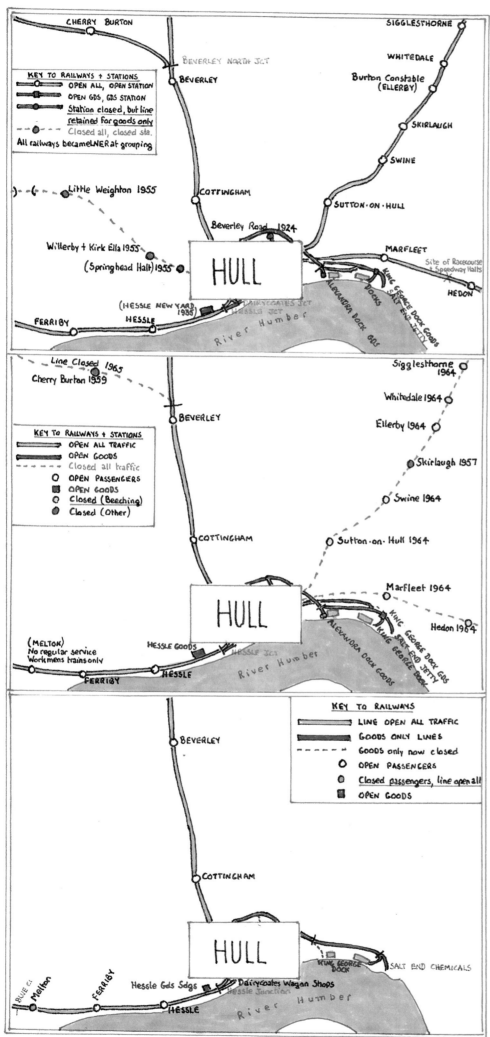

1916-1955

Following grouping the HULL & BARNSLEY's passenger service was diverted to Paragon resulting in Beverley Road closing in 1924. Following this the ex HULL & BARNSLEY service was progressively cut back and was closed to all traffic. The goods lines, however, continued in use since they were more convenient than the nearby ex NE line hampered by its many level crossings. A new hump yard was opened at Hessle in 1935.

It is interesting to note the similar appearance of this map with the map to 1865.

1956-1965

This map covers the Beeching Report and its implementation. Prior to the report, two intermediate stations were the only closures: Skirlaugh (1957) on the Hornsea branch and Cherry Burton (1959) on the line to York. The recommendation of the Beeching Report was reduction of the network to its 1850 state. The closures were quickly carried out, the two coastal branches closing in 1964 with the York line closing in 1965.

Again the close resemblance of this map to that of 1850 is uncanny.

1966-1991

With the network decimated by 1965, very little has happened over the last 25 years. However the 1935 new goods yard has been progressively closed until in 1991 it is but a handful of sidings. There have been other goods closures too as the map shows.

The Scarborough line has also been under threat from time to time but survives. Unlike many other centres there is no sign of any revival at Hull. There is still some dock goods traffic but it is restricted to the King George Dock. There is some rail-served industry.

effect of breaking the monopoly but still stifling development.

The railway family tree shows the development of the different railway companies at Hull and how at grouping all became part of the LONDON + NORTH EASTERN:

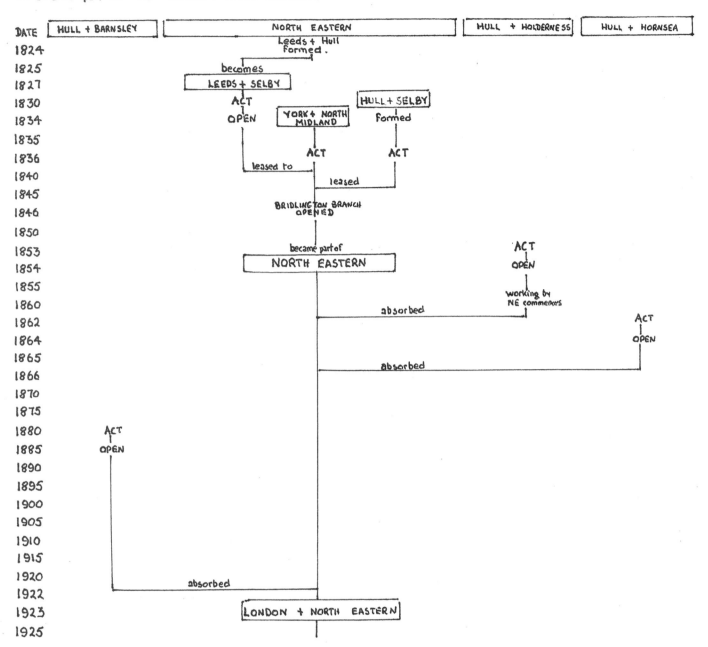

The maps showing the development of Hull are in two series. The first series shows the Hull district at a smaller scale than the normal general maps so that all these maps together with a brief commentary on each can be shown on a single spread. This highlights how development and rationalisation are precise mirror images of each other.

The second series of maps shows the central area and in addition to showing the railway development shows the growth of Hull's dock system. In this connection it is interesting to compare and contrast the railway and dock developments. With railways usually the last railway to open is the first to close and quite often the present-day position is very similar to that reached around 1850 and in very few places is this better illustrated than at Hull as the maps on pages 54 and 55 clearly show. With dock development, however, exactly the opposite prevails, the first docks opened, being of shallower depth, are usually the first to close and the later deep-water docks that can accommodate the larger vessels at all states of the tide are the ones to remain. In Hull the pre-railway docks have been closed sometime and in fact by the early 'eighties only Alexandra Dock (1883) and King George Dock (1914) were open and rail served. Now only the King George Dock retains a rail connection.

The notes relating to the earlier part of the second series of maps are presented as a chronological diary of events in an attempt to try and give as clear a picture as possible of the sequence of events leading to these vital initial developments which set the pattern for what was to follow.

TO 1846

29.12.1824 LEEDS + HULL Railroad launched. Capital of £500,000.

7.2.1825 Survey for LEEDS + HULL by George Stephenson, part of a plan to link Hull with Liverpool. Promoters unsure so strange rules of share allocation prevented progress; also wanted to wait and see how Liverpool + Manchester progressed.

11.12.1828 Now proposed as Leeds to Selby only, since journey to Hull could be by boat from that point.

20.3.1829 LEEDS + SELBY company formed (this was the LEEDS + HULL but with name changed to match new terminal point).

18.7.1829 New survey for Leeds - Selby by James Walker. Better route avoiding steep gradients and level crossings. New route adopted.

29.5.1830 LEEDS + SELBY ACT

11.8.1834 HULL + SELBY company formed, as it had become obvious Leeds + Selby was not to be extended and the boat journey from Selby to Hull would be a long one (up to five hours) and Hull could visualise dock traffic being lost to Goole.

22.9.1834 LEEDS + SELBY opened. Sandbanks cause frequent grounding of connecting boats to Hull at neap tides.

15.12.1834 LEEDS + SELBY line doubled and opened for goods. Hull dock traffic affected.

21.6.1836 HULL + SELBY ACT. Capital £533,333.

1.7.1840 HULL + SELBY officially opened. Passenger service commenced the following day. Hull terminus at MANOR HOUSE STREET.

19.8.1840 HULL + SELBY opened for goods. Hull goods station adjoined the passenger terminal.

9.11.1840 LEEDS + SELBY leased to George Hudson's YORK + NORTH MIDLAND. Leeds to Selby line reduced to goods only; passengers were routed onto the YORK + NORTH MIDLAND via Normanton!

9.4.1845 HULL + SELBY shareholders agree to lease the railway to YORK + NORTH MIDLAND in opposition to the directors who were in favour of a merger with the MANCHESTER + LEEDS which would have given a route between east and west coasts under a united management. The YORK + NORTH MIDLAND was of course a north to south route but the shareholders were of course influenced by the 10% return offered on their capital by the 'Hudson Company'.

30.6.1845 HULL + SELBY ACT for Bridlington branch.

1.7.1845 YORK + NORTH MIDLAND obtain perpetual lease of HULL + SELBY.

1846 RAILWAY DOCK opened by Hull Dock Company, near the HULL GOODS STATION.

18.6.1846 YORK - BEVERLEY ACT (YORK + NORTH MIDLAND). Line opened York to Market Weighton 4.10.1847 but the Beverley to Market Weighton section was not completed until 1865 (by the NORTH EASTERN).

6.10.1846 YORK + NORTH MIDLAND open Bridlington branch (later known as Scarborough branch).

1847-1850

22.7.1847 PARAGON STATION and LINES ACT. The accommodation at MANOR HOUSE STREET had become inadequate, and, at the same time the Hull centre was moving inland away from the docks. The lines authorised were: Hessle Junction to Hessle Road Junction; Cottingham Bridge Junction to a new terminus at Paragon Street via West Parade Junction; and from Cottingham Junction to West Parade Junction.

8.5.1848 The above lines and new station opened. Manor House Street retained for goods traffic together with the lines: Hessle Junction and from Cottingham Junction to Dairycoates Junction. Both lines would see some future passenger traffic.

1850 VICTORIA DOCK opened. This was the event influencing the next developments in central Hull.

1851-1853

1852 Extensions to VICTORIA DOCK opened.

30.6.1852 YORK + NORTH MIDLAND authorised to build a line round the outskirts of Hull to VICTORIA DOCK.

16.5.1853 VICTORIA DOCK BRANCH opened to goods traffic. The line ran from Anlaby Road Junction, on the Hull + Selby, crossed the Hull to Bridlington line at Victoria level crossing, circled the city and terminated at VICTORIA DOCK.

1.6.1853 Passenger service commenced on the Victoria Dock Branch. Starting from MANOR HOUSE STREET which was re-opened for passengers, it called at STEPNEY, SCULCOATES and SOUTHCOATES stations terminating at VICTORIA DOCK. The trains also picked up passengers at HESSLE ROAD, ANLABY ROAD and CEMETERY GATES but there is no record of actual stations built at these points. The initial service was seven trains per day in each direction with a standard fare for any length of journey. The service does not appear to have been very well patronised because before the end of the year the service was reduced to just four trains in each direction. At about this time a new curve was laid from West Parade Junction on the Bridlington line to Cemetery Gates and this enabled the Dock Branch passenger service to use Paragon station (or Paragon Street as it was sometimes known during this period). The exact date of this diversion of the service is not clear and for a time trains may well have used both PARAGON and MANOR HOUSE STREET. Hull thus now had for a short time no less than three terminal passenger stations: MANOR HOUSE STREET, PARAGON, and VICTORIA DOCK.

8.7.1853 HULL + HOLDERNESS authorised. This was to begin with an entirely independant company and not a satellite of the YORK + NORTH MIDLAND. It was to construct a line from Hull to Withernsea with connections at Hull to enable it to run to both PARAGON and VICTORIA DOCK.

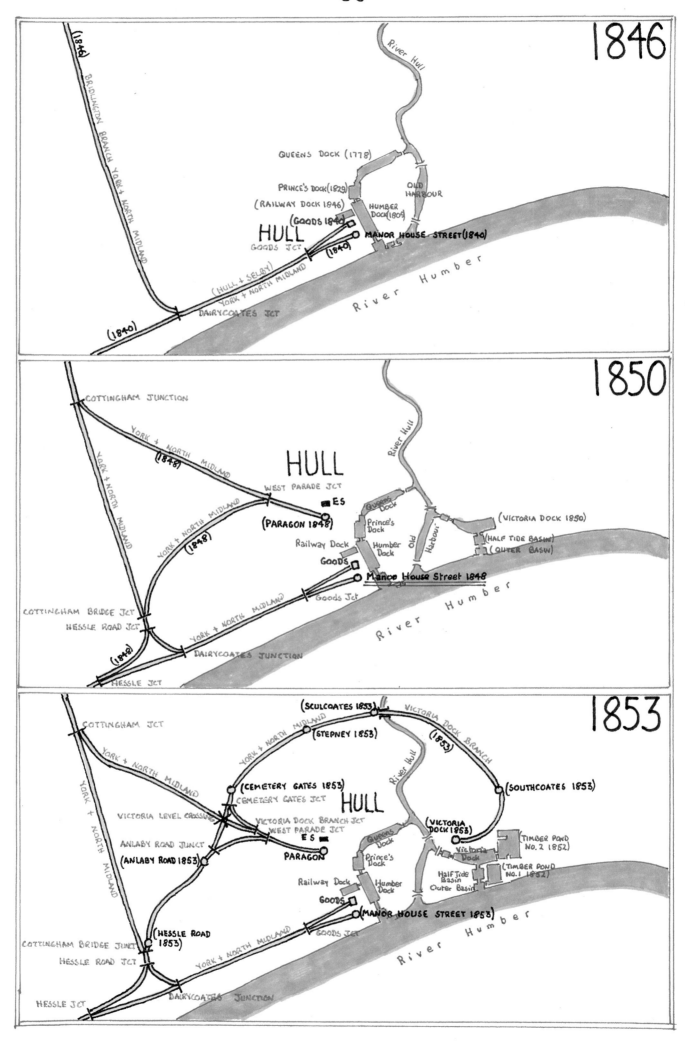

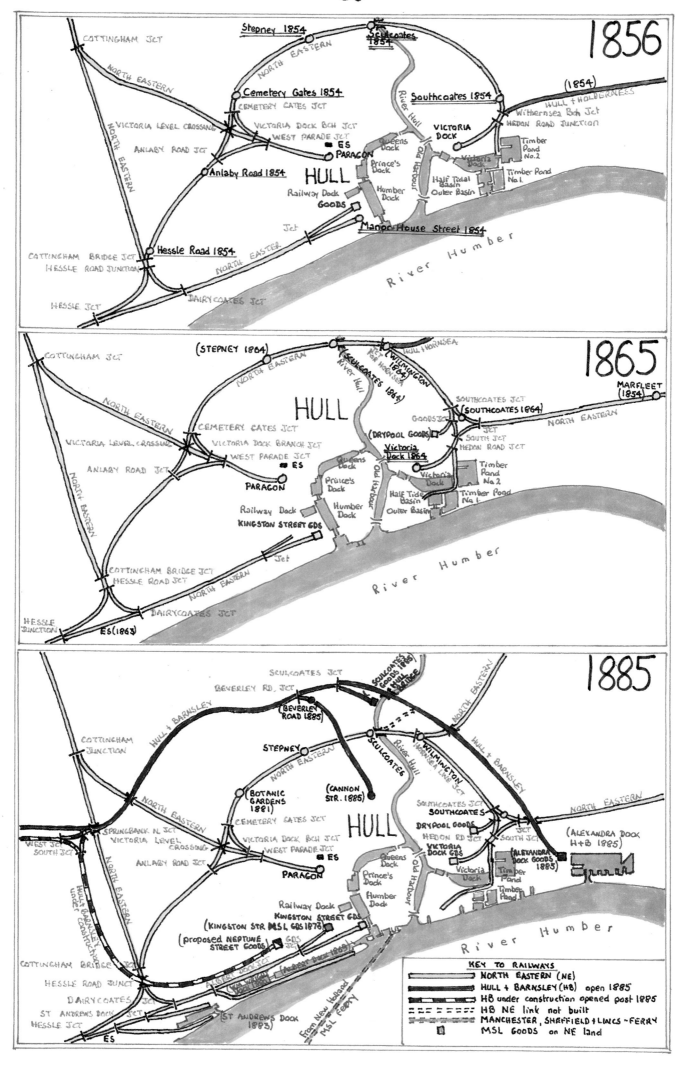

1854-1856

The year 1854 was a momentous one so far as the railways of Central Hull were concerned, with three major events:

24.6.1854 HULL + HOLDERNESS opened, between Hull and Withernsea. The railway had opened for traffic within twelve months of obtaining its Act, but of course the line was over level ground without engineering features. The Act had authorised connections into VICTORIA DOCK and PARAGON and in fact the RCH map of 1854 shows both these lines, but the PARAGON curve is a fiction at this period and it would be a further ten years before this was laid, authorised + brought into use.

31.7.1854 NORTH EASTERN ACT - formed by a merger of the YORK + NORTH MIDLAND, the Leeds Northern and the Malton + Driffield Junction, and other associated companies were quickly added.

11.1854 NORTH EASTERN withdraw the Hull Suburban service. Records do not indicate the precise date and what little evidence is available suggests a progressive withdrawal. The stations at Stepney, Sculcoates + Southcoates were downgraded to Goods stations. Hessle Road and Anlaby Road were closed to all traffic and would not be re-opened. Cemetery Gates was also closed to all traffic but the exact further fate of this location is not clear. VICTORIA DOCK remained open for the HULL + HOLDERNESS passenger traffic.

1857-1865

The next ten years saw the completion of the NORTH EASTERN network, which apart from new docks lines as new docks were opened would remain virtually unchanged for the next hundred years.

1.1.1860 From this date the NORTH EASTERN took over working of the HULL + HOLDERNESS.

30.6.1862 HULL + HORNSEA Act. This was really a satellite of the NORTH EASTERN.

7.7.1862 HULL + HOLDERNESS absorbed by NORTH EASTERN

30.1.1863 Decided that NORTH EASTERN service from WITHERNSEA would run into Paragon, but powers had lapsed and the Board of Trade refused to sanction opening of the curve until matters connected with signalling had been put right.

28.3.1864 HULL + HORNSEA opened. Worked by NORTH EASTERN and trains terminate at a new station WILMINGTON where the Hornsea line joined the VICTORIA DOCK BRANCH. Again Board of trade refuse to authorise running to PARAGON.

1.6.1864 WITHERNSEA trains commence using PARAGON. VICTORIA DOCK reduced to Goods

1.7.1864 HULL + HORNSEA trains commence running through to PARAGON. Stations at Stepney, Sculcoates and Southcoates re-opened to passengers. The situation re Cemetery Gates is unclear but not shown on RCH maps.

1.5.1865 NORTH EASTERN complete and open Beverley to Market Weighton (outside map area).

16.7.1866 HULL + HORNSEA fully absorbed by NORTH EASTERN.

1866-1885

The NORTH EASTERN had now established a railway monopoly at Hull and sought to maintain it by the excellence of the service it provided to other major company competitors who had obtained running powers. The service was in fact so good that these powers were not excercised. As a further example of the good relationship which the NORTH EASTERN sought to promote in 1873 the NORTH EASTERN provided the MANCHESTER, SHEFFIELD + LINCOLNSHIRE with a goods depot at KINGSTON STREET; this helped to stifle support from any attempts to break this monopoly. The NORTH EASTERN also established good relationships with the HULL DOCK COMPANY who owned all the Hull Docks and was active in opening new docks during this period : ALBERT (1869), WILLIAM WRIGHT (1880) and ST ANDREWS (1883). There were also plans for a new dock at Marfleet with the Dock Company and the railway co-operating.

But Hull Corporation were opposed to the monopoly and since at one stage they had given financial support to the dock company they had been able to dictate certain conditions and were able to block any merger between the Dock Company and the NORTH EASTERN. This tended to discourage projects which would have benefitted the port since the North Eastern could not be expected to expend considerable sums of money on a project which would then fall under the control of others. Then in 1880 the Hull Corporation were instrumental in obtaining an Act for a new railway, the HULL, BARNSLEY + WEST RIDING JUNCTION RAILWAY + DOCK COMPANY (later shortened to HULL + BARNSLEY). There was no real justification for this being authorised; in view of the high capital cost it should have been obvious it could not be able to service a capital (including borrowing) over £5,000,000, but it did get its ACT and opened from Cudworth to HULL in 1885. There were other feeder lines in the West Riding whilst at Hull there was a passenger terminus at Cannon Street and a goods station at ALEXANDRA DOCK alongside a new deep-water dock built by the railway on land provided by the HULL CORPORATION. In addition there was a further branch goods line to a depot at Neptune Street adjacent to the newer Hull Dock Co docks (opened during this period). This branch is shown as under construction on the RCH maps of 1885 and was probably opened the following year (1886). The NORTH EASTERN monopoly was broken, but at what a cost, as we shall see.

1886-1915

There was but little railway development during this period, except towards the end of the period. The reason for this was the continued anti-North Eastern attitude of Hull Corporation. With the opening of the HULL + BARNSLEY with its own dock the seeds of disaster had been sown. Parliament had insisted in authorising this new dock that an access line was constructed from the NORTH EASTERN. However, the HULL + BARNSLEY backed by Hull Corporation refused to put in this connection resulting in the NORTH EASTERN taking H+B to court as they were clearly in breach of law. The HULL + BARNSLEY now agreed to build the line but sought cramping conditions which the NORTH EASTERN refused to accept and withdrew from the court case to the jubilation of their opponents. However, the losers in this case were the HULL + BARNSLEY who lost access to the wide-reaching tentacles of the NORTH EASTERN.

Not satisfied that they were getting enough traffic (having cut off a good potential source) they entered a ruinous rate war with the HULL DOCK COMPANY who were owners of the rest of the Hull Docks. By the end of 1886 the only salvation for the DOCK COMPANY was to be taken over by a railway, whilst the HULL + BARNSLEY, being unable to pay its debenture interest, was threatened with receivership.

The only solution for both companies was merger with the NORTH EASTERN. The Dock Company had always enjoyed a good relationship with the NORTH EASTERN and after several attempts blocked by Hull Corporation the NORTH EASTERN took over the DOCK COMPANY in 1893. But even then in view of the stringent conditions laid down it meant that the new dock at Marfleet on which work commenced in the 1890's did not open until 1914. The NORTH EASTERN were reluctant to spend large sums of money over a short period without contributions from any other sources and then having to allow others to have an equal or greater control over an undertaking for which they had provided 100% of the finance.

Hull Corporation were able to block the merger of the NORTH EASTERN and HULL+ BARNSLEY and of course by this time they had become acknowledged experts at shooting themselves in the foot. A possible merger with the Midland was also blocked because of the unreasonable conditions insisted upon by the corporation. In the end of course the HULL + BARNSLEY was taken over by the NORTH EASTERN but not until 1922 as a prelude to grouping.

The table below gives dates of opening of the various Hull Docks, together with other details:-

DATE	NAME OF DOCK	OWNED BY	NOTES	
1778	QUEENS	HULL DOCK Co		
1809	HUMBER	HULL DOCK Co		BECAME PART OF
1829	PRINCE'S	HULL DOCK Co		NORTH EASTERN
1846	RAILWAY	HULL DOCK Co	built adjoining first Goods sta.	BY ACT OF 1893
1850	VICTORIA	HULL DOCK Co	Extended 1852	
1869	ALBERT	HULL DOCK Co	Riverside Quay opened 1907	
1880	WILLIAM WRIGHT	HULL DOCK Co	Named after Dock Co Chairman	
1883	ST ANDREWS	HULL DOCK Co	Used for fish traffic	
1885	ALEXANDRA	HULL+ BARNSLEY	Land provided by Hull Corpⁿ	BECAME NE
1914	KING GEORGE	NE and H+B JOINT	Opened by King George V	IN 1922

Other developments during this period were:

1896? NEWINGTON station opened. Opened as a private station. Only spasmodically included in Bradshaw. Later it was used, during several different periods, for excursion traffic and so trains to Bridlington via Hull could avoid the need to reverse.

1905 The Engine Shed adjoining Paragon was closed. A new shed at Botanic Gardens opened as replacement; probably at this time also Victoria Dock Branch Curve was re-aligned. Some authorities have suggested that the BOTANIC GARDENS station was a renaming of CEMETERY GATES, but the RCH maps indicate a slightly different site.

1907 Following dock improvements RIVERSIDE QUAY opened for boat trains in co-operation with other companies, in particular the LANCASHIRE + YORKSHIRE.

1912 The line between Sculcoates and Wilmington was remodelled to obviate one of the notorious level crossings. Following this the two stations mentioned were closed and replaced by a new WILMINGTON; this was midway between the two closed stations.

The 1915 map shows the railway network at its maximum development. Although some further new lines were built after this period they were part of rationalisation following grouping as will be seen.

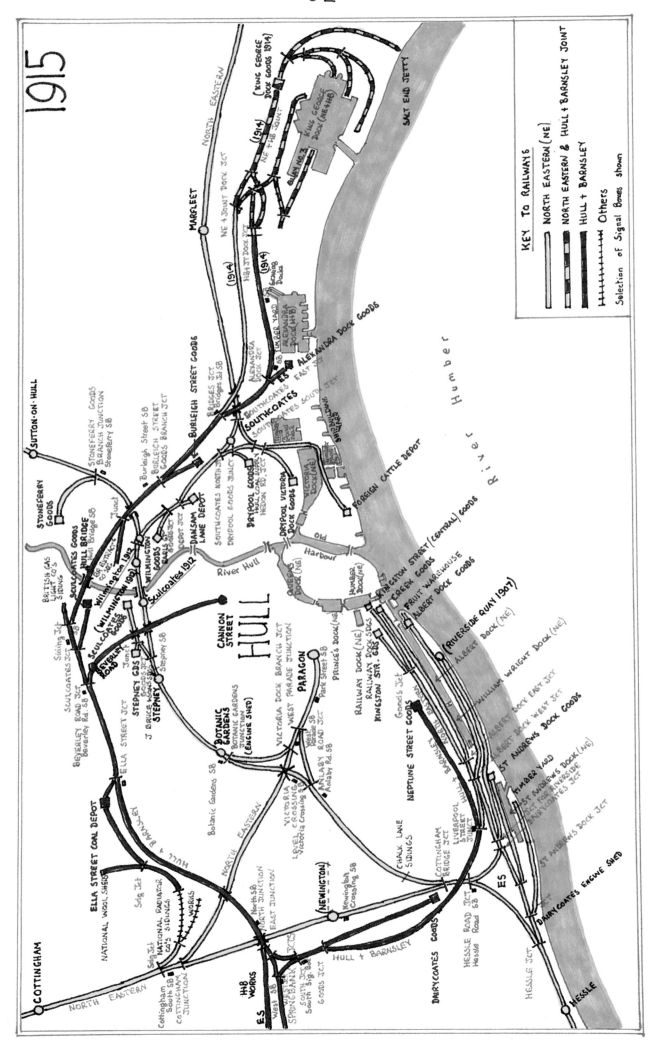

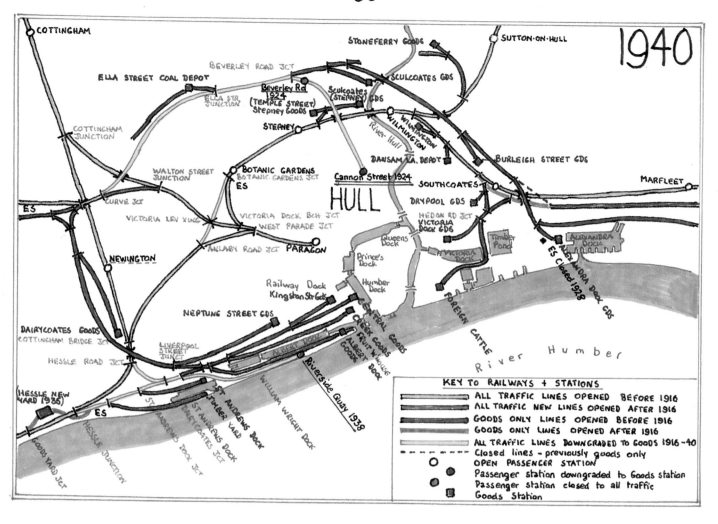

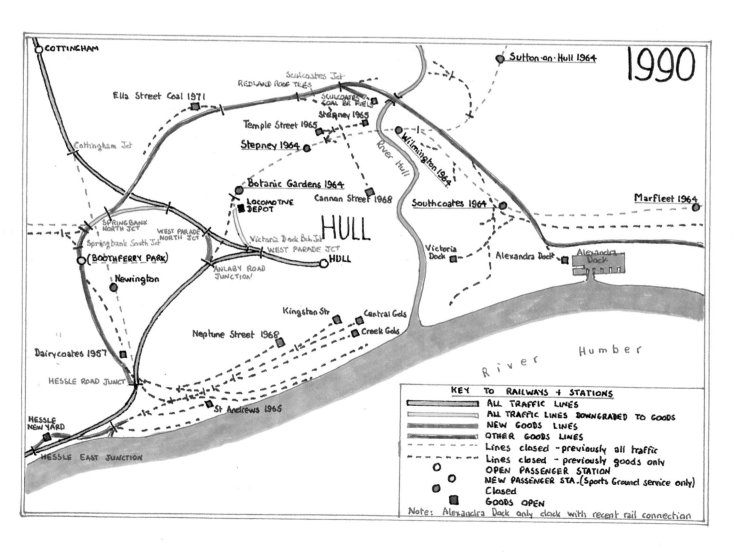

1916 - 1940

As already mentioned, the HULL + BARNSLEY was at last absorbed by the NORTH EASTERN in 1922 as a prelude to the grouping. Thus all docks and railways in the Hull area came under one management, control passing to the LONDON + NORTH EASTERN RAILWAY the following year. At the grouping almost a fifth of the NORTH EASTERN locomotive stock was shedded at Hull to cope with the busy passenger traffic and the very high volume of freight activity, Hull having been long recognised as the third port of Great Britain.

The first effects of grouping resulted in both rationalisation and making better use of resources. Rationalisation saw the closure of the Hull + Barnsley terminus at Cannon Street in 1924 with trains from Cudworth routed via a new curve, joining the Bridlington line at Walton Street Junction, into Paragon. Cannon Street, however, did remain open for goods traffic. Beverley Road intermediate station was closed completely, as it had never had a goods service.

At about the same time a connection was made from Southcoates directly into the ex North Eastern line to the King George Dock; this gave additional running lines to the dock and a direct access from some ex North Eastern lines previously unavailable without reversing. The old access from Bridges Junction was taken out of use.

The only other immediate result of grouping was some name changes in Goods stations to give every station a distinct identity. These are shown in tabular form below:

PRE-GROUPING RAILWAY	OLD NAME	NEW NAME	NOTES
GC (NE)	KINGSTON STREET (GC)	KINGSTON STREET	
NE	KINGSTON STREET (CENTRAL)	CENTRAL	
NE	STEPNEY	TEMPLE STREET	
NE	SCULCOATES	STEPNEY	H+B SCULCOATES retained its name

In the meantime the numerous level crossings on the Victoria Docks Docks Branch were, as a result of increased use of the roads, causing terrible congestion on the city roads. Hull Corporation were continually complaining about this. The LNER as with the NE before it had offered to do something but looked for some contribution from the Hull Corporation which they refused to give, so nothing was done. They railway tried to alleviate the situation partly by using the old H+B line where possible but this was not always possible with all goods traffic, and totally impossible with passenger trains to Withernsea + Hornsea. One final development did help to reduce goods trains over this docks branch was a new modern hump marshalling yard opened near Hessle in 1935.

1941 - 1990

Although rationalisation of passenger services had started in the 1930's on the Hull + Barnsley line, this had no effect on the central network because even after complete withdrawal of the passenger service in 1955 all the lines within the map area were retained for goods purposes.

As the map shows most of the goods depots were retained although traffic was shrinking with losses to both Immingham + Grimsby in addition to road haulage. Then came the Beeching Report in 1963 with both Hornsea and Withernsea branches scheduled for closure. These closures, both implemented in 1964, and the continued loss of freight volumes enabled the Victoria Docks branch to close entirely and all goods traffic to Alexandra and King George Docks could be routed over the old H+B line. This was on an embankment and had none of the level crossings of the older line. To further eliminate level crossings the original Bridlington branch line via Newington was closed and traffic from the Docks routed along the HB Neptune Street branch to make an entirely new connection at Hessle Road, whilst goods traffic for the Bridlington line could be routed by another new line from Anlaby Road onto the Bridlington line at West Parade North Junction.

A new passenger station was opened on the Neptune Street Goods line at Boothferry Park but this was for service to the adjoining sports ground only.

In the meantime all other goods stations were progressively closed and all that now remains is a goods line to the King George Dock and six sidings of the new Hessle Yard.

Looking to the future the prospects for Hull appear gloomy, the one remaining branch to Bridlington being under a closure threat more often than not, albeit it is not under threat at the time of writing. There is no sign of a revival of goods traffic. There is still an excellent rail service to London but other long-distance services are not so good. For example in the late 'eighties a Hull-Lancaster train gave a connection to Glasgow, but by leaving Hull only ten minutes sooner one could have an hour in London and reach Glasgow at the same time. In addition I have seen through passengers from Hull have to change at Leeds and then stand to Skipton. Due to its lack of use British Rail have now withdrawn this service !!

BARNSLEY

By the end of the eighteenth century Barnsley had developed as an important coal mining centre, with iron also being mined. The thick Barnsley coal seams had resulted in early exploitation where they outcropped and the industrialisation of the area was one of the earliest in Great Britain. Barnsley differs from most railway centres in that up to very recent times the movement of passengers has always been of secondary consideration compared to the movement of coal. Even the recent changes have been influenced by exhaustion of coal in the Barnsley area with the centre of the mining area moving steadily eastwards into the concealed coalfield as the development maps clearly show. In view of the relative importance of freight traffic, goods-only lines are indicated on all maps, helping to illustrate the effects that the coal industry had on the railway network.

1799-1838

This first period up to 1838 includes no railway development but illustrates the canal system of the times together with the connecting tramways and wagonways built to serve the mining and associated industries. In the meantime the NORTH MIDLAND railway was authorised by an ACT of 4·7·1836 to construct a railway from Derby to Leeds.

1839-1845

1. 7.1840 NORTH MIDLAND opened for passengers and goods with stations at ROYSTON + NOTTON and BARNSLEY. However, this station was only called BARNSLEY; it was not at BARNSLEY but at Cudworth. This did nothing to help distribute Barnsley coal. In some cases coal carried by rail from Durham was cheaper. There was a demand for railways which to begin with were held at bay by powerful canal interests. But these negative policies could not prevail for long.

10.5.1844 NORTH MIDLAND becomes part of MIDLAND

1846-1850

7. 8.1846 SHEFFIELD ROTHERHAM BARNSLEY WAKEFIELD HUDDERSFIELD + GOOLE (SRBWHG) authorised to connect points of its title.

1.5.1847 Northern portion of SRBWHG leased to MANCHESTER + LEEDS.

9.7.1847 MANCHESTER + LEEDS becomes LANCASHIRE + YORKSHIRE (LY) so the northern portion of SRBWHG effectively became part of the LY but not fully absorbed until 2.8.1858.

22.7.1847 The southern portion of SRBWHG becomes SOUTH YORKSHIRE, DONCASTER + GOOLE with power to change its name to — SOUTH YORKSHIRE RAILWAY + RIVER DUN NAVIGATION, the canal company having decided it was better to join forces with the railway rather than oppose it. The name change was contingent upon half the railway capital being subscribed and was effected 19·4·1850. The company was usually known simply as the SOUTH YORKSHIRE (SY).

1.1.1850 SRBWHG northern portion opened by LY for passengers. Trains ran from Horbury Junction to BARNSLEY with stations at CRIGGLESTONE, HAIGH and DARTON. Due to a recession the line was single only and it would be over fifty years before it was doubled throughout and the connection in the Huddersfield direction was laid.

15.1.1850 The LY BARNSLEY opened for Goods. Branch to SILKSTONE opened for goods.

1.2.1850 SY opened for goods from the south to Elsecar Junction, ELSECAR branch opened for goods.

30.6.1850 SY opened to Aldham Junction and part of the Moor End branch: both sections for goods only.

At this point in time the SRBWHG lines constructed served precisely the same points and with the same outlets as the canal system shown on the first map. The Thurgoland Collieries had also been served by a short branch from the MANCHESTER, SHEFFIELD + LINCOLNSHIRE (MSL) since 1847.

1851-1855

1. 7.1851 SY opened to end on junction with LY at Barnsley. Passenger service started; stations opened at WOMBWELL and ARDSLEY.

4.1852 SY Goods branch opened to MOOR END.

15.5.1854 MSL line from Barnsley Junction opened for goods traffic to Silkstone and Dodworth.

1.7.1854 MSL: the above line opened for passengers. Stations at SILKSTONE and DODWORTH.

4.9.1854 SY BLACKBURN VALLEY LINE opened to all traffic. Passenger stations at SMITHLEY (later became DOVECLIFFE) and at WESTWOOD.

1.10.1854 MIDLAND Barnsley replaced by new station, nearby site. New name based on location - CUDWORTH.

1. 1.1855 SY opened additional station on Blackburn Valley line called HANGMAN'S STONE, but renamed BIRDWELL + HOYLAND the following month.

21. 4.1855 LY line now doubled throughout except Woolley Tunnel.

1.11.1855 MSL Barnsley branch opened for passengers to station at SUMMER LANE.

5.12.1855 MSL Barnsley branch goods service extended to Summer Lane.

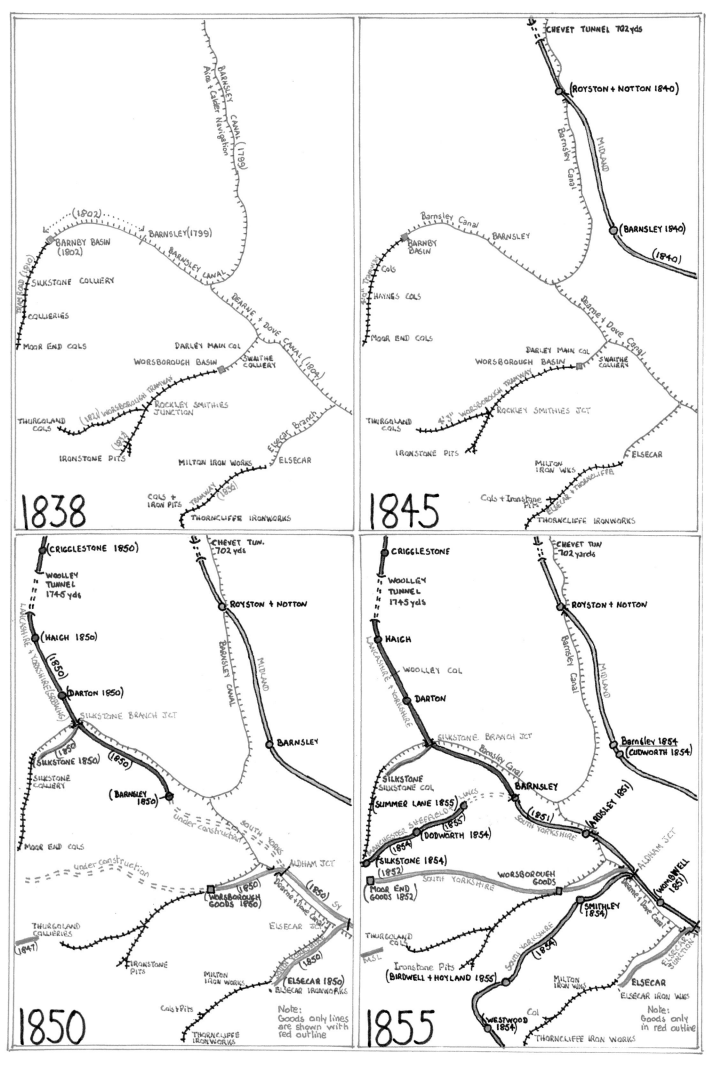

1838

1845

1850

Note:
Goods only lines
are shown with
red outline

1855

Note:
Goods only
in red outline

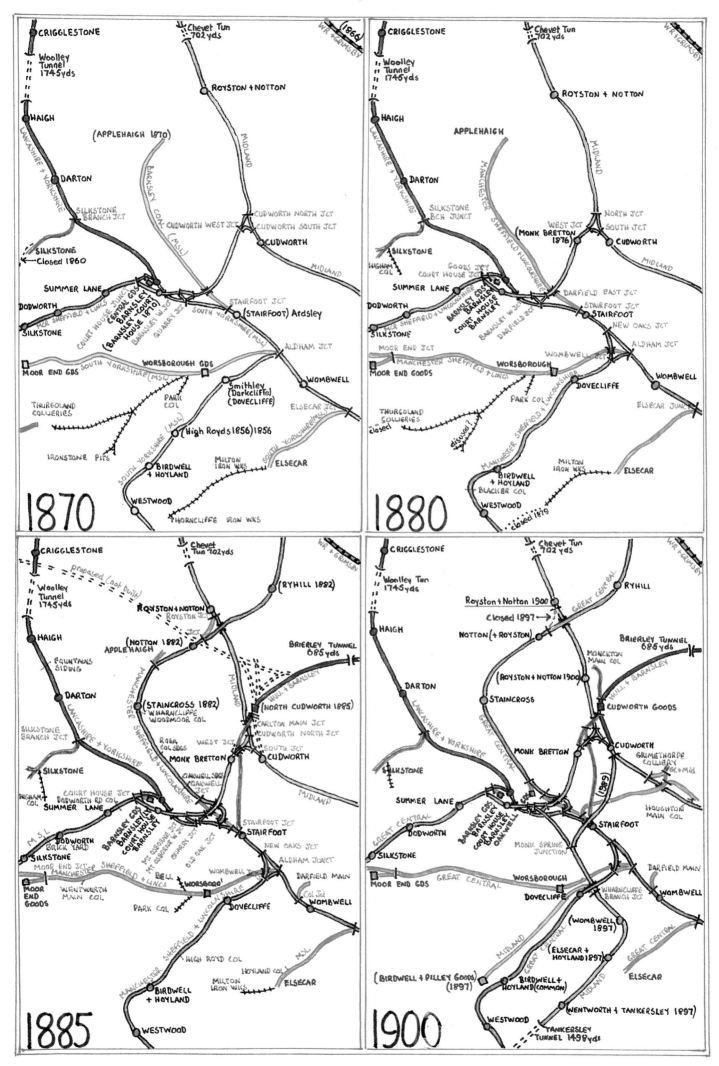

1856-1870

1.7.1856 New station on Blackburn Valley Line at HIGH ROYDS appeared in Bradshaw but only for two months. It appears likely it was used to carry workpeople and may in fact have been used before and after these dates for that purpose. At that time there were sidings and a local colliery of that name on the site of the station.

12.2.1857 MANCHESTER SHEFFIELD + LINCOLNSHIRE (MSL) opened for Goods to BARNSLEY REGENT STREET. This terminus remained a Goods Station and was later renamed CENTRAL.

2.8.1858 SRBWHG (northern portion) fully absorbed into LANCASHIRE + YORKSHIRE (LY).

1.12.1859 MSL opened to passengers into BARNSLEY (LY station).

22.7.1861 BARNSLEY COAL Railway - ACT. This was intended to serve collieries in the area between the LY and MIDLAND lines, from Ardsley to Wakefield, but was curtailed in its passage through parliament to a short branch, under 5 miles long, from the SOUTH YORKSHIRE (SY) to APPLEHAIGH.

13.7.1863 Transfer of BARNSLEY COAL to SOUTH YORKSHIRE authorised.

23.6.1864 Transfer of SY to MSL authorised.

1.2.1866 WEST RIDING + GRIMSBY JOINT opened. Authorised 7.8.1862. Agreed to be leased jointly by MSL and GREAT NORTHERN on 28.2.1866, effective from the date of opening.

28.6.1869 MIDLAND branch opened from Cudworth South Junction to Court House Junction at Barnsley and Cudworth North Junction to Cudworth West Junction both opened for goods traffic.

2.5.1870 Above lines opened to passenger traffic; station opened at BARNSLEY COURT HOUSE.

31.5.1870 Connections from QUARRY JUNCTION (MSL) to MIDLAND line in each direction to enable MIDLAND and MSL to use either station at Barnsley.

22.1.1870 MSL open BARNSLEY COAL from Ardsley to APPLEHAIGH.

1.10.1870 ARDSLEY renamed STAIRFOOT.

1871-1880

1.12.1871 STAIRFOOT: Station rebuilt just to the south of the previous station.

16.7.1874 SY fully absorbed by MSL.

1.5.1876 MIDLAND open MONK BRETTON station.

1.12.1879 MSL new curve from NEW OAKS JUNCTION to WOMBWELL MAIN JUNCTION to avoid the need to reverse for trains from Barnsley to Sheffield via the Blackburn Valley line.

2.8.1880 MSL Worsborough Goods Branch extended from Moor End Junction, 3/4 mile east of the terminus, to join the Barnsley line of the MSL at Silkstone West Junction (just off the map).

26.8.1880 HULL, BARNSLEY + WEST RIDING JUNCTION RAILWAY + DOCK COMPANY (HB) - ACT

1881-1885

1881 By this date there was a definite shift of the centre of the coal industry eastwards. Barnsley itself was still an active area but some pits to the west were reaching exhaustion; but these were more than balanced by new pits to the east extending into the concealed coalfield. This is reflected by the abandonment, by this date, of most of the old tramways together with the falling into disuse of the MSL Thurgoland branch.

1.8.1882 MSL line from Lee Lane Junction to Nostell, Old Oaks Junction to Oakwell Junction and Royston Curve opened for Goods. A passenger service commenced the following month from Barnsley via Old Oaks + Oakwell to Nostell. Stations were opened at RYHILL, NOTTON and STAINCROSS.

20.7.1885 HULL + BARNSLEY lines opened to Goods. Further lines and connections were planned as the 1885 map shows, but none of these, except the line to Monckton Main and the direct connection to Cudworth (Midland) were completed as the 1900 map shows.

27.7.1885 HB opened for passenger traffic. Only station NORTH CUDWORTH but all trains ran through to the Midland station and soon ceased calling at North Cudworth which became a goods station.

1886-1900

4.7.1892 MSL Goods line opened: Stairfoot to Houghton Main Colliery. Later a connection was made from this line to Grimethorpe Colliery where it became a joint line with the MIDLAND branch from Storr's Mill Junction.

1.7.1896 MSL: OAKWELL - Goods branch and Depot opened.

12.4.1897 MIDLAND Chapeltown branch extended to Barnsley West Junction, and Birdswell + Pilley branch opened for goods traffic.

1.7.1897 Passenger service Barnsley to Sheffield (MIDLAND) commenced. Stations at WOMBWELL, ELSECAR + HOYLAND and WENTWORTH + TANKERSLEY.

1.8.1897 MANCHESTER SHEFFIELD + LINCOLNSHIRE becomes GREAT CENTRAL.

6.8.1897 MIDLAND Cudworth Station South Junction to Monkspring Junction opened to all traffic.

1901-1919

Before covering the events of this period, two matters relating to the 19th century remain to be recorded. Both were in 1897.

1897 GREAT CENTRAL (GC) Royston curve closed but retained as a siding.

6.8.1897 DEARNE VALLEY - ACT

19.3.1901 BRACKENHILL (LIGHT) - ACT

16.8.1901 GC - OLD MILL LANE GOODS - Depot and branch opened

19.3.1902 DEARNE VALLEY (DV) - Brierley Junction to Houghton Colliery Junction opened for goods.

2.3.1902 LANCASHIRE + YORKSHIRE (LY) - second Woolley Tunnel opened, Crigglestone Junction to Horbury + Ossett opened for Goods traffic.

1.7.1902 LY Crigglestone Junction to Horbury + Ossett opened for passenger traffic. This opening finally completed the connections proposed in the S R BWHG ACT of 1846 !!

6.3.1905 LY open Dearne Valley Junction Railway from Crofton Junction to Shafton Junction for Goods. Connection with DV.

13.3.1905 DV remainder of lines within map area opened for goods traffic.

3.7.1905 MIDLAND - Line opened for goods from Royston Junction to Crigglestone Junction. (Before these works started at the turn of the century ROYSTON + NOTTON station had been rebuilt one mile to the south). This line was part of a grand plan for a new main line to Scotland via BRADFORD, avoiding LEEDS and reducing by some miles the distance from LONDON to CARLISLE. It was deferred by the war and never completed beyond Thornhill.

1905 One further event of 1905 affecting BARNSLEY but just outside the map area was the opening of the first part of a new hump shunting yard at WATH by the GREAT CENTRAL.

13.9.1906 GC brought into use remodelled junction layout at Wombwell main to enable traffic from the Wath - Barnsley main line, travelling in either direction to gain access to either the Worsborough branch or the Blackburn Valley line without the need to reverse.

1.7.1909 MIDLAND line from Royston Junction brought into use for passenger traffic.

31.12.1909 GC - Moor End Goods closed together with associated spur. Through line retained for traffic.

3.6.1912 LY + DV commence passenger service over all DV main line and LY connecting line. Stations/Halts opened: RYHILL GREAT HOUGHTON and GRIMETHORPE

1.7.1914 BRACKENHILL (LIGHT) opened to Goods; Depot at ACKWORTH MOOR TOP. The line served Wentworth Colliery and was worked by the NORTH EASTERN. At about the same time a short spur was opened from the GRIMSBY + WEST RIDING to also service Wentworth Colliery.

1.1.1917 MIDLAND passenger service on the 'new main line' from Royston Junction withdrawn as a war-time economy measure. It would be restored in 1920.

The development outlined from 1880 was almost exclusively associated with colliery connections, some laid to new sources of supply but mainly constructed at the instigation of the colliery owners who sought to ensure that most of the collieries had connections to at least two railways, making sure that competitive rates were obtained. The BARNSLEY COAL, the HULL + BARNSLEY and the DEARNE VALLEY were all promoted by these motives; the latter company in fact was solely a promotion of the colliery owners. From the map it is clear that the DV in the Barnsley area alone made connection with each of the four major companies in the area: The HB at Brierley; LY, the working company, at Shaftholme, whilst the MSL and MIDLAND were both joined at Grimethorpe and Houghton Main. In addition, what the map does not show is the running powers exercised over parts of the DV by the GREAT NORTHERN and the NORTH EASTERN.

The 1919 Map, so far as colliery lines are concerned, is based upon a MIDLAND map of that date and does not therefore always show all colliery lines connecting to foreign railways, but even so it is easy to see that few collieries have connection with only one railway. Two further multiple connections are noted below:

(1) Ryhill Main, Hodroyd and Monckton Main were served by HULL + BARNSLEY; then through Ryhill Main Sidings which were jointly owned by and with connections to the MIDLAND and GREAT CENTRAL; and finally by stub lines that led to a wharf on the independant Barnsley Canal of the AIRE + CALDER NAVIGATION.

(2) Hemsworth Colliery as can be seen was served by a spur from the GRIMSBY + WEST. RIDING giving both GREAT NORTHERN and GREAT CENTRAL access. It was also served by the BRACKENHILL (LIGHT) which made connection to the SWINTON + KNOTTINGLEY JOINT owned by the MIDLAND and NORTH EASTERN.

Finally a word about Engine Sheds. These were at BARNSLEY (GC) adjoining the LY station and was also used by the LY (and later LMS until about 1933); CUDWORTH (HB) situated near to the Goods station. The final shed was unique as it was not built until LMS days and was the only entirely new shed built by that grouping company. Site was between Midland + HB lines south of Royston station. Known as ROYSTON or sometimes CARLTON.

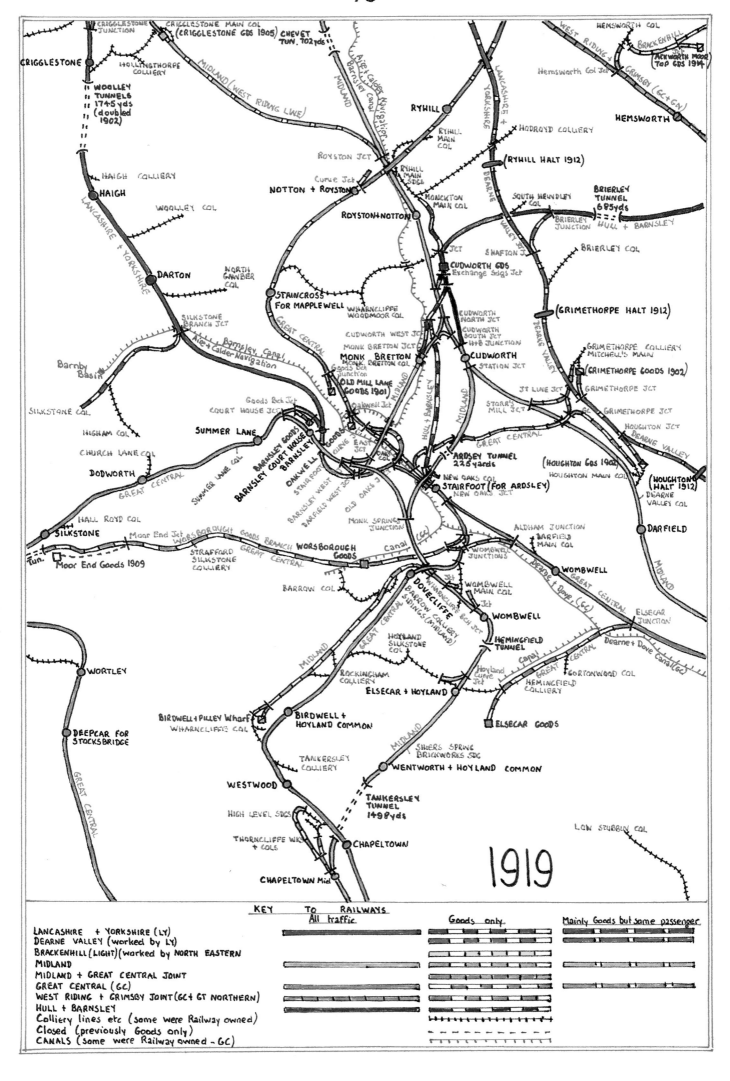

CRIGGLESTONE
CRIGGLESTONE MAIN COL
(CRIGGLESTONE GDS 1905)
CRIGGLESTONE JUNCTION
CHEVET TUN. 702yds
HEMSWORTH COL
WEST RIDING
BRACKENHILL
ACKWORTH MOOR TOP GDS 1914

HOLLINGTHORPE COLLIERY
MIDLAND (WEST RIDING LINE)
AIRE CALDER NAVIGATION
BARNSLEY CANAL
MIDLAND
LANCASHIRE + YORKSHIRE
Hemsworth Col Jct
GRIMSBY (GC + GN)
HEMSWORTH

WOOLLEY TUNNELS 1745yds (doubled 1902)
RYHILL
RYHILL MAIN COL
HODROYD COLLIERY
(RYHILL HALT 1912)

HAIGH COLLIERY
HAIGH
WOOLLEY COL
ROYSTON JCT
Curve Jct
NOTTON + ROYSTON
RYHILL MAIN SDGS
MONCKTON MAIN COL
SOUTH HEINDLEY COL
BRIERLEY TUNNEL 685yds
BRIERLEY JUNCTION HULL + BARNSLEY

DARTON
NORTH GAWBER COL
ROYSTON+NOTTON
JCT
SHAFTON JCT
DEARNE VALLEY
BRIERLEY COL

SILKSTONE BRANCH JCT
Aire + Calder Navigation
Barnsley Canal
GREAT CENTRAL
STAINCROSS FOR MAPPLEWELL
WHARNCLIFFE WOODMOOR COL
CUDWORTH GDS Exchange Sdgs Jct
SHAFTON JCT
GRIMETHORPE HALT 1912

Barnby Basin
SILKSTONE COL
COURT HOUSE JCT
CUDWORTH WEST JCT
MONK BRETTON JCT
MONK BRETTON
MONK BRETTON COL
CUDWORTH NORTH JCT
CUDWORTH SOUTH JCT H+B JUNCTION
CUDWORTH STATION JCT
GRIMETHORPE COLLIERY MITCHELL'S MAIN
(GRIMETHORPE GOODS 1902)

HIGHAM COL
SUMMER LANE
Goods Bch Jct
Goods Bch Junction
OLD MILL LANE GOODS 1901
Oakwell Jct
JT LINE JCT
STARR'S MILL JCT
GC GRIMETHORPE JCT
HOUGHTON JCT
DEARNE VALLEY

CHURCH LANE COL
Summer Lane Col
BARNSLEY COURT HOUSE
BARNSLEY
OAKWELL
CURVE JCT
EAST JCT
GREAT CENTRAL
ARDSLEY TUNNEL 225 yards
(HOUGHTON GDS 1902)
HOUGHTON MAIN COL
HOUGHTON (HALT 1912)

DODWORTH
GREAT CENTRAL
Stairfoot West
Barnsley West Jct
Barfield West Jct
OLD OAKS JCT
NEW OAKS COL
STAIRFOOT (FOR ARDSLEY)
NEW OAKS JCT
DEARNE VALLEY COL

HALL ROYD COL
SILKSTONE
Moor End Jct
WORSBOROUGH GOODS BRANCH GREAT CENTRAL
STRAFFORD SILKSTONE COLLIERY
WORSBOROUGH GOODS
MONK SPRINGS JUNCTION
Canal (GC)
ALDHAM JUNCTION
BARFIELD MAIN COL
DARFIELD

Tun.
Moor End Goods 1909
BARROW COL
DOVECLIFFE
Wharncliffe Bch Jct
BARROW COLLIERY SDGS (MIDLAND)
WOMBWELL JUNCTIONS
WOMBWELL MAIN COL
Dearne + Dove (GC)
WOMBWELL
Dearne + Dove Canal (GC)
ELSECAR JUNCTION
MIDLAND

WORTLEY
GREAT CENTRAL
MIDLAND
HOYLAND SILKSTONE COL
ROCKINGHAM COLLIERY
Barrow Col Jct
WOMBWELL
HEMINGFIELD TUNNEL
Hoyland Curve Jct
HEMINGFIELD COLLIERY
GORTONWOOD COL
GREAT CENTRAL

DEEPCAR FOR STOCKSBRIDGE
BIRDWELL + PILLEY Wharf
WHARNCLIFFE COL
BIRDWELL + HOYLAND COMMON
ELSECAR + HOYLAND
ELSECAR GOODS

TANKERSLEY COLLIERY
MIDLAND
SHIERS SPRING BRICKWORKS SDG
WENTWORTH + HOYLAND COMMON

WESTWOOD
TANKERSLEY TUNNEL 1498yds
LOW STUBBIN COL

HIGH LEVEL SDGS
THORNCLIFFE WKS + COLS
CHAPELTOWN

CHAPELTOWN Mid.

1919

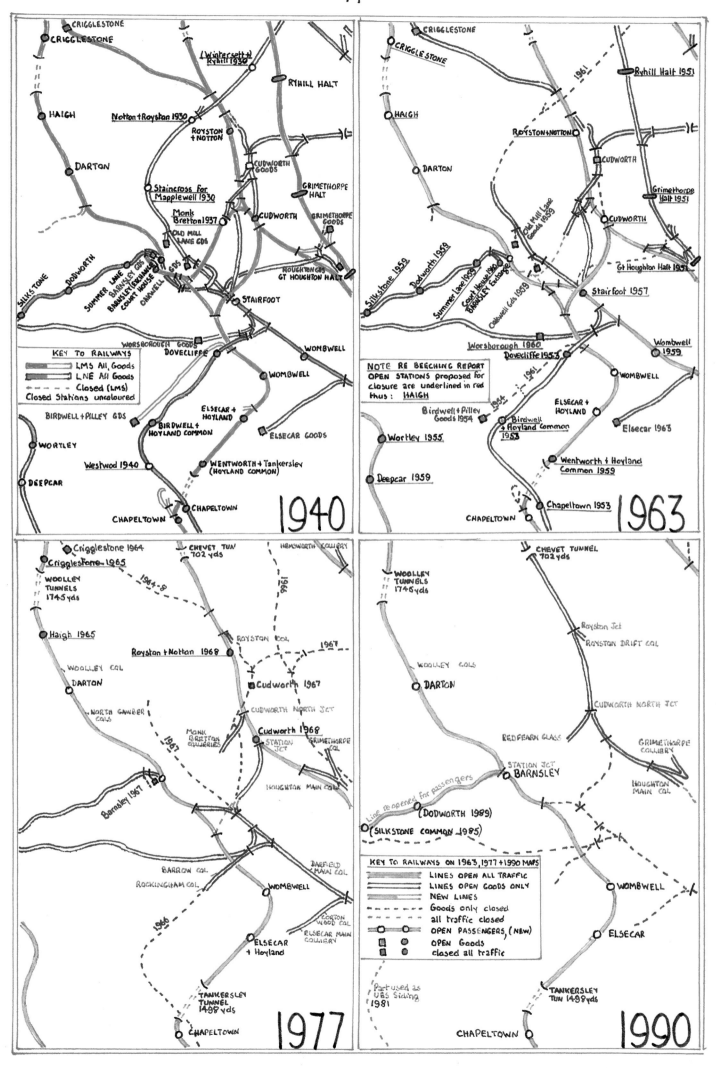

1920-1940

Grouping had little effect on the railway network around Barnsley and in fact most collieries continued to have access to competitive links for their traffic, either LMS or LNE.

Further evidence of the eastward shift of the centre of the coal industry occurred throughout the period but the reduced volumes of traffic were not fully reflected in rationalisation of the network in the west, the only closure being the Silkstone branch which closed in 1937 except for a short spur.

The remaining changes were the withdrawal of passenger services from the ex-Barnsley Coal line in 1930, but this line had not been built with a passenger service in mind and it continued to carry quite a heavy volume of coal traffic, in particular at the Barnsley end. But it also carried good volumes of coal from the Monckton Main group of collieries (see notes on page 69). There were two other intermediate passenger stations closed: Westwood on the LNE Blackburn Valley line in 1940, and Monk Bretton had closed in 1937.

1941-1963

This period covers the war years, nationalisation, and finishes with the publication of the Beeching Report in 1963. During the war years and the immediate post-war period the movement of coal increased in importance due to the lack of foreign exchange to buy petrol, and even passenger services enjoyed a brief honeymoon period in the wake of public owned railways. Looking first at passenger services - progressive withdrawal of both entire lines and intermediate stations started in the 1950's, although the Royston to Thornhill service had been withdrawn in 1946. First to go in the 'Fifties was the Dearne Valley line in 1951, followed by the LNE Blackburn Valley line in 1953. Then in 1959 the Penistone - Barnsley passenger service was withdrawn whilst in the meantime there were closures of intermediate stations on other lines which, however, did continue to carry passenger traffic. In view of all these closures the Beeching proposals for the area were relatively quite modest: The Barnsley - Wath line having lost its intermediate stations would be reduced to goods only; The Midland main line would loose its intermediate stations and stopping service but retain through express services; and HAIGH and CRIGGLESTONE on the Barnsley - Wakefield line were scheduled for closure. Turning to goods rationalisation, there were few of these during this period and in fact the only lines to go were where collieries had previously been served by both LMS and LNE; quite often one of the lines was closed. Again this map does not reflect the coal industry move to the east, so that by 1970 all pits within the borough of BARNSLEY would be closed.

1964 - 1977

This period saw, on the passenger front, all the Beeching proposals implemented. CRIGGLESTONE and HAIGH were both closed in 1965 whilst ROYSTON + NOTTON and CUDWORTH closed in 1968 along with the withdrawal of the Leeds to Sheffield stopping train service via the ex MIDLAND main line. The LNE Wath line remained in use for passenger services but in practice only carried diverted traffic to assist maintenance schedules on regular passenger lines, and the Midland main line was progressively reduced to a similar status. BARNSLEY was thus left with a solitary through line; although other passenger lines passed through the area they had no stations or connections with the area. On the goods rationalisation, the process of closing duplicate lines was continued. The goods lines which remained often became changed in character particularly in the west, where they no longer served pits but acted as feeder and distribution lines serving the WATH HUMP YARD which was located to the east of the map area just beyond Elsecar Junction.

1978 - 1990

The use of new yards and merry-go-round trains during this period has resulted in closure of WATH YARD and made its feeder and distribution lines redundant. Most of the previous goods-only lines have gone with the exception of the stubs serving Grimethorpe + Houghton Main. There has also been rationalisation on the passenger lines in the area. The ex-MSL main line closed completely in 1981, whilst the Midland main line has been reduced to just 2 goods branch serving collieries at ROYSTON and GRIMETHORPE, and part of the line has been closed to all traffic. This well engineered line capable of carrying trains at speeds of 100mph has closed rather than the line to the east with its numerous colliery subsidence slacks, but the loss of the passenger stopping trains probably sounded its death knell as the alternative route carries local services. Even so this is one of the very few pre-1850 lines in the country to close. One positive development; following closure of the MSL main line, the Penistone - Barnsley line (closed to passengers 1959) was upgraded to again carry passengers and Huddersfield to Sheffield trains were rerouted this way. New stations were opened - SILKSTONE COMMON in 1985 followed by the re-opening of DODWORTH in 1989, and Barnsley had regained its junction status.

1991 - FUTURE

Looking to the future one can only envisage further contraction; when economically reachable coal resources on the MIDLAND stub become exhausted complete closure of the line will follow.

MANCHESTER

Outside London, MANCHESTER has always been the railway centre with the largest number of lines radiating from it, its closest rival in this respect being Glasgow. Although it does not have the central complexities of Carlisle, its development and growth was continuous up to the First World War. If its latest Metro-link plans are implemented, it will by the mid-'nineties be one of the few places to have more stations in 1995 than in 1905. Manchester also had the distinction of having the first railway in the modern sense, since its first railway fulfilled the three qualifying criteria of steam traction, working to a timetable, and having the movement of passengers as its primary objective.

In the chronology which follows dates have been checked but opening dates of the early intermediate stations must be treated with some reserve. Early intermediate stations tended to be stopping places only without platforms or buildings and timetables also are not fool-proof in deciding when a station opened or closed.

TO 1840

5.5.1826 LIVERPOOL + MANCHESTER (LM) is authorised.

15.9.1830 LM official opening. Passenger service commenced two days later. Goods service started on 1st December.

23.8.1831 MANCHESTER, BOLTON + BURY CANAL NAVIGATION + RAILWAY (MBBCN) authorised to build a railway following the canal route of its title.

6.5.1833 GRAND JUNCTION (GJ) authorised. Did not build a railway in the area but would later absorb the LM.

4.7.1836 MANCHESTER + LEEDS (ML) authorised.

5.5.1837 SHEFFIELD, ASHTON-UNDER-LYNE + MANCHESTER (SAULM) authorised. Often referred to as the SHEFFIELD.

30.6.1837 MANCHESTER + BIRMINGHAM (MB) obtains its Act.

29.5.1838 MBBCN opened from SALFORD (New Bailey Street) to Bolton. AGECROFT and CLIFTON stations may have opened later, but it appears they were both in use before the end of the year.

4.7.1839 ML opened from a terminus in OLDHAM ROAD to Littleborough. There were no intermediate stations within the map area, nor were any stations opened for a number of years.

4.7.1840 MB opened from a temporary terminus at TRAVIS STREET to another temporary terminus at STOCKPORT, since viaduct across the Mersey was incomplete. The temporary Stockport station was on the site of what became HEATON NORRIS. In addition there was an intermediate station at RUSHFORD but this also turned out to be temporary since it was soon replaced.

Thus at the end of 1840 there were four railways in MANCHESTER each with its separate terminus and this initial lack of co-operation between the railways would continue to be an inconvenience to Mancunians for many years to come.

1841-1845

This next period of only five years saw further active development in MANCHESTER's railway network and the start of a long period of inter-company rivalry and competition. Quite often the aim appeared not to build a railway except as a last resort but to prevent the others from doing it.

17.11.1841 SAULM opened from TRAVIS STREET to GODLEY (temporary station) with intermediate stations at FAIRFIELD, ASHTON, DUKINFIELD (later known as DOG LANE) and NEWTON. The SAULM were to share the MB terminus under construction at STORE STREET but the MB refused to share the line into the terminus from ARDWICK.

8.5.1842 STORE STREET (also known as Bank Top) opened (SAULM + MB Joint), TRAVIS STREET closed.

10.5.1842 STOCKPORT to the south opened by MB, the viaduct at Stockport having been finally completed.

24.12.1842 GODLEY to Broadbottom opened by SAULM.

15.2.1843 STOCKPORT (EDGELEY) opened as a temporary station. Later in the year RUSHFORD replaced by LONGSIGHT (MB).

1.1.1844 ML line from MILES PLATTING to Hunt's Bank, to be site of VICTORIA station.

4.5.1844 LM line from Liverpool Road Junction to join ML. VICTORIA (ML) opened; LIVERPOOL ROAD (LM) and OLDHAM ROAD (ML) both now reduced to goods stations. MBBCN trains use junction with LM to also run into VICTORIA from 19th July.

10.5.1844 MIDLAND Incorporated. It would however be many years before any Midland lines reached the area.

6.6.1844 MANCHESTER, BURY + ROSSENDALE authorised.

19.7.1844 ASHTON STALEYBRIDGE + LIVERPOOL JUNCTION authorised.

1.7.1845 MANCHESTER + LEEDS absorbs MBBCN.

21.7.1845 MANCHESTER SOUTH JUNCTION + ALTRINCHAM authorised. Capital provided by SAULM and MB.

21.7.1845 MANCHESTER BURY + ROSSENDALE changes its name to EAST LANCASHIRE (EL).

21.7.1845 HUDDERSFIELD + MANCHESTER authorised.

8.8.1845 LIVERPOOL + MANCHESTER absorbed by GRAND JUNCTION.

24.11.1845 MB open branch from near their Cheadle station to Poynton. (Not on 1845 map - but see later maps extended south)

30.12.1845 SAULM open branch to STALEY BRIDGE (original style) stations at DUKINFIELD and ASHTON. Dukinfield (Dog Lane) Closed.

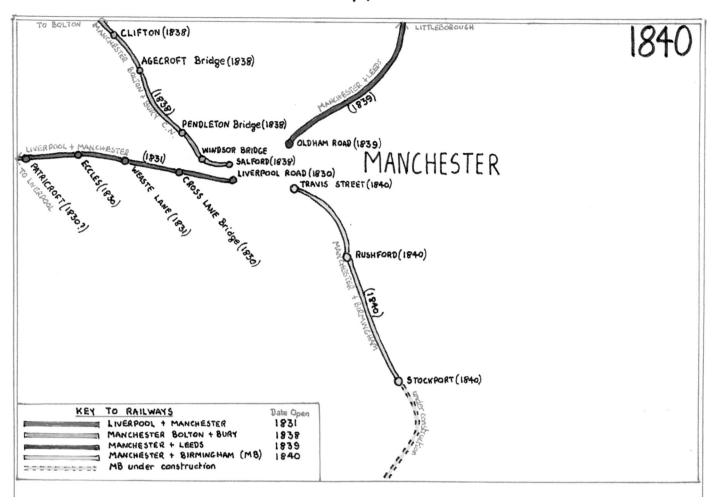

1840

TO BOLTON
CLIFTON (1838)
AGECROFT Bridge (1838)
LITTLEBOROUGH
PENDLETON Bridge (1838)
MANCHESTER + LEEDS (1839)
WINDSOR BRIDGE
OLDHAM ROAD (1839)
LIVERPOOL + MANCHESTER (1831)
SALFORD (1838)
MANCHESTER
PATRICROFT (1830?)
ECCLES (1830)
WEASTE LANE (1831)
CROSS LANE Bridge (1830)
LIVERPOOL ROAD (1830)
TO LIVERPOOL
MANCHESTER BOLTON + BURY C.N. (1838)
TRAVIS STREET (1840)
RUSHFORD (1840)
MANCHESTER + BIRMINGHAM (1840)
STOCKPORT (1840)
under construction

KEY TO RAILWAYS	Date Open
LIVERPOOL + MANCHESTER	1831
MANCHESTER BOLTON + BURY	1838
MANCHESTER + LEEDS	1839
MANCHESTER + BIRMINGHAM (MB)	1840
MB under construction	

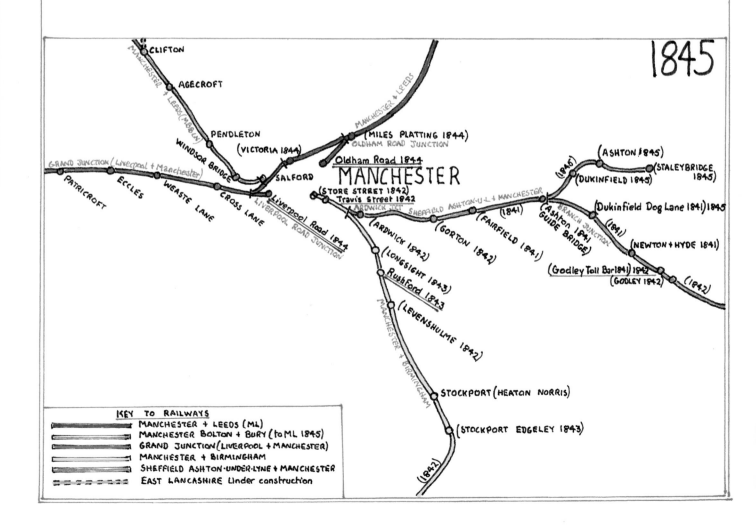

1845

CLIFTON
AGECROFT
MANCHESTER + LEEDS (MBBCo)
PENDLETON
WINDSOR BRIDGE
(MILES PLATTING 1844)
OLDHAM ROAD JUNCTION
(VICTORIA 1844)
MANCHESTER + LEEDS
(ASHTON 1845)
GRAND JUNCTION (LIVERPOOL + MANCHESTER)
PATRICROFT
ECCLES
WEASTE LANE
CROSS LANE
SALFORD
Oldham Road 1844
MANCHESTER
(1845)
STALEYBRIDGE 1845
(DUKINFIELD 1845)
LIVERPOOL ROAD 1844
(STORE STREET 1842)
Travis Street 1842
SHEFFIELD ASHTON-U-L + MANCHESTER
(ASHTON 1841
GUIDE BRIDGE)
BRANCH JUNCTION
Dukinfield Dog Lane 1841) 1845
LIVERPOOL ROAD JUNCTION
ARDWICK JCT
(ARDWICK 1842)
(FAIRFIELD 1841)
(1841)
(1841)
NEWTON + HYDE 1841
(GORTON 1842)
(LONGSIGHT 1843)
(Godley Toll Bar 1841) 1842
RUSHFORD 1843
(GODLEY 1842)
(1842)
(LEVENSHULME 1842)
MANCHESTER + BIRMINGHAM
STOCKPORT (HEATON NORRIS)
(STOCKPORT EDGELEY 1843)
(1842)

KEY TO RAILWAYS	
MANCHESTER + LEEDS (ML)	
MANCHESTER BOLTON + BURY (to ML 1845)	
GRAND JUNCTION (LIVERPOOL + MANCHESTER)	
MANCHESTER + BIRMINGHAM	
SHEFFIELD ASHTON-UNDER-LYNE + MANCHESTER	
EAST LANCASHIRE Under construction	

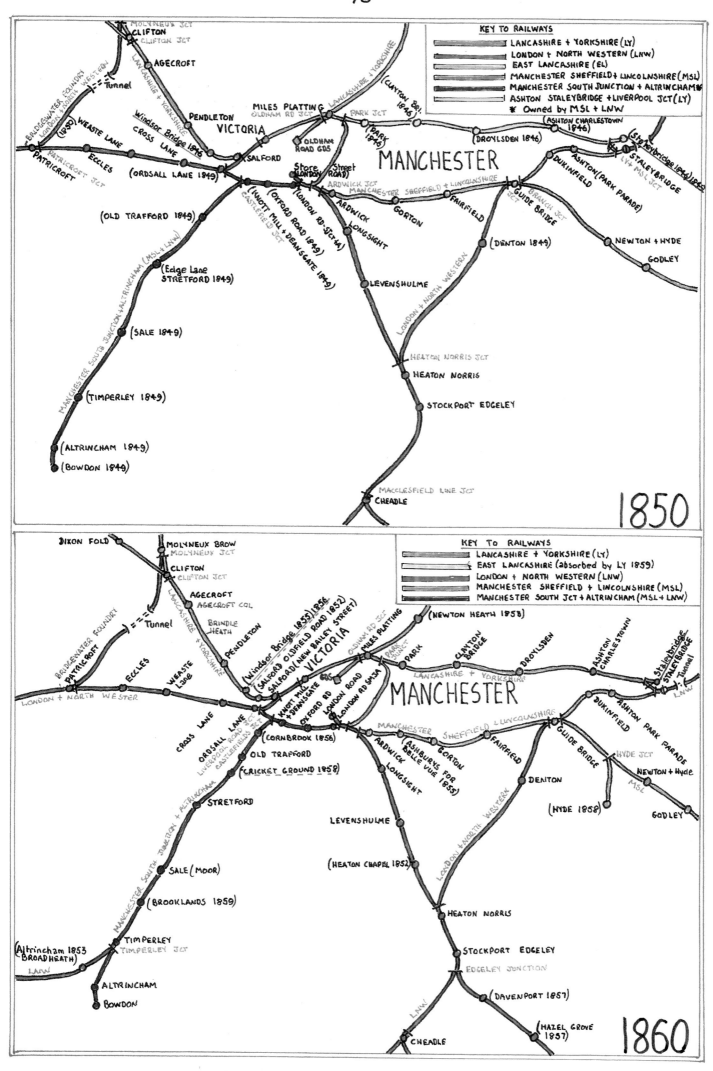

1846-1850

13.4.1846 ASHTON STALEYBRIDGE + LIVERPOOL JUNCTION (ASLJ) opened from Miles Platting to Ashton (Charlestown). Reference sources quote the company name as STALYBRIDGE but this would appear incorrect as all old maps, both Railway and Ordnance Survey, spell with an 'E' in the middle. Intermediate stations at PARK, CLAYTON BRIDGE and DROYLSDEN.

16.7.1846 MANCHESTER BUXTON MATLOCK + MIDLAND JUNCTION (MBMMJ) authorised. The first step by the MIDLAND to make progress in the direction of MANCHESTER. There was an additional ACT on 22.7.1846.

16.7.1846 GRAND JUNCTION and MANCHESTER + BIRMINGHAM combine with the London + Birmingham to form the 'Premier Line', the LONDON + NORTH WESTERN (LNW).

22.7.1846 The SHEFFIELD, ASHTON-UNDER-LYNE + MANCHESTER combines with various other railways to become the MANCHESTER, SHEFFIELD + LINCOLNSHIRE (MSL)

28.9.1846 EAST LANCASHIRE (EL) opened from CLIFTON to Bury.

5.10.1846 ASLJ opened from ASHTON to a terminus at STALEYBRIDGE.

9.7.1847 MANCHESTER + LEEDS becomes LANCASHIRE + YORKSHIRE, at the same time absorbing several other concerns. In the map area the ASLJ was one of the companies absorbed at that time.

9.7.1847 HUDDERSFIELD + MANCHESTER absorbed by LNW.

22.7.1847 MANCHESTER + SOUTHPORT (MS) is authorised.

18.12.1848 LY link from MILES PLATTING to join LNW between Ardwick Junction and London Road, as Store Street was now known. A passenger service used the line to give a cross-city service, but was of short duration due to the obstructive attitude of the LNW.

31.12.1848 MSL GORTON WORKS brought partly into use, and Engine Shed established on an adjoining site.

26.7.1849 MANCHESTER SOUTH JUNCTION + ALTRINCHAM (MSJA) Oxford Road to Altrincham opened. Further openings on 1.8 and 1.9. The company remained independant but was owned and worked by MSL + LNW, but most of the early working was by the MSL. Although a connection was established at LONDON ROAD together with platforms it faced away from the LNW + MSL joint station and was little used, most trains terminating at OXFORD ROAD.

1.8.1849 LY + MSL establish a connection at Staley Bridge. LY trains then used the MSL station but later from 1878 they reverted to using their own station.

1.8.1849 LNW open HUDDERSFIELD + MANCHESTER to Staley Bridge. Trains ran into VICTORIA via LY rather than LONDON ROAD.

1.8.1849 LNW Heaton Norris to Guide Bridge opened. Trains then used MSL to Staleybridge giving a route to Yorkshire.

2.2.1850 LNW PATRICROFT to Molyneux Junction. Regular passenger service started at this time but lasted only a few months due to obstructive tactics of LY; it became in effect a goods branch as a result, although it did in later days see use by some holiday and excursion trains during the summer months.

1851-1860

3.7.1851 WARRINGTON + ALTRINCHAM (WA) authorised.

31.12.1852 LY ARDWICK passenger service appears to have terminated by this date.

3.7.1853 WA becomes WARRINGTON + STOCKPORT (WS). Despite the changed name it never progressed beyond Altrincham.

1.11.1853 WS reaches Wilderspool (later became BROADHEATH) at Altrincham.

3.7.1854 MS absorbed jointly by EL and LY.

1.5.1854 WS BROADHEATH to TIMPERLEY connecting with MSJA opened to all traffic.

31.7.1854 STOCKPORT DISLEY + WHALEY BRIDGE is authorised.

9.6.1857 SDWB opened STOCKPORT to Whaley Bridge.

10.8.1857 OLDHAM ASHTON + GUIDE BRIDGE authorised. There had been several schemes to give better access to MANCHESTER from Oldham than that provided by the steeply graded LY branch. MSL were most interested but being, as so often was the case, short of funds made an agreement with LY. When MSL sought also to involve LNW, LY 'took their bat home' and it became a MSL and LNW venture.

1.3.1858 MSL at last open a branch in their own name - Hyde Junction to HYDE. But it soon became a joint line.

13.8.1859 EL is absorbed by LY.

13.8.1859 WS leased to and absorbed by the LNW.

15.5.1860 MARPLE NEW MILLS + HAYFIELD JUNCTION authorised. This was another MSL promotion destined to become a joint line and was to be a continuation of the Hyde Branch mentioned above (see 1.3.1858).

15.5.1860 STOCKPORT + WOODLEY JUNCTION authorised. Yet a further MSL proposal destined to become one of original founder constituents of the CHESHIRE LINES COMMITTEE (CLC).

14.6.1860 CHESHIRE MIDLAND authorised. A further founder constituent of the CLC.

In most railway centres following the establishment of the main network, usually in place by 1851, any further development tended to be spasmodic. But this did not happen at MANCHESTER where further development was a continuous process right up to the start of World War I.

1861-1870

1. 1.1861 LANCASHIRE + YORKSHIRE (LY) Agecroft station closed. Normally in a complex development, specific station closures do not call for comment, but Agecroft's closure and also that of Windsor Bridge (whose final closure was shown as 1856) are a little odd since both stations continued to appear on RCH maps for many years. Agecroft in fact is on some early 20c maps. A possible explanation is retention as staff halts for engine shed staff.

22. 7.1861 STOCKPORT TIMPERLEY + ALTRINCHAM JUNCTION (STAJ) authorised. The line was to make an end on junction with STOCKPORT + WOODLEY JUNCTION (SWJ). Both lines would become part of the CHESHIRE LINES COMMITTEE (CLC).

31. 7.1861 OLDHAM ASHTON + GUIDE BRIDGE (OAGB) opened. Vested in MANCHESTER SHEFFIELD + LINCOLNSHIRE (MSL) and LONDON + NORTH WESTERN (LNW) on 30·6·1862.

12. 5.1862 CHESHIRE MIDLAND (CM) opened from Bowdon to the south. Continuation of MANCHESTER SOUTH JUNCTION + ALTRINCHAM (MSJA).

5. 8.1862 MANCHESTER NEW MILLS + HAYFIELD JUNCTION (MNMHJ) opened from end on junction at HYDE (MSL) to Compstall near Marple.

12. 1.1863 SWJ opened from Woodley Junction to a station at PORTWOOD.

1. 2.1863 HYDE JUNCTION station opened (MSL) but strangely it served only the branch line.

13. 7.1863 First mention of CHESHIRE LINES in GREAT NORTHERN (CHESHIRE LINES) ACT. Involved GREAT NORTHERN (GN) in what to that time had been MSL project.

14. 6.1864 MACCLESFIELD BOLLINGTON + MARPLE (MBM) authorised to construct a line from COMPSTALL (near Marple) to Macclesfield

1. 9.1864 LNW opened line from ECCLES JUNCTION to Wigan. Intermediate station at WORSLEY (in map area).

1. 7.1865 MNMHJ opened to New Mills. Compstall closed and replaced by MARPLE.

5. 7.1865 CLC TRANSFER ACT. SWJ, CM, STAJ together with three others grouped with MSL + GN as owners. Power to admit MIDLAND.

1. 8.1865 LY SALFORD to VICTORIA opened. At last trains from Bolton and Bury could reach MANCHESTER.

1. 12.1865 CLC PORTWOOD to DEANSGATE JCT (Altrincham) opened. Line was authorised 22·7·1861 STAJ (see above).

1. 2.1866 MSL GODLEY to APETHORNE JUNCTION opened. Transferred to CLC on 10·8·1866.

1. 2.1866 CLC SKELTON JUNCTION to BROADHEATH JUNCTION (with LNW) opened.

16. 7.1866 MANCHESTER + STOCKPORT (M+S) authorised. An MSL scheme which lapsed but later revived by MIDLAND and MSL (see 1·4·1875).

18. 7.1866 MIDLAND becomes partner in CLC.

1. 8.1866 LNW opened EDGELEY (Stockport) to NORTHENDEN and junction with CLC.

10. 11.1866 STOCKPORT, DISLEY + WHALEY BRIDGE absorbed by LNW

15. 8.1867 CHESHIRE LINES ACT authorises CLC as fully independant.

24. 6.1869 Hyde Junction to New Mills (MSL and MNMHJ) vested in SHEFFIELD + MIDLAND COMMITTEE (SMC) -owners MSL and MIDLAND.

2. 8.1869 MBM opened from junction near closed Compstall station to Macclesfield via ROSE HILL.

1871-1880

25. 5.1871 MBM vested jointly in MSL and NORTH STAFFORDSHIRE known as the MACCLESFIELD COMMITTEE.

1. 8.1873 CLC SKELTON WEST JCT (Altrincham) to Partington Jct opened to passengers (had opened to Goods on 1·3·1873).

5. 8.1873 MANCHESTER SOUTH DISTRICT authorised. Revamp of earlier scheme to serve Cheadle area. Was to become CLC but the GN would not agree. Then to be SMC but MSL reluctant. Became MIDLAND but part transferred to CLC later!!

2. 9.1873 CLC line opened from Warrington to CORNBROOK from whence trains ran over MSJA to OXFORD ROAD.

5. 7.1874 LNW Roe Green Junction near Worsley to Bolton opened to all traffic.

1. 4.1875 SMC ROMILEY to BREDBURY opened to passenger traffic, having already opened to goods on 15·2·1875.

2. 8.1875 SMC ASHBURYS JCT to ROMILEY, Reddish Junction to Brinnington Junction opened to passengers (Goods 17·5·1875).

14. 2.1876 LNW Denton Junction to Crowthorn Junction (OAGB) opened.

11. 8.1876 MANCHESTER SOUTH DISTRICT (MSD) vested in SMC. Powers also granted 17·7·1877 for GN to have part control.

9. 7.1877 CLC line from CORNBROOK junction to new CENTRAL station brought into use.

11. 8.1877 MSD now vested in MIDLAND.

4. 11.1877 LY loop line VICTORIA to THORPS BRIDGE JUNCTION opened to all traffic.

1. 7.1878 CLC Cornbrook to OLD TRAFFORD (MSJA) opened to all traffic.

22. 7.1878 STALYBRIDGE to be rebuilt as MSL + LNW, and LY not involved. LY had re-used its old station from 1·10·1869.

1. 9.1879 LY MANCHESTER to BURY opened. Manchester terminus DUCIE BRIDGE - later became part of VICTORIA.

1. 1.1880 MIDLAND opened MSD line between Throstle Nest Jct (CLC) to HEATON MERSEY JUNCTION to all traffic.

17. 5.1880 LY Thorps Bridge Junction to Oldham direct opened to all traffic. Stations at DEAN LANE and FAILSWORTH.

1. 7.1880 CLC open new CENTRAL station. Previous temporary station becomes Goods Depot.

Also opened 1·2·1879 MSL SKELTON North Junction to Timperley enabling MSL to run a circular service via its several joint lines.

A glance at the 1880 map suggests that by this time all railway development in MANCHESTER must be complete. But this was far from the case. Steady continuous development would continue at virtually the same rate for three further decades.

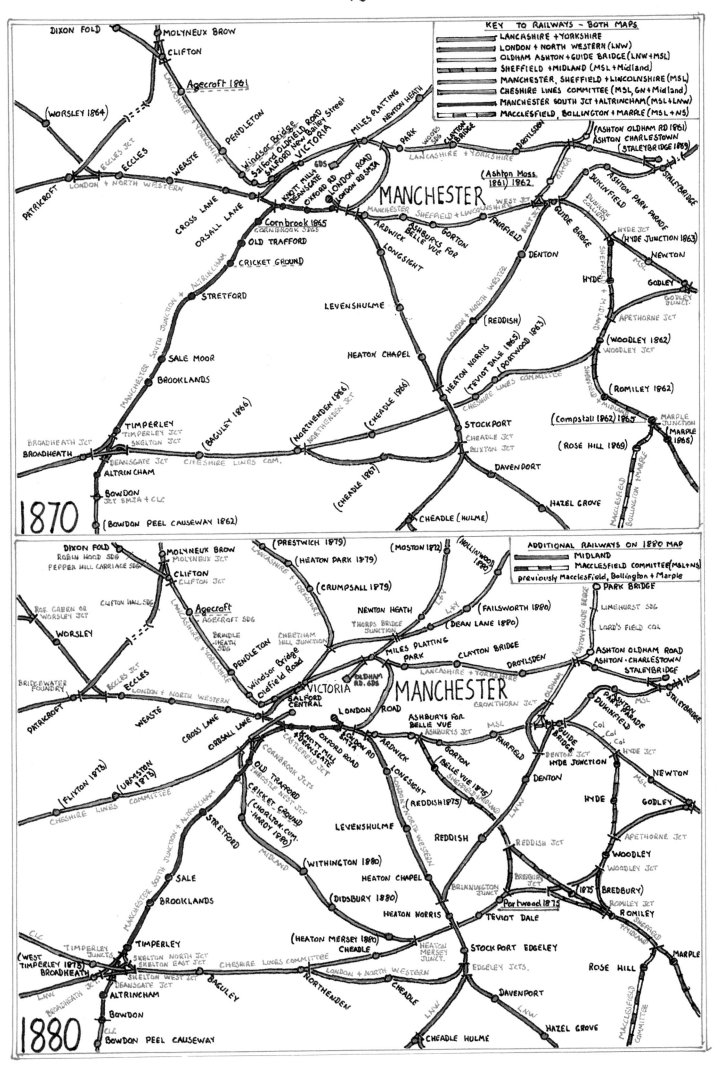

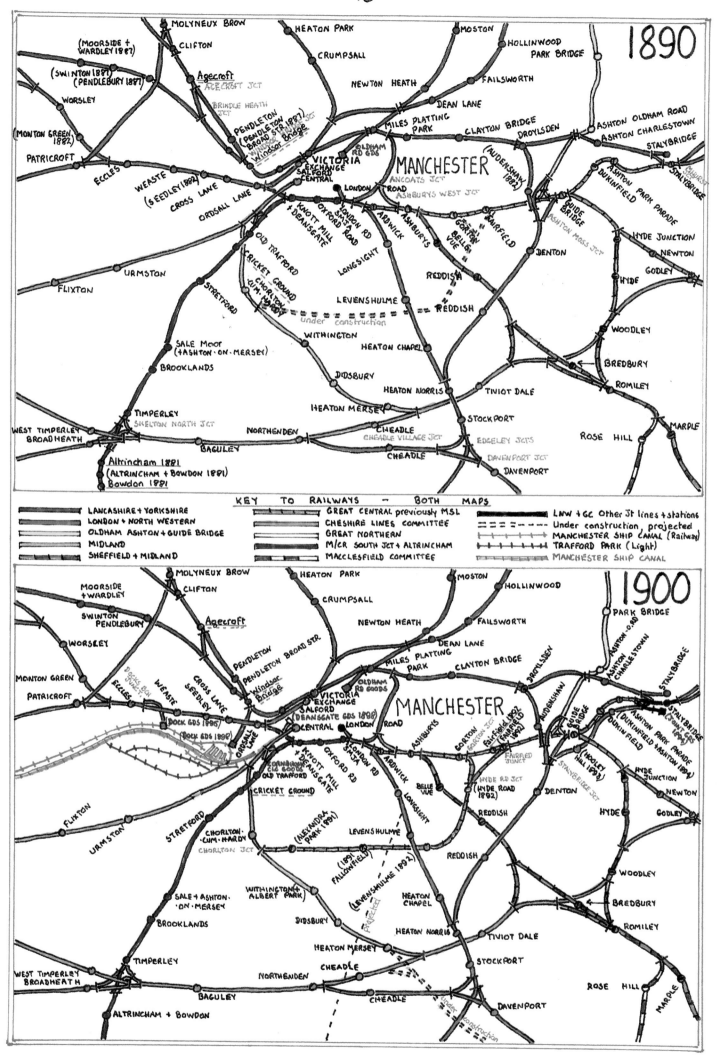

1881-1890

1. 1.1881 CHESHIRE LINES COMMITTEE (CLC) opened Cornbrook to Cornbrook Goods

15. 3. 1881 LONDON + NORTH WESTERN (LNW) opened Denton Junction to Droylsden for goods. Droylsden later became a joint station. The following year the LNW opened an intermediate passenger station at AUDENSHAW. MIDLAND Heaton Mersey Jct in use.

3. 4. 1881 MANCHESTER SOUTH JUNCTION + ALTRINCHAM (MSJA) Altrincham and Bowden stations closed. Replaced by ALTRINCHAM + BOWDON.

1. 11. 1882 LNW Denton to Dukinfield opened avoiding Guide Bridge (not shown on map); exact route not clear. Effectively taken on to Stalybridge in 1893 (see 1900 map) may have followed initial part of the route shown on that map but may have followed line of what became a short goods branch near Guide Bridge.

1. 3. 1884 LANCASHIRE + YORKSHIRE (LY) open enlarged VICTORIA but have told LNW after using it for 40 years that they no longer can. As a result of this LNW open EXCHANGE station in June 1884.

6. 8. 1885 MANCHESTER SHIP CANAL obtains Royal Assent. Included within its ACT was incorporation of the MANCHESTER SHIP CANAL RAILWAYS. Work in cutting the canal did not start for two years. Early lines built at this time were contractors' railways and mostly remained outside the canal railway system (MSC).

3. 8. 1886 LNW quadrupled track Huddersfield to Stalybridge opened. At Stalybridge the extra tracks took the form of a second double track line at the other side of the valley.

3. 6. 1887 LY opened from Windsor Bridge Junction to Hindley with stations at PENDLETON BROAD STREET, PENDLEBURY, SWINTON and MOORSIDE + WARDLEY.

1. 7. 1889 MIDLAND opened from Ashburys West Junction on MSL to Ancoats Junction (with LY) enabling MIDLAND trains to run into Victoria. Also at this time the MIDLAND opened various Goods Depots in this area.

1891-1900

A comparison of the 1890 and 1900 maps appears to indicate very few new lines were opened during this period. However, that is an illusion, since in actual miles of track laid this was probably the most active to date, but this is not obvious from the map. The MSC was responsible for a big slice of this development, laying some 200 miles of track in the docks area and most of it within the map area. But the canal influence also affected all the other main line companies in making connections with the MSC, each requiring parliamentary approval and all presenting some engineering snags to be overcome, the LY route through a densely populated district and mainly by tunnel causing greatest difficulty.

Bearing this in mind it may come as a surprise that any other railways opened at all. But the MSL at last got another line actually opened in MANCHESTER in its own name! The line from Chorlton opened to Fallowfield in 1891 and on to Fairfield and Gorton the following year. Fairfield station was rebuilt so that it could serve trains using both lines. There were intermediate stations at ALEXANDRA PARK, FALLOWFIELD, LEVENSHULME and HYDE ROAD. With the opening of this line there was a fourth change of ownership in the line from Throstle Nest Junction to Chorlton Junction which passed from the MIDLAND to the CHESHIRE LINES COMMITTEE.

In 1893 the LNW completed and opened the whole of its Guide Bridge avoiding line between Denton Junction and Stalybridge with connections at Stalybridge in each direction with the MSL line. A joint LNW and MSL Goods station was opened to the south of the passenger station. Part of this line had opened in 1882 (see note above 1.11.1882).

The MIDLAND were also active during this period in building its line from Disley to HEATON MERSEY involving the over two miles long Disley Tunnel amongst other engineering difficulties, but the line did not open until the turn of the century.

Although the LY opened no new lines except the MSC connection it was active in seeking parliamentary approval for quadrupling various sections of main line, and work on some of these commenced in the late 1890's.

The remaining events during the period were as follows:

1. 8. 1897 MANCHESTER SHEFFIELD + LINCOLNSHIRE becomes GREAT CENTRAL

1898 GREAT NORTHERN Goods Depot opened at DEANSGATE on a site close to CENTRAL station. A small engine shed was opened alongside but had to be closed shortly afterwards due to objections from the corporation.

1900 LONDON + NORTH WESTERN were projecting a new railway from a junction to be made just to the south of LONGSIGHT to serve the Cheadle commuter traffic in the area which the original MANCHESTER SOUTH DISTRICT proposals had sought to tap.

1901-1912

Although the railway development during this period was not quite so active as the previous six decades there were some developments not shown on the map which are worthy of record. These were:

(1) Additional lines and sidings were added throughout the period to the MANCHESTER SHIP CANAL RAILWAYS and the associated TRAFFORD PARK ESTATE lines. This involved extra freight works through the various main line railways. The scale of increased traffic can be judged by the fact that MSC railway freight increased from 1.5 million tons in 1901 to over 3.5 million tons in 1912.

(2) A great deal of quadrupling of track took place during this period. Five different sections of the LANCASHIRE + YORKSHIRE were thus dealt with during the period. The Great Central too widened its line between Ardwick and Fairfield besides expanding the locomotive works at Gorton and building a new Wagon and Carriage works, these being located close to the site of Dunkirk Colliery (shown on the map) near Guide Bridge.

(3) The final development not shown on the map was the increased frequency of suburban stopping services to places such as Altrincham, Bury, Bolton, Oldham, etc.

1902 MIDLAND – Line from Disley to a junction at HEATON MERSEY station; New station at CHEADLE HEATH; Connection from near Cheadle Heath station to join the CHESHIRE LINES COMMITTEE (CLC). All these lines opened to all traffic.

1903 GREAT CENTRAL (GC) Spur from Timperley to Skelton North Junction closed to all traffic.

1904 CLC opened new connection to Trafford Park Estate system to replace the inconvenient MSC connection.

1905 LANCASHIRE + YORKSHIRE (LY) Park Junction to Philips Park Junction opened for goods traffic.

1909 LONDON + NORTH WESTERN (LNW) – Slade Junction to Wilmslow opened to all traffic with stations at MAULDETH ROAD, EAST DIDSBURY and GATLEY. An additional station at BURNAGE was opened the following year.

1909 LY – By this date the fly-over connections at Cheetham Hill and the new line to VICTORIA were in place. Exact date of opening is unclear. Not shown on a map of 1901 but included on a map of 1911.

1910 GC Throstle Nest South Junction to Trafford Park opened for goods.

1910 LNW – MAYFIELD passenger station opened to relieve pressure on LONDON ROAD.

1911 GC ASHTON MOSS JCT and curve opened to all traffic giving a cut off route from the OLDHAM ASHTON + GUIDE BRI. line to the LY towards MANCHESTER. The final new line until BR days.

Although within the map area there were around fifty railways incorporated, most of them were absorbed by the LY or LNW or became a joint undertaking in which the MANCHESTER SHEFFIELD + LINCOLNSHIRE (later GC) were involved. The family tree below traces the growth of the LNW and LY in the area. ACT gives parliamentary authorisation year and OPEN the year of first substantial opening; any later openings are normally excluded:

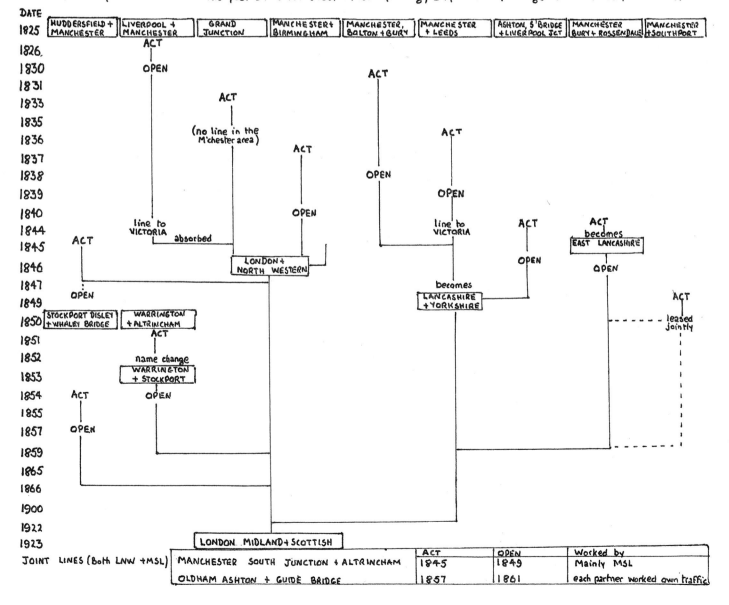

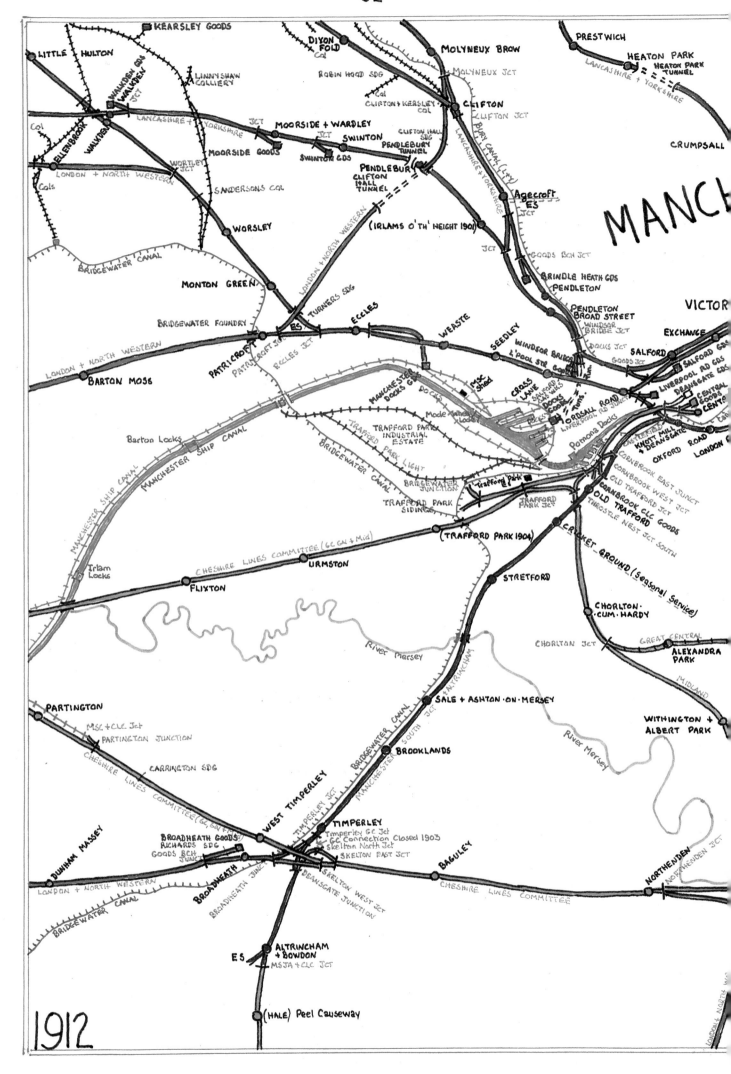

LITTLE HULTON
KEARSLEY GOODS
DIXON FOLD
Col
MOLYNEUX BROW
PRESTWICH
HEATON PARK
HEATON PARK TUNNEL
Lancashire + Yorkshire
LINNYSHAW COLLIERY
ROBIN HOOD SDG
MOLYNEUX JCT
WALKDEN GDS WALKDEN
WALKDEN JCT
Col
CLIFTON + KEARSLEY Col
CLIFTON
CLIFTON JCT
CRUMPSALL
LANCASHIRE + YORKSHIRE JCT
MOORSIDE + WARDLEY
SWINTON
JCT
CLIFTON HALL SDG
PENDLEBURY TUNNEL
Bury Canal (LY)
Lancashire + Yorkshire
Col
ELLENBROOK
WALKDEN
WORTLEY JCT
MOORSIDE GOODS
SWINTON GDS
PENDLEBURY
CLIFTON HALL TUNNEL
AGECROFT ES JCT
MANCH
Cols
LONDON + NORTH WESTERN
SANDERSONS Col
(IRLAMS O'TH' HEIGHT 1901)
JCT
GOODS BCH JCT
BRINDLE HEATH GDS
PENDLETON
WORSLEY
London + North Western
PENDLETON BROAD STREET
VICTOR
BRIDGEWATER CANAL
MONTON GREEN
WINDSOR BRIDGE JCT
EXCHANGE
BRIDGEWATER FOUNDRY
ES TURNERS SDG
ECCLES
WEASTE
SEEDLEY
WINDSOR BRIDGE
DOCKS JCT
SALFORD
SALFORD GDS
LIVERPOOL RD GDS
DEANSGATE GDS
PATRICROFT
ECCLES JCT
PATRICROFT SDG
L'POOL STR GOODS
SALFORD GOODS WALLS
GOODS JCT
LONDON + NORTH WESTERN
BARTON MOSS
MSC SHED
CROSS LANE
SALFORD GOODS WALLS
ORDSALL RD JUNCT
CENTRAL GOODS
CENTO
MANCHESTER DOCKS G
DOCKS G
Mode Wheel Locks
DOCKS EAST
LIVERPOOL RD JUNCT
KNOTT MILL + DEANSGATE
LONDON
Barton Locks
MANCHESTER SHIP CANAL
TRAFFORD PARK LIGHT
TRAFFORD PARK INDUSTRIAL ESTATE
DOCKS JCT
Pomona Docks
CORNBROOK EAST JUNCT
OXFORD ROAD
MANCHESTER SHIP CANAL
BRIDGEWATER CANAL
BRIDGEWATER JUNCTION
Trafford Park
TRAFFORD PARK JCT
CORNBROOK WEST JCT
CORNBROOK CLC GOODS
OLD TRAFFORD CLC JCT
OLD TRAFFORD
Irlam Locks
TRAFFORD PARK SIDINGS
(TRAFFORD PARK 1904)
THROSTLE NEST JCT SOUTH
CHESHIRE LINES COMMITTEE (GC GN + Mid)
URMSTON
CRICKET GROUND (Seasonal Service)
FLIXTON
STRETFORD
CHORLTON CUM HARDY
River Mersey
CHORLTON JCT
GREAT CENTRAL
ALEXANDRA PARK
MIDLAND
PARTINGTON
SALE + ASHTON ON MERSEY
WITHINGTON + ALBERT PARK
MSC + CLC Jct
PARTINGTON JUNCTION
BRIDGEWATER CANAL
River Mersey
CARRINGTON SDG
BRIDGEWATER CANAL SOUTH
BROOKLANDS
CHESHIRE LINES COMMITTEE (GC GN + ?)
WEST TIMPERLEY
TIMPERLEY JCT
MSJA + ALTRINCHAM
DUNHAM MASSEY
BROADHEATH GOODS
RICHARDS SDG
GOODS BCH JUNCT
TIMPERLEY
Timperley GC Jct
GC Connection Closed 1903
Skelton North Jct
SKELTON EAST JCT
BAGULEY
NORTHENDEN
NORTHENDEN JCT
BROADHEATH JUNC
SKELTON WEST JCT
DEANSGATE JUNCTION
CHESHIRE LINES COMMITTEE
LONDON + NORTH WESTERN
BROADHEATH
BRIDGEWATER CANAL
ES
ALTRINCHAM + BOWDON
MSJA + CLC JCT
LONDON + NORTH W

(HALE) Peel Causeway

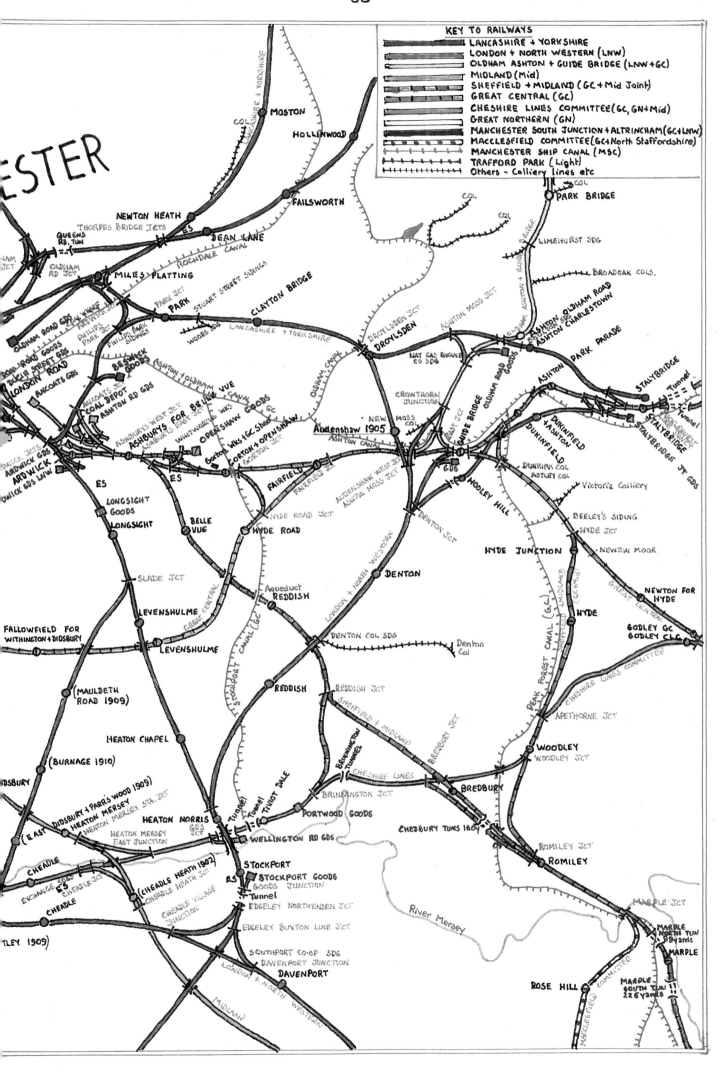

KEY TO RAILWAYS
- LANCASHIRE + YORKSHIRE
- LONDON + NORTH WESTERN (LNW)
- OLDHAM ASHTON + GUIDE BRIDGE (LNW + GC)
- MIDLAND (Mid)
- SHEFFIELD + MIDLAND (GC + Mid Joint)
- GREAT CENTRAL (GC)
- CHESHIRE LINES COMMITTEE (GC, GN + Mid)
- GREAT NORTHERN (GN)
- MANCHESTER SOUTH JUNCTION + ALTRINCHAM (GC + LNW)
- MACCLESFIELD COMMITTEE (GC + North Staffordshire)
- MANCHESTER SHIP CANAL (MSC)
- TRAFFORD PARK (Light)
- Others – Colliery lines etc

The Family Tree for the GREAT CENTRAL takes a different form, and is effectively divided into three parts. To the left are the joint undertakings showing formation, date GC(MSL) become joint owner, and other owning company; in the centre the GREAT CENTRAL itself; with the CHESHIRE LINES COMMITTEE to the right

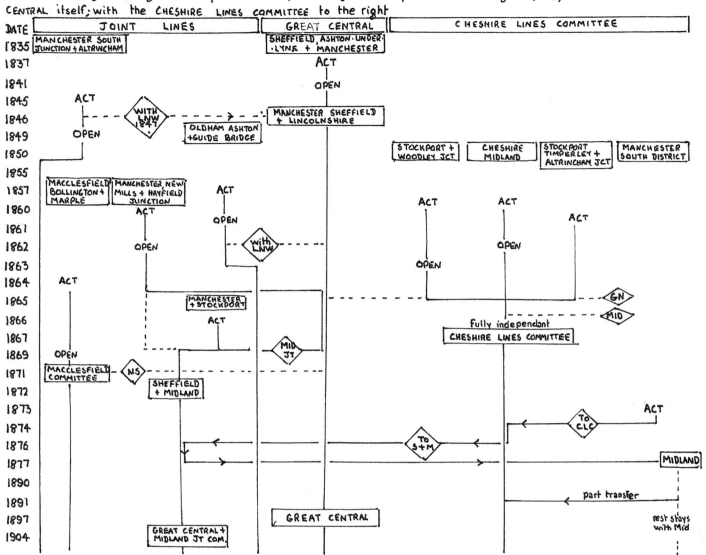

The table below sets out available engine shed information:

No.	Name / Location	Co.	Opened	Closed	Used by	Notes
1	CORNBROOK	CLC	1880	1895	MSL	Later replaced by Trafford Park - see 4 below
2	HEATON MERSEY	CLC + MID	1889	1968	GC+MID	GC for CLC, Midland for own line, Midland also known as CHEADLE
3	STOCKPORT TIVIOT DALE	CLC	1866	1889	MSL	Used for banking engines after closure
4	TRAFFORD PARK	CLC	1894	1968	GC,GN,Mid	GN used after stopped in using No.18 below. Replacement for No.1
5	GORTON	GC	1848	1968		Also loco works on nearby site
6	LONGSIGHT	LNW	1841	1965		Site of modern Diesel + Electric depots (BR)
7	PATRICROFT	LNW	1885	1968		Built to cope with Longsight + Ordsall Lane overspill
8	STOCKPORT EDGELEY	LNW	1883	1968		To save engines running light from Longsight
9	ALTRINCHAM ✻	GC	? pre	1929?	LNW	presumed it became redundant when service electrified
10	ORDSALL LANE	LNW	1848	1904		phased out when 7 opened
11	VICTORIA	LNW	1844	1858		Cramped site and enlargement of station led to closure
12	MANCHESTER	MIDLAND	1870	1956		Later known as BELLE VUE in LMS days
13	AGECROFT	LY	1889	1966		Replaced No.17 below
14	MILES PLATTING	LY	1839	1878		Replaced by No.15 below. Now BR Depot
16	VICTORIA	LY	1844	1858		Cramped site + enlarged station led to closure - see also 11 above
17	SALFORD	LY	1849	1890		Replaced by 13 above
18	DEANSGATE	GN	?			Short time opened only. Corporation objections. Used No.4
19	MODE WHEEL	MSC	1893			Also works and wagon shops - these two parts now closed
20	BARTON DOCK	MSC	1982			Opened following split of system

✻ Also known as BOWDON + ALTRINCHAM

Before looking at events during the periods covered by the final four maps, it is appropriate to mention the part played by Manchester's canals in the city's railway development. In many areas the canals opposed the railways, and though this policy sometimes gained a short respite it was of a transient nature only. In Manchester, however, the canals either co-operated with the railways or turned themselves into a railway. The MANCHESTER BOLTON + BURY CANAL NAVIGATION + RAILWAY is an obvious example of the latter solution, eventually passing to the LY. The MSL (later the GREAT CENTRAL) also acquired substantial canal holdings, many of which were in the Manchester area including the Peak Forest, the Macclesfield, the Stockport, the Ashton + Oldham and the Ashton. Then the Manchester South Junction, just a short line linking together the two LNW lines, was invited by the Bridgewater Canal to continue its line alongside the canal to Altrincham which it did whilst changing its name to become MANCHESTER SOUTH JUNCTION + ALTRINCHAM. The Huddersfield canal was acquired by the LNW, whilst the MANCHESTER SHIP CANAL had its own railway system. Only the Rochdale Canal remained independant of railway influence.

1913-1922

The period covered by the map is split into two unequal periods to enable pre-grouping and post-grouping events to be distinguished. In this first period there was one station opened at WOODLANDS ROAD (1913) on the Bury line; and two wartime closures at Stalybridge (LY) and Cheadle (LNW) both in 1917. At Stalybridge trains on the LY now ran into the joint station.

1923-1940

The immediate effects of grouping in the MANCHESTER area were nil except for name changes to enable two stations with the same name now under one management to be distinguished. Then in the 'thirties there were a few closures of intermediate stations mainly those on the very fringe of the area. These closures were, however, more than balanced by additional stations on the commuter lines. The MSJA gained two new stations when the line was electrified. These were NAVIGATION ROAD (Altrincham) and DANE ROAD (Sale); in addition the Cricket Ground station which had been a seasonal stopping place was upgraded to the status of a full station and renamed WARWICK ROAD. The Bury line also gained an additional station when BOWKER VALE opened in 1938. Finally in this list of new stations the CLC line gained CHASSEN ROAD in 1934 and UNITED FOOTBALL GROUND the same year. This latter station was used only on first team Saturdays during the football season.

Manchester again during this period failed to conform to the national pattern since whilst during this period Manchester was showing a net gain in number of passenger stations most other places were recording an overall reduction in passenger stations open.

1941-1947

Most areas lost some wayside stations as a war-time economy measure, but here again Manchester was almost an exception. Weaste closed to passengers in 1942 and to goods in late 1947.

1948-1963

During this period, Manchester, for the only time in its development history, conformed to the normal pattern, with route closures, other lines reduced to goods only, and closure of intermediate stations on some lines which retained passenger services. But nonetheless stations affected were proportionately less than seen elsewhere. Only two routes appear to have closed completely: Patricroft - Molyneux Brow (closed due to tunnel collapse) and the ex LNW Guide Bridge by-pass line to Stalybridge which was a duplicate route. In this latter case the line may in fact have been retained for goods traffic beyond 1963 as information on this point is unclear.

Routes reduced to goods only were few in number as the map shows and some of the lines shown had always been mainly concerned with goods traffic. The principal downgrading was the ex-MSL Chorlton to Gorton and Fairfield line, but following withdrawal of passenger services it increased in importance in providing a route from all the Manchester lines to what had become MANCHESTER's most important group of marshalling sidings at Trafford Park. Incidentally it is strange that MANCHESTER in its strategic position at the convergence of so many different routes has never had a major marshalling yard.

Intermediate station closures too were fairly modest. Including the Beeching proposals the passenger situation during the period is summarised in the following table:

STATIONS OPEN IN 1941 (1st January)	111
Stations closed 1941 to 1963 (inclusive)	25
STATIONS OPEN at the end of 1963 (31st December)	86
Proposed for closure in the BEECHING REPORT	40
STATIONS to be retained if Beeching Report is fully implemented	46

The surprising result following the Beeching proposals is examined in relation to the final two maps.

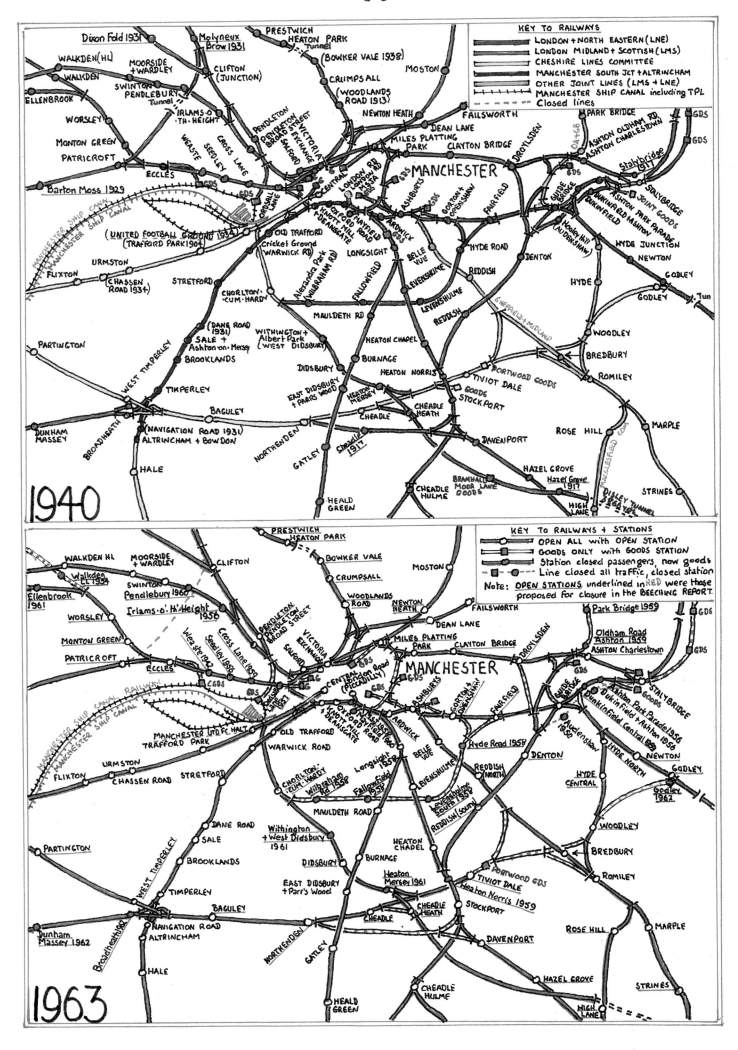

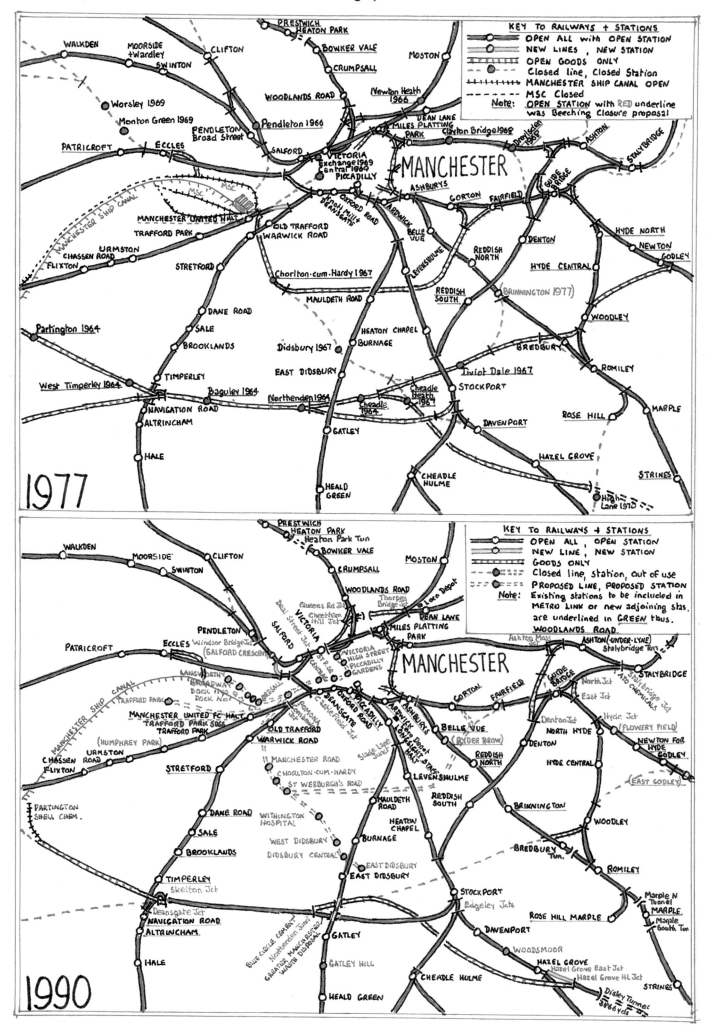

1964-1977

Following the Beeching Report, Manchester again reverted to its established pattern of nonconformity to the large-scale rationalisation seen elsewhere.

Although in this period a number of routes were lost to all traffic, these were a relatively small proportion and were all duplicate routes with the exception of goods curves linking routes from which passenger traffic had long been withdrawn or had never been utilised for other than casual passenger traffic. As for the Beeching proposals - well, these were largely ignored. As noted previously the Beeching Report recommended the closure of forty of the 86 passenger stations remaining open within the map area at that date. But only seventeen of these closures were in fact implemented. Even with these seventeen stations, six of them were on routes that would be retained or later re-opened for passenger traffic, a further three were on routes still open to freight, whilst a further three are proposed to re-open in the 1990's.

In many places, particularly where some of the Beeching proposals were not implemented, there was a tendency to have compensating closures elsewhere. But that did not happen in MANCHESTER, except in rational-isation of the central stations which were not usually covered in the report.

A nadir was reached in 1969 but since that date there has been only one closure: High Lane on the fringe of the area. This station closed on 5th January 1970 but had been scheduled for earlier closure.

However, even before this low point had been reached, Manchester was looking to expand its network by a rapid transit system akin to such existing systems as the Liverpool Underground or the Glasgow Subway. In 1966 a working party was set up by the Minister of Transport to look at the better utilisation of existing lines and a new underground link between VICTORIA and PICCADILLY. An ambitious scheme in 1968 was a product of the working party. But approval was not obtained due to construction envisaged was to be to main line standards. Similar schemes elsewhere including Liverpool obtained approval due to being more budget conscious.

However, from the mid-seventies new stations were planned on many of the suburban commuter routes. In 1977 the first of these new stations opened at BRINNINGTON.

1978-1990

In looking at this final period, we look first at closures. These were all restricted to lines which had previously suffered the withdrawal of passenger services. The principal closure has been the Warrington-Stockport-Godley line resulting from a tunnel near Stockport being declared unsafe. The South Manchester loop, although falling into disuse, is still open. Other closures have all been connecting goods loops.

Turning to the positive side, two new lines have been built. The first was the chord line at HAZEL GROVE enabling trains for Sheffield to leave Manchester by the old ex-LNW route via Stockport and Davenport to Hazel Grove and then switch to the ex-Midland line to Sheffield. The other new line was the connection from the ex-LY line at WINDSOR BRIDGE to ORDSALL LANE enabling trains from the west to use PICCADILLY which is now the main station in MANCHESTER. VICTORIA is gradually having its long-distance services withdrawn, retaining only local services.

Two goods-only lines have also been upgraded: these are the Midland line from the new chord connection at Hazel Grove to the south, and Stockport to Altrincham via Northenden, Skelton and Deansgate Junctions.

In addition GREATER MANCHESTER in co-operation with the PTE and BR have continued to open new stations. These have been: SALFORD CRESCENT (serving the University area), HUMPHREY PARK (between Urmston and Trafford Park), RYDER BROW, FLOWERY FIELD and EAST GODLEY. Further new stations are planned to open at WOODSMOOR and GATLEY HILL.

Finally a new METRO-LINK service is planned and will be brought progressively into use from 1991. This is a light rapid transport system based on the London DOCKLANDS lines and will be a combination of different types of development. In some cases existing BR lines will be converted to the new system (MANCHESTER-BURY). Another type of development will be for BR and METRO-LINK services to share a route (MANCHESTER-ALTRINCHAM). A third type of development will be utilisation of redundant BR track (OLD TRAFFORD-EAST DIDSBURY) thus limiting the entirely new lines which in any event will cost less in real terms compared to the abortive 1966-68 scheme. The map shows the proposed system which is planned to be completed by 1995.

1991 + FUTURE

If all MANCHESTER'S METRO-LINK plans are implemented together with the anticipated additional stations on the Trafford Park line, plus the possibility of additional intermediate halts on existing lines, it appears that by 1995 the number of stations in the map area might well exceed those shown on the 1912 maximum development map.

The final map is also noteworthy in that it shows no less than sixteen passenger routes leaving the map area.

CHESTER

CHESTER at the start of its railway development was not a natural focal point. The line from Crewe was a rural branch, the main line serving the north besides Liverpool and Manchester passing well to the east. The other early line was also of only branch status, Birkenhead being a small place albeit with potential for growth. However, with the mail line routed via CHESTER and the rapid growth of Birkenhead, lines were attracted into Chester to link into these two routes and CHESTER's development as a railway centre was assured.

TO 1840

6. 5.1833 GRAND JUNCTION is authorised.

31. 8.1835 GREAT WESTERN authorised.

30. 6.1837 CHESTER + CREWE authorised.

12. 7.1837 CHESTER + BIRKENHEAD obtains its Act.

1. 7.1840 GRAND JUNCTION absorb CHESTER + CREWE.

22. 9.1840 CHESTER + BIRKENHEAD opened, but not to the public until December. It made an end-on junction with GRAND JUNCTION at CHESTER. Each company had its own station, these being at either side of Brook Street. There were intermediate stations at MOSTON (possible name at opening - but later became MOLLINGTON), CAPENHURST, SUTTON (also later to change its name) and HOOTON.

1.10.1840 GRAND JUNCTION opened from Crewe to junction at CHESTER as noted above. There was just one intermediate station, within the map area, at WAVERTON.

Also shown on this first map are tramways (horse-drawn) serving collieries to an outlet at Connah's Quay on the River Dee. The Dee between Chester and Connahs Quay had been improved to carry regular traffic.

1841-1850

4. 7.1844 CHESTER + HOLYHEAD authorised. After arguments about the Royal Mail route to Ireland, this proposed line which followed the level route along the coast of North Wales was preferred. It was this choice of the mail line which led to Chester becoming a railway centre resulting in the intense development of the next six years.

6. 8.1844 NORTH WALES MINERAL obtains its Act.

30. 6.1845 SHREWSBURY, OSWESTRY + CHESTER JUNCTION is authorised.

26. 6.1846 BIRKENHEAD, LANCASHIRE + CHESHIRE JUNCTION authorised.

16. 7.1846 GRAND JUNCTION merges with the Manchester + Birmingham and the London + Birmingham to form the LONDON + NORTH WESTERN.

22. 7.1846 MANCHESTER SHEFFIELD + LINCOLNSHIRE formed.

28. 8.1846 Amalgamation of the NORTH WALES MINERAL and the SHREWSBURY, OSWESTRY + CHESTER JUNCTION to form the SHREWSBURY + CHESTER.

4. 11.1846 CHESTER + HOLYHEAD opened from CHESTER to SALTNEY JUNCTION to enable the SHREWSBURY + CHESTER to run into CHESTER by virtue of the running powers obtained.

4. 11.1846 SHREWSBURY + CHESTER opened from RUABON to SALTNEY JUNCTION. There was an intermediate station at SALTNEY and a short goods branch to wharves on the Dee, serving railway purposes and local industry. A small engine shed was also built on the banks of the Dee, but was only used for a few years.

9. 7.1847 MOLD authorised. To be purchased by CHESTER + HOLYHEAD on completion. To be worked by LONDON + NORTH WESTERN.

22. 7.1847 BIRKENHEAD, LANCASHIRE + CHESHIRE JUNCTION absorb CHESTER + HOLYHEAD.

1. 5.1848 CHESTER + HOLYHEAD opened from SALTNEY JUNCTION to Bangor. There was at this stage only one intermediate station within the map area at QUEEN'S FERRY.

1. 8.1848 CHESTER + HOLYHEAD open WEST LOOP at CHESTER from Tunnel Junction to Brook Lane Junction, but ownership of this line immediately passes to a JOINT COMMITTEE (see next entry).

1. 8.1848 CHESTER GENERAL station opens, the two earlier stations closing. The station and all approach lines come under a JOINT COMMITTEE (LONDON + NORTH WESTERN, SHREWSBURY + CHESTER, CHESTER + HOLYHEAD and BIRKENHEAD, LANCASHIRE + CHESHIRE JUNCTION).

14. 9.1849 MOLD opened from MOLD JUNCTION to Mold, passes to CHESTER + HOLYHEAD in accordance with agreement. It was worked by LONDON + NORTH WESTERN. There was an intermediate station opened at BROUGHTON.

18. 12.1850 BIRKENHEAD LANCASHIRE + CHESHIRE JUNCTION opened from CHESTER (from a junction to the south on the Crewe line) to Walton Junction. Intermediate stations, within the map area were opened at DUNHAM (later became DUNHAM HILL) and FRODSHAM.

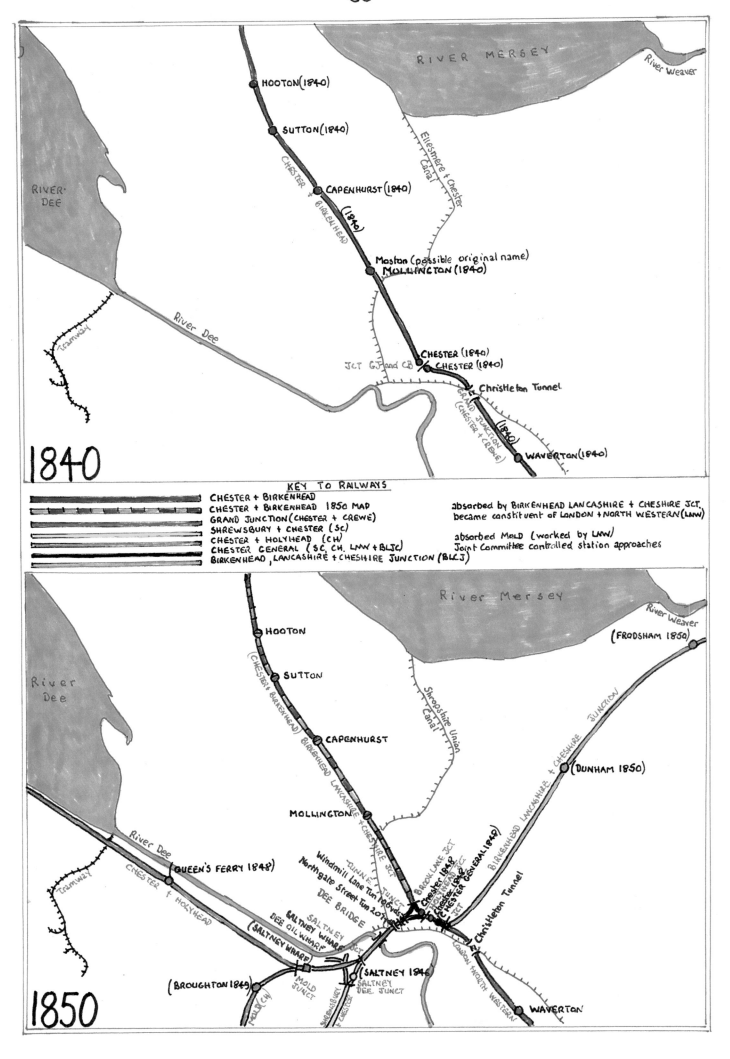

1840

KEY TO RAILWAYS

CHESTER + BIRKENHEAD
CHESTER + BIRKENHEAD 1850 MAP
GRAND JUNCTION (CHESTER + CREWE)
SHREWSBURY + CHESTER (SC)
CHESTER + HOLYHEAD (CH)
CHESTER GENERAL (SC, CH, LNW + BLJC)
BIRKENHEAD, LANCASHIRE + CHESHIRE JUNCTION (BLCJ)

absorbed by BIRKENHEAD LANCASHIRE + CHESHIRE JCT.
became constituent of LONDON + NORTH WESTERN (LNW)

absorbed MOLD (worked by LNW)
Joint Committee controlled station approaches

1850

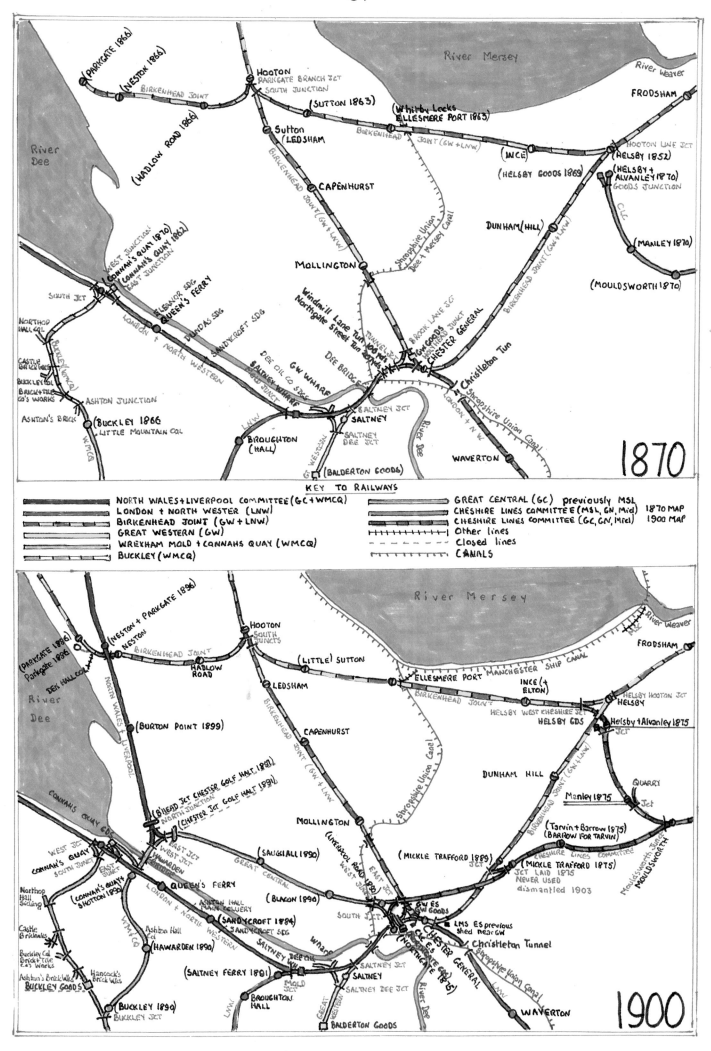

KEY TO RAILWAYS

▬▬▬ NORTH WALES + LIVERPOOL COMMITTEE (GC + WMCQ)	▬▬▬ GREAT CENTRAL (GC) previously MSL
▬▬▬ LONDON + NORTH WESTER (LNW)	▬▬▬ CHESHIRE LINES COMMITTEE (MSL, GN, Mid) 1870 MAP
▬▬▬ BIRKENHEAD JOINT (GW + LNW)	▬▬▬ CHESHIRE LINES COMMITTEE (GC, GN, Mrel) 1900 MAP
▬▬▬ GREAT WESTERN (GW)	+++ Other lines
▬▬▬ WREXHAM MOLD + CONNAHS QUAY (WMCQ)	- - - Closed lines
▬▬▬ BUCKLEY (WMCQ)	++++ CANALS

1851-1870

All the lines opened during this period had no direct effect on the development of Chester; none of them actually reached Chester and all were located on the fringes of the area.

1. 9. 1854 SHREWSBURY + CHESTER absorbed by GREAT WESTERN.

1. 1. 1859 CHESTER + HOLYHEAD vested in LONDON + NORTH WESTERN from this date.

1. 8. 1859 BIRKENHEAD LANCASHIRE + CHESHIRE JUNCTION becomes BIRKENHEAD.

1. 1. 1860 BIRKENHEAD becomes BIRKENHEAD JOINT and is vested jointly in GREAT WESTERN and LONDON + NORTH WESTERN.

14. 6. 1860 BUCKLEY authorised. This was an ACT to convert the horse tramway shown on the maps of 1840 and 1850 into a railway. The railway was to be worked by the WREXHAM MOLD + CONNAHS QUAY with which it would make an end on connection. This latter company was at this time in course of being authorised.

11. 7. 1861 WEST CHESHIRE incorporated. Would become part of the CHESHIRE LINES COMMITTEE before the line was opened.

7. 8. 1862 WREXHAM MOLD + CONNAHS QUAY authorised.

7. 6. 1862 BUCKLEY opened for goods traffic. The line using the steep grades and curves of the old tramway always remained a goods-only line, although passenger traffic was authorised and some summer Saturday trains used the line in later days. Connections were made with the LNW at CONNAH'S QUAY where a goods depot was opened. The LNW also had its own connection to the Goods Depot.

1. 7. 1863 BIRKENHEAD JOINT opened from HELSBY to HOOTON with stations at SUTTON, WHITBY LOCKS (later became ELLESMERE PORT) and INCE.

5. 7. 1865 CHESHIRE LINES Transfer Act: Various railways including WEST CHESHIRE are vested in the MANCHESTER, SHEFFIELD + LINCOLNSHIRE and GREAT NORTHERN as CHESHIRE LINES COMMITTEE. MIDLAND became an equal partner 18·7·1866.

1. 1. 1866 WREXHAM MOLD + CONNAHS QUAY opened to Goods from the south to make an end on junction with the BUCKLEY at Ashton Junction. Opened to passengers 1·5·1866. There was a terminal passenger station at BUCKLEY. The two railways were worked as one but retained their separate identities.

1. 10. 1866 BIRKENHEAD JOINT opened branch from HOOTON to PARKGATE. Intermediate stations at NESTON and HADLOW ROAD.

1. 9. 1869 CHESHIRE LINES COMMITTEE opened West Cheshire via Mouldsworth to Helsby for goods traffic.

22. 6. 1870 The above line opened to passengers. Stations: MOULDSWORTH, MANLEY and HELSBY + ALVANLEY.

During this period there were two additional stations opened on existing lines: HELSBY (Birkenhead Joint, in 1852) and (on the LNW Chester to Holyhead line) CONNAHS QUAY in 1870. The map also shows some name changes.

1871-1900

14. 6. 1871 CHESHIRE LINES COMMITTEE. Helsby + Alvanley to Helsby West Cheshire Junction opened for goods traffic.

5. 8. 1873 BUCKLEY leased to WREXHAM MOLD + CONNAH'S QUAY (WMCQ).

2. 11. 1874 CHESHIRE LINES COMMITTEE - Mouldsworth Junction to Chester Northgate opened for goods traffic.

1. 5. 1875 CLC Mouldsworth Junction to CHESTER NORTHGATE opened to passengers. Intermediate stations at Tarvin + Barrow (name changed later to BARROW for TARVIN) and MICKLE TRAFFORD. A connecting spur from Mickle Trafford leading to Chester via Birkenhead Joint was laid but not used until it had been taken out and then relaid 94 years later.

1. 5. 1875 CLC Manley and Helsby + Alvanley CLOSED to passengers. Line and stations retained for goods. This was a result of the BIRKENHEAD JOINT blocking CLC passenger running powers to Birkenhead.

28. 7. 1884 MANCHESTER SHEFFIELD + LINCOLNSHIRE - Chester and Connah's Quay line authorised.

31. 7. 1885 Additional WIRRAL Act authorising line from Bidston to HAWARDEN BRIDGE (Railway incorporated 1883).

19. 4. 1886 BIRKENHEAD JOINT - Line from new station at PARKGATE opened to West Kirby.

12. 8. 1889 WIRRAL TRANSFER ACT. Powers granted 31·7·1885 passed to MSL + WMCQ known initially as WIRRAL COMMITTEE, became DEE + BIRKENHEAD COMMITTEE in 1894. Changed in 1895 to NORTH WALES + LIVERPOOL (NWL).

31. 3. 1890 WMCQ open HAWARDEN LOOP from BUCKLEY JUNCTION (new station) to CONNAH'S QUAY + SHOTTON with a goods branch to Connah's Quay Goods and an intermediate station at HAWARDEN.

31. 3. 1890 MSL CHESTER NORTHGATE to junction with WMCQ near Hawarden Bridge opened. Also opened Chester avoiding line. Stations at LIVERPOOL ROAD, BLACON and SAUGHALL, and GOLF CLUB HALT was opened the following year.

18. 5. 1896 NWL opened from Bidston to HAWARDEN BRIDGE JUNCTION and a triangular junction layout giving direct access to CHESTER. Intermediate station at NESTON + PARKGATE. Later a GOLF CLUB HALT was added at the North Junction and BURTON POINT was opened in 1899.

1. 8. 1897 MANCHESTER SHEFFIELD + LINCOLNSHIRE becomes GREAT CENTRAL.

Stations opened during this period on existing lines were: LNW - SANDYCROFT (1884) and SALTNEY FERRY (1891); whilst on the Chester to Walton Junction line of the BIRKENHEAD JOINT - MICKLE TRAFFORD opened in 1889 (close to the CLC station).

Name changes: Sutton became LITTLE SUTTON; Ince became INCE + ELTON.

The map shows the network at its maximum but there would be further intermediate stations opened during the twentieth century.

1901-1922

The period covered by the next map is split into two periods, the first period taking the story to the eve of grouping. However, before turning to the 20th century, one matter whose roots are firmly in the 1890's needs to be mentioned. This was the opening of the MANCHESTER SHIP CANAL and its railways. Although there was very little development of the canal's railways in the 19th century, two short spurs had been built, both in the nature of sidings as the 1900 map shows. But with the turn of the century considerable development took place. The map just shows the main lines. They never carried passenger traffic.

Turning to the network during this period there are only two events to record. First in 1903 the Mickle Trafford connection from the CLC to the Birkenhead Joint was removed. Because of a disagreement between the CLC and Birkenhead Joint it had never been used. It was to be re-instated but that was 66 years into the future. The other event was the absorption by the GREAT CENTRAL of the WREXHAM MOLD + CONNAHS QUAY and the NORTH WALES AND LIVERPOOL by an Act of 22.7.1904 and effective from 1.1.1905.

The only other events to note were the opening of additional intermediate stations: BALDERTON (Gt Western, in 1901), SHOTTON (LNW, in 1907) and WELSH ROAD (GC, and later to become SEALAND in 1919).

1923-1940

This period effectively spans the grouping influence since by 1940 the railways were firmly under government control. One strange effect of grouping in the Chester area was that six pre-grouping railways continued as six post-grouping railways insuring effectively against even the minor rationalisation seen elsewhere.

Further openings of intermediate stations were: HAWARDEN BRIDGE (LNE, in 1924), HELSBY (CLC, re-opened in 1936), UPTON-BY-CHESTER (BIRKENHEAD JOINT, in 1939) and STANLOW + THORNTON (BIRKENHEAD JOINT, in 1940). This last station may in fact have opened somewhat earlier as an unadvertised halt.

There were no closures except possibly the Golf Halts but as these never appeared in Bradshaw the exact closure date is unclear and has been guessed to be at the start of World War II.

1941-1947

This short period saw only two events: First the closure of Helsby (CLC) after only re-opening in 1936; and the building of a new line! This latter development in 1942 was a connecting spur at Mickle Trafford. This was not, however, as some authorities have stated, the relaying of the spur removed in 1903 and noted above. It was a spur which allowed goods traffic from the Birkenhead Joint line to run onto the CLC line and thence to the LNE (ex-Great Central) network.

1948-1963

During this period following nationalisation leading up to the Beeching Report, the railways in the Chester area followed the national pattern. There were closures of unremunerative branch lines and intermediate stations on the main lines.

During this period two branches closed to passengers: The Hooton-West Kirby service was the first casualty in 1956, and the branch closed entirely in 1962; Passenger services were withdrawn between Chester and Mold in 1962, goods traffic finishing at the same time except for a spur to Broughton serving lineside industries. Two goods only branches also closed during this period - the Buckley line to Connahs Quay and the short ex-GW Saltney branch. Most lines remaining open lost one or more intermediate stations: The Warrington line lost both Dunham Hill and Mickle Trafford in the early 50's, whilst at the same time the Manchester line's Mickle Trafford closed along with Barrow. On the Crewe to Holyhead line, Waverton closed in 1959 and Sandycroft two years later, whilst the Wrexham-Bidston line lost Burton Point in 1955. Even the Birkenhead line suffered a closure - Mollington in 1960 - and only the Hooton-Helsby line retained its full complement of stations. Before looking at the Beeching proposals one strange event needs to be recorded — a station OPENED and in 1963! Helsby (ex CLC) opened for the third time.

Turning finally to the Beeching proposals, as they affected the Chester area were very modest. Chester Northgate was scheduled for closure but not the services using it. Up to this point Chester's railway network consisted of two entirely different networks without any physical connection between them and a logical economy was to arrange for all lines to run into CHESTER GENERAL. The remaining proposals are simply told and consisted of the withdrawal of the Hooton-Helsby passenger service and closure of the stations: LITTLE SUTTON, ELLESMERE PORT, STANLOW + THORNTON, INCE + ELTON, HELSBY and FRODSHAM. The report contained one very surprising omission in that it did not include Helsby CLC. If this station had remained open and the other closures followed through, one wonders where passenger trains for Helsby would have come from or gone to! One can only surmise that the Good Doctor could not believe that any passenger station could have opened in 1963, and not only that but one that had already closed twice already.

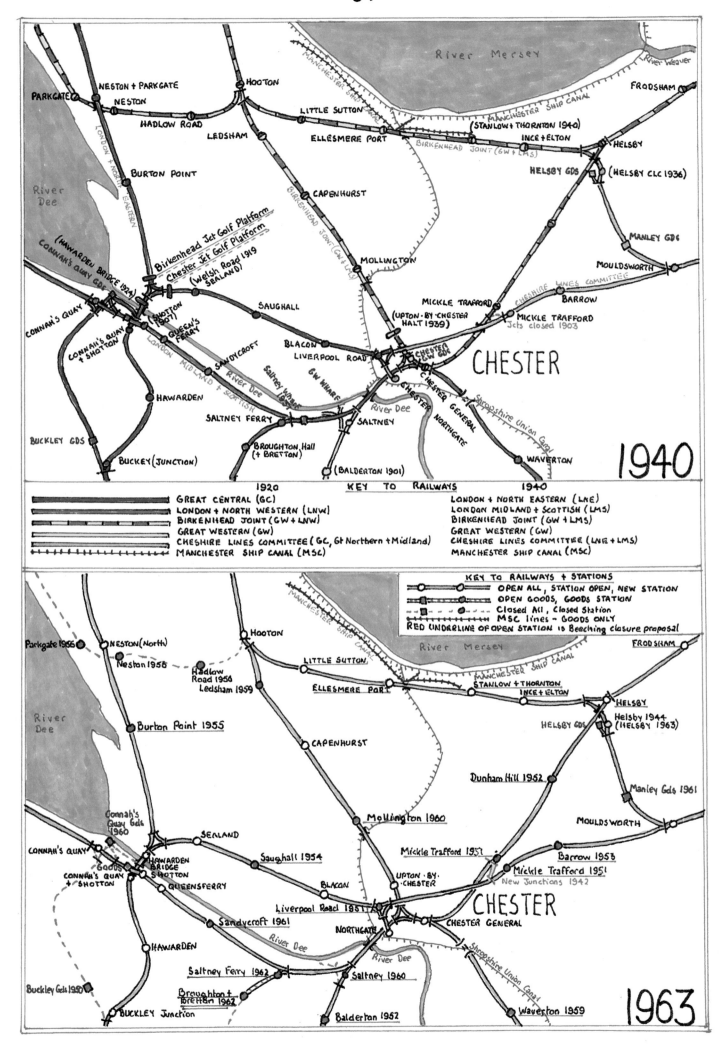

KEY TO RAILWAYS

1920		1940
GREAT CENTRAL (GC)		LONDON + NORTH EASTERN (LNE)
LONDON + NORTH WESTERN (LNW)		LONDON MIDLAND + SCOTTISH (LMS)
BIRKENHEAD JOINT (GW + LNW)		BIRKENHEAD JOINT (GW + LMS)
GREAT WESTERN (GW)		GREAT WESTERN (GW)
CHESHIRE LINES COMMITTEE (GC, Gt Northern + Midland)		CHESHIRE LINES COMMITTEE (LNE + LMS)
MANCHESTER SHIP CANAL (MSC)		MANCHESTER SHIP CANAL (MSC)

1940

KEY TO RAILWAYS + STATIONS

OPEN ALL, STATION OPEN, NEW STATION
OPEN GOODS, GOODS STATION
Closed All, Closed Station
MSC lines - GOODS ONLY
RED UNDERLINE OF OPEN STATION is Beeching closure proposal

1963

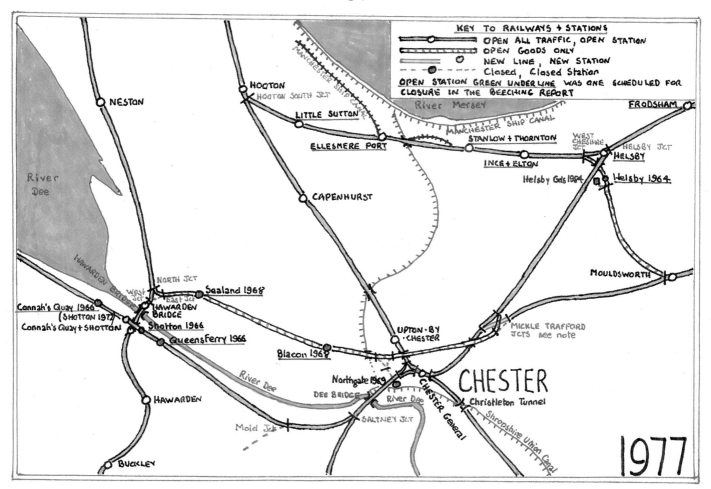

KEY TO RAILWAYS & STATIONS

- OPEN ALL TRAFFIC, OPEN STATION
- OPEN GOODS ONLY
- NEW LINE, NEW STATION
- Closed, Closed Station

OPEN STATION GREEN UNDERLINE WAS ONE SCHEDULED FOR CLOSURE IN THE BEECHING REPORT

NESTON
HOOTON
Hooton South Jct
LITTLE SUTTON
ELLESMERE PORT
CAPENHURST
River Mersey
Manchester Ship Canal
STANLOW + THORNTON
INCE + ELTON
WEST CHESHIRE JCT
HELSBY JCT
HELSBY
Helsby Gds 1984
Helsby 1964
FRODSHAM
MOULDSWORTH
River Dee
HAWARDEN BRIDGE
Connah's Quay 1966 (SHOTTON 1972)
Connah's Quay + Shotton
West Jct
North Jct
East Jct
Sealand 1968
HAWARDEN BRIDGE
Shotton 1966
Queensferry 1966
Blacon 1968
UPTON · BY · CHESTER
MICKLE TRAFFORD JCTS see note
HAWARDEN
River Dee
Northgate 1969
DEE BRIDGE
River Dee
SALTNEY JCT
CHESTER General
CHESTER
Christleton Tunnel
Shropshire Union Canal
Mold Jct
BUCKLEY

1977

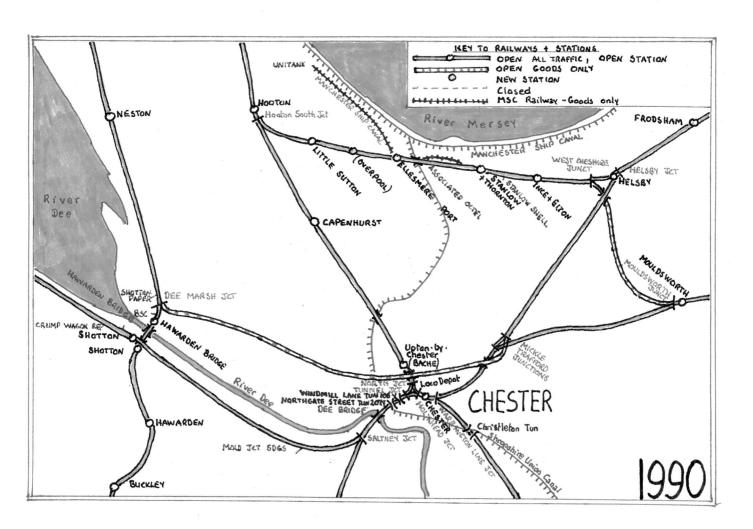

KEY TO RAILWAYS & STATIONS

- OPEN ALL TRAFFIC, OPEN STATION
- OPEN GOODS ONLY
- NEW STATION
- Closed
- MSC Railway ~ Goods only

NESTON
UNITANK
HOOTON
Hooton South Jct
LITTLE SUTTON
(OVERPOOL)
ELLESMERE PORT
CAPENHURST
Manchester Ship Canal
River Mersey
Manchester Ship Canal
Associated Octel
STANLOW SHELL
STANLOW + THORNTON
INCE + ELTON
WEST CHESHIRE JUNCT
HELSBY JCT
HELSBY
FRODSHAM
MOULDSWORTH
MOULDSWORTH JUNCT
River Dee
HAWARDEN BRIDGE
Shotton PAPER
B.S.C.
DEE MARSH JCT
CRUMP WAGON REP
SHOTTON
Shotton
HAWARDEN BRIDGE
River Dee
Upton · by · Chester (BACHE)
NORTH JCT
Loco Depot
MICKLE TRAFFORD JUNCTIONS
HAWARDEN
WINDMILL LANE TUNNEL
NORTHGATE STREET TUN
DEE BRIDGE
Mold Jct Sdgs
SALTNEY JCT
BIRKENHEAD LINE JCT
CHESTER
Christleton Tun
Shropshire Union Canal
BUCKLEY

1990

1964 - 1977

In the aftermath of the Beeching Report, Chester's pattern of conformity with the national trend in development and rationalisation was shattered.

It will be recalled that the Beeching Report had recommended the closure of Northgate but retention of its routes; the report was, however, silent on how implementation was to be achieved. This in fact presented some considerable difficulty due to the lack of any connection between the routes into Northgate and those into General. First another connection was built at Mickle Trafford; this effectively just meant relaying the 1875 connection which had been removed in 1903 without ever being brought into use. Thus after 94 years Manchester trains were able to run into CHESTER GENERAL. However, this did nothing to solve the problem of the Bidston and Wrexham services. In the event this was tackled in a different way. The line from Northgate to Hawarden Jct was closed to passengers (resulting in the loss of Sealand and Blacon stations) but the line was retained for goods traffic to Birkenhead. Associated with this, but rather as an afterthought, Shotton station was closed and later re-opened on a site adjoining the Wrexham to Bidston station so that in theory at any rate passengers from Chester could reach Bidston by travelling on the North Wales line and changing trains at Shotton. In this complex re-organisation the east to west curve at Hawarden Bridge was closed. The only other line to be closed to all traffic was the goods stub from Mold Junction.

Other changes were closure of Helsby (ex CLC) station for the third time in 1964 but the line from Mouldsworth to West Cheshire Junction was retained for goods. There was also the loss of intermediate stations on the Holyhead line, Connah's Quay and Queensferry both closing in 1966.

It will be noted thus far that although NORTHGATE had closed as recommended in the Beeching report and there had been some closures, recommendations from the report were significant by their absence. This continued to be the case, for none of the other closure proposals was ever put into effect!

1978 - 1990

This period has seen stagnation at CHESTER. Nothing has happened apart from Upton-by-Chester being re-named as BACHE and a new station at OVERPOOL on the Hooton to Helsby line. All the passenger lines carry good and regular services and as can be seen little of the overall network has been lost, just stations.

1991 - FUTURE

Looking to the future no plans for further development are in the pipe-line, but the present network appears to be secure.

LINCOLN

In railway terms Lincoln conforms to the normal pattern of development in so far as its main network was fully in place by the end of 1850. Further routes were then added over a period of many years but these later routes with just one exception have now all gone, and even the exception serves the same places as the one pre-1850 route to close. In effect therefore the 1850 and 1990 maps are identical in the places served. The central area had complexities of yards, engine sheds, private sidings and junctions that stretched across the Witham Gap, so that in addition to the general maps in this chapter there is a second series covering the central area and its frustrating level crossings.

Having established Lincoln's conformity to the national pattern there is still one oddity in that it was 1846 before Lincoln was reached by a railway line, which in view of its strategic geographical position and its early development as a route focal point appears strange. Its importance as a route centre was very firmly established by mid-way through the third century as the first map shows. This shows that in Roman times it was already the meeting point of four main roads and three secondary roads. In addition it was a junction of four waterways, the River Witham forming a natural waterway but connected to the Trent by the Foss Dyke to the west and to the Welland and Cambridge by a further canal, the Car Dyke, aiming south.

The Witham Gap gave a natural route through the limestone ridge, whilst at Lincoln the river was only twelve feet above sea-level and therefore tidal. In addition the watershed between the Trent and the Witham was but 17 feet at its lowest point which in ancient times would put Lincoln on a tidal island when there was a particularly high spring tide. This provided one of the obvious canal routes developed by the Romans which continued to be used for goods traffic until the 1970's. Nor should the importance of these water routes be underestimated since they were sufficient during the middle ages to make LINCOLN England's fourth port.

It is in the light of this background that one becomes surprised that it was 1846 before the iron road reached Lincoln. This was not for the lack of schemes and in fact there was nowhere in England of comparable size that spawned so many schemes either to reach it or pass through it making use of the Witham Gap. The first proposal for a railway affecting Lincoln was as early as 1821 - the CAMBRIDGE + LINCOLN; this was followed by two later schemes routed via Cambridge and Lincoln to link LONDON with YORK. Then in 1835 a survey was undertaken for the GREAT NORTHERN (an earlier company with this name) for a route from LONDON to YORK, and passing through LINCOLN, but it failed to gain parliamentary approval in the 1836 session. There now arose a fierce competition over the merits of various routes to the north and the arrival on the scene of the infamous George Hudson, the Railway King. He made alliances on all sides in an effort to stifle what would become the Great Northern fearing that the direct route would drain traffic from his railways. In the end the GREAT NORTHERN obtained its authorisation but even then it would suffer under the notorious Octuple Agreement for pooling traffic.

In addition one must put some of the blame on Hudson for the level crossing chaos at Lincoln. The early proposals all planned to pass through Lincoln on an embankment but failed to get sanction. In the meantime, due to the delaying tactics employed, the MIDLAND was the first railway to reach Lincoln which it did on the level. At this time no level crossing was involved but it was obvious that later lines would seek to make a junction with the Midland and level crossings would follow. So they did. Chronology up to 1848 follows:

10. 5.1844 MIDLAND incorporated, the amalgamation of three existing companies. It opened no new lines until 1846 but was active in promoting several lines and extensions including the NOTTINGHAM + LINCOLN in 1845. This had been an earlier proposal of the MIDLAND COUNTIES authorised in 1836 but which had lapsed.

26. 6.1846 GREAT NORTHERN authorised including the Lincoln Loop line.

22. 7.1846 MANCHESTER SHEFFIELD + LINCOLNSHIRE formed. This was the merger of several companies including the GREAT GRIMSBY + SHEFFIELD JUNCTION and its proposed MARKET RASEN + LINCOLN extension.

3. 8.1846 MIDLAND - official opening of the branch from Nottingham. Hudson had boasted he would open a railway to Lincoln whilst others were still talking about it. Actually the GN and MIDLAND branches had both been seeking parliamentary approval at the same time, but whilst MIDLAND Bill was unopposed, GN was delayed for a year. The railway opened to the public on 4.8.1846 and there were within the map area intermediate stations at COLLINGHAM, SWINDERBY, THORPE and HYKEHAM.

1. 1.1847 MANCHESTER SHEFFIELD + LINCOLNSHIRE name used from this. Merger had been approved 22.7.1846 (see above).

17.10.1848 GREAT NORTHERN opened from Werrington Junction, near Peterborough, to Boston and LINCOLN; station located just to the north of the Midland Station.

18.12.1848 MANCHESTER SHEFFIELD + LINCOLNSHIRE opened from Market Rasen to an end-on junction with the MIDLAND. There were two level crossings; at Pelham Street, where GREAT NORTHERN was also crossed, and at High Street where MIDLAND met.

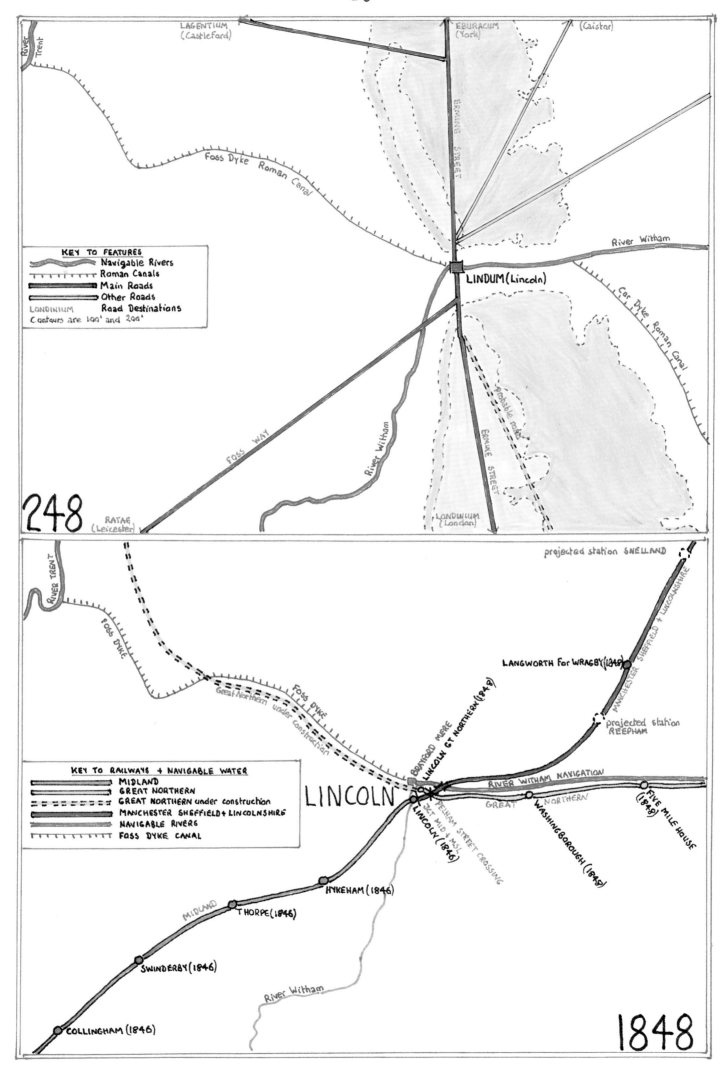

KEY TO FEATURES

~~~~~~~~ Navigable Rivers
~~~~~~~~ Roman Canals
▬▬▬▬▬ Main Roads
━━━━━━ Other Roads
LONDINIUM   Road Destinations

Contours are 100' and 200'

LAGENTIUM (Castleford)
EBURACUM (York)
(Caistor)
River Trent
Foss Dyke Roman Canal
ERMINE STREET
LINDUM (Lincoln)
River Witham
Car Dyke Roman Canal
FOSS WAY
River Witham
Probable road
ERMINE STREET
LONDINIUM (London)
RATAE (Leicester)

248

---

projected station SNELLAND
River Trent
Foss Dyke
MANCHESTER SHEFFIELD + LINCOLNSHIRE
Great Northern under construction
Foss Dyke
LANGWORTH for WRAGBY (1848)
projected station REEPHAM
BRAYFORD MERE
LINCOLN GT NORTHERN (1849)
PELHAM STREET CROSSING
RIVER WITHAM NAVIGATION
GREAT NORTHERN
FIVE MILE HOUSE (1848)
WASHINGBOROUGH (1848)

KEY TO RAILWAYS + NAVIGABLE WATER

▬▬▬▬▬ MIDLAND
━━━━━━ GREAT NORTHERN
▬ ▬ ▬ GREAT NORTHERN under construction
▬▬▬▬▬ MANCHESTER SHEFFIELD + LINCOLNSHIRE
~~~~~~ NAVIGABLE RIVERS
~~~~~~ FOSS DYKE CANAL

LINCOLN
JCT MID + MSL
LINCOLN (1846)
HYKEHAM (1846)
MIDLAND
THORPE (1846)
SWINDERBY (1846)
River Witham
COLLINGHAM (1846)

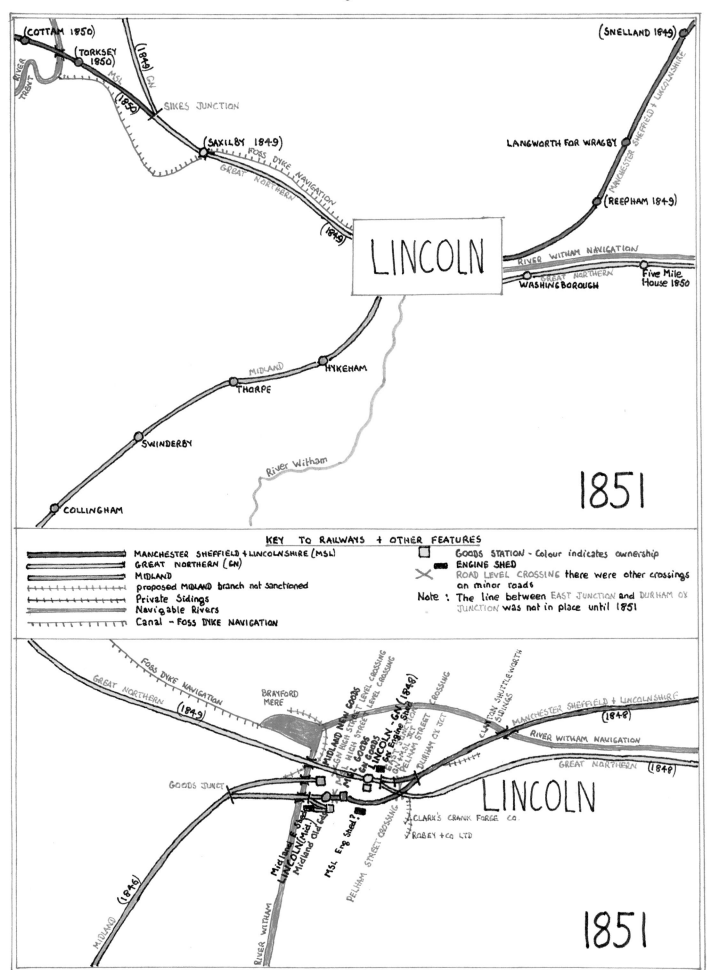

(COTTAM 1850)
(TORKSEY 1850)
(1849) GN
MSL
(1850)
SIKES JUNCTION
RIVER TRENT
(SAXILBY 1849)
FOSS DYKE NAVIGATION
GREAT NORTHERN
(1849)

(SNELLAND 1849)
MANCHESTER SHEFFIELD + LINCOLNSHIRE
LANGWORTH FOR WRAGBY
(REEPHAM 1849)

LINCOLN

RIVER WITHAM NAVIGATION
GREAT NORTHERN
WASHINGBOROUGH
Five Mile House 1850

MIDLAND
HYKEHAM
THORPE
SWINDERBY
River Witham
COLLINGHAM

1851

KEY TO RAILWAYS + OTHER FEATURES

- MANCHESTER SHEFFIELD + LINCOLNSHIRE (MSL)
- GREAT NORTHERN (GN)
- MIDLAND
- proposed MIDLAND branch not sanctioned
- Private Sidings
- Navigable Rivers
- Canal - FOSS DYKE NAVIGATION

- GOODS STATION - Colour indicates ownership
- ENGINE SHED
- X ROAD LEVEL CROSSING there were other crossings on minor roads
- Note : The line between EAST JUNCTION and DURHAM OX JUNCTION was not in place until 1851

FOSS DYKE NAVIGATION
GREAT NORTHERN
(1849)
BRAYFORD MERE
MIDLAND NEW GOODS
GN HIGH STREET LEVEL CROSSING
MSL HIGH STREET LEVEL CROSSING
GN GOODS
LINCOLN - GN (1848)
GN Engine Shed
GN + MSL JCT
EAST JUNCTION
PELHAM STREET
DURHAM OX JCT
CLAYTON SHUTTLEWORTH SIDINGS
MANCHESTER SHEFFIELD + LINCOLNSHIRE (1848)
RIVER WITHAM NAVIGATION
GREAT NORTHERN (1848)

GOODS JUNCT

LINCOLN

Midland E. Shed ?
LINCOLN (Mid.)
Midland Old Goods
MSL Eng Shed ?
PELHAM STREET CROSSING
CLARK'S CRANK FORGE CO.
ROBEY + CO LTD

MIDLAND (1846)
RIVER WITHAM

1851

1849-1851

The first event of this short period was on 1·2·1849 when REEPHAM and SNELLAND stations were opened on the MSL line. These had not been quite ready when the line opened in mid-December 1848 although both were part of the planned line, and were therefore shown as projected on the 1848 map.

The next event was on 9th April 1849 when the GREAT NORTHERN (GN) opened from Lincoln to a junction with the MSL at Gainsborough. It was then the intention after using the MSL to cross the Trent to proceed towards Doncaster but the GN found their way blocked by the hunting interests and it would be some time before the line could be completed. One must feel sympathy for the GN with everyone turned against them; they had rushed to complete the loop line taking a level course rather than a direct course between Boston and Lincoln only to be blocked at Gainsborough. So they had both an incomplete line and a twisting route which was never able to provide express running. This handicap ensured it would be the only pre-1850 route to close. There was one intermediate station on the new section of line at SAXILBY.

The final event shown on the general map of 1851 was the MSL line from Sykes Junction (known as SIKES JUNCT at first) to Clarborough Junction; it opened on 7th August 1850 with intermediate stations at TORKSEY and COTTAM. One further matter remains to be recorded although there is some doubt about it. This was the possible closure of FIVE MILE HOUSE in late 1850. The station did not appear in Bradshaw during 1851 and for several years afterwards. It does appear possible, however, that it continued as an unadvertised halt serving the village of Fiskerton across the River Witham using a local ferry service.

The detailed map of the central area shows other developments during this period:
The MIDLAND, the first railway to reach LINCOLN, established a small cramped goods area to the south of the passenger lines and station with an engine shed close to the river. The engine shed remained on this same site until final closure in BR days, but the goods facilities were soon replaced to the north of the station. The date the new goods opened is not known but a map dated 1846 shows it as under construction at that time. The MIDLAND and the GN both sought to build branches to connect with canal and river traffic at BRAYFORD MERE and the map shows the line of the earliest MIDLAND proposal which, however, failed to gain parliamentary sanction. A later joint MIDLAND and GN scheme was approved but does not appear to have been built.

The GREAT NORTHERN initially had a goods depot to the south of the passenger station with an engine shed to the north. Both these were replaced as traffic increased because eventually the city of Lincoln were able to ensure that shunting across the level crossing was prohibited.

The MANCHESTER SHEFFIELD + LINCOLNSHIRE opened its first goods depot at the opposite side of the High Street to the Midland station. The earliest engine shed is thought to have been at an adjoining site, but it could have been on the site shown as old shed (on 1905 map) from the outset but it was definitely established at this latter site by the mid 1850's. The MSL had originally intended to join the GN half a mile outside Lincoln and run into their station. However, the GN refused running powers to MSL, perhaps because they combined against the GN in the notorious Octuple Agreement. The MSL were thus involved in engineering works by having to approach Lincoln through a cutting in the limestone ridge rather than the level, less costly original proposal. The MSL then as a 'tit for tat' joined the Midland line, crossing the GN on the level without making any connection with it. However, common sense eventually prevailed and the two companies established the Lincoln East to Durham Ox chord line which was brought into use in 1851.

The central area map shows the three earliest private sidings, one linked to the MSL, and the others to the GN. Many years passed before any further private sidings came into use.

Finally a few words about the notorious level crossings. As mentioned, Pelham Street was only a minor road in 1850 and it was not expected that a great deal of railway traffic would cross the High Street at the Midland MSL crossing since MSL trains would be concentrated into the GN station and on to Sykes Junction and there joining their own line to Retford. The GN High Street Level Crossing, however, was obviously going to see quite intensive use, by both GN + MSL trains. With these possibilities in mind the GREAT NORTHERN, before building the line, suggested to the city that they would lower the railway 5' at the crossing point and that the High Street should be highered by about thirteen feet. However, a special vestry meeting of St Marks voted against this proposal. There were fears that such alterations would depreciate the value of properties in the area. The meeting went beyond this and insisted on a level crossing. In later years when the authorities of Lincoln were trying to eliminate the level crossing the GN could respond that authority for the crossing had been by the local people who had refused to sanction the GN alternative of a bridge. The congestion still involved with this crossing must therefore be shared by George Hudson and the people of Lincoln as equally to blame.

The basic LINCOLN railway network was now in place.

1852-1885

As with many railway centres, Lincoln, after a period of intense activity between 1846 and 1851, had only two major events affecting it during the next thirty years.

The first of these events was in 1867 when the GREAT NORTHERN (GN) opened its line to Honnington with intermediate stations at WADDINGTON and HARMSTON. A station was also opened at BRACEBRIDGE but appears to only have ever handled goods traffic. On later maps Bracebridge is just shown as sidings, used by the Gas Works on the up side and by Thompson's on the down side. There were also further sidings serving the Bracebridge Brickworks and these were located mid-way between Bracebridge and Waddington. The building of the line was partly the result of some local agitation to provide Lincoln with a shorter and speedier link with London, than that provided by the Loop line whose disadvantages inherent in its curving course following the river Witham have already been commented upon. The new line did in fact reduce the journey time to London, and 4¾ hours in 1864 became only 3½ hours when the new route opened.

The other main development of the period was in 1882 with the opening of the GREAT NORTHERN + GREAT EASTERN line from Lincoln to Spalding and March. The main instigator of the line was the GREAT EASTERN (GE) which company needed access to coal supplies which were entirely absent from its operating area. At this time there was a strong possibility of a merger between the GN and GE but in the event it came to nothing. However, one of the side effects of this was transfer of the portion of the loop line north of Lincoln into joint GN + GE ownership. The new line to the south was in effect a duplicate route of the loop line but gave the GN a shorter route to Peterboro' and a route to Boston avoiding the twists and turns of the loop line, and though no shorter provided a speedier service for through traffic. Stations were opened at BRANSTON + HEIGHINGTON, POTTER HANWORTH, NOCTON + DUNSTON and BLANKNEY + METHERINGHAM. There was also a Lincoln Avoiding Line to ease the passage of through goods traffic and the route quickly developed an intensive mineral traffic, coal from the Yorkshire coalfield to the Great Eastern area being the main traffic.

One final minor event during this period was the re-opening of FIVE MILE HOUSE in 1865 although as mentioned earlier it appears likely that during its closed period it remained in use as an unadvertised halt, since it does appear on more than one railway map whilst it was closed.

The 1885 map gives some information about sidings which had come into use by that date. This information is somewhat patchy. North of Lincoln it is taken from an RCH map of 1885 and can therefore be regarded as accurate if not comprehensive for this area. To the south the information is from various sources and of somewhat later date so some sidings shown may not have been brought into use until post-1885.

1886-1905

This period contained only one major event marking the maximisation of Lincoln's railway network.

This was the opening of the LANCASHIRE DERBYSHIRE + EAST COAST (LD-EC). This railway was authorised 5-8-1891 to build a railway to an ambitious scheme from the docks at Manchester via Chesterfield and Lincoln to the east coast at Sutton where a new harbour would be built. It had wide support including the colliery owners always keen to support competition which helped to cut their transport costs. The GE gave support also, including finance, as they too were anxious to seek competitive coal supplies. In the event the railway was never completed except for the central section linking Chesterfield to Lincoln; this opened in 1896 and there were intermediate stations, in the map area, at CLIFTON-ON-TRENT and SKELLINGTHORPE and, in the following year (1897), an additional station opened at DODDINGTON + HARBY. The LDEC always enjoyed good relationships with the bigger companies but ultimately the lack of funds forced it to seek absorption and strangely the least likely candidate, the GREAT CENTRAL (GC — name had been changed by this time from MANCHESTER SHEFFIELD + LINCOLNSHIRE in 1897), became owners from 1.1.1907.

Before continuing the story of Lincoln's network it is appropriate to look at how this network development of the last sixty years had affected Central Lincoln, and the detailed map of the central area concentrates on these matters. It shows Goods Stations, Engine Sheds, Private Sidings, Junctions and Signal Boxes.

In the meantime the level crossings, with increases in both road and railway traffic, were continuing to cause increasing chaos in the High Street. The GN as mentioned earlier had to stop shunting across their High Street Level Crossing and the railway companies were asked to provide footbridges in the interests of pedestrian safety. The GN provided footbridges at Pelham Street and High Street but the MIDLAND (or MSL) crossing never had a footbridge. However, in practice little use was made of the footbridges; the people of Lincoln, having selected a level crossing, were jolly well going to use it.

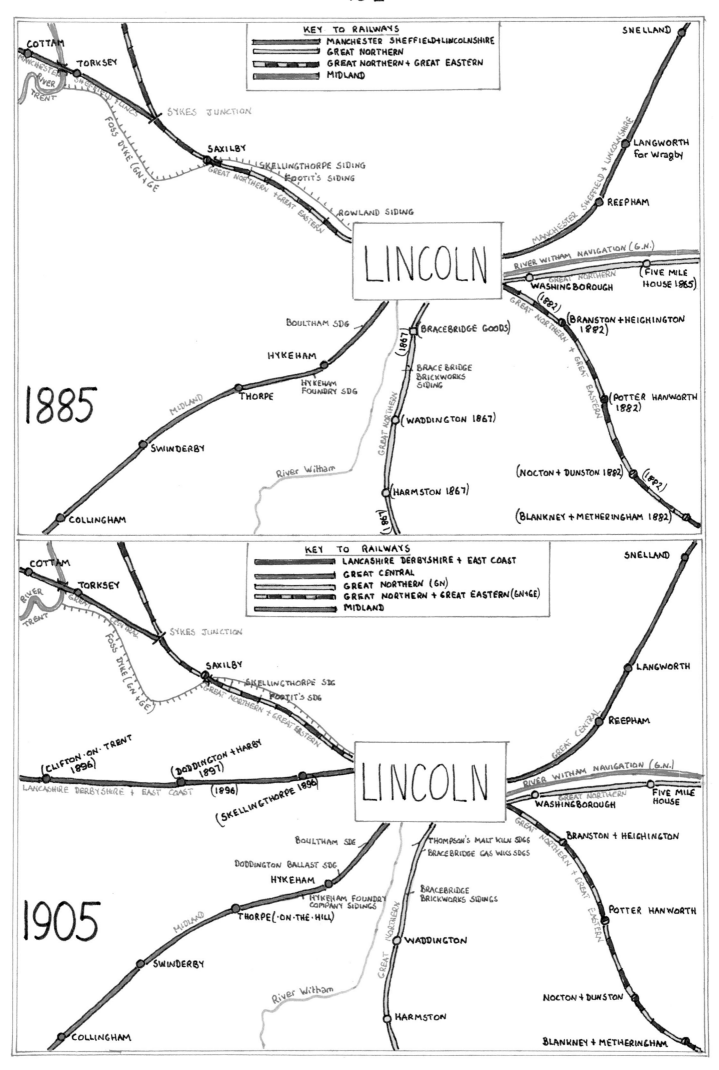

KEY TO RAILWAYS
- MANCHESTER SHEFFIELD + LINCOLNSHIRE
- GREAT NORTHERN
- GREAT NORTHERN + GREAT EASTERN
- MIDLAND

COTTAM
TORKSEY
MANCHESTER SHEFFIELD FLINS
RIVER TRENT
FOSS DYKE (GN+GE
SYKES JUNCTION
SAXILBY
SKELLINGTHORPE SIDING
BOOTIT'S SIDING
GREAT NORTHERN + GREAT EASTERN
ROWLAND SIDING

SNELLAND
LANGWORTH for Wragby
MANCHESTER SHEFFIELD + LINCOLNSHIRE
REEPHAM

LINCOLN

RIVER WITHAM NAVIGATION (G.N.)
GREAT NORTHERN
WASHINGBOROUGH
FIVE MILE HOUSE 1965)
(1882)
(BRANSTON + HEIGHINGTON 1882)
GREAT NORTHERN + GREAT EASTERN

BOULTHAM SDG
HYKEHAM
HYKEHAM FOUNDRY SDG
BRACEBRIDGE GOODS)
(1867)
BRACEBRIDGE BRICKWORKS SIDING
(POTTER HANWORTH 1882)

1885

MIDLAND
THORPE
GREAT NORTHERN
(WADDINGTON 1867)

SWINDERBY
River Witham
(NOCTON + DUNSTON 1882)   (1882)

(HARMSTON 1867)

COLLINGHAM
(1867)
(BLANKNEY + METHERINGHAM 1882)

KEY TO RAILWAYS
- LANCASHIRE DERBYSHIRE + EAST COAST
- GREAT CENTRAL
- GREAT NORTHERN (GN)
- GREAT NORTHERN + GREAT EASTERN (GN+GE)
- MIDLAND

COTTAM
TORKSEY
RIVER TRENT
GREAT CENTRAL
FOSS DYKE (GN+GE)
SYKES JUNCTION
SAXILBY
SKELLINGTHORPE SDG
BOOTIT'S SDG
GREAT NORTHERN + GREAT EASTERN

SNELLAND
LANGWORTH
GREAT CENTRAL
REEPHAM

(CLIFTON·ON·TRENT 1896)
(DODDINGTON + HARBY 1897)
LANCASHIRE DERBYSHIRE + EAST COAST   (1896)
(SKELLINGTHORPE 1896)

LINCOLN

RIVER WITHAM NAVIGATION (G.N.)
GREAT NORTHERN
WASHINGBOROUGH
FIVE MILE HOUSE
BRANSTON + HEIGHINGTON
GREAT NORTHERN + GREAT EASTERN

BOULTHAM SDE
DODDINGTON BALLAST SDG
HYKEHAM
HYKEHAM FOUNDRY COMPANY SIDINGS
THOMPSON'S MALT KILN SDGS
BRACEBRIDGE GAS WKS SDGS
BRACEBRIDGE BRICKWORKS SIDINGS
GREAT NORTHERN
POTTER HANWORTH

1905

MIDLAND
THORPE (·ON·THE·HILL)
WADDINGTON

SWINDERBY
River Witham
NOCTON + DUNSTON

HARMSTON

COLLINGHAM
BLANKNEY + METHERINGHAM

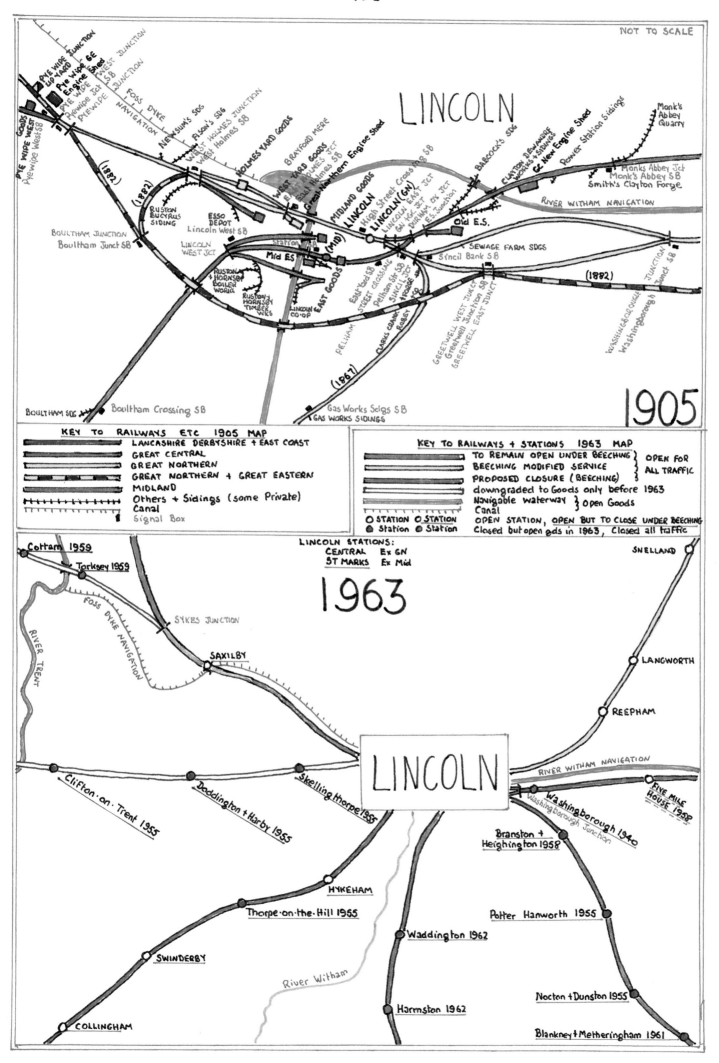

NOT TO SCALE

LINCOLN

1905

KEY TO RAILWAYS ETC 1905 MAP
- LANCASHIRE DERBYSHIRE + EAST COAST
- GREAT CENTRAL
- GREAT NORTHERN
- GREAT NORTHERN + GREAT EASTERN
- MIDLAND
- Others + Sidings (some Private)
- Canal
- Signal Box

KEY TO RAILWAYS + STATIONS 1963 MAP
- TO REMAIN OPEN UNDER BEECHING } OPEN FOR ALL TRAFFIC
- BEECHING MODIFIED SERVICE
- PROPOSED CLOSURE (BEECHING)
- downgraded to Goods only before 1963
- Navigable waterway } OPEN GOODS
- Canal
- O STATION O STATION OPEN STATION, OPEN BUT TO CLOSE UNDER BEECHING
- ● Station ● Station Closed but open gds in 1963, Closed all traffic

LINCOLN STATIONS:
CENTRAL   Ex GN
ST MARKS   Ex Mid

1963

LINCOLN

NEW LINES

NEW LINES in Central Lincoln from 1852 were: The Honnington GREAT NORTHERN(GN) line opened from Sincil Junction, to the east of the station, and used the route already followed by the first two GN sidings (as shown on the 1851 map). The next new lines were those of the GREAT NORTHERN + GREAT EASTERN (GN+GE). The main line diverged to the south from Pye Wipe Junction and skirted the city on an embankment. At this time also connections were laid to enable traffic from the east to reach the MANCHESTER SHEFFIELD + LINCOLNSHIRE (MLS) + GN yards without the need to negotiate the central level-crossings. The GN also laid two connections linking the line with the Loop Line to Boston. These joined the GN+GE at GREETWELL. The final addition, the LANCASHIRE DERBYSHIRE + EAST COAST, joined the GN+GE at Pye Wipe.

GOODS

GOODS development during this period was substantial. Although the MIDLAND yard did not increase very much, having no through traffic, a new goods line to the south of the station was opened which served various private sidings in the vicinity. The MSL, whilst retaining its original EAST GOODS, opened a WEST GOODS near the Holmes at the opposite side of the main line to the GN. The GN facilities showed the most expansion and the yard at HOLMES covered a large area between the main line and the Foss Dyke. The final two railways to reach Lincoln, the GREAT EASTERN (GE) and the LANCASHIRE DERBYSHIRE + EAST COAST (LDEC), both had yards at Pyewipe.

ENGINE SHEDS

ENGINE SHEDS - Early evidence on this topic is rather patchy. The MIDLAND shed as already noted was in situ by 1847 and though altered and rebuilt remained on the same site until closure in 1959. The GN engine shed near the station was replaced by the one shown on the map in 1873. Information on the MSL (or GREAT CENTRAL [GC] as it became) is not so clear. The shed shown as 'old' probably dated from very early days and the 'new' shed was brought into use in 1893. Both sheds continued in use until 1939 when the old shed was closed. The present depot is on approximately the same site as this old MSL shed. Finally the GE used an area near Pyewipe Jct from shortly after opening of the joint line although the actual shed was not brought into use until 1907. The shed had a short life, closing just after grouping in 1924, but continued as a stabling and signing-on point into the 1930's.

1906 - 1940

Lincoln is one of the few places not to justify a 1940 map. During this period there were no changes at all in the railway network and very few other events of note. As already noted, the LD+EC became part of the GREAT CENTRAL in 1907 and grouping brought all Lincoln's railways except the MIDLAND into the LONDON + NORTH EASTERN, but these were just name changes. It might be thought that with most of the city's railways falling into one group that some rationalisation would have followed, but apart from some minor economies with engine sheds as noted above nothing at all happened. Finally, following the outbreak of war the only event affecting the network during this quite long period occurred, the closure of WASHINGBOROUGH in 1940.

1941 - 1963

This period opened as a continuation of the previous period without either development or rationalisation and continued until the end of 1954. Then at last the BR rationalisation programmes began to have an effect on Lincoln. But even now the full network of lines remained intact although some lines lost their services to passengers entirely and, where passenger services were retained, many of the intermediate stations closed altogether whilst others were reduced to handling goods traffic only as a prelude to complete closure. Undoubtedly it was Lincoln's importance as a focal point of through goods traffic which preserved the network during this period when most places lost some routes.

The events from 1955 and onwards are tabulated below in chronological order:

1955 Thorpe-on-the-Hill closed; Clifton-on-Trent, Doddington + Harby and Skellingthorpe closed and withdrawal of the passenger service on the ex LDEC line (the line and stations continued in use for goods traffic); Potter Hanworth and Nocton + Dunston closed.

1958 Branston + Heighington closed; Five Mile House closed except for excursion traffic which continued for a further six years. The Pelham Street Flyover (road) was constructed enabling road traffic to avoid one of the notorious level crossings. The rail flat crossing at this point remained.

1959 Cottam and Torksey stations closed and passenger services on the line withdrawn, but the line continued in use for goods traffic.

1961 Blankney + Metheringham closed.

1962 Waddington and Harmston stations closed.

1963 The BEECHING REPORT:

The 1963 map shows the extent of the report's proposals as they would affect Lincoln. The lines remaining open to passengers in 1963 are distinguished from those to remain and those where the passenger service was proposed to be modified or withdrawn. These proposals had a very mixed fate and initially at any rate it appeared that most of the Good Doctor's report was ignored.

1963-1977

The detailed Beeching Report closure proposals affecting Lincoln were:

1. Withdrawal of passenger service on the loop line to the south.
2. Withdrawal of the passenger service between Lincoln and Nottingham.
3. Modification of the passenger service between Lincoln and Grimsby.

These proposals would lead to closure of stations at: COLLINGHAM, SWINDERBY, HYKEHAM, LINCOLN ST MARKS and FIVE MILE HOUSE (already closed except for some seasonal excursion trains). The intermediate station at SAXILBY was also scheduled for closure.

As already noted Lincoln largely ignored the Beeching Report and it was 1985 before the first station closure was implemented. Admittedly a prompt start appeared to be made in 1964 with the complete closure of FIVE MILE HOUSE, but this cannot really be counted since it had been closed to regular passenger traffic some six years earlier. But the passenger traffic continued on the line until December 1969 and the portion of the line within the map area continued in use for goods traffic to the end of the period.

None of the other proposals were carried out during this period and this neglect graphically illustrates the report's glaring failure in looking at closures in splendid isolation rather than a part of the overall network. Lincoln had, as mentioned earlier, developed strategic importance as a cross roads for through goods traffic and at the time of the report's publication there had been but little reduction in through freight workings although the pattern of that traffic had changed. The Doncaster to East Anglia coal traffic had reduced but iron and steel traffic to Scunthorpe had increased. This latter traffic reached Lincoln via the ex-LDEC line and required reversal at Pyewipe Junction. In addition the Nottingham line had retained intermediate stations enjoying some patronage, whilst the Honnington line stations had closed. It was therefore decided to lay a connecting spur at Newark onto the Midland Lincoln line with a threefold purpose of: Running trains from Kings Cross into ST MARKS LINCOLN (as the ex-Midland station was now known); to continue local services; and to divert the iron and steel traffic via this route. This made ST MARKS Lincoln's main station and the removal of the closure threat of this line would enable BR to close two lines, the Honnington line which closed in the 1960's and the ex-LDEC, but the latter remained open until into the next period for some coal traffic.

In 1965 the intermediate stations on the Market Rasen line were all closed, although not scheduled for closure in the Beeching report. The line remained open, however, for both passenger and freight traffic. SAXILBY station remained open and in 1975 the station at METHERINGHAM was re-opened. One final closure remains to be noted on the general map and that was the severance of the Sykes Junction to Clarborough Junction freight-only line, but spurs at both ends of this line were retained to serve industry.

Turning to the effect of rationalisation on the central area there was comparatively little effect upon this at this stage.

The line from Sincil Junction was closed in 1967 but a short spur survived until about 1971 to serve the private sidings in that area. In 1969 Sincil Junction to Washingborough Junction closed with the withdrawal of the loop line passenger services, and access to the line for goods purpose was via Greetwell Junctions. The other line closures in the central area were the goods-only branches to St Marks and West Yard which both closed in 1965. Private sidings were also progressively closed so that by the end of the period there was little private siding traffic within the city. The remaining goods depots in the central area appear to have all closed by the end of 1966 with the exception of the ex-GREAT NORTHERN HOLMES YARD, but even here it was progressively reduced in size.

One matter of desperate urgency was the increasing chaos caused to High Street road traffic with its two level crossings. Some easing of the situation had been gained in 1958 with the Pelham Street flyover, and further easing of the situation had been expected with the Beeching Report proposal to close ST MARKS. However, as we have seen, ST MARKS became the principal station at Lincoln and the new rail traffic routes mentioned above appeared, to begin with, to increase the traffic delays in the High Street.

At the end of 1977 the rationalisation of passenger lines serving Lincoln had been reduced to almost an exact carbon copy of the 1851 layout, the only difference being the replacement of the Lincoln loop line to the south by the ex GN+GE route; but the replacement route was serving the same needs, but by a shorter and more convenient route.

The High Street Level Crossing problem remained unsolved mainly through a lack of communication between road and rail interests in appreciation of the other party's overall strategy.

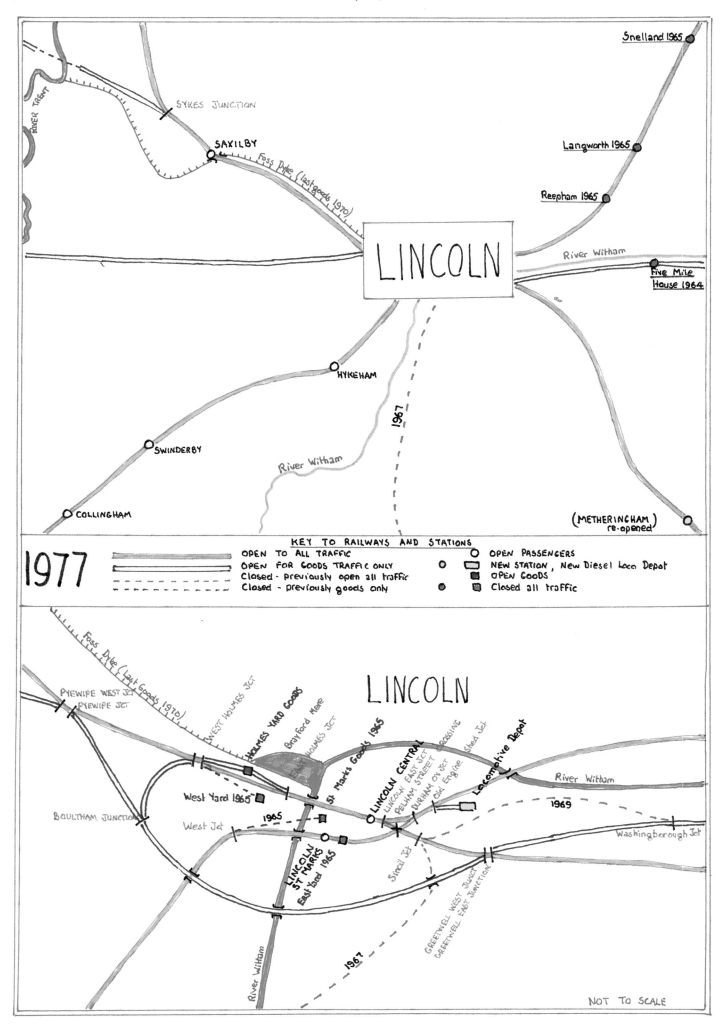

Snelland 1965

Langworth 1965

Reepham 1965

SYKES JUNCTION

SAXILBY

RIVER TRENT

Foss Dyke (last goods 1970)

LINCOLN

River Witham

Five Mile House 1964

HYKEHAM

1967

SWINDERBY

River Witham

COLLINGHAM

(METHERINGHAM) re-opened

1977

KEY TO RAILWAYS AND STATIONS

OPEN TO ALL TRAFFIC   ○ OPEN PASSENGERS

OPEN FOR GOODS TRAFFIC ONLY   ◉ ▭ NEW STATION, New Diesel Loco Depot

Closed - previously open all traffic   ◼ OPEN GOODS

Closed - previously goods only   ◉ ▨ Closed all traffic

LINCOLN

Foss Dyke (Last Goods 1970)

PYEWIPE WEST JCT

PYEWIPE JCT

WEST HOLMES JCT

HOLMES YARD GOODS

Brayford Mere

EAST HOLMES JCT

St Marks Goods 1965

LINCOLN CENTRAL

LINCOLN EAST JCT

PELHAM STREET CROSSING

DURHAM OX JCT

Old Engine Shed Jct

Locomotive Depot

River Witham

West Yard 1965

BOULTHAM JUNCTION

West Jct

1965

LINCOLN ST MARKS 1965

East Yard 1965

Sincil Jct

1969

Washingborough Jct

GREETWELL WEST JUNCTION

GREETWELL EAST JUNCTION

River Witham

1967

NOT TO SCALE

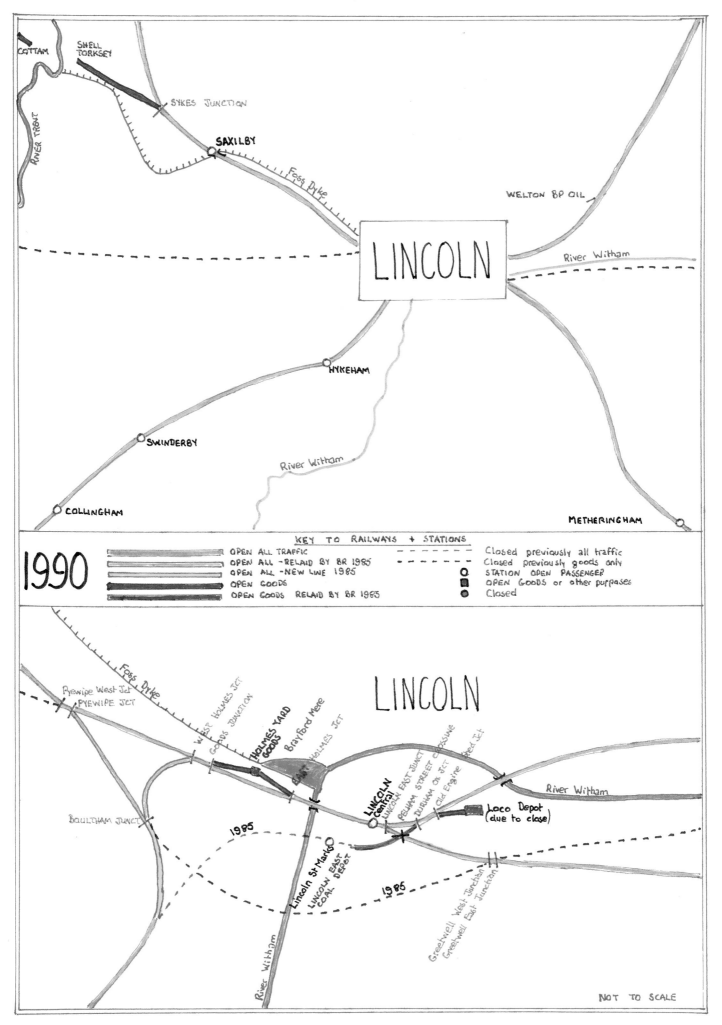

COTTAM

SHELL TORKSEY

RIVER TRENT

SYKES JUNCTION

SAXILBY

Foss Dyke

WELTON BP OIL

LINCOLN

River Witham

HYKEHAM

SWINDERBY

River Witham

COLLINGHAM

METHERINGHAM

KEY TO RAILWAYS + STATIONS

1990

OPEN ALL TRAFFIC
OPEN ALL - RELAID BY BR 1985
OPEN ALL - NEW LINE 1985
OPEN GOODS
OPEN GOODS RELAID BY BR 1985

Closed previously all traffic
Closed previously goods only
STATION OPEN PASSENGER
OPEN GOODS or other purposes
Closed

LINCOLN

Foss Dyke

Pyewipe West Jct
PYEWIPE JCT

WEST HOLMES JCT
GOODS JUNCTION

HOLMES YARD GOODS

Brayford Mere

HOLMES JCT

LINCOLN CENTRAL

LINCOLN EAST JUNCT

PELHAM STREET CROSSING

DURHAM OX JCT

SHED JCT

Old Engine

Loco Depot
(due to close)

River Witham

BOULTHAM JUNCT

1985

Lincoln St Marks

LINCOLN EAST COAL DEPOT

River Witham

1985

Greetwell West Junction
Greetwell East Junction

NOT TO SCALE

1978-1990

At most railway centres a nadir in rationalisation occurs during the period between the Beeching Report and the late 1960's or the early 1970's; this is then normally followed with the subsequent period showing some revival particularly with the opening of new suburban stations. Lincoln did not follow that pattern at all. As already noted rationalisation of the railway had been slow to affect Lincoln due to its strategic importance as a focal point of through freight traffic. Lincoln now failed to conform to the national pattern since through goods traffic was substantially reduced. The steel traffic virtually ceased in 1974 and other traffic also reduced so that by 1985 through goods volumes were down to one-fifth of those seen in 1963. With regard to any revival at Lincoln, as seen elsewhere, this could not be expected due to Lincoln's relative isolation, and the lack of any suburban potential. In the meantime the level crossings on High Street remained a nightmare.

It is within this background that the developments of this period need to be considered.

Looking first at events shown on the General Map of 1990, the Goods-only Lincoln Loop line had by 1977 been cut back to a spur reaching only as far as Bardney. Even that spur was little used by that time and was closed very shortly afterwards. The other line loss was the ex-LANCASHIRE DERBYSHIRE & EAST COAST goods line. This line had had its through steel traffic diverted in the mid-60's as already noted but had continued to carry some coal traffic and other freight in connection with MARNHAM Power Station, but this latter traffic mainly tended to use the Derbyshire outlet and this led to the closure of the connection to Lincoln by 1980. The remaining freight-only spurs to Torksey and to Cottam both remain in use.

The reduction in goods traffic also had its effects on the lines in the centre of Lincoln and at last enabled some alleviation of the level crossing difficulties to be tackled. But the central developments at this time were also influenced by the inadequacy of St Marks, whilst unused capacity was available at the superior LINCOLN CENTRAL station. The result of these factors was the authorisation of a £2 million scheme to divert all trains to CENTRAL and the closure of St Marks together with its level crossing! At last a Beeching closure proposal would be implemented. A new line was built from the Midland line to join the south goods loop at Boultham Junction and the curves from that point to West Holmes Junction and Pyewipe Junction were relaid enabling London trains to use CENTRAL station. The short stub line from Durham Ox Junction terminating before the High Street was also relaid and was designated for use as a coal depot. The remainder of the line forming the goods south loop was closed together with the line to St Marks and the central portions of the goods lines shown on the General Map. Holmes Yard remains in use handling sundries and the remaining local goods traffic.

THE FUTURE

The remaining network at LINCOLN appears secure. All the passenger lines continue to carry some goods, but in greatly reduced volumes. The lines all carry reasonable passenger services. The Locomotive Depot at Lincoln is scheduled for closure.

NOTTINGHAM

NOTTINGHAM, in common with most railway centres, had a unique set of circumstances affecting its development. In the first place, however, there was a major conformity to the national pattern in that the city's network of 1851, so far as passenger lines are concerned, closely resembles that proposed for the 1990's. There are, however, a few features in the development story which merit comment and explanation before looking at the chain of events in detail. The first of these is the comparatively late date of 1846 before NOTTINGHAM was on a through route, and even then it was of branch line status; very strange, bearing in mind the size, importance, and geographic location of Nottingham. This was partly the result of the excellent canal communications the city enjoyed; and early canal opposition caused the main line to pass Nottingham to the west. Stemming from this was the development of the location known as TRENT as an important route centre. The importance of this location has persisted into present age and remains of greater significance than Nottingham itself. A second factor was that for a long time the city was in a monopoly area, being the exclusive preserve of the MIDLAND. But the third factor, with the city at the fringe of the coalfield, attracted other railways into the area to share its remunerative coal traffic in spite of MIDLAND opposition.

TO 1846

21. 6. 1836 MIDLAND COUNTIES (MC) - Authorised. The scheme was for a line from Rugby via Leicester to Trent, with lines from there to Derby, Nottingham and up the Erewash Valley together with other branches. These latter branches were dropped by the promoters to stifle opposition of the NORTH MIDLAND, and from this time the line to Derby was considered as the main line, with NOTTINGHAM regarded as a branch.

4. 7. 1836 NORTH MIDLAND (NM) - Authorised.

30. 5. 1839 MC: Official opening between Derby and NOTTINGHAM.

4. 6. 1839 MC: Opened to the public between Derby and NOTTINGHAM. There were intermediate stations, within the map area, at: BURROWASH (became BORROWASH), BREASTON (name soon changed to SAWLEY), LONG EATON (the first of three different stations with this name) and BEESTON. Before the end of the year an additional station had been opened. This was at DRAYCOTE (later to become DRAYCOTT).

5. 5. 1840 MC: Opened between TRENT JUNCTION and Leicester (and to Rugby by 30th June); connections to both Derby and NOTTINGHAM opened. The through trains from the south ran to Derby where onward connections to Birmingham and Leeds were available. Passengers from and to NOTTINGHAM had to travel via Derby, accentuating the city's branch line status.

10. 5. 1844 MC merges with NM and Birmingham + Derby Junction to form MIDLAND. The three railways met at Derby which became the natural headquarters of the new company but did little but emphasise the branch status of NOTTINGHAM.

4. 8. 1845 EREWASH VALLEY - Authorised. This was the revival of one of the MC original branches which had been dropped to appease the NM. Instigated by the valley colliery owners to obtain outlets for their coal, it was absorbed by the MIDLAND shortly afterwards before construction was started.

26. 6. 1846 GREAT NORTHERN - Authorised (GN)

16. 7. 1846 LONDON + NORTH WESTERN (LNW) formed.

16. 7. 1846 AMBERGATE, NOTTINGHAM + BOSTON + EASTERN JUNCTION (ANBEJ) - Authorised as an amalgamation of various schemes to bring a railway into NOTTINGHAM from the east.

27. 7. 1846 MANCHESTER SHEFFIELD + LINCOLNSHIRE formed. Thus within five weeks all the remaining railways to reach the city were formed.

3. 8. 1846 MIDLAND opened between NOTTINGHAM and Lincoln with stations, within the map area, at CARLTON, BURTON JOYCE, LOWDHAM and THURGARTON. The line was opened, not for local convenience, but to make things difficult for the GN. The line engineer, George Stephenson, made one of his queer recommendations with the suggestion that the line to Lincoln should start ¼ mile west of the terminal station with trains from NOTTINGHAM backing out of the station and then running past it to Lincoln!

1847-1854

26. 9. 1847 MIDLAND open EREWASH VALLEY line. A contemporary map shows stations, within the map area, at SANDIACRE (later to become STAPLEFORD + SANDIACRE), STANTON (to become STANTON GATE), ILKESTON JUNCTION (from whence a short branch to ILKESTON opened at the same time), SHIPLEY (became SHIPLEY GATE), HEANOR JUNCTION (possibly only open for a short period and closure date is unclear) and LANGLEY MILL. Numerous colliery branches were opened and a selection of some of the longer lasting ones are shown on the map. A station called LONG EATON was also opened on this line. This was to the north of the later station and became TOTON for LONG EATON whilst the earlier LONG EATON

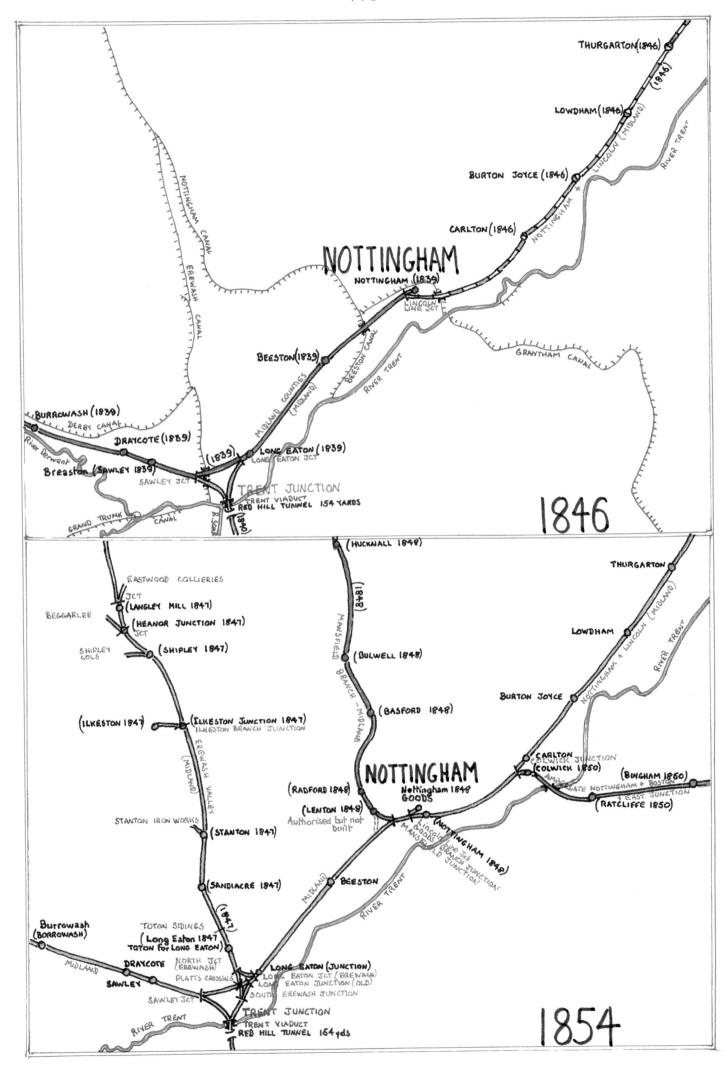

THURGARTON (1846)

LOWDHAM (1846)

BURTON JOYCE (1846)

CARLTON (1846)

NOTTINGHAM CANAL

EREWASH CANAL

RIVER TRENT

LINCOLN (MIDLAND)

NOTTINGHAM (MIDLAND)

NOTTINGHAM

NOTTINGHAM (1839)

LINCOLN LINE JCT

BEESTON (1839)

MIDLAND COUNTIES (MIDLAND)

BEESTON CANAL

RIVER TRENT

GRANTHAM CANAL

BURROWASH (1839)

DERBY CANAL

DRAYCOTE (1839)

River Derwent

Breaston (Sawley 1839)

LONG EATON (1839)

(1839)

LONG EATON JCT

SAWLEY JCT

TRENT JUNCTION

GRAND TRUNK CANAL

R. Soar

(1840)

TRENT VIADUCT

RED HILL TUNNEL 154 YARDS

1846

HUCKNALL 1848

EASTWOOD COLLIERIES

JCT (LANGLEY MILL 1847)

BEGGARLEE

(HEANOR JUNCTION 1847) JCT

SHIPLEY COLS

(SHIPLEY 1847)

THURGARTON

LOWDHAM

(1848)

MANSFIELD BRANCH - MIDLAND

BULWELL 1848

BURTON JOYCE

(ILKESTON 1847)

(ILKESTON JUNCTION 1847) ILKESTON BRANCH JUNCTION

EREWASH VALLEY (MIDLAND)

(BASFORD 1848

NOTTINGHAM + LINCOLN (MIDLAND)

RIVER TRENT

NOTTINGHAM

CARLTON (COLWICK 1850)

COLWICK JUNCTION

AMBERGATE NOTTINGHAM + BOSTON + EAST JUNCTION

(BINGHAM 1850)

(RADFORD 1848)

Nottingham 1848 GOODS

(RATCLIFFE 1850)

STANTON IRON WORKS

(LENTON 1848)

Authorised but not built

LINCOLN LINE JCT GOODS BRANCH JUNCTION

(NOTTINGHAM 1848) NOTTINGHAM + MANSFIELD BRANCH JUNCTION

(STANTON 1847)

MIDLAND

BEESTON

SANDIACRE 1847

RIVER TRENT

Burrowash (BORROWASH)

TOTON SIDINGS

(1847)

MIDLAND

DRAYCOTE

(Long Eaton 1847 TOTON for LONG EATON)

NORTH JCT (EREWASH)

LONG EATON (JUNCTION)

SAWLEY

PLATTS CROSSING

LONG EATON JCT (EREWASH) LONG EATON JUNCTION (OLD)

SAWLEY JCT

SOUTH EREWASH JUNCTION

RIVER TRENT

TRENT JUNCTION

TRENT VIADUCT

RED HILL TUNNEL 154 yds

1854

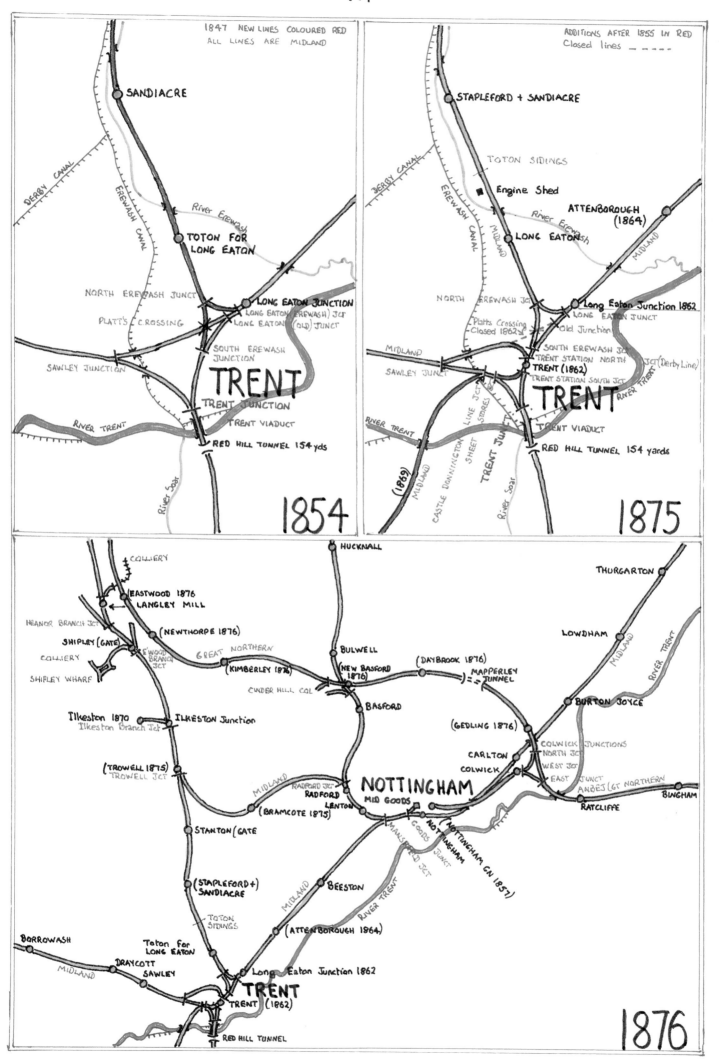

1854

1875

1876

station on the Derby-NOTTINGHAM line became known as LONG EATON JUNCTION. This date also saw the second stage in the development of TRENT with a second triangular junction giving access to the Erewash Valley line from both NOTTINGHAM and the south. However, this second triangle of lines suffered from two defects; first there was no access to Derby without reversing and as the two triangles of lines overlaid each other there was a flat crossing at PLATT's CROSSING which would cause increasing congestion as traffic increased.

2.10.1848 MIDLAND opened branch to Kirkby-in-Ashfield and on to a terminus at Mansfield one week later. Within the map area stations were opened at LENTON, RADFORD, BASFORD, BULWELL and HUCKNALL.

22.5.1848 Four months earlier the inconvenient reversal of Lincoln trains ended with the opening of a new passenger station at NOTTINGHAM on the through line. The original terminus became a goods station.

15.7.1850 AMBERGATE, NOTTINGHAM + BOSTON + EASTERN JUNCTION - The ambitious aims of this railway having been reduced from the aims proclaimed in its title, a line linking NOTTINGHAM with GRANTHAM was opened. A shortage of funds resulted in the line joining the MIDLAND at COLWICK JUNCTION with running powers over the MIDLAND into NOTTINGHAM. Within the map area there were intermediate stations at RATCLIFFE and BINGHAM.

From the time of its authorisation the AMBERGATE company had had covetous eyes cast upon it by both the MIDLAND and GREAT NORTHERN (GN). Eventually the influence of one of the main shareholders of the AMBERGATE ensured agreement was reached with the GN. But the MIDLAND 'dirty tricks' department found a legal loophole to prevent the GN exercising AMBERGATE running powers and then so harassed the AMBERGATE at Nottingham that they were compelled to convey goods traffic to COLWICK by horse and cart. Finally at the end of 1854 a lease was agreed with the GN taking effect from April 1855.

A final development during the period was the steady growth of Toton sidings which as early as 1850 had assumed importance in connection with Midland coal traffic.

1855-1876

As with many railway centres, following the intense activity in development up to the early 1850's, the next two decades saw comparatively little change in the railway network. Such development as did take place was mainly exploitation of coal traffic and/or the MIDLAND 'dirty tricks' department directed against the GN. This had commenced before the GN was authorised, with the infamous George Hudson delaying passage of the GN bill through parliament, and was followed by opening the Lincoln line into GN territory. This was followed by the notorious Octuple Agreement designed to starve the GN of revenues. The sharp practice with the AMBERGATE which resulted in a wasteful line having to built parallel to the MIDLAND line has been noted. Further examples were to follow.

1857 GN build and open line from COLWICK to NOTTINGHAM LONDON ROAD. The MIDLAND connection is severed.

1860 AMBERGATE, NOTTINGHAM + BOSTON + EASTERN JUNCTION changes its name to NOTTINGHAM + GRANTHAM RAILWAY + CANAL. Company had been leased to the GN. It was never fully absorbed and retained its identity until grouping.

1862 The most important event of this year was the remodelling of the TRENT JUNCTION layout. A station was opened at TRENT for interchange purposes, the notorious PLATT's CROSSING was abolished and new SAWLEY JUNCTION gave access to both northern and southern approaches of the new station enabling traffic to enter or leave the complex to or from any of the converging lines. LONG EATON JUNCTION station was closed and TOTON became LONG EATON.

The other event of the year saw Phase I of the Midland's latest 'dirty tricks' campaign directed against any GN encroachment. GN were proposing a line from COLWICK to Codnor Park. The MIDLAND, who were using the GN line to KINGS CROSS pending completion of their LONDON extension, offered GN running powers over its own lines with effect from 1863.

1865 MIDLAND; TRENT to Weston-on-Trent authorised.

1868 MIDLAND Phase II of MIDLAND 'dirty tricks' plan hatched in 1862. Their own LONDON line now being in use they cancelled at short notice the GN running powers over their lines which had been operative since 1863.

1869 MIDLAND opened TRENT to Weston-on-Trent. Extended to join main line near Repton in 1873.

1870 MIDLAND closed the short Ilkeston branch. Open goods branch to Shipley Collieries

1872 GN in response to MIDLAND moves of 1868 obtain authorisation for a much more comprehensive set of lines compared to those proposed ten years earlier. In addition to the line to Codnor Park, lines to Derby and up the Leen Valley were agreed. These would enable the GN to obtain a full share of all coal traffic.

MIDLAND obtain authorisation for a line from NOTTINGHAM to Saxby which would form the southern portion of a route giving a main line connection between London and the North via NOTTINGHAM.

1875 MIDLAND opened the Radford to TROWELL loop; this would give access from the above route northwards into the main line. There was according to RCH maps an intermediate station at BRAMCOTE, although most other information sources make no mention of this.

1875 The first portion of the GREAT NORTHERN (GN) lines authorised in 1872 opened to Goods Traffic between COLWICK and Pinxton with sorting sidings at Eastwood.

1876 GN open above line to passengers from 1st August. Intermediate stations at GEDLING (later became GEDLING + CARLTON), DAYBROOK FOR ARNOLD + BESTWOOD, NEW BASFORD (later became BASFORD + BULWELL), KIMBERLEY, NEWTHORPE · GREASLEY + SHIPLEY GATE, and EASTWOOD ROAD + LANGLEY MILL.

1877-1888

This period saw further additions to the railway network, the GN completing its network of lines authorised in 1872. In addition both the GN and MIDLAND built numerous colliery branches in competition with each other as the 1888 map clearly shows. Meanwhile the MIDLAND at last put NOTTINGHAM on a through main line from LONDON.

1877 MIDLAND branch opened to Watnall Colliery.

1878 GN - Line from AWSWORTH JUNCTION to Derby opened to all traffic. Intermediate stations at : AWSWORTH, ILKESTON (later known as ILKESTON NORTH) and WEST HALLAM.

Colwick station became NETHERFIELD + COLWICK. A goods depot and engine shed brought into use by GN within the Colwick triangle of lines.

1879 GREAT NORTHERN + LONDON + NORTH WESTERN JOINT line opened to all traffic from SAXONDALE JUNCTION to Bottesford North and Welham Junctions. Intermediate station at BINGHAM ROAD. The LONDON + NORTH WESTERN opened a goods depot at NOTTINGHAM and an engine shed at COLWICK alongside the GN Shed.

MIDLAND line from LONDON ROAD JUNCTION at NOTTINGHAM to Saxby opened to all traffic. Intermediate stations opened at EDWALTON and PLUMTREE. This opening at last put NOTTINGHAM on a main through line between London and the North. Local services along this line were always sparse, its main purpose being to serve as an express passenger line and for freight.

1880 MIDLAND re-opened Ilkeston Branch - station now known as ILKESTON TOWN. There was further connection from the North to the re-opened station and a new line from BENNERLEY JUNCTION to join the earlier Watnall Colliery Branch. Intermediate stations were at KIMBERLEY and WATNALL. It was thus now possible to travel from Ilkeston Town to NOTTINGHAM by two routes — via KIMBERLEY and BASFORD or via TROWELL.

1882 GN - LEEN VALLEY line opened including a passenger service from 1st October. Intermediate stations within the map area were at BULWELL FOREST, BESTWOOD COLLIERY, BUTLERS HILL and HUCKNALL (later became HUCKNALL TOWN to distinguish it from the MIDLAND and (later) GREAT CENTRAL stations).

1886 GN - Nutbrook Colliery branch opened.

NOTTINGHAM SUBURBAN authorised (25/6) promoted by local interests. GN were to work the line for 55% of the receipts with power to purchase it (which they never did).

The map showing the position at the close of the period is based on a Railway Clearing House map of 1889. This also shows railways under construction or projected. The date has been altered since the map shows NOTTINGHAM SUBURBAN as under construction following a different alignment, but it was opened to all traffic before the end of 1889. Other features shown on the map are several colliery branches together with branches to the Stanton Iron Works by both the MIDLAND and GN. LONG EATON station moved ¼ mile south; the old station became goods only but would soon be swallowed up in the continued expansion of the TOTON SIDINGS used for marshalling MIDLAND coal trains to all parts of the country southwards.

1889 - 1905

1889 NOTTINGHAM SUBURBAN opened to all traffic in early December. Stations at THORNEYWOOD, ST ANN'S WELL and SHERWOOD. The line was heavily engineered with steep gradients and soon became redundant with the opening of the GREAT CENTRAL and the expansion of NOTTINGHAM's tramway system.

1890 MIDLAND - Branch to Ripley opened to all traffic with a station at HEANOR. Later (1905) a spur branch was laid to enable passenger trains to terminate at LANGLEY MILL as the 1905 map shows.

1891 GN opened its HEANOR BRANCH to all traffic. This was an extension of the Nutbrook Colliery line (see above 1886). In addition to the terminal station at HEANOR there was an intermediate station at MARLPOOL.

1893 With construction of the MANCHESTER SHEFFIELD + LINCOLNSHIRE (MSL) LONDON EXTENSION under way, some MSL trains used the GN Gedling line to run into NOTTINGHAM.

1897 MSL becomes GREAT CENTRAL (GC)

1899 GC opens its main line to LONDON. In the area this had involved great expense with three tunnels and several substantial viaducts. Within the map area stations were opened at HUCKNALL CENTRAL, BULWELL COMMON, NEW BASFORD, CARRINGTON, ARKWRIGHT STREET and RUDDINGTON. The GN built a connection to the main station (as yet incomplete) and a new HIGH LEVEL LONDON ROAD station.

1900 VICTORIA on GC main line opened. This was a joint station (GC and GN).

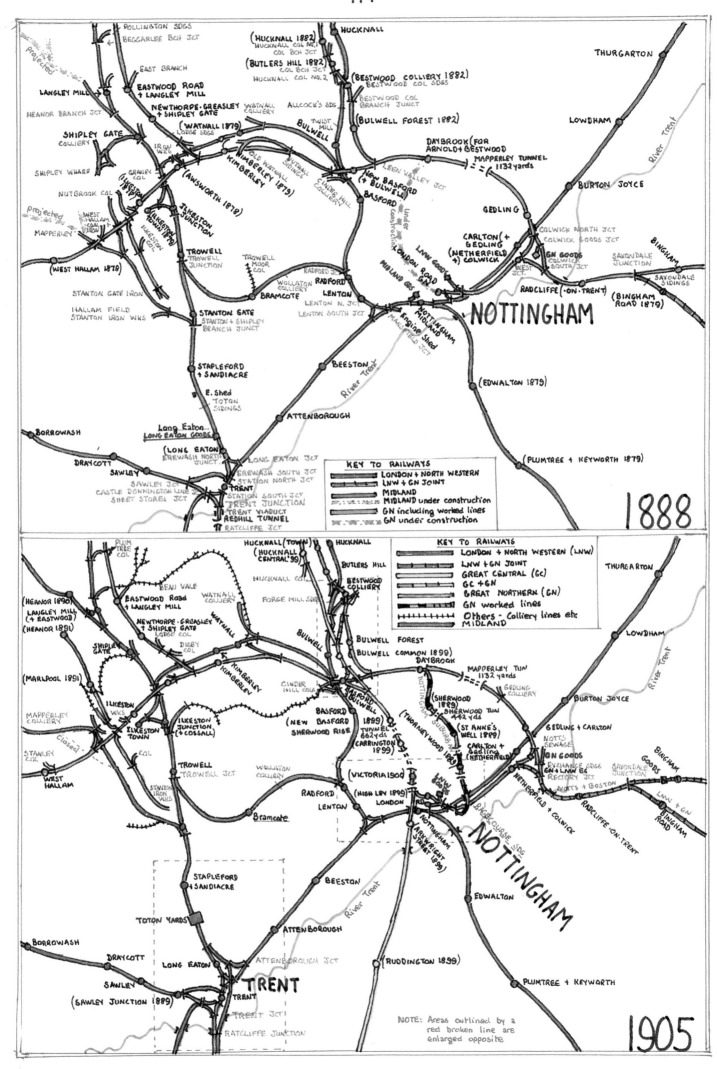

KEY TO RAILWAYS

	LONDON + NORTH WESTERN
	LNW + GN JOINT
	MIDLAND
	MIDLAND under construction
	GN including worked lines
	GN under construction

1888

KEY TO RAILWAYS

	LONDON + NORTH WESTERN (LNW)
	LNW + GN JOINT
	GREAT CENTRAL (GC)
	GC + GN
	GREAT NORTHERN (GN)
	GN worked lines
	Others - Colliery lines etc
	MIDLAND

NOTE: Areas outlined by a red broken line are enlarged opposite

1905

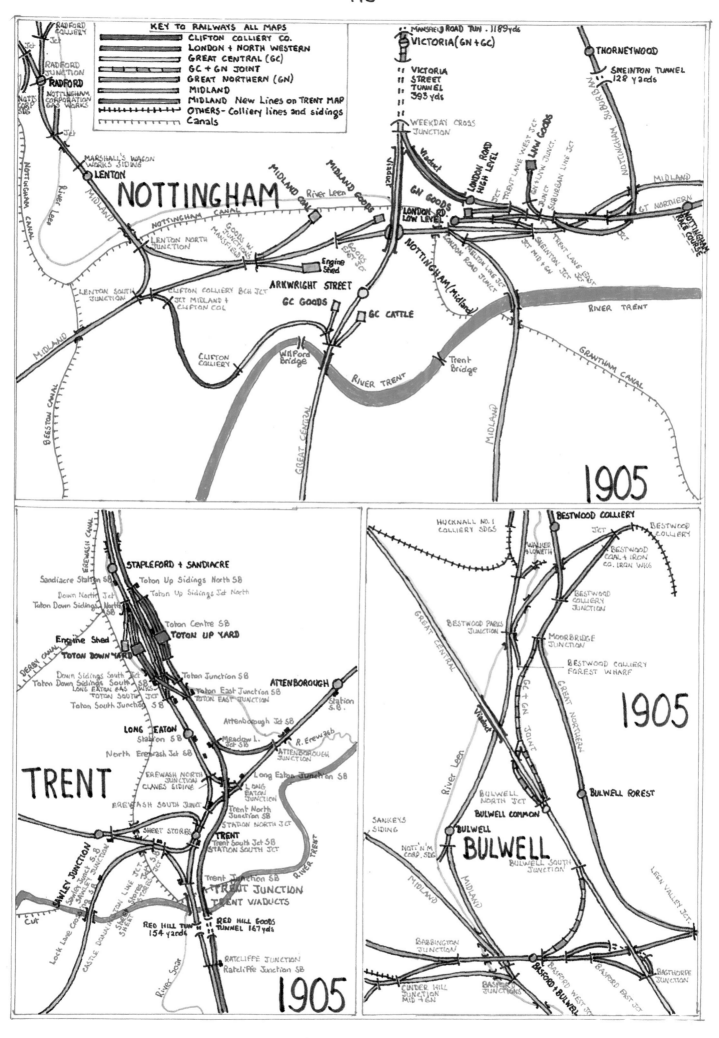

1901 MIDLAND opened further connections at TRENT but these are commented upon below in association with the TRENT enlargement map of 1905.

To complete the development picture it remains to note the opening dates of additional intermediate stations on the existing lines where these have not already been recorded:

ATTENBOROUGH on the MIDLAND Nottingham to Derby line opened in 1864, whilst SAWLEY JUNCTION on the same line was opened in 1889. TROWELL opened in 1875 when the LOOP LINE opened. BRAMCOTE was a private station probably opened with the line. The precise closure date is unclear. NOTTINGHAM RACECOURSE on the GREAT NORTHERN is problematic. RCH and Clinker refer to Race Course Siding from an early date but other sources refer to a station for 100 years. Probably it was a siding serving the Race Course which was used by passenger services on race days. It has been shown this way on the maps — indicated by the dotted red underlining.

Although 1905 appears an early date for maximum development, it is so far as NOTTINGHAM is concerned; almost too late, since rationalisation started in 1900 although this does not show on the maps since this was a steady and continuous reduction in local passenger services. The reasons for this are obvious with three separate passenger lines running north from the city through an area which would have had some problem supporting one. The city tramway system was yet a further factor resulting in rationalisation of these services.

Although some lines were built in the 20th century these were all short colliery branches.

Before looking at rationalisation in detail it is appropriate to comment briefly on the 1905 enlargement maps of the area's most complex locations.

NOTTINGHAM

The map of Nottingham shows why the GREAT CENTRAL London Extension through Nottingham was one of the most costly sections of line ever built, with the high cost of land added to the heavy engineering features of tunnels and viaducts. The GN connecting line was also costly being entirely on a viaduct. The MIDLAND line between Lenton North and South Junctions was originally authorised at the same time as the Mansfield Line but the connection was not built until many years later and did not open for traffic until 1869 but it took many years longer before it was shown on RCH maps and any use would appear to have been for the odd goods train.

There is some doubt about the layout of the GN and MIDLAND connections at NOTTINGHAM. In fact the RCH shows a connection requiring two reversals. The connection shown on the maps, however, is that indicated on MIDLAND DISTANCE diagrams. It could be that both are correct, the MIDLAND showing the later layout which was not altered in RCH records.

One final point: LONDON ROAD LOW LEVEL became redundant and confined mainly to goods after HIGH LEVEL opened, but it continued in use for some terminating services for many further years.

TRENT

TOTON SIDINGS for remarshalling coal trains to LONDON and the south was developed from around 1850 and by early in the 1870's it already comprised some twenty-five miles of sidings. Expansion continued over the next sixty years so that by the early 1930's siding mileage had increased to 65. This spectacular increase in coal traffic at TOTON, where the yards eventually handled as many as 10,000 wagons per day, was causing increasing strain on the junction layout at TRENT, which in addition to the heavy freight traffic was the meeting place of five passenger lines. Difficulty arose due to the close proximity of the various junctions. This could mean that a long coal train held at an exit route might easily foul a junction (or sometimes two junctions) to the rear. The main line to the south had earlier been quadrupled with the eastern pair of tracks being designated as goods lines. Then in 1901 a further remodelling was undertaken to enable south-bound goods from the yards to be able to avoid the Trent complex of junctions entirely. The map shows the new lines and the signal boxes after the modifications had taken place. Finally by this date Toton Engine Shed was the MIDLAND's largest freight shed. This is a position it still occupies under BRITISH RAIL into the 1990's.

BULWELL

This enlargement shows part of the Leen Valley with the lines of three companies crossing and re-crossing each other, the main objective being coal traffic although each line carried passenger traffic. However, as mentioned above local passenger services were progressively withdrawn, starting about 1900.

Another point of interest shown was the obvious exchange of traffic between the GREAT NORTHERN and GREAT CENTRAL with two separate fly-over connections to facilitate traffic exchange without interfering with through traffic. It should not be thought that the MIDLAND - GN connections had traffic exchange in mind; these simply enabled the two companies to compete for traffic from the same colliery. In fact, as a result of the MIDLAND 'dirty tricks' campaign against the GN relationships between the companies stayed cool for the remainder of their independant existence.

1906-1922

The period covered to the next map, dated 1940, is divided into two periods, pre-grouping and post-grouping. Both periods show continued rationalisation of passenger stations, although in most cases lines were retained because of their importance to coal traffic. In the chronology that follows, temporary wartime closures have been ignored.

1911 LENTON Closed to passengers but the station continued to handle goods traffic until 1951.

1916 SHERWOOD and THORNEYWOOD closed to all traffic following complete withdrawal of NOTTINGHAM SUBURBAN line passenger service. The remaining station on the line, ST ANN'S WELL, also, of course, closed to passengers, but it remained open for goods traffic.

1917 KIMBERLEY (Midland) reduced to goods only and WATNALL closed to all traffic. The line between Kimberley (Midland) and Bennington Junction was closed to all traffic although a short spur at Bennington serving the colliery there was retained.

1923-1940

1926 LANGLEY MILL (RIPLEY LINE PLATFORM) and HEANOR (Midland) both closed to passengers. Heanor remained in use as a goods station.

1928 MARLPOOL closed to all traffic (LNE Heanor Branch).
CARRINGTON (always a passenger station only) was closed.

1929 BULWELL FOREST closed to passengers but remained open for goods traffic.

1930 SAWLEY (LMS) Closed to all traffic. BULWELL HALL closed. This halt had a short life as it did not open until the post-grouping period. The precise opening date is not known.

1931 This year saw complete withdrawal of the un-remunerative service on the ex-GN Leen Valley line and with it the closure of stations: HUCKNALL TOWN, BUTLER'S HILL and BESTWOOD COLLIERY. The line remained open for coal traffic.

1938 HEANOR (LNE) passenger service withdrawn but line and station remained in use for goods.

The only positive development during this period was at TOTON where the two yards were mechanised to improve handling capacity, the project being completed shortly before the outbreak of World War II.

1941-1963

During this period the steady closure of passenger stations continued. There was also some goods rationalisation in particular where collieries had previously been served by both LMS + LNE. Another factor affecting coal traffic was the exhaustion of deposits in the west and the movement of the centre of mining activity eastwards into the concealed coalfield. But there were some new spurs opened as a result of this shift to the east to partly balance the closures in the west.

1941 EDWALTON - Closed to passengers but remained open for goods traffic.

1944 LONDON ROAD LOW LEVEL reduced to goods only. Had been little used since opening of the HIGH LEVEL station in 1899.

1947 ILKESTON TOWN - closed to all traffic together with projecting spurs.

1948 SHIPLEY GATE - closed all traffic.

1949 PLUMTREE - closed all traffic

1951 KIMBERLEY - goods closed. Entire line closed three years later. NOTTINGHAM SUBURBAN LINE closed completely. Also during the year BINGHAM ROAD was closed to all traffic, the line being closed to all traffic by 1962.

1953 Lenton Goods closed completely.

1960 Colwick Junction to Basford closed to passengers; GEDLING + CARLTON station closed to all traffic; DAYBROOK closed to passengers but retained for goods. Through goods traffic on ex-GN Leen Valley line ended, although traffic at Bestwood Colliery continued for a while but was routed northwards via Hucknall.

1963 EASTWOOD + LANGLEY MILL and NEWTHORPE GREASLEY + SHIPLEY GATE closed to passengers but remained open for goods. HUCKNALL CENTRAL and BULWELL COMMON closed. Closure of several colliery branches in the east affected by this date.

BEECHING PROPOSALS:

Passenger stations to close: BORROWASH, DRAYCOTT, BURTON JOYCE, LOWDHAM, THURGARTON, CARLTON + NETHERFIELD, WEST HALLAM, ILKESTON NORTH, AWSWORTH, KIMBERLEY, LANGLEY MILL + EASTWOOD, ILKESTON JUNCTION + COSSALL, TROWELL, STANTON GATE, STAPLEFORD + SANDIACRE, LONG EATON, RADFORD, BULWELL MARKET, HUCKNALL BYRON, BASFORD + BULWELL, NEW BASFORD and NOTTINGHAM VICTORIA. ARKWRIGHT STREET was a strange omission from the closure list, as it would have been a station without a passenger service, but it did in fact close during the year but was later re-opened.

The report recommended retention of the LMS main line through NOTTINGHAM but closure of the ex-LNE line. In the event both were lost. The report does not mention withdrawal of the LINCOLN service but just closure of all the stations. The Beeching proposals for NOTTINGHAM were in fact strangely inconsistent.

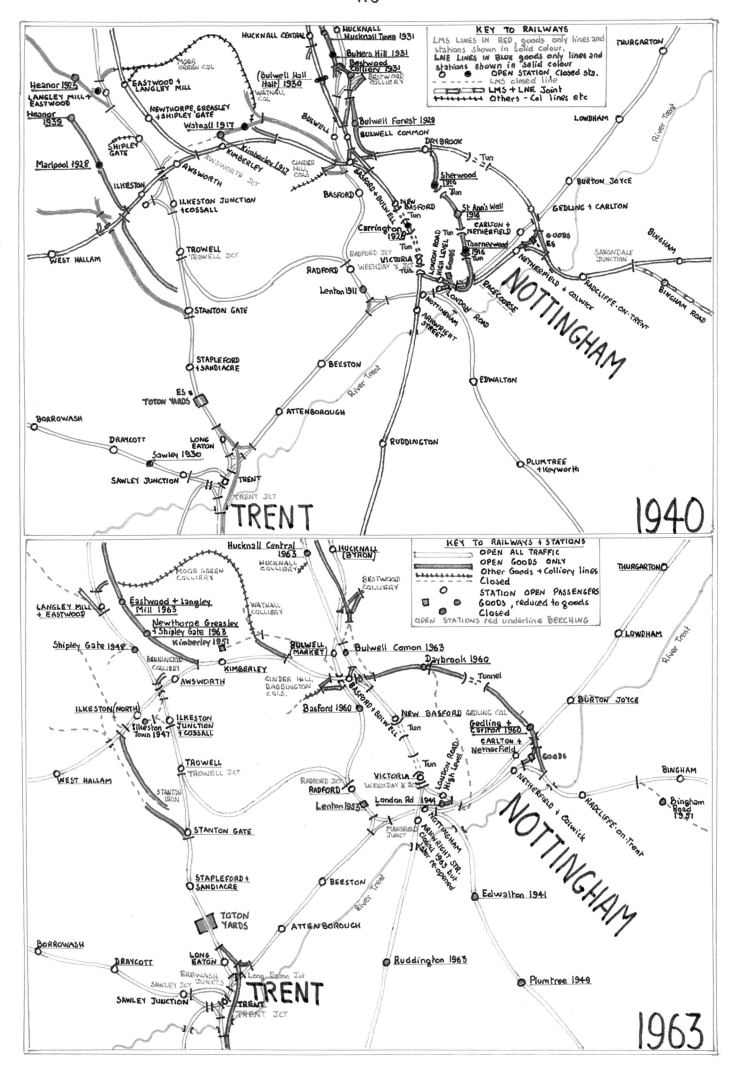

KEY TO RAILWAYS
LMS LINES IN RED goods only lines and stations shown in solid colour.
LNE LINES IN BLUE goods only lines and stations shown in solid colour
○ OPEN STATION ● Closed sta.
—— LMS closed line
▭▭▭ LMS + LNE Joint
+++++ Others - Col lines etc

1940

KEY TO RAILWAYS + STATIONS
OPEN ALL TRAFFIC
OPEN GOODS ONLY
+++++ Other Goods + Colliery lines
—— Closed
○ STATION OPEN PASSENGERS
● GOODS, reduced to goods
● Closed
OPEN STATIONS red underline BEECHING

1963

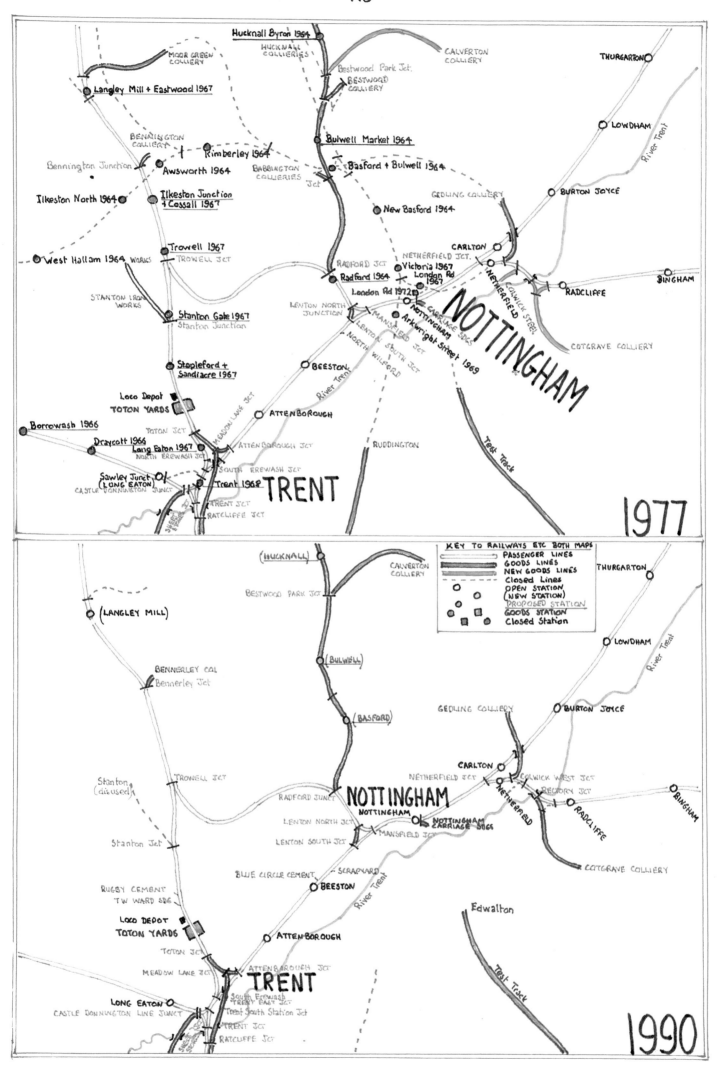

1977

1990

1964 - 1977

This period saw most of the Beeching proposals implemented, in addition to rationalisation of the station and line situation at NOTTINGHAM. The Midland main line to the south was regrettably lost, so that Nottingham lost both its main lines and was once again reduced, in effect, to branch line status. But the Lincoln line was saved.

TRENT, although losing some of its junction connections, is still important as a route focal point. The Toton Yards have been reduced in size but both UP and DOWN yards continue in use, whilst the Toton diesel freight locomotive depot is reputed to be the largest in Western Europe.

During the period there have been some new colliery lines brought into use, due to continued eastward shift of mining into the concealed coalfield. Also a number of rail-served power stations have been brought into use within the area or just outside it. A number of these developments are indicated on the map.

1964 RADFORD, BULWELL MARKET and HUCKNALL BYRON closed to all traffic. The Radford-Trowell loop continued to carry passenger traffic, but the line north from Radford reduced to goods traffic only. Ex-GN Colwick to London Road closed. Junction at Colwick to Midland line re-instated so that Newark trains could use the ex-Midland station (1965).
    BASFORD + BULWELL, KIMBERLEY, AWSWORTH, ILKESTON NORTH and WEST HALLAM closed to all traffic, most of line taken out of use and all closed by 1968. NEW BASFORD closed to all traffic, but line remained open.

1966 Intermediate stations at BORROWASH and DRAYCOTT closed. By this time the ex-GN line north to Pinxton had been closed entirely.

1967 LONDON ROAD Closed together with connection to VICTORIA which was also closed. ARKWRIGHT STREET was re-opened.
    The stopping passenger service on the Erewash Valley line and, although the line continued in use for all traffic, the intermediate stations of LONG EATON, STAPLEFORD + SANDIACRE, STANTON GATE, TROWELL, ILKESTONE JUNCTION + COSSALL and LANGLEY MILL + EASTWOOD were closed. SAWLEY JUNCTION becomes LONG EATON. MIDLAND Old Main Line south from NOTTINGHAM was closed to all traffic although section of track south of Edwalton was retained as a test track.

1968 TRENT Closed and junction layout simplified. Remaining portion of ex GN Leen Valley line closed entirely. By this time Castle Donnington line had been reduced to goods only. The local passenger service along the line had in fact been withdrawn in the early 1930's but the line continued to carry diverted passenger traffic into the late 1960's but the precise date this traffic ceased is unclear.

1969 ARKWRIGHT STREET Closed. All traffic on ex GC main line ceased. But a goods spur from Rudding southwards was kept as a siding serving industrial users. This spur was later progressively cut back.

1970 COLWICK Engine Shed Closed.

1972 LONDON ROAD GOODS closed (Old Low Level passenger station).
    During the period there were new lines to serve collieries at CALVERTON and COTGROVE.

1978 - 1990

This period saw only two minor closures both relative to goods-only branches in the western part of the area. In addition some further rationalisation at TOTON has followed the introduction of merry-go-round trains serving the local power stations. But TOTON still has its UP and DOWN yards serving the identical purpose of marshalling coal trains for the south which they had from establishment in 1850. The locomotive Depot continues as BR's largest. The station at LANGLEY MILL has been re-opened.

The final map shows some of the current industrial users of railway facilities including collieries still rail-connected.

1991 - THE FUTURE

Currently there are proposals to re-instate a local passenger service to Mansfield utilising the ex-Midland Leen Valley line which though still open is restricted to goods traffic. Nevertheless this will entail building a new line to the north near Annesley where the line has been severed where it passed through an unsafe tunnel. The line will have stations at BASFORD, BULWELL and HUCKNALL on the sites of the previously closed stations of the same names.

The remaining network appears secure.

SHREWSBURY

From earliest times SHREWSBURY has been an important route centre, so it is no surprise that with the coming of the railways it developed into an important railway centre with lines radiating from it to all points of the compass. In view of this it is, however, strange to note the late start to this development. By 1851, the date nationally when the main line network was in place, only two lines had reached Shrewsbury. The only explanation for this was that Shrewsbury's network was in the main, initially, the result of local enterprise evidenced by Shrewsbury being the first element in the railway companies linking it with places such as Chester, Hereford and Birmingham.

SHREWSBURY, although an important route centre, was relatively isolated making the ultimate railway pattern very simple. This has meant it has been possible to use a somewhat smaller scale for the general maps in this chapter. This in turn has enabled this chapter to include, besides Shrewsbury, the Wellington-Coalbrookdale area often regarded as the cradle of the industrial revolution. Also to cover the UK's largest new town – TELFORD.

1844-1850

6.8.1844 NORTH WALES MINERAL (NWM) – Authorised. This railway never reached SHREWSBURY but it would shortly amalgamate to form the SHREWSBURY + CHESTER which became the first railway to reach Shrewsbury.

30.6.1845 SHREWSBURY OSWESTRY + CHESTER JUNCTION (SOCJ) – Authorised.

1.8.1846 LONDON + NORTH WESTERN (LNW) formed. This was one of the two railways which would ultimately monopolise the area and the one wielding the greatest early influence. The other company, the GREAT WESTERN (GW), had obtained its Act in 1835, but its early influence affecting the area was off-stage.

27.7.1846 SHREWSBURY + CHESTER (SC) formed, an amalgamation of the NWM and SOCJ. There appears to be some doubt about the date as alternative dates quoted include 27.6.1846 and 28.8.1846. The confusion is due to the fact that parliamentary sanction and effective dates were often different. The date shown in this chronology is the date of the ACT.

3.8.1846 SHREWSBURY + BIRMINGHAM (SB) – ACT

3.8.1846 SHREWSBURY + HEREFORD (SH) – ACT

3.8.1846 SHROPSHIRE UNION RAILWAY + CANAL (SUC) ACT. This was an amalgamation of canals authorised to build a line from SHREWSBURY to Stafford. Between Shrewsbury and Wellington the line would be a joint one built in conjunction with the SB (see above).

2.7.1847 SUC is leased to LNW effectively becoming part of that railway.

16.10.1848 SC opened between SHREWSBURY and Ruabon (ie the SOCJ portion of the line). Within the map area there were intermediate stations at BASCHURCH and LEATON and a temporary station at SHREWSBURY just north of the later joint station. Early maps also show OLD WOODS WHARF but the opening date of this is unclear although it appears certain it was open by 1850.

1.6.1849 LNW opened the SUC line from SHREWSBURY, and an end-on junction with the SC, to Stafford. The line between SHREWSBURY and WELLINGTON was joint with the SB. Intermediate stations at: UPTON MAGNA, WALCOT and at ADMASTON (early records show this station as ADMASTON SPA). On the solely LNW portion of the line there were stations at: HADLEY, TRENCH CROSSING and DONNINGTON.
At the same date the SB opened to OAKENGATES. Official records of the GW also show that on the same date Madeley Junction to Lightmoor opened. However, it would appear that this was the take-over by the GW of an existing private tramway which was not upgraded until 1854. RCH maps also show HOLLINGWOOD west of OAKENGATES, but this appears an error, but indicates the line was in use for goods to beyond the position of MADELEY JUNCTION by this date and used for exchange of tramway traffic. The line opened for passenger traffic to Wolverhampton on 12th November 1849.

1851-1860

20.4.1852 SH opened SHREWSBURY to Ludlow. Intermediate stations: CONDOVER, DORRINGTON and LEEBOTWOOD.

20.8.1853 WELLINGTON + SEVERN JUNCTION (WSJ) incorporated.

20.8.1853 SHREWSBURY + CREWE (LNW) line authorised.

20.8.1853 SEVERN VALLEY (SV) authorised

1.6.1854 SB Madeley Junction to Coalbrookdale opened; intermediate stations at MADELEY and LIGHTMOOR JUNCTION. LIGHTMOOR to COALBROOKDALE was actually opened by GW in November after absorption of SB by GW.

1.9.1854 SB vested in GW from this date by an ACT dated 7.8.1854.

29.7.1856 SHREWSBURY + WELSHPOOL – ACT.

1.5.1857 WSJ opened Ketley Junction to Lightmoor Junction. Intermediate stations: KETLEY, LAWLEY BANK and HORSEHAY

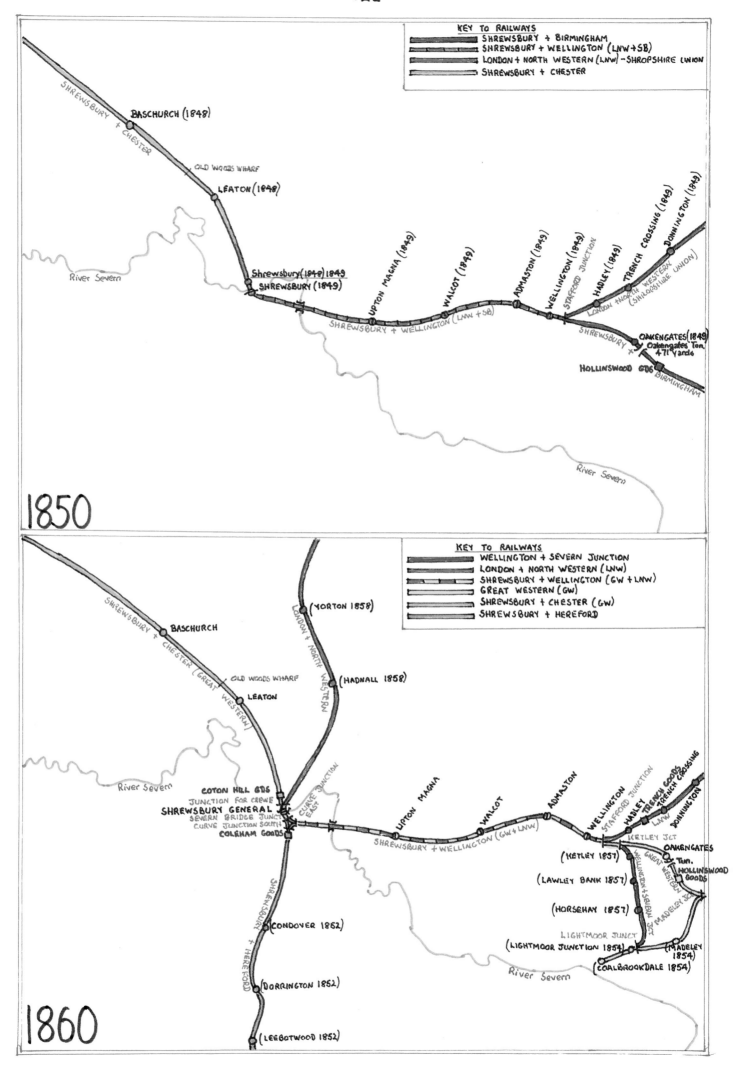

KEY TO RAILWAYS
- SHREWSBURY + BIRMINGHAM
- SHREWSBURY + WELLINGTON (LNW+SB)
- LONDON + NORTH WESTERN (LNW) - SHROPSHIRE UNION
- SHREWSBURY + CHESTER

BASCHURCH (1848)

OLD WOODS WHARF

LEATON (1848)

SHREWSBURY + CHESTER

River Severn

Shrewsbury (1848) 1849
SHREWSBURY (1849)

UPTON MAGNA (1849)

WALCOT (1849)

SHREWSBURY + WELLINGTON (LNW + SB)

ADMASTON (1849)

WELLINGTON (1849)

STAFFORD JUNCTION

HADLEY (1849)

TRENCH CROSSING (1849)

DONNINGTON (1849)

LONDON + NORTH WESTERN (SHROPSHIRE UNION)

SHREWSBURY +

OAKENGATES (1849)
Oakengates Tun.
471 Yards

HOLLINSWOOD GDS

BIRMINGHAM

River Severn

1850

KEY TO RAILWAYS
- WELLINGTON + SEVERN JUNCTION
- LONDON + NORTH WESTERN (LNW)
- SHREWSBURY + WELLINGTON (GW + LNW)
- GREAT WESTERN (GW)
- SHREWSBURY + CHESTER (GW)
- SHREWSBURY + HEREFORD

SHREWSBURY + CHESTER (GREAT WESTERN)

BASCHURCH

OLD WOODS WHARF

LEATON

(YORTON 1858)

LONDON + NORTH WESTERN

(HADNALL 1858)

River Severn

COTON HILL GDS
JUNCTION FOR CREWE
SHREWSBURY GENERAL
SEVERN BRIDGE JUNCT
CURVE JUNCTION SOUTH
COLEHAM GOODS

CURVE JUNCTION EAST

UPTON MAGNA

WALCOT

ADMASTON

WELLINGTON

STAFFORD JUNCTION

HADLEY

TRENCH GOODS
TRENCH CROSSING

SHREWSBURY + WELLINGTON (GW + LNW)

KETLEY JCT

LNW

DONNINGTON

(KETLEY 1857)

WELLINGTON + SEVERN JCT

GREAT WESTERN

OAKENGATES
Tun.
HOLLINSWOOD
GOODS

(LAWLEY BANK 1857)

(HORSEHAY 1857)

MADELEY JCT

LIGHTMOOR JUNCT

(LIGHTMOOR JUNCTION 1854)

(MADELEY 1854)

(COALBROOKDALE 1854)

SHREWSBURY + HEREFORD

(CONDOVER 1852)

River Severn

(DORRINGTON 1852)

1860

(LEEBOTWOOD 1852)

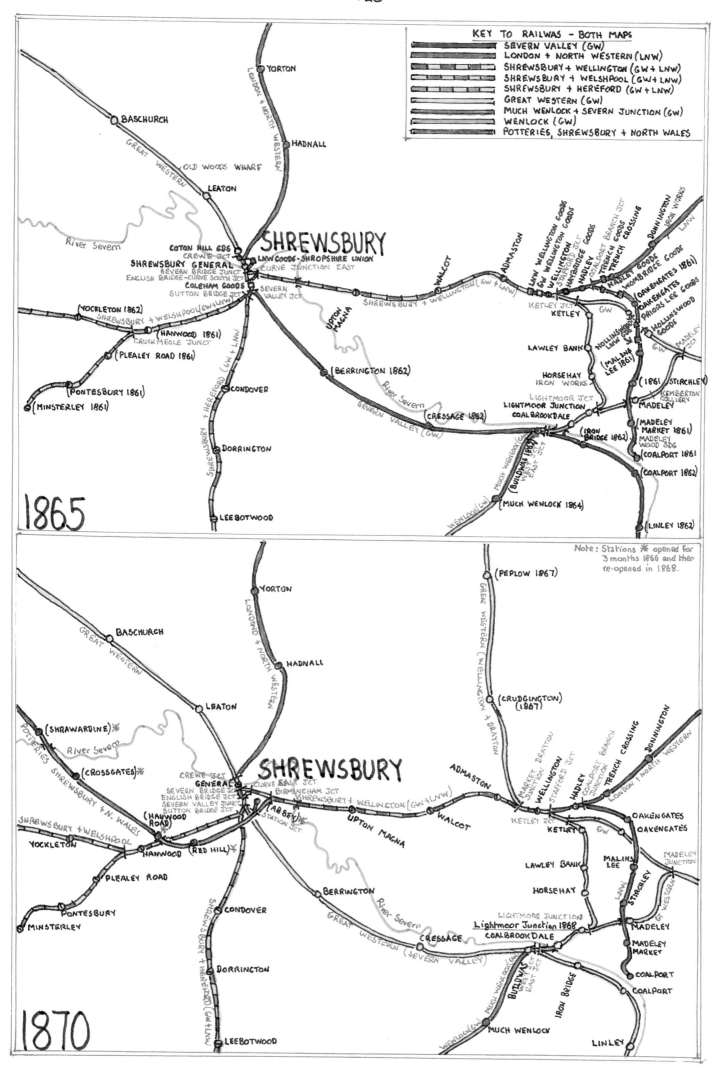

KEY TO RAILWAYS - BOTH MAPS
SEVERN VALLEY (GW)
LONDON + NORTH WESTERN (LNW)
SHREWSBURY + WELLINGTON (GW + LNW)
SHREWSBURY + WELSHPOOL (GW + LNW)
SHREWSBURY + HEREFORD (GW + LNW)
GREAT WESTERN (GW)
MUCH WENLOCK + SEVERN JUNCTION (GW)
WENLOCK (GW)
POTTERIES, SHREWSBURY + NORTH WALES

1865

Note: Stations ✳ opened for
3 months 1866 and then
re-opened in 1868.

1870

Some authorities suggest that the Horsehay to Lightmoor section did not open until the following year. This date maybe when this portion of line (previously a tramway) was authorised for passenger traffic, but it is clear that the whole line was opened for goods traffic from May 1857. Shortly afterwards the GREAT WESTERN (GW), who worked the railway from the outset, began a WELLINGTON → LIGHTMOOR (where the trains reversed) - Shifnal passenger train service.

14. 6.1860 WEST MIDLAND (WM) - Act. Although this company did not penetrate the area, it became a joint lessor of the WELLINGTON + SEVERN JUNCTION (WSJ) together with the GW in 1861, and leased other lines in the area.

2. 11. 1860 SEVERN VALLEY (SV) leased to WM.

1861 - 1865

14. 4.1861 SHREWSBURY + WELSHPOOL (SWpl) opened from Sutton Bridge Junction on the SHREWSBURY + HEREFORD (SH) to MINSTERLEY with intermediate stations at HANWOOD and PONTESBURY, with an additional station opened at PLEALEY ROAD later in the year. Here again there is a conflict of opinion on the actual opening date. This may have been due to the Inspecting Officer's report, which passed the railway but not for passengers until the SH was doubled (with which it connected at Sutton Bridge). However, SH had been doubled and passed, so the SWpl, in technical breach, commenced a passenger service without written consent (not received until a year later).

17. 6.1861 LONDON + NORTH WESTERN (LNW) open branch from HADLEY to COALPORT. Intermediate stations at OAKENGATES, MALINS LEE, MADELEY MARKET and Goods stations at Haybridge, Wombridge, Priors Lee (serving the Iron Works) and at HOLLINSWOOD (close to the GW Goods station).

22. 7. 1861 WENLOCK - Act.

1. 8.1861 WSJ leased jointly to GW + WM.

27. 1. 1862 SWpl opened from SHREWSBURY (Cruckmeole Jct) to Buttington Junction. There was one intermediate station within the map area - at YOCKLETON.

1. 2. 1862 SV (WM) opened from SHREWSBURY (Severn Valley Jct) to Hartlebury. Intermediate map area stations opened at: BERRINGTON, CRESSAGE, BUILDWAS, IRON BRIDGE, COALPORT (opposite side of river to LNW station) and LINLEY.

1. 2. 1862 MUCH WENLOCK + SEVERN JUNCTION (MWSJ) (Authorised 21.7.1859) - Opened BUILDWAS to MUCH WENLOCK.

1. 7.1862 SHREWSBURY + HEREFORD leased to GW, LNW and WM. Date of Act 29.7.1862.

29. 7.1862 WEST SHROPSHIRE MINERAL - Act. The first step towards what would become the 'Potts Line'.

7. 8.1862 WELLINGTON + DRAYTON (WD) - Authorised.

1. 8 1863 WEST MIDLAND absorbed by GW.

14. 7.1864 SWpl purchased by LNW.

1. 10.1864 WENLOCK opened between COALBROOKDALE + BUILDWAS worked by GW together with MWSJ but not absorbed until 1896.

1. 11.1864 GW COALBROOKDALE used for through services. The 1854 opening shown may have been goods only.

5. 12.1864 WENLOCK opened from MUCH WENLOCK to PRESTHOPE. Opened onwards to Marsh Farm Jct in 1867. Worked by GW.

5. 7.1865 SWpl vested jointly in GW and LNW.

1866 - 1870

16. 7.1866 West Shropshire Minerals together with other schemes were combined into a new railway: POTTERIES, SHREWSBURY + NORTH WALES authorised to link the points of its title (PSNW).

30. 7.1866 WD absorbed by GW.

13. 8.1866 PSNW opened from SHREWSBURY (ABBEY) to Llanymynech. Intermediate map area stations at RED HILL, HANWOOD ROAD, CROSSGATES and SHRAWARDINE. Also link from ABBEY to Shrewsbury + Wellington line.

12. 12.1866 PSNW closed after under four month's operations! (Due to financial pressures.)

1. 11.1867 WD (GW) opened from WELLINGTON (Market Drayton Junction) to Market Drayton. Intermediate map area stations at PEPLOW and CRUDGINGTON.

1. 12.1868 PSNW re-opened.

4. 7.1870 SHREWSBURY + HEREFORD vested in GW and LNW.

With the end of this period the railway net-work reached its maximum, and during the subsequent eighty years there was very little change. The PSNW would close and re-open and the SNAILBEACH 2'3¾" narrow gauge line would open and have its ups and downs, but these would be the network's only changes. There were of course some further station openings (mainly in the 1930's). Also by this date all area railways except the PSNW were in the hands of the GW or the LNW or these two companies jointly. Grouping also had no effect since all that happened was that the LNW became LMS.

Finally it should be noted that the 1870 map and some subsequent maps do not show goods stations. There were no goods-only lines within the area as at the map date.

1871-1885

5. 8.1873 SNAILBEACH DISTRICT RAILWAYS (SDR) Incorporated to build a narrow gauge line, 2'3¾" from Pontesbury on the SHREWSBURY + WELSHPOOL (SWpl), where exchange sidings were laid in, to SNAILBEACH. Additional lines were also planned but none of them materialised.

31.12.1877 SDR opened throughout by this date. The exact date is not recorded. It served besides the Snailbeach Mine, a further mine known as Crownest, and a short spur midway along its length served a smelting works.

22. 6.1880 POTTERIES SHREWSBURY + NORTH WALES (PSNW) again closed due to financial difficulties and because lack of maintenance made the line unsafe for passenger traffic. Track etc remained in situ in the hope of some rescue package materialising.

1886-1915

7. 8.1888 SHROPSHIRE RAILWAYS COMPANY incorporated to acquire PSNW from the Official Receiver. But no cash could be raised to enable it to be re-opened.

1. 7.1892 WELLINGTON + SEVERN JUNCTION, which had been leased to GREAT WESTERN (GW) and WEST MIDLAND, now became fully vested in the GW.

1. 7.1896 WENLOCK vested in GW.

24. 2.1908 GW open goods branch from Hollinswood to Stirchley.

11. 2.1909 Light Railway Order granted to take over SHROPSHIRE (ex PSNW).

13. 4.1911 SHROPSHIRE re-opened, now known as SHROPSHIRE + MONTGOMERYSHIRE (Light). Previous stations were re-opened with some name changes and with additional stopping places. Within the map area the stations were: ABBEY (terminus), SHREWSBURY WEST (new), MEOLE BRACE (new - and the following year a connection with the SWpl was added in place of the old Birmingham Junction connection with the SW), RED HILL, CRUCKTON (new), FORD + CROSSGATES (previously known as Crossgates) and SHRAWARDINE. HANWOOD ROAD was also re-opened.

22. 3.1915 Shifnal to Lightmoor closed as a war-time economy measure. Madeley station closed.

One or two other matters remain to be recorded to complete the story to this point. LIGHTMOOR JUNCTION had closed to passengers in the 1860's; it was re-opened as LIGHTMOOR PLATFORM in 1907. Abbey Foregate closed to passengers in 1912 but its importance increased as a goods station (it had opened to passengers about 1890; the precise date has not been ascertained).

A NOTE ABOUT DATES OF EVENTS

In preparing a chronology of events it is often difficult to establish dates, as even where references are available opening dates quoted from several reliable sources can be in conflict. Some of the difficulties were touched upon in the Author's Introduction with particular reference to Railway Clearing House maps, but as work on this volume has progressed the errors noted on RCH maps have mounted steadily. For example a RCH map of England + Wales dated 1940 obtained as a prime source document for stations open at all centres as at that date has been found to be full of mistakes. In the Manchester area alone over twenty errors were noted including several stations included on the map which closed before the end of World War I. Other maps often omit both lines and stations opened in the two or three years before the map date.

Dates of line openings have also involved substantial difficulty because opening of the line can have at least four different meanings, and unless the type of opening is specified one can find different dates quoted for opening by various authorities, where each is correctly quoting a different type of opening. At SHREWSBURY this has caused particular difficulty and some of these instances have been mentioned in the chronology.

Once a railway had been constructed, it had, before it could run a public passenger service, to be inspected by the Railway Inspectorate. It was not always passed at this inspection, although it could be passed subject to the Railway confirming certain matters had been attended to. Sometimes a further inspection was needed. Sometimes the Railway may have considered that on fulfilment of contingencies a public service could commence, but this may have needed confirmation by the Inspecting Officer and thus in spite of a public service it could not be said to be officially open until proper consent was received. Then there were Official openings where shareholders were feted and speeches made, but this type of opening could take place before inspection, which might prohibit the later commenced advertisement giving notice of opening to public passenger services. Even with regard to opening to public services, goods and passenger openings could in fact be at widely differing dates. Even in looking at public opening to passenger services there could be a difference between the advertised date,

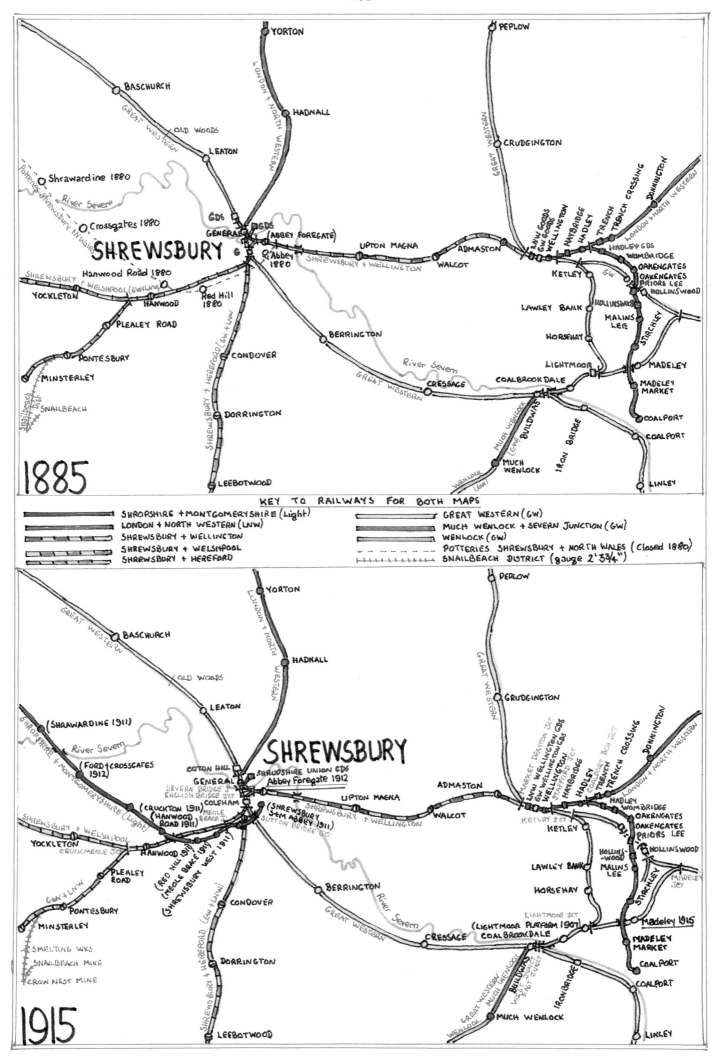

1885

PEPLOW
YORTON
BASCHURCH
GREAT WESTERN
OLD WOODS
HADNALL
LEATON
LONDON + NORTH WESTERN
Shrawardine 1880
River Severn
Potteries Shrewsbury & NW
Crossgates 1880
GDS
GENERAL
(GDS
SHREWSBURY
(ABBEY FOREGATE)
Q'Abbey 1880
UPTON MAGNA
ADMASTON
SHREWSBURY + WELLINGTON
WALCOT
Hanwood Road 1880
Red Hill 1880
YOCKLETON
HANWOOD
SHREWSBURY + WELSHPOOL (GWHLNW)
PLEALEY ROAD
PONTESBURY
BERRINGTON
River Severn
CONDOVER
GREAT WESTERN
CRESSAGE
SHREWSBURY + HEREFORD (GW + LNW)
MINSTERLEY
SNAILBEACH
Snailbeach Dist
DORRINGTON
COALBROOKDALE
LEEBOTWOOD
MUCH WENLOCK
WENLOCK (GW)
BUILDWAS
IRON BRIDGE
MUCH WENLOCK (GW)
CRUDGINGTON
TRENCH CROSSING
DONNINGTON
LONDON + NORTH WESTERN
LNW GOODS
GW GOODS
WELLINGTON
HADLEY
TRENCH
HADLEY GDS
WOMBRIDGE
KETLEY
OAKENGATES
OAKENGATES PRIORS LEE
GW
HOLLINSWOOD
HOLLINSWOOD
LAWLEY BANK
MALINS LEE
STIRCHLEY
HORSEHAY
MADELEY
LIGHTMOOR
MADELEY MARKET
COALPORT
COALPORT
LINLEY
GREAT WESTERN

KEY TO RAILWAYS FOR BOTH MAPS

SHROPSHIRE + MONTGOMERYSHIRE (Light)
LONDON + NORTH WESTERN (LNW)
SHREWSBURY + WELLINGTON
SHREWSBURY + WELSHPOOL
SHREWSBURY + HEREFORD

GREAT WESTERN (GW)
MUCH WENLOCK + SEVERN JUNCTION (GW)
WENLOCK (GW)
POTTERIES SHREWSBURY + NORTH WALES (Closed 1880)
SNAILBEACH DISTRICT (gauge 2' 3¾")

1915

PEPLOW
YORTON
GREAT WESTERN
BASCHURCH
OLD WOODS
LONDON + NORTH WESTERN
HADNALL
LEATON
(SHRAWARDINE 1911)
SHROPSHIRE + MONTGOMERYSHIRE (Light)
River Severn
(FORD + CROSSGATES 1912)
COTON HILL
SHROPSHIRE UNION GDS
SHREWSBURY
GENERAL
Abbey Foregate 1912
SEVERN BRIDGE + ENGLISH BRIDGE JCT
(CRUCKTON 1911)
(HANWOOD ROAD 1911)
COLEHAM
MEOLE BRACE JCT
(SHREWSBURY ABBEY 1911)
SUTTON BRIDGE JCT
SUTTON BRIDGE JG
UPTON MAGNA
ADMASTON
SHREWSBURY + WELLINGTON
WALCOT
MARKET DRAYTON JCT
LNW WELLINGTON GDS
GW WELLINGTON GDS
STAFFORD JCT
HADLEY
COALPORT BCH JCT
TRENCH CROSSING
DONNINGTON
LONDON + NORTH WESTERN
HADLEY
WOMBRIDGE
OAKENGATES
OAKENGATES PRIORS LEE
YOCKLETON
SHREWSBURY + WELSHPOOL
CRUCK MEOLE JCT
HANWOOD
(RED HILL 1911)
(MEOLE BRACE 1911)
(SHREWSBURY WEST 1911)
PLEALEY ROAD
GW + LNW
GW + LNW
KETLEY JCT
KETLEY
HNBRIDGE
HOLLINS-WOOD
HOLLINSWOOD
LAWLEY BANK
MALINS LEE
MADELEY JCT
STIRCHLEY
PONTESBURY
SHREWSBURY + HEREFORD (GW + LNW)
CONDOVER
BERRINGTON
River Severn
GREAT WESTERN
HORSEHAY
MINSTERLEY
SMELTING WKS
SNAILBEACH MINE
CROW NEST MINE
DORRINGTON
CRESSAGE
(LIGHTMOOR PLATFORM 1907)
LIGHTMOOR JCT
COALBROOKDALE
MADELEY 1915
MADELEY MARKET
COALPORT
COALPORT
LEEBOTWOOD
GREAT WESTERN MUCH WENLOCK
WENLOCK WEST JUNCT
BUILDWAS WEST JUNCT
BUILDWAS EAST JUNCT
IRONBRIDGE
MUCH WENLOCK
LINLEY

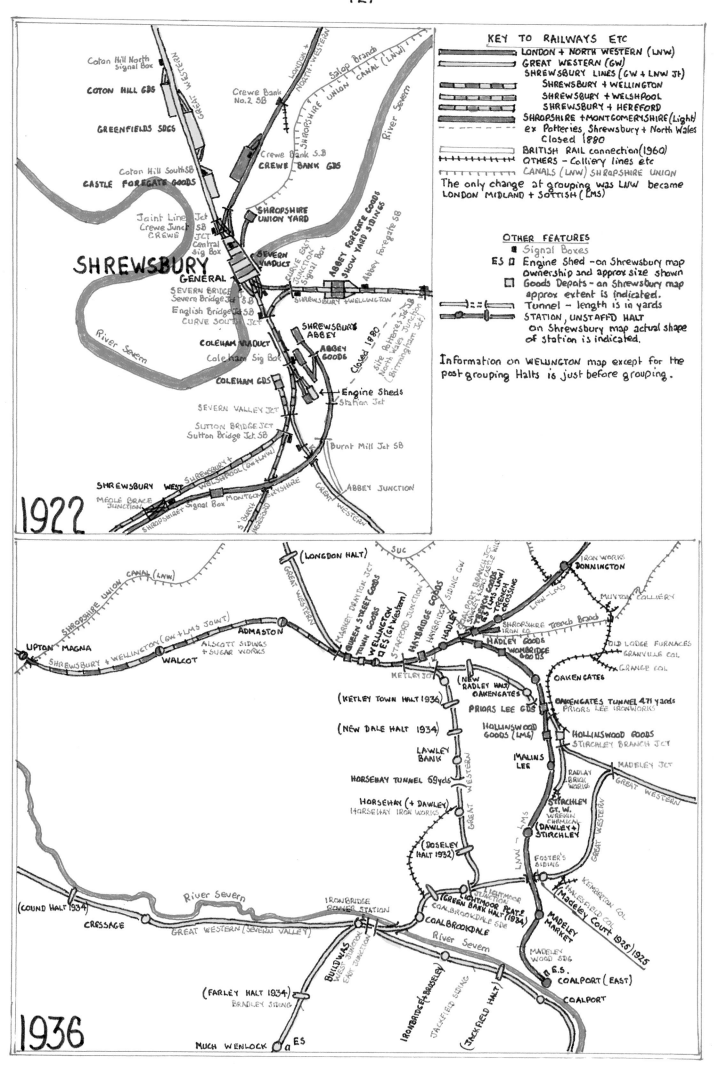

KEY TO RAILWAYS ETC
LONDON + NORTH WESTERN (LNW)
GREAT WESTERN (GW)
SHREWSBURY LINES (GW + LNW Jt)
  SHREWSBURY + WELLINGTON
  SHREWSBURY + WELSHPOOL
  SHREWSBURY + HEREFORD
SHROPSHIRE + MONTGOMERYSHIRE (Light)
ex Potteries Shrewsbury + North Wales
  Closed 1880
BRITISH RAIL connection (1960)
OTHERS - Colliery lines etc
CANALS (LNW) Shropshire Union
The only change at grouping was LNW became
LONDON MIDLAND + SCOTTISH (LMS)

OTHER FEATURES
■ Signal Boxes
ES ☐ Engine Shed —on Shrewsbury map
         Ownership and approx size shown
    ☐ Goods Depots —on Shrewsbury map
         approx extent is indicated.
         Tunnel – length is in yards
         STATION, UNSTAFF'D HALT
         on Shrewsbury map actual shape
         of station is indicated.

Information on WELLINGTON map except for the
post grouping Halts is just before grouping.

SHREWSBURY
GENERAL
1922

1936

the actual opening date and the date from which opening was sanctioned if this is subsequent to the actual opening date.

Closure dates for passenger services are usually somewhat easier thanks to Clinker's Register. However, goods closures are fraught with difficulty as services were often terminated years before official closure.

All these points need bearing in mind in studying the chronology of the various centres. Except where otherwise stated, both opening and closing dates are those which the author has considered to be the actual date of opening or closing for public advertised passenger services.

FAMILY TREE OF THE GREAT WESTERN IN SHREWSBURY DISTRICT

ACT shows year of authorisation. OPEN - first section opened or all opened; later openings mentioned only if substantial and at a much later date. Openings by GW itself are excluded except with independant concerns opened after absorption. Dotted line shows leased, solid line absorption.

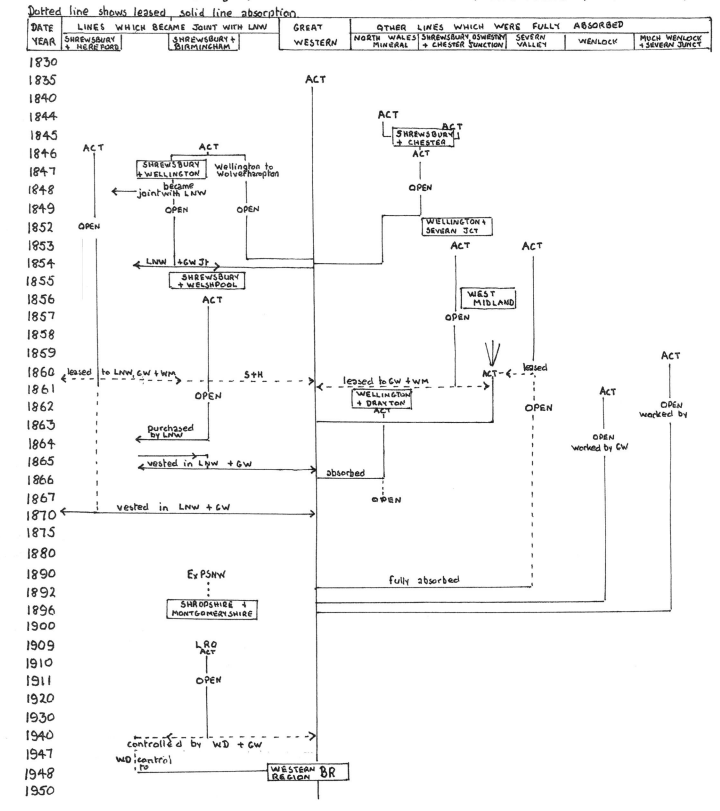

ENGINE SHEDS

Details of the Engine Sheds of the area are given in tabular form below:

NAME / LOCATION	OWNER- SHIP	OPENED	CLOSED	NOTES
SHREWSBURY (SALOP)	LNW	1852	1967	Shrewsbury + Hereford origins, joint GW + LNW shed built in 1855. This was soon split and became two adjoining sheds. Known also as COLEHAM and as SALOP.
SHREWSBURY	GW	1852	1967	See notes above re origins. GW shed always known as SHREWSBURY.
SHREWSBURY - ABBEY	PSNW	1866	1880	Potteries Shrewsbury + North Wales - close to goods station. Closed with the railway. When railway re-opened as SHROPSHIRE + MONTGOMERY shed at Kinnerley.
COALPORT	LNW	1861	1952	Opened and closed at the same time as the branch passenger services.
TRENCH	LNW	unclear	1943	Sub-shed to Shrewsbury. Also known as Trench Crossing.
WELLINGTON	GW	1849	1964	Possibly Shrewsbury + Birmingham origins if opening date correct. If so new shed opened 1876.
MUCH WENLOCK	GW	1862	1951	One authority quotes the shed to be of West Midland origins. But this is an error. Probably built by GW who worked lines from Much Wenlock from their opening.

1915-1940

During this period some of the opening dates of GREAT WESTERN Halts are unclear, therefore events are recorded under company headings.

LONDON + NORTH WESTERN. The only change so far as the LNW was concerned was at the grouping when the LNW became one of the major constituents of the LONDON MIDLAND + SCOTTISH.

SNAILBEACH DISTRICT. This line struggled throughout the period, being semi-derelict for part of the time, its fortunes depending on the industries it served. In addition it suffered increasing competition from local road haulage operators.

SHROPSHIRE + MONTGOMERYSHIRE (Light). In spite of opening an additional halt at Shoot Hill, passenger traffic steadily declined in the post-war period and passenger services were withdrawn in 1933 although the line remained open for goods. World War II brought the line its heaviest useage, the line being worked, from 1940, by the WAR DEPARTMENT and the GREAT WESTERN jointly.

GREAT WESTERN - The GW alone of the grouping companies sought, on a large scale, to counter the effects of road competition by opening unstaffed halts which could produce additional revenue whilst at the same time not incurring any additional staff costs. In 1925 the Madeley branch, which had closed to passengers as a war-time economy measure, was re-opened to passengers together with MADELEY station now known as MADELEY COURT. However, passenger traffic lasted only three months but the line remained in use for goods and is in fact still in use for that purpose (1990). Other halts opened in the 1930's (with dates where known) were at: ELLERDINE (1930), ROWTON and LONGDON on the Drayton line; NEW HADLEY on the Birmingham line; COUND (1934) on the Severn Valley line; FARLEY (1934) and WESTWOOD (1935) on the Much Wenlock line; KETLEY TOWN (1936), NEW DALE (1934), DOSELEY (1932) and GREEN BANK on the Wellington to Lightmoor line; and STANWARDINE and OLD WOODS on the Chester line. Thus during the period, and in spite of closure of the SHROPSHIRE + MONTGOMERYSHIRE to passengers, the number of area passenger stations increased.

1941-1963

Although Shrewsbury retained its network of lines virtually intact into the early 1960's, its comparative isolation meant that local services and branch lines could not compete with road traffic, thus 90% of the area's stations closed during this period. Once branch line passenger services were withdrawn the inevitable complete closure of all but through routes would follow. This is indicated in the chronology that follows (goods station closures are not normally included unless a precise closure date has been confirmed):

1946 SNAILBEACH closed except for a short spur worked by Shropshire County Council with a tractor

1951 WESTWOOD HALT closed.

1951 PLEALEY ROAD, PONTESBURY and MINSTERLEY closed with closure of branch to passengers. Goods service retained.

1952 OAKENGATES (Market Street), MALINS LEE, DAWLEY + STIRCHLEY, MADELEY MARKET and COALPORT (East) with withdrawal of branch passenger service. Progressive closure to goods followed and by the map date Stirchley to the terminus was closed completely with the remainder scheduled for early closure.

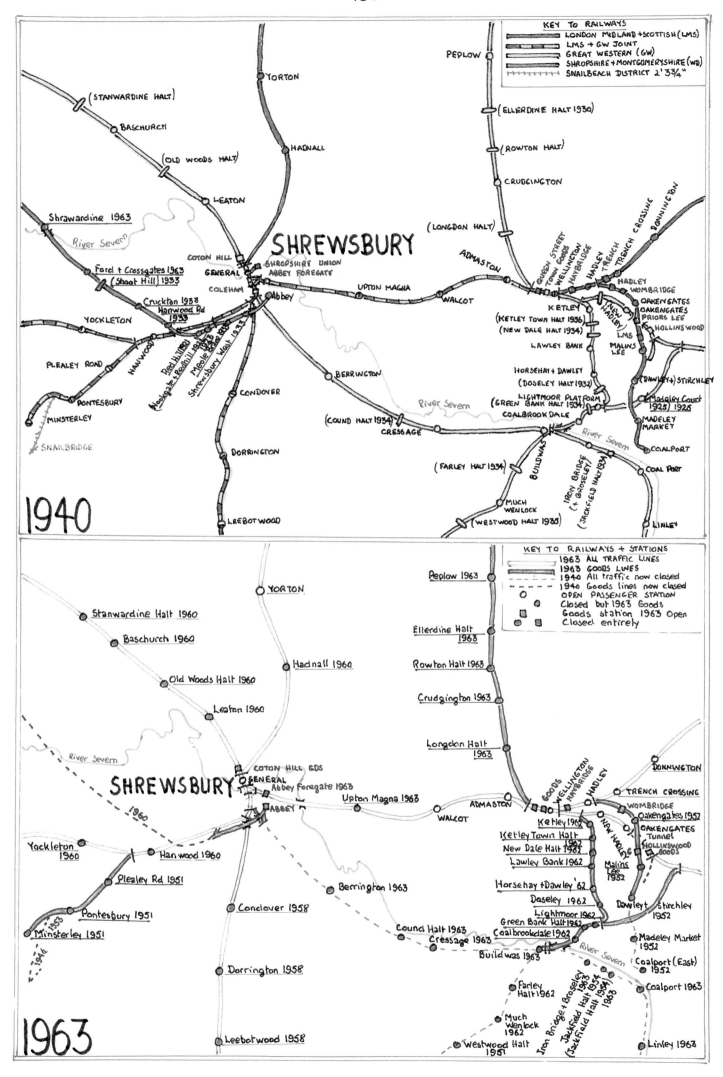

KEY TO RAILWAYS
LONDON MIDLAND + SCOTTISH (LMS)
LMS + GW JOINT
GREAT WESTERN (GW)
SHROPSHIRE + MONTGOMERYSHIRE (WD)
SNAILBEACH DISTRICT 2'3¾"

1940

PEPLOW
(ELLERDINE HALT 1930)
(ROWTON HALT)
CRUDGINGTON
(LONGDON HALT)
ADMASTON
QUEEN STREET
TOWN GOODS
WELLINGTON
HAYBRIDGE
HADLEY
TRENCH
TRENCH CROSSING
DONNINGTON
KETLEY
(NEW HADLEY)
(KETLEY TOWN HALT 1936)
(NEW DALE HALT 1934)
LMS
HADLEY
WOMBRIDGE
OAKENGATES
OAKENGATES
PRIORS LEE
HOLLINSWOOD
LAWLEY BANK
MALINS LEE
HORSEHAY + DAWLEY
(DOSELEY HALT 1932)
(DAWLEY +) STIRCHLEY
LIGHTMOOR PLATFORM
(GREEN BANK HALT 1934)
COALBROOKDALE
(MADELEY COURT 1925) 1925
MADELEY MARKET
River Severn
COALPORT
COAL PORT
BUILDWAS
(FARLEY HALT 1934)
IRON BRIDGE
(+ BROSELEY)
(JACKFIELD HALT 1934)
MUCH WENLOCK
(WESTWOOD HALT 1935)
LINLEY

YORTON
(STANWARDINE HALT)
BASCHURCH
(OLD WOODS HALT)
HADNALL
LEATON
Shrawardine 1963
River Severn
Ford + Crossgates 1963
(Shoot Hill) 1933
COTON HILL
GENERAL
SHROPSHIRE UNION
ABBEY FOREGATE
SHREWSBURY
COLEHAM
Abbey
UPTON MAGNA
WALCOT
Cruckton 1938
Hanwood Rd 1933
YOCKLETON
HANWOOD
Red Hill(s)
Meole Brace 1931
Noobyth + Redhill 1935
Shrewsbury West 1932
BERRINGTON
PLEALEY ROAD
PONTESBURY
CONDOVER
(COUND HALT 1934)
CRESSAGE
MINSTERLEY
SNAILBRIDGE
DORRINGTON
LEEBOTWOOD

KEY TO RAILWAYS + STATIONS
1963 ALL TRAFFIC LINES
1963 GOODS LINES
1940 All traffic now closed
1940 Goods lines now closed
OPEN PASSENGER STATION
Closed but 1963 Goods
Goods station 1963 Open
Closed entirely

1963

Peplow 1963
Ellerdine Halt 1963
Rowton Halt 1963
Crudgington 1963
Longdon Halt 1963
DONNINGTON
WELLINGTON
HAYBRIDGE
HADLEY
TRENCH CROSSING
ADMASTON
GOODS
WOMBRIDGE
WALCOT
Ketley 1962
New Hadley
Oakengates 1952
OAKENGATES Tunnel
Ketley Town Halt 1962
New Dale Halt 1962
Lawley Bank 1962
HOLLINSWOOD GOODS
Malins Lee 1952
Horsehay + Dawley '62
Doseley 1962
Dawley + Stirchley 1952
Lightmoor 1962
Green Bank Halt 1962
Coalbrookdale 1962
Madeley Market 1952
Coalport (East) 1952
Coalport 1963
Buildwas 1963
River Severn
Farley Halt 1962
Iron Bridge + Broseley 1963
Jackfield Halt 1954 1963
Much Wenlock 1962
Westwood Halt 1951
Linley 1963

YORTON
Stanwardine Halt 1960
Baschurch 1960
Old Woods Halt 1960
Hadnall 1960
Leaton 1960
River Severn
1960
Coton Hill GDS
GENERAL
Abbey Foregate 1963
SHREWSBURY
Abbey
Upton Magna 1963
Yockleton 1960
Hanwood 1960
Plealey Rd 1951
Pontesbury 1951
Minsterley 1951
1960
Condover 1958
Berrington 1963
Cound Halt 1963
Cressage 1963
Dorrington 1958
Leebotwood 1958

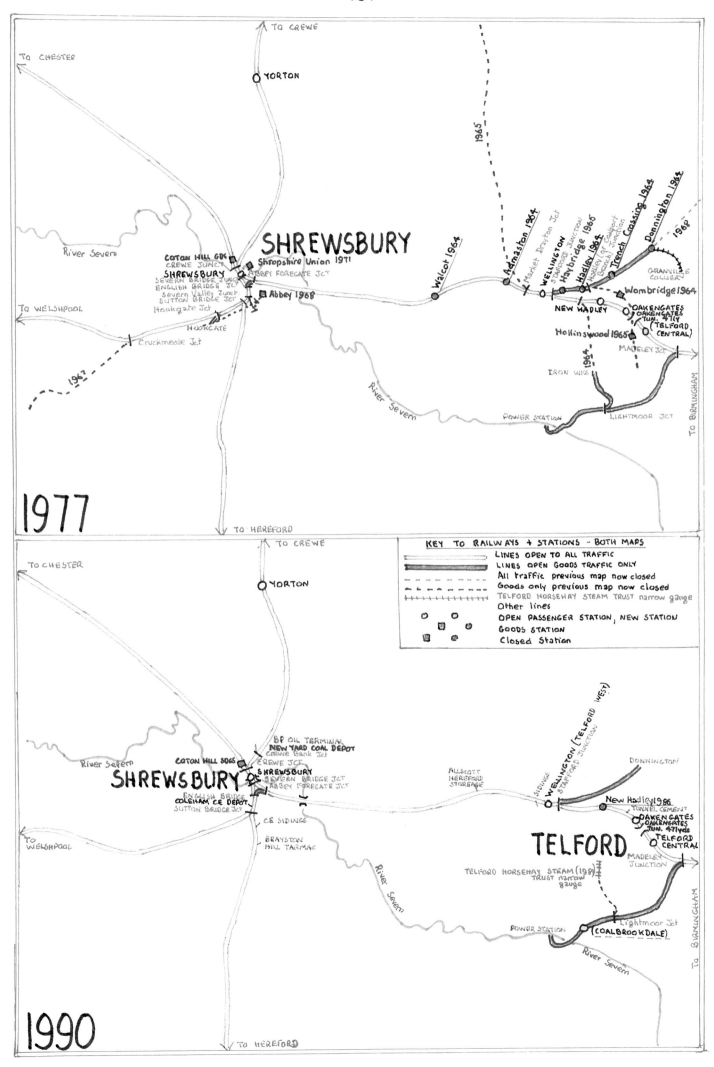

1977

1990

KEY TO RAILWAYS + STATIONS - BOTH MAPS

LINES OPEN TO ALL TRAFFIC
LINES OPEN GOODS TRAFFIC ONLY
All traffic previous map now closed
Goods only previous map now closed
TELFORD HORSEHAY STEAM TRUST narrow gauge
Other lines
OPEN PASSENGER STATION, NEW STATION
GOODS STATION
Closed Station

1953 SNAILBEACH Closed completely

1954 Jackfield Halt replaced by new halt nearby due to subsidence.

1958 Condover, Dorrington and Leebotwood closed.

1960 SHROPSHIRE + MONTGOMERYSHIRE - Closed completely except Abbey to Hookgate. New connection at SHREWSBURY so that Severn Valley goods trains could use Abbey Goods. Leaton, Oldwoods, Baschurch, Stanwardine, Hadnall, Yockleton, Hanwood, all closed.

1962 Coalbrookdale (ex GW), Green Bank, Doseley, Horsehay + Dawley, New Dale, Ketley Town, Ketley and Lightmoor all closed together with all passenger trains on Wellington to Buildwas line. Line retained for goods.

1963 Peplow, Ellerdine, Rowton, Crudgington, Longdon, Upton Magna, Berrington, Cound, Cressage, Buildwas, Iron Bridge + Broseley, Jackfield, Linley, and Coalport all closed. Passenger services withdrawn fully from Wellington - Drayton line with complete closure planned. Severn Valley line closed completely. One further closure actually implemented in late 1962 was the Much Wenlock line and the stations/halts at Farley and Much Wenlock. This line was closed completely.

With so much already gone BEECHING had little left to recommend. The proposals were:

1. Withdrawal of local service between SHREWSBURY and CREWE and the consequent closure of Yorton.

2. Withdrawal of local service between WELLINGTON and Stafford and closure of Tirench Crossing and Donnington

3. Withdrawal of local service between SHREWSBURY and WELLINGTON - but!! without closing the only two stations on the line, WALCOT and ADMASTON. One can only assume this had some connection with the proposed marshalling yard scheduled for WALCOT, although in the event this was not built.

4. Modification of the SHREWSBURY to Aberystwyth service.

None of these proposals affected the line network since in all cases through passenger traffic would continue.

1964 - 1977

Dealing first with the Beeching proposals: The SHREWSBURY to Crewe local service was retained, but the other two local services were withdrawn 1964 and the stations at Walcot, Admaston and Hadley were closed and the proposed closures of Trench Crossing and Donnington. The proposed modification of the Aberystwyth service had no effect on the line or station situation in the area. 1964 also saw complete closure of the exLNW Coalport branch and most of the ex GW Ketley to Lightmoor line, except a short spur to Horsehay serving an Iron Works. Wombridge Goods closed.

1965 saw complete closure of the WELLINGTON to Drayton line and the closure of goods stations at Haybridge and Hollinswood (ex GW); BR threaten to build new TELFORD station on the site.

1967 Minsterley branch closed completely.

1968 WELLINGTON to Stafford closed entirely although a short spur to Donnington was retained. Abbey Goods to Hookgate, the final remnant of the SHROPSHIRE + MONTGOMERYSHIRE, closed — effective closure could have been earlier since access to Hookgate was available from the Welshpool line.

1971 The final closure of the period was the Shropshire Union Goods thought to have been the original terminus for passenger traffic pending the opening of GENERAL Joint station.

It remains to record one solitary development of the period. TELFORD CENTRAL was opened to serve the rapidly expanding new town, on the site of the old goods station. However, it took BR ten years to implement their stated intentions and in the meantime the needs of TELFORD were restricted to Telford suffixes added to the stations at WELLINGTON and OAKENGATES.

1978 - 1990

During this period little has happened to disturb the railway scene. The Horsehay goods spur was closed, but a short stretch of line in the vicinity was re-opened as narrow gauge by TELFORD HORSEHAY STEAM TRUST in the early 1980's. Madeley Junction to Buildwas is still in use for coal traffic serving the power station. A small positive event has been the re-opening of COALBROOKDALE station but only as a non-advertised station - there is no regular service. New Hadley closed in 1986. Following the further expansion of TELFORD, WELLINGTON now has (TELFORD WEST) added to its title. The 1990 map shows all the above features and the various rail-served industries in the area.

1991 - FUTURE

There are plans to extend the TELFORD HORSEHAY STEAM TRUST narrow gauge line to the south as funds permit.

A SHREWSBURY SIGNALLING CENTRE is planned which will eliminate semaphore signals and result in the closure of many of the remaining signal boxes in the area.

The latest development from a leaked report in the press in January 1992 on the aspect of privatisation of the railways envisages both TELFORD and SHREWSBURY being withdrawn from the Inter-city network and this could put further lines in jeopardy, so the future looks somewhat insecure.

BIRMINGHAM

BIRMINGHAM, from the birth of railways, has been an important railway centre and that importance has been retained into the 1990's. In common with most centres, however, Birmingham had its own unique set of circumstances which decided the pattern of development.

In many areas, where mining and heavy industries had developed, this led to the need to improve the means of moving both raw materials and finished products. Canals were the earliest method of dealing with this problem, and in many railway centres one notes how often a canal network was in place before the railways and this network was often fed by tramways. Birmingham, however, was in a unique position in this respect being remote from the coast in all directions and lacking even the attribute of a navigable river. These special factors needed a special solution and led to the development of trunk canals linking Birmingham with London, Bristol, Mersey and Humber together with an intensive network of branch canals serving industrial needs. It was, moreover, a network which continued to expand even after the coming of the railways. The central network which came under control of the LONDON + NORTH WESTERN in the late 1840's provided increased local movement of raw materials and finished products From customer's premises built alongside the canals to railway wharves where they were transhipped for long-distance transportation. On the LONDON + NORTH WESTERN's BIRMINGHAM CANAL NAVIGATION, trade carried steadily increased throughout the 19th century rising to over 8·5 million tons per annum. Although a decline then set in, over a million tons was still carried each year into the early 1950's.

The canal network also had another influence on Birmingham's railway development in that most of its early trunk lines carried no local support, no doubt influenced by the excellence of the canal system which was serving local needs and providing good returns on local capital. Apart from this the canal system itself was improving and expanding with the construction of a new main line engineered by Telford to speed traffic to Wolverhampton by a shorter route and no doubt this obtained a first priority on available local funds.

The first map shows the canal network at its maximum development in the early 1860's. The main lines, however, were all in place before the end of the 18th century. In the key to the canals a distinction has been made to highlight those which became railway controlled.

One final comment on the railway development of Birmingham is of interest, although not of any consequence, that from a comparatively early date the city was served by just three railways - LONDON + NORTH WESTERN, MIDLAND and GREAT WESTERN. Was it a matter of coincidence that these were also, from early times, the three largest of the British Railway Companies?

1820-1840

During the 1820's three railway schemes were gestated with the objective of reaching Birmingham from Liverpool, Manchester and London. The first of these had the greedy concept of feeding into the Liverpool + Manchester at Warrington, making the Manchester project redundant, and this became the GRAND JUNCTION. But the other two also obtained parliamentary sanction and together they formed the constituents of the LONDON + NORTH WESTERN.

6. 5. 1833 GRAND JUNCTION authorised (GJ).

6. 5. 1833 LONDON + BIRMINGHAM (LB) authorised.

16. 6. 1834 GJ and LB junction between the two lines in Birmingham is authorised.

31. 8. 1835 GREAT WESTERN (GW) - Act. Would ultimately become one of three railways sharing the BIRMINGHAM traffic.

22. 4. 1836 BIRMINGHAM + GLOUCESTER (BG) - Act.

19. 5. 1836 BIRMINGHAM + DERBY JUNCTION (BDJ) authorised. The only early trunk line with local support.

30. 6. 1837 MANCHESTER + BIRMINGHAM (MB) authorised. This company line never reached the district in spite of its title, but as mentioned above it was the third company, which together with the GJ and LB would merge to form the LONDON + NORTH WESTERN.

4. 7. 1837 GJ opened to passengers from Warrington to a temporary terminus at Vauxhall. Line not opened for goods traffic until January 1838. Due to the absence of engineering features and the avoidance of large centres of population, the cost of construction was low and dividends paid were high.

9. 4. 1838 LB to BIRMINGHAM opened to a station at CURZON STREET adjoining the GJ station in course of being constructed. Was opened throughout to London 24·6·1838. GJ terminus opened.

5. 8. 1839 BDJ - Official opening Derby to HAMPTON to give route to London. Public traffic started one week later.

17. 9. 1840 BG opened from the South to Cofton.

17. 12. 1840 BG further opening to a temporary terminus at CAMP HILL with intermediate stations: LONGBRIDGE, LIFFORD and MOSELEY.

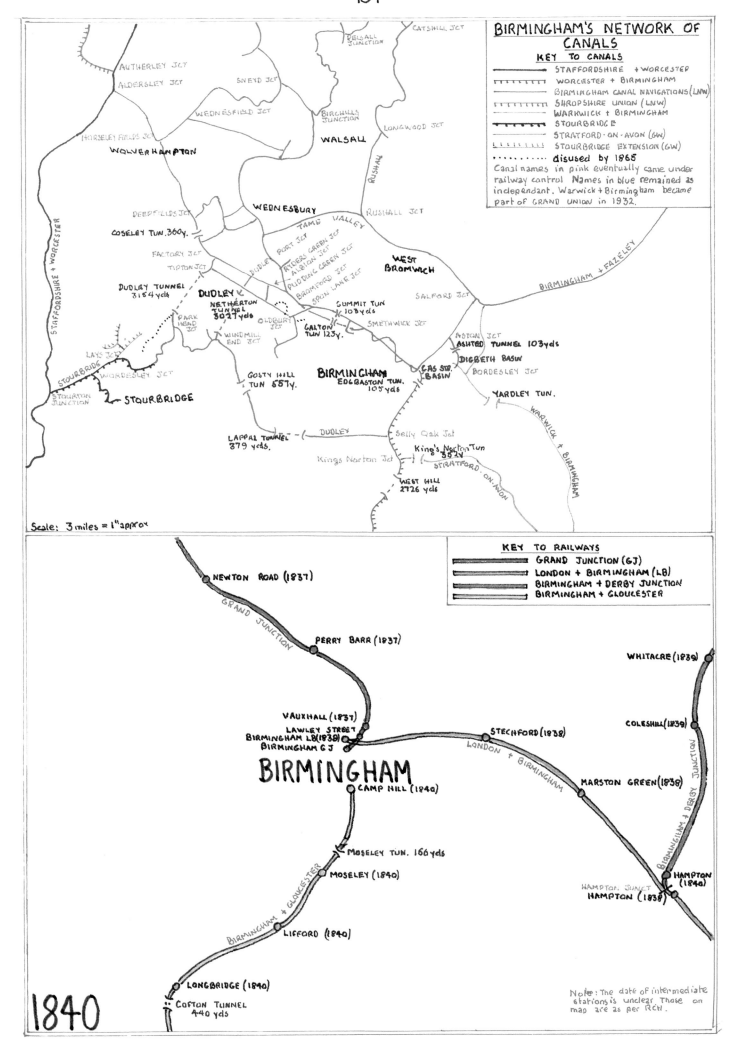

BIRMINGHAM'S NETWORK OF CANALS

KEY TO CANALS

- STAFFORDSHIRE + WORCESTER
- WORCESTER + BIRMINGHAM
- BIRMINGHAM CANAL NAVIGATIONS (LNW)
- SHROPSHIRE UNION (LNW)
- WARWICK + BIRMINGHAM
- STOURBRIDGE
- STRATFORD-ON-AVON (GW)
- STOURBRIDGE EXTENSION (GW)
- disused by 1865

Canal names in pink eventually came under railway control. Names in blue remained as independant. Warwick + Birmingham became part of GRAND UNION in 1932.

AUTHERLEY JCT
ALDERSLEY JCT
SNEYD JCT
CATSHILL JCT
PELSALL JUNCTION
WEDNESFIELD JCT
BIRCHILLS JUNCTION
HORSELEY FIELDS JCT
LONGWOOD JCT
WOLVERHAMPTON
WALSALL
RUSHALL
DEEPFIELDS JCT
WEDNESBURY
RUSHALL JCT
COSELEY TUN. 360y.
TAME VALLEY
FACTORY JCT
PORT JCT
RYDERS GREEN JCT
ALBION JCT
WEST BROMWICH
TIPTON JCT
DUDLEY
PUDDING GREEN JCT
BIRMINGHAM + FAZELEY
DUDLEY TUNNEL 3154 yds
BROMFORD JCT
SPON LANE JCT
SALFORD JCT
NETHERTON TUNNEL 3027 yds
SUMMIT TUN. 103 yds
OLDBURY JCT
PARK HEAD JCT
WINDMILL END JCT
GALTON TUN 123y.
SMETHWICK JCT
ASTON JCT
STAFFORDSHIRE + WORCESTER
ASHTED TUNNEL 103 yds
LAYS JCT
DIGBETH BASIN
WORDESLEY JCT
GOSTY HILL TUN 557y.
BIRMINGHAM
GAS ST. BASIN
BORDESLEY JCT
STOURBRIDGE
STOURTON JUNCTION
STOURBRIDGE
EDGBASTON TUN. 105 yds
YARDLEY TUN.
WARWICK + BIRMINGHAM
LAPPAL TUNNEL 379 yds.
DUDLEY
SELLY OAK JCT
KING'S NORTON TUN 552y
Kings Norton Jct
STRATFORD-ON-AVON
WEST HILL 2726 yds

Scale: 3 miles = 1" approx

KEY TO RAILWAYS

- GRAND JUNCTION (GJ)
- LONDON + BIRMINGHAM (LB)
- BIRMINGHAM + DERBY JUNCTION
- BIRMINGHAM + GLOUCESTER

NEWTON ROAD (1837)
GRAND JUNCTION
PERRY BARR (1837)
WHITACRE (1839)
VAUXHALL (1837)
LAWLEY STREET
BIRMINGHAM LB (1838)
STECHFORD (1838)
COLESHILL (1839)
BIRMINGHAM GJ
BIRMINGHAM
LONDON + BIRMINGHAM
CAMP HILL (1840)
MARSTON GREEN (1838)
BIRMINGHAM + DERBY JUNCTION
MOSELEY TUN. 166 yds
BIRMINGHAM + GLOUCESTER
MOSELEY (1840)
HAMPTON (1840)
HAMPTON JUNCT.
HAMPTON (1838)
LIFFORD (1840)
LONGBRIDGE (1840)
Cofton Tunnel 440 yds

Note: The date of intermediate stations is unclear. Those on map are as per RCH.

1840

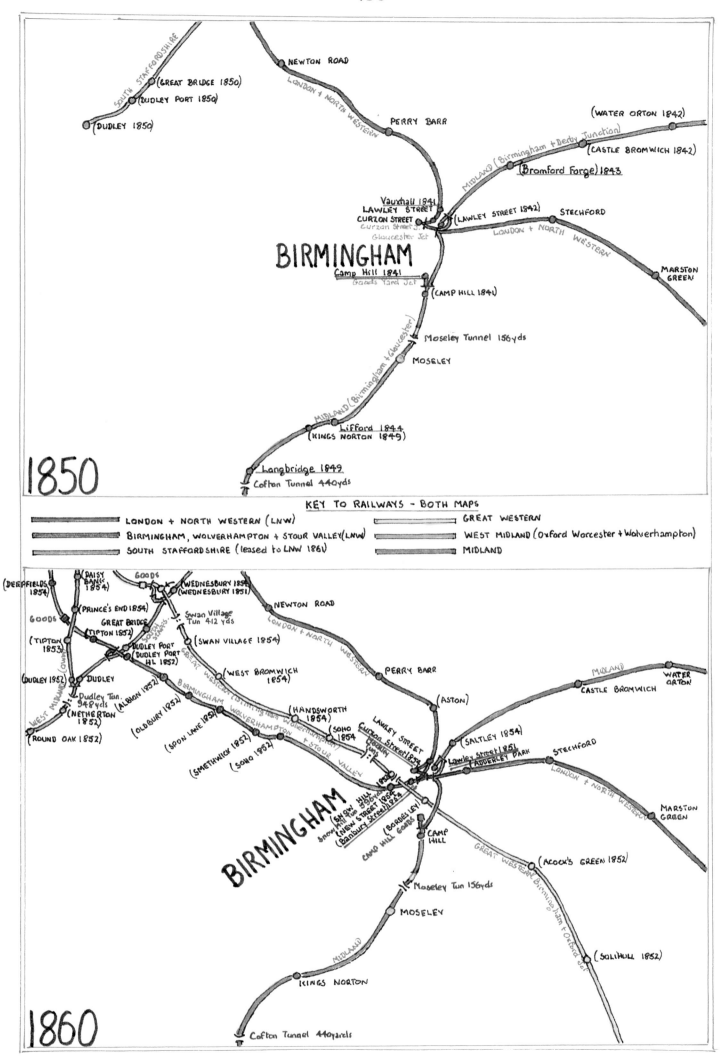

1850

KEY TO RAILWAYS - BOTH MAPS

LONDON + NORTH WESTERN (LNW)

BIRMINGHAM, WOLVERHAMPTON + STOUR VALLEY (LNW)

SOUTH STAFFORDSHIRE (leased to LNW 1861)

GREAT WESTERN

WEST MIDLAND (Oxford Worcester + Wolverhampton)

MIDLAND

1860

1841-1850

16. 8. 1841 BIRMINGHAM + GLOUCESTER (BG) opened to a junction with the LONDON + BIRMINGHAM (LB), known initially as Gloucester Junction - later became GRAND JUNCTION. Camp Hill terminus becomes a goods depot on what effectively was a short branch. A new CAMP HILL passenger station was opened to the south of the junction to the old terminus. Vauxhall closed to passengers before the end of the year, but the exact date of closure is not recorded.

10. 2. 1842 BIRMINGHAM + DERBY JUNCTION (BDJ) opened from Whitacre to LAWLEY STREET with intermediate stations at — WATER ORTON and CASTLE BROMWICH. An additional station was opened later at Bromford Forge but this closed in 1843, although remaining in use as a goods station.

11. 4. 1842 BDJ opened inclined connection with GJ so that goods trains from Whitacre did not have to travel via Hampton. The connection from the railway shown on the map to enable BDJ trains to run to CURZON STR. was opened at this time but not used for passenger traffic until 1851. This later development followed the formation of the MIDLAND and its subsequent steady growth, its size having a profound influence on all the railways it made connections with.

10. 5. 1845 MIDLAND formed. An amalgamation of BDJ, North Midland and Midland Counties.

1. 7. 1845 BG leased to MIDLAND.

4. 8. 1845 OXFORD WORCESTER + WOLVERHAMPTON (OWW) - Act.

16. 7. 1846 LONDON + NORTH WESTERN (LNW) formed - A merger of LB, GRAND JUNCTION and Manchester + Birmingham.

3. 8. 1846 BG fully absorbed by MIDLAND. BIRMINGHAM WOLVERHAMPTON + STOUR VALLEY (BWSV) - Authorised.

3. 8. 1846 SOUTH STAFFORDSHIRE JUNCTION (SSJ) - Act. BIRMINGHAM + OXFORD JUNCTION (BOJ) - Authorised.

6. 10. 1846 SSJ name changed to SOUTH STAFFORDSHIRE (SS) following merger with TRENT VALLEY, MIDLAND + GRAND JCT which had also obtained its Act on 3·8·1846.

12. 11. 1846 BIRMINGHAM WOLVERHAMPTON + DUDLEY (BWD) - also authorised 3·8·1846 agreed lease to GREAT WESTERN (GW).

1. 11. 1847 SS opened first section - Bescot to Walsall (outside the map area).

31. 8. 1848 BOJ fully absorbed by GW. BWD fully absorbed by GW.

4. 1849 First Longbridge station closed. Lifford station had already closed in late 1844. KINGS NORTON opened.

1. 3. 1850 SS Pleck Junction to DUDLEY opened with stations at DUDLEY PORT and GREAT BRIDGE within the map area. It was the first line opened in BIRMINGHAM (within the map area) since 1842, although several lines were in course of construction. It had been a period of promotions, in-fighting and mergers.

1851-1860

1. 5. 1851 MIDLAND - Saltley curve in use for passenger trains which from this date ran into the LNW station. Lawley Street reduced to a goods only station.

2. 1852 BWVS opened for goods BIRMINGHAM to Bushbury via Wolverhampton. Opened to passengers on 1st July '52. Intermediate stations (map area) at: SOHO, SMETHWICK, SPON LANE, OLDBURY, ALBION, DUDLEY PORT (HIGH LEVEL) and TIPTON. An additional station at DEEPFIELDS opened in 1854; had by this time been leased to LNW.

1. 10. 1852 GW (Projected OBJ) opened to SNOW HILL. Initial intermediate map area stations: ACOCK'S GREEN and SOLIHULL. ✱

16. 11. 1852 OWW opened from Stourbridge Junction to DUDLEY for goods traffic and to passengers on 20·12·1852. There were two intermediate stations within the map area at ROUND OAK and NETHERTON.

9. 1853 SS and BWVS connection opened at DUDLEY PORT.

1. 12. 1853 OWW opened DUDLEY to TIPTON, and Junction at DUDLEY between SS and OWW opened.

1. 6. 1854 LNW NEW STREET opened. Curzon Street closed to passengers but retained as goods. NEW STREET is also used by MIDLAND trains.

1. 7. 1854 OWW from TIPTON to Wolverhampton opened to passengers (Goods since April). Additional stations at DAISY BANK and PRINCE'S END.

14. 11. 1854 GW SNOW HILL to junction OWW at Priestfield. Stations: SOHO, HANDSWORTH, WEST BROMWICH, SWAN VILLAGE and WEDNESBURY. This line and the 1·10·1852 opening (✱ above) were mixed gauge lines.

1855 LNW temporary ticket platform, which had been opened at Banbury Street pending the completion of NEW STREET, closed.

1. 6. 1859 GW goods connection with LNW at WEDNESBURY.

14. 6. 1860 STOURBRIDGE - Authorised.

16. 6. 1860 OWW merged with Worcester + Hereford and Newport, Abergavenny + Hereford to form WEST MIDLAND (WM). Shortly afterwards it was agreed that the WM would merge with the GW; due to technicalities it would be three years before this became effective, but in the meantime the companies agreed they would work as a single undertaking.
GW moves to take the Broad gauge north from Wolverhampton were abandoned.

The chart which follows and the chart on page 140 show how just three railways – LONDON + NORTH WESTERN, MIDLAND and GREAT WESTERN – developed their influence in the area by merger and acquistion. A continuous line thus: ———— shows the railway fully absorbed, - - - - shows line leased, ... shows line worked or opening of the line after it had been absorbed. Openings: usually only the first or principal opening is shown, restricted to the lines within the area covered by the general maps. ACT indicates year of parliamentary authorisation.

FAMILY TREE OF THE LONDON MIDLAND + SCOTTISH

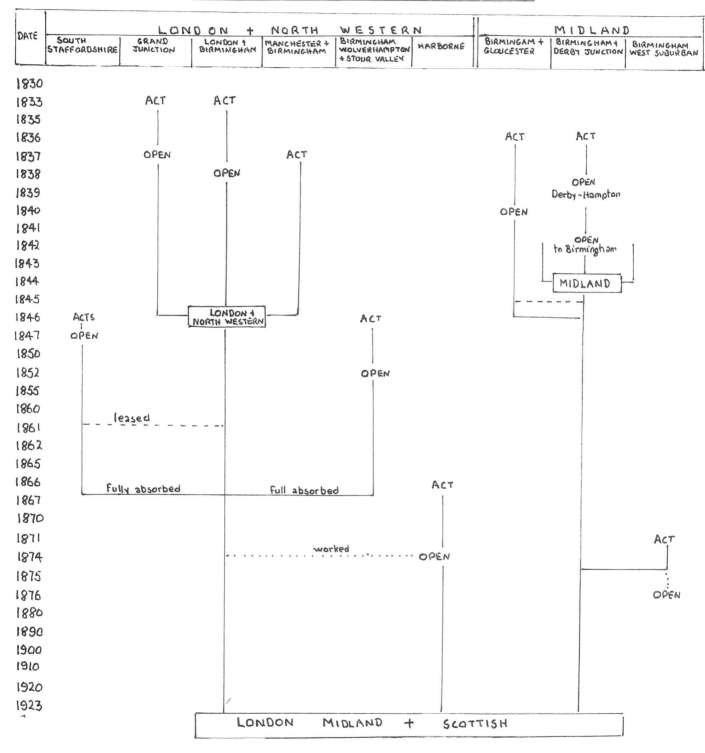

There was just one other railway in which the MIDLAND were joint owners with the GREAT WESTERN. This was the HALESOWEN. This railway had a complex history – most of its originally projected line became parts of various other railways supported and ultimately absorbed by the GREAT WESTERN. The original railway got its ACT in 1865 as HALESOWEN + BROMSGROVE BRANCH RAILWAY and was to connect Netherton to Bromsgrove by way of Halesowen. The only common factor with this and the line eventually built was HALESOWEN. North of this point were GW-inspired lines, the DUDLEY + OLDBURY JUNCTION (became OLDBURY) and NETHERTON + HALESOWEN (partly the creation of the WEST MIDLAND). The line opened November 1883 and was worked from the outset by MIDLAND and GW. It was vested in those two companies jointly in 1906.

TO 1840

This first map of the central area of Birmingham emphasises the growth of its canal network. Prominent to the north-west is the new direct main line (opened in 1839) of the Birmingham Canal with the earlier contour canal and its branches, alongside which industries had grown up, continuing to serve local needs. The continued growth of the canal system will also be noted — the duplicate canal being built to the NE to ease traffic flows on a system in use 24 hours per day.

The new railways are interesting in one respect relative to Birmingham's two terminal stations, that from the south being located north of that from the north.

1841-1850

This period saw little railway development but it is interesting that all were joined to each other; this cooperation was no doubt partly influenced by the routes not being in conflict with each other. On the canal side the duplicate route was now opened together with several branches and basins outside the central area.

Camp Hill terminus became a goods depot when the line projected on the 1840 map was opened.

One final point is that all through routes required reversal at Birmingham and it would be many years before this problem was fully solved.

1851-1875

A period of continuous development in the city railway network now dominated by just three companies: MIDLAND, GW and LNW. The canal system continued to play an important part in short-haul traffic to the various railway wharves where it joined the rail system for long-distance travel. All the railways were planned to be connected but the planned route between GW and LNW — the final link — was never completed due to a dispute between the two companies.

Some local suburban traffic was also developed during the period.

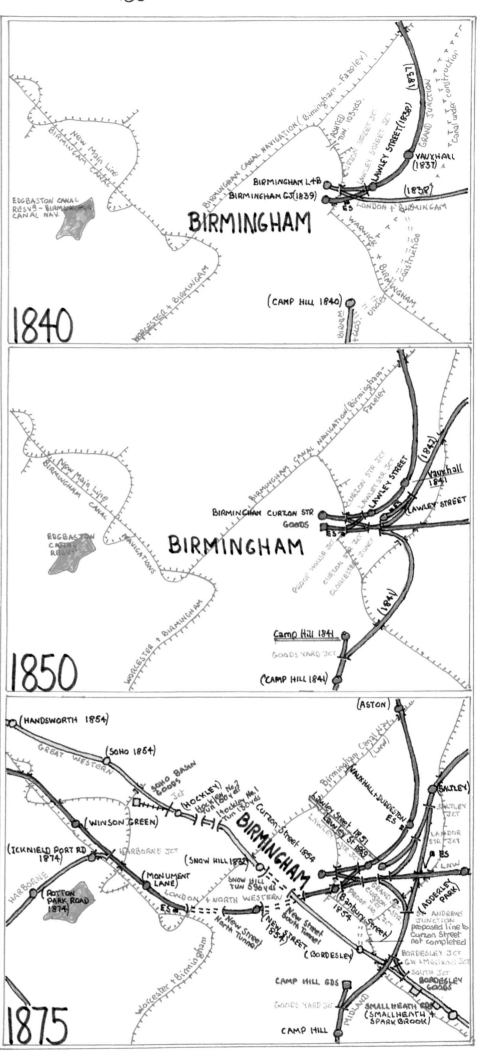

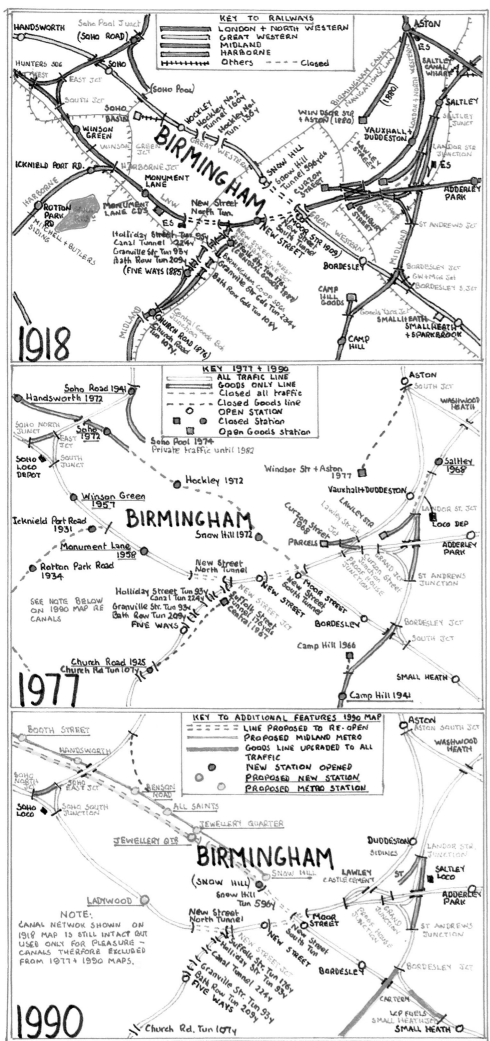

1876-1918

This map shows maximum development of the central area and apart from MOOR STR, opened in 1909, it could have been dated at almost any date post 1890.

It is again interesting to note the number of goods branches constructed to link-up with the canal network reflecting the increase of canal freight which continued to a zenith about 1900.

The two main additions to the railway network were: LNW - SOHO to PERRY BARR enabling goods traffic to avoid NEW ST, and the MIDLAND West Suburban which at last enabled MIDLAND through trains to call at NEW STREET without the need to reverse. Some of the central jcts not shown on this map are on 1977 map.

1919 -1977

This map covers the period co-inciding with the decline of railways. This had started during 1914-18 WAR, continuing during the 1930's. After a short World War II respite steady shrinkage followed, accelerated under BEECHING. However, BIRMINGHAM central area had only one big casualty, the old GW main line. This now ended at MOOR STREET. Canal goods traffic had by this time all gone, so the canal network has been excluded from the final two maps. It should be noted, however, that the canals of the area do remain intact but are now devoted to pleasure activities.

1978-1990

The final map of the central area shows some re-generation of the network and in addition further planned re-opening of lines and stations together with a planned MIDLAND METRO system.

The Birmingham-Gloucester line, which had been down-graded to goods only, has been restored to passenger use and SNOW HILL has re-opened. It is planned to extend the re-opened line to give SNOW HILL main-line status, so that Wolverhampton services do not need to take the contorted route via St Andrew's Jct if approaching the city via SMALL HEATH. The METRO system is dealt with on the general map page.

FAMILY TREE OF THE GREAT WESTERN IN BIRMINGHAM DISTRICT

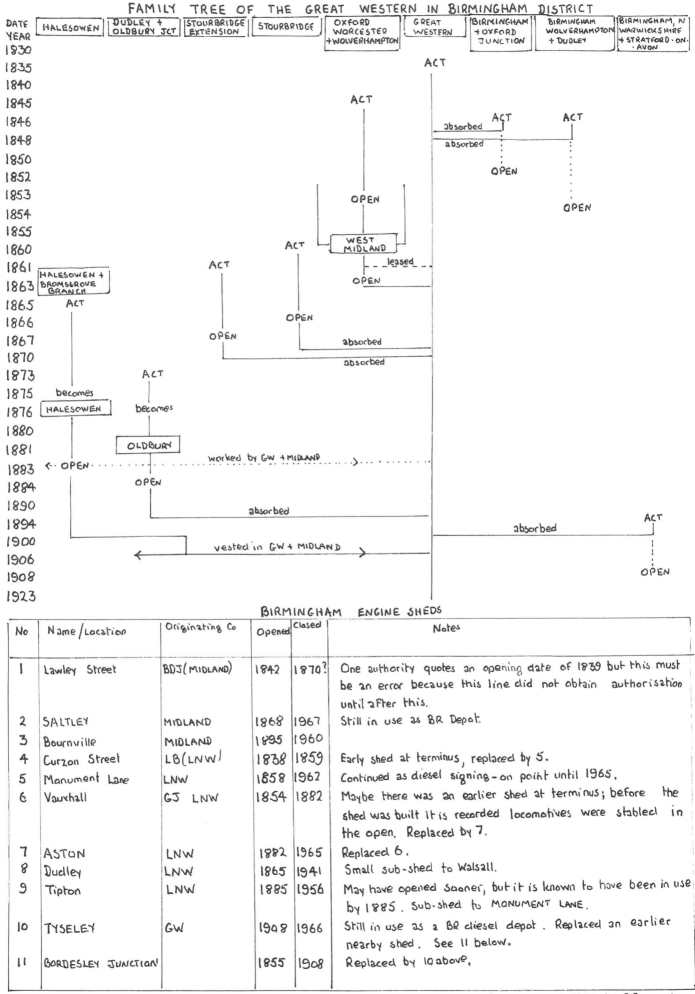

BIRMINGHAM ENGINE SHEDS

No	Name/Location	Originating Co	Opened	Closed	Notes
1	Lawley Street	BDJ (MIDLAND)	1842	1870?	One authority quotes an opening date of 1839 but this must be an error because this line did not obtain authorisation until after this.
2	SALTLEY	MIDLAND	1868	1967	Still in use as BR Depot.
3	Bournville	MIDLAND	1895	1960	
4	Curzon Street	LB (LNW)	1838	1859	Early shed at terminus, replaced by 5.
5	Monument Lane	LNW	1858	1962	Continued as diesel signing-on point until 1965.
6	Vauxhall	GJ LNW	1854	1882	Maybe there was an earlier shed at terminus; before the shed was built it is recorded locomotives were stabled in the open. Replaced by 7.
7	ASTON	LNW	1882	1965	Replaced 6.
8	Dudley	LNW	1865	1941	Small sub-shed to Walsall.
9	Tipton	LNW	1885	1956	May have opened sooner, but it is known to have been in use by 1885. Sub-shed to MONUMENT LANE.
10	TYSELEY	GW	1908	1966	Still in use as a BR diesel depot. Replaced an earlier nearby shed. See 11 below.
11	BORDESLEY JUNCTION		1855	1908	Replaced by 10 above.

In addition to the two ex-steam depots at TYSELEY and SALTLEY currently in use as at 1990 by BR, extra depot has been opened at SOHO.

1861-1875

2.1861 SOUTH STAFFORDSHIRE (SS) leased to LONDON + NORTH WESTERN (LNW). Also WEST MIDLAND (WM) leased to GREAT WESTERN.

1.8.1861 STOURBRIDGE EXTENSION (SX) - Authorised.

2.6.1862 LNW opened line to Sutton Coldfield from a junction at ASTON. The initial intermediate stations were at: GRAVELLY HILL, ERDINGTON and WYLDE GREEN; an additional station at CHESTER ROAD was opened at the end of the following year.

30.6.1862 MIDLAND obtained authorisation for a line from Landor Street Junction to St Andrews Junction so that any through trains from the north to Gloucester could avoid calling at NEW STREET and the consequent need to reverse.

1.4.1863 STOURBRIDGE opened from Stourbridge Junction to Cradley (worked under agreement with GREAT WESTERN and WM).

1.6.1863 STOURBRIDGE - Hayes Lane Goods branch opened.

1.8.1863 WEST MIDLAND completely absorbed by GREAT WESTERN (GW). Act of 13.7.1863.

1864 MIDLAND spur between Landor Street Junction and St Andrews Junction opened to all traffic. The exact date the line was brought into use is unclear.

1.11.1864 GW - BIRMINGHAM to Wolverhampton passenger trains restricted to 'narrow' gauge.

5.7.1865 HALESOWEN + BROMSGROVE - Act. This was an ambitious scheme, but parts of its powers were taken over by other railways under GW influence and only many years later was the six-mile remnant of the line built (See 1876 for new Act and change of name).

1.1.1866 STOURBRIDGE - opened CRADLEY to OLD HILL.

28.6.1866 HARBORNE - Act.

1.9.1866 GW - SWAN VILLAGE to Horsefields Junction with LNW opened. Swan Village Basin - line opened.

1.4.1867 SX OLD HILL to HANDSWORTH and also junction with LNW opened.

15.7.1867 SS Fully absorbed by LNW. BIRMINGHAM WOLVERHAMPTON + STOUR VALLEY fully absorbed by LNW.

1.3.1869 LNW LAWLEY STREET station closed to passengers.

1.7.1870 STOURBRIDGE and SX both fully absorbed by GW.

31.7.1871 BIRMINGHAM WEST SUBURBAN (BWS) - Authorised.

21.7.1873 DUDLEY + OLDBURY JUNCTION (DOJ) - Authorised.

10.8.1874 HARBORNE opened. Worked by LNW but remained independant until grouping. There were stations at: ICKNEILD PORT ROAD, ROTTON PARK ROAD, HAGLEY ROAD and the terminal station HARBORNE.

1.7.1875 BWS vested in MIDLAND. This was the line that would enable through trains to call at NEW STREET without the need to reverse.

1876-1898

3.4.1876 MIDLAND open BWS. Stations: GRANVILLE STREET, CHURCH ROAD, SOMERSET ROAD, SELLY OAK, STIRCHLEY STREET; two months later station opened at LIFFORD.

13.7.1876 HALESOWEN + BROMSGROVE becomes HALESOWEN to be worked jointly by MIDLAND and GW.

1.3.1878 GW open NETHERTON to OLD HILL and OLD HILL to HALESOWEN.

10.5.1879 GW open WITHYMOOR Goods Branch.

1.7.1879 MIDLAND (having absorbed Wolverhampton, Walsall + Midland in 1874) opened triangular junction from WATER ORTON + CASTLE BROMWICH to Walsall. Intermediate map area station at PENNS.

1.3.1880 LNW ASTON to WINDSOR STREET GOODS opened.

11.8.1881 DOJ name changed to OLDBURY.

10.9.1883 HALESOWEN opened. Intermediate stations at HUNNINGTON and RUBERY.

7.11.1884 OLDBURY (GW) opened for goods traffic. Passenger traffic commenced the following May.

1.7.1885 MIDLAND close GRANVILLE STREET and open FIVE WAYS. LIFFORD changed to Gloucester Line later in the year.

1.7.1887 MIDLAND - WORCESTER WHARF GOODS opened - later became CENTRAL (canal and railway traffic exchange).

3.10.1887 LNW - Soho Pool Goods branch opened.

1.3.1888 LNW - SOHO to PERRY BARR connections opened goods, passengers 1.4.1889.

1892 MIDLAND BWS improvements including new connections at LIFFORD. NORTHFIELD closed 1893.

1.7.1894 OLDFIELD fully absorbed by GW.

25.8.1894 BIRMINGHAM, NORTH WARWICKSHIRE + STRATFORD-ON-AVON (BNWSA) - Authorised.

1.4.1897 MIDLAND - New Saltley Curve and burrowing junction. NEW STREET becomes LNW and MIDLAND joint, but maps continue to show NEW STREET as LNW owned with MIDLAND running powers.

1.7.1897 BNWSA is fully absorbed by GW. However, a further decade would pass before the line was completed and opened. Apart from goods branches this would become the last line to be built in the area.

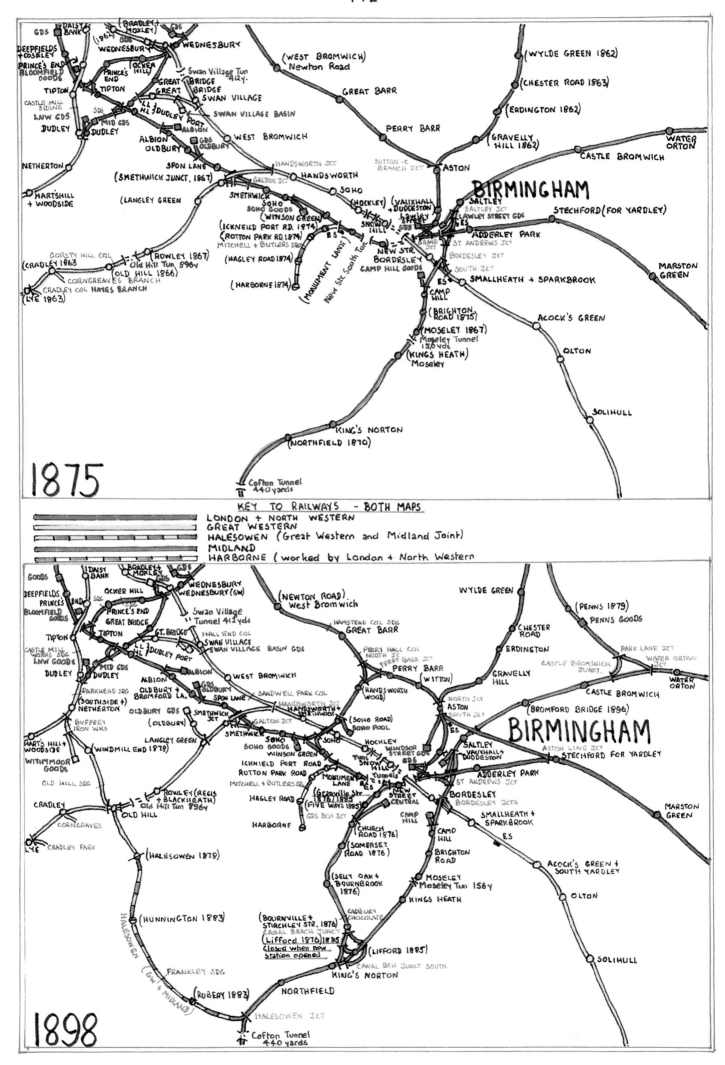

1875

KEY TO RAILWAYS - BOTH MAPS

LONDON + NORTH WESTERN
GREAT WESTERN
HALESOWEN (Great Western and Midland Joint)
MIDLAND
HARBORNE (worked by London + North Western

1898

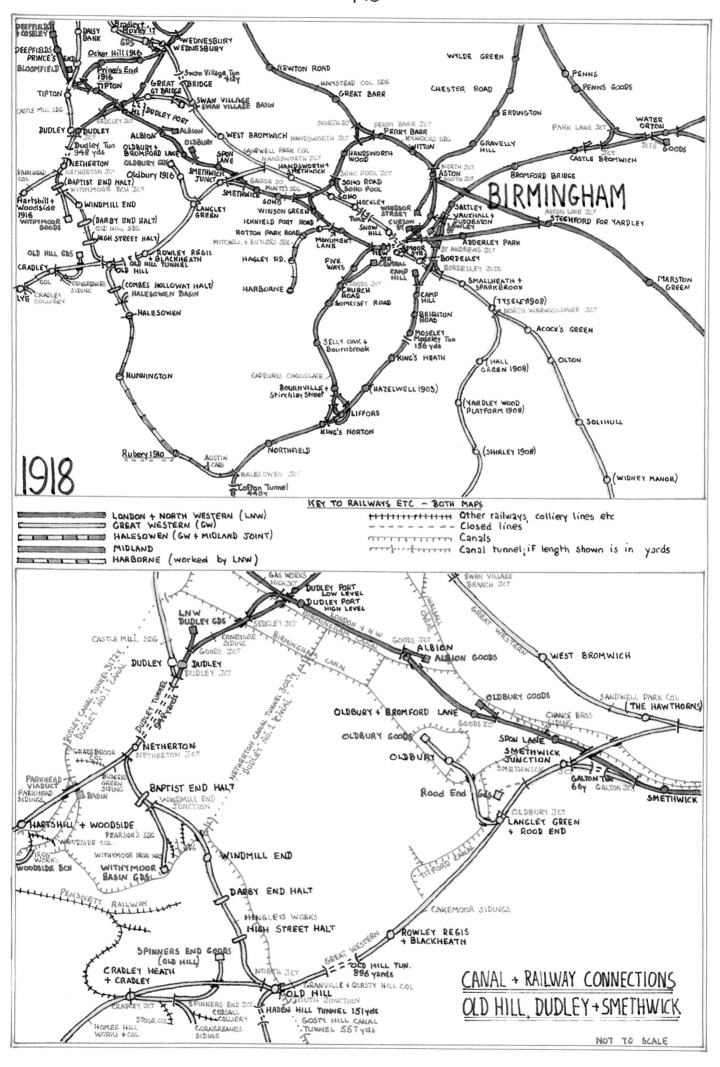

1918

KEY TO RAILWAYS ETC – BOTH MAPS

- LONDON + NORTH WESTERN (LNW)
- GREAT WESTERN (GW)
- HALESOWEN (GW + MIDLAND JOINT)
- MIDLAND
- HARBORNE (worked by LNW)

- +++++++++++ Other railways, colliery lines etc
- – – – – – – Closed lines
- Canals
- Canal tunnel; if length shown is in yards

CANAL + RAILWAY CONNECTIONS
OLD HILL, DUDLEY + SMETHWICK

NOT TO SCALE

1899-1918

1. 7.1900 BIRMINGHAM, NORTH WARWICKSHIRE + STRATFORD·ON·AVON (BNWSOA) absorbed by GREAT WESTERN (GW).

2. 4.1902 GW open HALESOWEN BASIN branch for goods, illustrating quite graphically the continuing importance of the area's extensive canal network in carrying bulky local cargoes to railway wharves and transhipment to rail for long-distance haulage. Canal carriage reached a zenith about this time, and from this point in time a steady decline set in. Nevertheless in no other area of the UK was the canal zenith not reached until such a late date, as in most areas the coming of railways resulted in decline of canal traffic from the mid 1840's or even earlier.

29. 7.1906 HALESOWEN now vested in GW and MIDLAND, effective from the previous month (30th June).

1. 8.1907 GW open SPINNERS END Goods Branch from CRADLEY. The goods depot at the end of the branch was also known as OLD HILL.

9.12.1907 GW opened BNWSOA for goods traffic.

1. 7.1908 BNWSOA opened to passenger traffic. Stations at: HALL GREEN, YARDLEY WOOD PLATFORM and SHIRLEY.

22. 3.1909 MIDLAND opened direct line from WATER ORTON to Kingsbury for goods traffic. Passenger traffic commenced two months later (from 3rd May).

1. 7.1909 GW opened MOOR STREET to deal with passenger services off BNWSOA line.

1. 4.1910 Rubery station on the HALESOWEN joint line was closed to passengers; however, workmen's trains were continued until 1936, but not shown in Bradshaw for April 1910 or any subsequent Bradshaw.

The rail network of BIRMINGHAM had now reached its maximum extent and though some new stations and halts would be opened, these would be more than balanced by closures. The suburban branch network in particular was in this period increasingly affected by road competition.

Before looking at the closures of the period, it is appropriate to mention the earliest rationalisation of any main line in the UK; although this is just outside the map area, it is shown on the 1840 map: The WHITACRE-HAMPTON line. Constructed as a main line feeding into the LONDON + BIRMINGHAM, it soon became redundant when MIDLAND opened more direct lines to both BIRMINGHAM and London. It was singled in the 1840's, and the always scanty passenger service was withdrawn at the end of 1916.

The closures noted below were regarded as war·time economy measures, but passenger services were not re-instated. However, all the affected lines continued to carry goods traffic:

1916   Ocker Hill (LNW), Oldbury (GW), Prince's End (LNW), Hartshill + Woodside (GW).

1917   Bradley + Moxley (GW).

The next map shows the importance of canal and railway integration in the OLD HILL, DUDLEY and SMETHWICK area. It is not dated and some features not in existance together at the same time are included to show the zenith of development. 1910 would be the most appropriate year for dating if a year needed to be selected.

THE RAILWAY BULLY BOYS I : CAPTAIN MARK HUISH of the LONDON + NORTH WESTERN

The LONDON + NORTH WESTERN claimed the title of THE PREMIER LINE. The justification of this claim, however, depends on the basis of assessment and the date. However, if one examines the claim during its early days throughout the period when Huish was in charge, and the basis of assessment the use of bully·boy tactics, it can be said that indisputably the LONDON + NORTH WESTERN was THE PREMIER LINE.

Initially three lines were planned to meet at BIRMINGHAM from Liverpool, Manchester and London. The first of these, having received enormous help from the LIVERPOOL - MANCHESTER, changed its plans to link into this railway thus making the Manchester scheme redundant; this became the GRAND JUNCTION. Compared to the other two companies its route was devoid of engineering difficulties and, passing few sizeable places, the cost of land was cheap. Its line was soon opened and large dividends were paid and big cash resources accumulated enabling it to purchase The Liverpool + Manchester and other smaller connecting Lancashire co's. Lead by its Secretary, Huish, the GRAND JUNCTION now used its muscle to create difficulties for the other Birmingham companies. For example, the MANCHESTER + BIRMINGHAM were promised running powers into BIRMINGHAM if they built their line into Crewe. But as soon as this was done the agreement was rescinded. Eventually of course the three Birmingham companies amalgamated to form the LONDON + NORTH WESTERN. Huish retained his influence as secretary of the new company. With the overthrow of Hudson, Huish took charge of the anti-GREAT NORTHERN faction which became known as the Euston Square Confederacy which by the notorious Octuple Agreement was specifically designed to starve the GREAT NORTHERN of traffic and revenues.

Up to this point in time the GRAND JUNCTION and its successor the LONDON + NORTH WESTERN had indulged only in sharp practice and questionable and ungentleman like tactics; it now turned its attention to violent

and illegal means in efforts to extend its influence. The smaller companies attacked in this way either fell into LONDON + NORTH WESTERN hands through fear of the inevitable consequences, or, if they resisted, the LNW policy was to find ways of starving them of traffic and revenues, battering them into submission or financial ruin. In this process rigged meetings were used and on one occasion a forged seal at an illegal meeting was used to overturn or try and overturn a decision which had parliamentary approval. A typical example of deliberately organised violence when a smaller company sharing a station with the LNW refused to conform, they had notices torn down and staff forcibly ejected from the station and prevented from entering their own shared premises. On another occasion men were prevented laying track by an organised gang of toughs. Even when taken to court they were adept at finding legal loopholes or so delaying matters that by the time justice was obtained it was too late. Readers interested will be able to find full details of these and other similar events in THE HISTORY OF THE GREAT WESTERN RAILWAY by E.T. Macdermot.

1919-1940

This period saw no changes at all in the network. However, as happened elsewhere, passenger services came under threat from road competition, and suburban lines in particular saw reduction and withdrawal of passenger services and station closures. But such lines as were affected remained open for goods traffic and/or the long-distance services. One suburban line, the MIDLAND WEST SUBURBAN, had already gained increased importance as it had enabled MIDLAND through trains to call at NEW STREET without the need to reverse. This development increased in importance following grouping, but it nevertheless failed to save the inner suburban stations on the line from closure.

1919 Hunnington on the HALESOWEN line closed. A station at LONGBRIDGE came into use shortly afterwards. To begin with it was unadvertised and used to convey work-people to the nearby Austin Works.

1925 Church Road closed (Western Suburban line). SPRING ROAD (GW) opened by this date.

1927 Combes Holloway and Halesowen closed and regular passenger trains withdrawn but the line remained in use for goods traffic and work-people's unadvertised trains.

1930 Somerset Road (Western Suburban) closed.

1931 Icknield Port Road closed (Harborne line). GW open HAWTHORNS (for football traffic).

1934 Harborne branch passenger traffic withdrawn. Consequent closure of stations: Rotton Park Rd., Hagley Road and Harborne. Remained open for goods. WHITLOCK'S END (GW) opened in 1936.

1939 LEA HALL opened (LMS) to serve new housing development. Lifford closed in 1940.

1941-1963

This period saw further passenger station closures, but the entire line network remained intact until December 1963 when the Harborne branch closed completely, having lost its passenger service in 1934 as noted above.

1941 Closures: Hazelwell, King's Heath, Moseley, Brighton Road, Camp Hill, Handsworth Wood, Soho Road.

1944 Five Ways - closed.

1945 Newton Road - closed.

1949 Soho (ex LMS) - closed.

1957 Winson Green - closed.

1958 Monument Lane closed. Halesowen workmen's services ended.

1960 Albion closed. Langbridge workmen's services ended; later a LONGBRIDGE main line station would be built.

1962 Daisy Bank + Bradley, Prince's End + Coseley, Tipton (ex GW) and Blowers Green - all closed. Passenger services on this line were withdrawn but the line has retained goods traffic into the 1990's.

1963 Harborne line closed completely.

The final event of the period, the BEECHING REPORT, had very little effect on BIRMINGHAM. Of course the inevitable modifications to passenger services in the area were included in the report. These, however, were all with one exception main lines and had no effect upon the network.

The exception was withdrawal of the DUDLEY to OLD HILL passenger service and closure of stations at: DUDLEY, BAPTIST END HALT, WINDMILL END HALT (this former full station had been reduced to halt status in 1952 because it was at this time it became HALT), DARBY END HALT, and HIGH STREET HALT (OLD HILL). There were no other station closure proposals contained in the report, except PENNS.

However, as will be seen in the next period these proposals were soon implemented together with other closures. BEECHING's main effect in fact came from BR no longer being common carriers and resulted in the steady closure of goods branches and spurs which continue through the final two periods.

1940

KEY TO RAILWAYS 1940 MAP
- ▬▬▬ LONDON MIDLAND + SCOTTISH (LMS)
- ▭▭▭ GREAT WESTERN (GW)
- ▭▭▭ HALESOWEN (LMS + GW JOINT)
- ◯ STATION
  STATION OPEN - SPECIAL SERVICES ONLY
  ✱ Workmen's trains   † Sporting activities

KEY TO RAILWAYS 1963 MAP
- ◯▬▬ OPEN ALL TRAFFIC + OPEN PASSENGER STATION
- ▭▭▭ GOODS ONLY 1940 and 1963
- ▬▬▬ ALL TRAFFIC IN 1940 - GOODS ONLY IN 1963
- ▪--◗--●--▫ STATION STILL IN USE GOODS IN 1963
  Goods only now closed ; Closed stations

1963

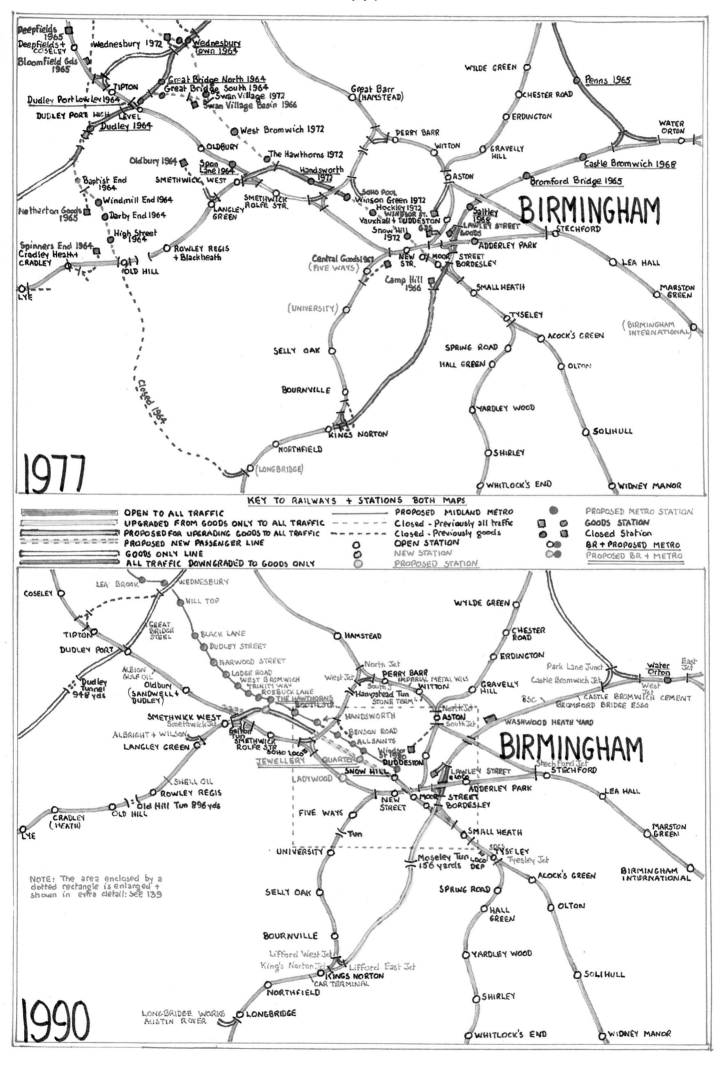

1977

BIRMINGHAM

Deepfields 1965
Deepfields + COSELEY
Bloomfield Gds 1965
Wednesbury 1972
Wednesbury Town 1964
TIPTON
Dudley Port Low Lev 1964
DUDLEY PORT HIGH LEVEL
Dudley 1964
Great Bridge North 1964
Great Bridge South 1964
Swan Village 1972
Swan Village Basin 1966
West Bromwich 1972
OLDBURY
Oldbury 1964
Spon Lane 1964
SMETHWICK WEST
The Hawthorns 1972
Handsworth 1972
Baptist End 1964
Windmill End 1964
Darby End 1964
Netherton Goods 1965
SMETHWICK ROLFE STR.
LANGLEY GREEN
Spinners End 1964
Cradley Heath + CRADLEY
High Street 1964
ROWLEY REGIS + Blackheath
OLD HILL
LYE
Great Barr (HAMSTEAD)
PERRY BARR
WITTON
Soho Pool
Winson Green 1972
Hockley 1972
WINDSOR ST. 1965
Vauxhall + DUDDESTON
Snow Hill 1972
Central Goods 1967 (FIVE WAYS)
Camp Hill 1966
(UNIVERSITY)
SELLY OAK
BOURNVILLE
KINGS NORTON
NORTHFIELD
(LONGBRIDGE)
Closed 1964
ASTON
Bromford Bridge 1965
Saltley 1968
LAWLEY STREET GOODS
NEW ST.
MOOR STREET
Bordesley
ADDERLEY PARK
STECHFORD
LEA HALL
SMALL HEATH
TYSELEY
ACOCK'S GREEN
SPRING ROAD
HALL GREEN
OLTON
YARDLEY WOOD
SOLIHULL
SHIRLEY
WHITLOCK'S END
WIDNEY MANOR
MARSTON GREEN
(BIRMINGHAM INTERNATIONAL)
WYLDE GREEN
CHESTER ROAD
ERDINGTON
GRAVELLY HILL
Penns 1965
WATER ORTON
Castle Bromwich 1968

KEY TO RAILWAYS + STATIONS BOTH MAPS

OPEN TO ALL TRAFFIC
UPGRADED FROM GOODS ONLY TO ALL TRAFFIC
PROPOSED FOR UPGRADING GOODS TO ALL TRAFFIC
PROPOSED NEW PASSENGER LINE
GOODS ONLY LINE
ALL TRAFFIC DOWNGRADED TO GOODS ONLY

PROPOSED MIDLAND METRO
Closed - Previously all traffic
Closed - Previously goods
OPEN STATION
NEW STATION
PROPOSED STATION

PROPOSED METRO STATION
GOODS STATION
Closed Station
BR + PROPOSED METRO
PROPOSED BR + METRO

1990

BIRMINGHAM

LEA BROOK
WEDNESBURY
HILL TOP
COSELEY
TIPTON
DUDLEY PORT
GREAT BRIDGE STEEL
BLACK LANE
DUDLEY STREET
HARWOOD STREET
Dudley Tunnel 948 yds
ALBION GULF OIL
Oldbury (SANDWELL + DUDLEY)
LODGE ROAD
WEST BROMWICH TRINITY WAY
ROEBUCK LANE
THE HAWTHORNS (BOOTHSTER)
SMETHWICK WEST
Smethwick Jct.
Galton
SMETHWICK ROLFE STR.
ALBRIGHT + WILSON
LANGLEY GREEN
SOHO LOCO
JEWELLERY QUARTER
SHELL OIL
ROWLEY REGIS
Old Hill Tun 896 yds
CRADLEY (HEATH)
OLD HILL
LYE
HAMSTEAD
North Jct.
West Jct.
PERRY BARR
South
Hampstead Tun
STONE TERM.
HANDSWORTH
BENSON ROAD
ALL SAINTS
SOHO LOCO
Windsor St. 1990
LADYWOOD
SNOW HILL
FIVE WAYS
NEW STREET
Tun
UNIVERSITY
Moseley Tun 156 yards
SELLY OAK
BOURNVILLE
Lifford West Jct.
King's Norton Jct.
Lifford East Jct.
KINGS NORTON CAR TERMINAL
NORTHFIELD
LONGBRIDGE WORKS AUSTIN ROVER
LONGBRIDGE
IMPERIAL METAL WKS
WITTON
North Jct.
ASTON
South Jct.
WASHWOOD HEATH YARD
Stech Ford Jct.
LAWLEY STREET + LOCO
STECHFORD
ADDERLEY PARK
MOOR STREET
Bordesley
SMALL HEATH
SDGS
TYSELEY LOCO DEP
Tyseley Jct.
ACOCK'S GREEN
SPRING ROAD
HALL GREEN
OLTON
YARDLEY WOOD
SOLIHULL
SHIRLEY
WHITLOCK'S END
WIDNEY MANOR
MARSTON GREEN
BIRMINGHAM INTERNATIONAL
LEA HALL
WYLDE GREEN
CHESTER ROAD
ERDINGTON
GRAVELLY HILL
Park Lane Junct.
Castle Bromwich Jct.
BSC
CASTLE BROMWICH CEMENT
Bromford Bridge Esso
BSC
Water Orton
East Jct.
West Jct.

NOTE: The area enclosed by a dotted rectangle is enlarged + shown in extra detail: see 139

1964-1977

As already mentioned, the BEECHING REPORT had little impact on the area's line network or on passenger stations. In fact, the number of station closures not in the report outnumbered those in the report by a considerable margin and to a greater extent than elsewhere. This pattern was further accentuated by a development aspect, the modernisation and electrification of the BIRMINGHAM to Euston main line. The result of this was loss of SNOW HILL's long-distance passenger traffic and its consequent reduction to a suburban terminus on a duplicate route even on that basis. Chronology of events follows:

1964 Was a busy year on the closure front with the implementation of all but one of the Beeching closures: Dudley, Baptist End, Windmill End, Darby End and High Street (OLD HILL). Also there were an equal number of closures of non-Beeching stations at Great Bridge (both stations), Wednesbury Town, Dudley Port Low Level and Spon Lane. Only the last of these stations retained a passenger service along its line although all retained a goods service but in some cases this was for only a few months. The year also saw many goods branches closed or cut back including Spinners End, Oldbury (short spur retained), Old Hill to Longbridge and Hayes Lane branch at Lye.

1965 Penns closed (the last of the Beeching proposals) together with passenger services along the line. Bromford Br also closed having handled only race traffic for many years. Goods branches also continued to close. The closures included Blowers Green to Old Hill, together with the Withymoor branch, and including goods depots at Deepfields, Bloomfields and Lifford.

1966 Goods Depots closed: Camp Hill and Swan Village Basin.

1967 Further Goods closures included Central. Main line electrification complete - SNOW HILL became doomed.

1968 Castle Bromwich closed, but line continued in use for both passengers and goods. Goods traffic continued to decline and Dudley to Wolverhampton (ex-GW already reduced to goods only) was closed fully except for a short spur retained at Dudley.

1969 Although there were no closures it was about this time that King's Norton to Bordesley line reduced to goods only with Bristol-Derby services all now routed via the WESTERN SUBURBAN line.

1972 This year saw the final closures before a modest resurgence of development. The closures were all on the GW main line between Wolverhampton and SNOW HILL: Wednesbury, Swan Village, West Bromwich, The Hawthorns, Handsworth, Winson Green, Hockley and Snow Hill. The line between SMETHWICK WEST and Winson Green was retained for goods traffic and to serve sidings near Soho Pool; the rest was closed completely.

Towards the end of the period a modest revitalisation commenced with one entirely new station, BIRMINGHAM INTERNATIONAL, serving Exhibition Centre and Airport, and there were two re-openings: UNIVERSITY (on the site of Somerset Road) and LONGBRIDGE (on the main line and site of the first station of that name). A short spur of the old HALESOWEN was still retained for goods traffic serving the car works there.

1978 - 1990

As in most large conurbations this period has seen a continuation of the modest revival noted at the close of the previous period assisted by local authority subsidies of the remaining suburban network, and this has resulted in increased utilisation of more intensive services. Also the King's Norton - Bordesley line has been upgraded to all traffic. But the most significant event has been the alterations to make MOOR STR. a through station and the re-opening of SNOW HILL. The 1990 map shows these events together with a selection of private user's rail connections. The current Locomotive Depots are also shown.

It remains to record the area's final passenger station closure, Water Orton, little used for many years. Included amongst the goods closures of the period were Soho Pool (had already been reduced to private siding traffic), Windsor Street (1989), and the Tipton-Wednesbury line.

1991 - FUTURE

There is considerable development envisaged for the future. First it is proposed that the line through SNOW HILL to SMETHWICK WEST would be upgraded (the portion now goods only) or re-opened together with a new spur at SMETHWICK enabling trains via SNOW HILL to rejoin the main line at that point. There will be new stations on this line at JEWELLERY QUARTER (on the site of Hockley) and THE HAWTHORNS (on the site of GW Handsworth Junction). On the main line Monument Lane is planned to re-open as LADYWOOD.

In addition there is a proposed MIDLAND METRO between SNOW HILL and Wolverhampton which within the map area will follow the route of the closed GW main line and include seventeen new stations. If the scheme is implemented as planned the number of stations within the map area will be getting close to the number open at maximum development in 1915.

YARMOUTH + LOWESTOFT

Neither of these two places could be described as an important railway centre and their close proximity and similarity make it convenient to deal with them together. They also provide a contrast in development pattern to some of the more industrial centres. The main industries of the area are fishing and agriculture but associated, in part, with the coming of the railways, tourism and leisure have played an increasing part in local economy.

The navigable rivers and canals of the area, as in many places, had their influence on the early development and resulted in the decline to some extent in the use of Yarmouth as Norwich's port and its replacement by LOWESTOFT. This is reflected in the fact that the railway reached YARMOUTH before LOWESTOFT, but by 1860 LOWESTOFT, with improvements to the harbour completed and the new cut open giving better water routes to Norwich, the railway communications too had become superior. From 1860 inland waterways showed a steady decline in amount of goods traffic carried. To illustrate the position navigable waterways have been included on the first two maps, but excluded from later general maps.

TO 1850

The first railway event to affect the area was parliamentary authority granted in 1836 to the EASTERN COUNTIES (EC) to build a line from London to YARMOUTH. However, it opened only as far as Colchester and it was left to other locally inspired companies to build all the early lines in the area.

18.6.1842 YARMOUTH + NORWICH (YN) - Authorised to build a line between the points of its title. The selected route appears strange but was no doubt planned to ultimately serve both YARMOUTH and LOWESTOFT and save mileage by having part of the route from Norwich common to both places. It formed part of EC route.

1.5.1844 YN opened from Norwich to YARMOUTH (VAUXHALL). There were intermediate stations within the map area at: BRUNDALL, BUCKENHAM, CANTLEY, REEDHAM and BERNEY ARMS.

30.6.1845 YN merges with Norwich + Brandon (who had built another portion of the incompleted EC line) to form the NORFOLK.

30.6.1845 LOWESTOFT RAILWAY + HARBOUR (LRH) - Act

3.5.1847 LRH opened to goods from a junction at REEDHAM to LOWESTOFT together with a short Docks Branch.

1.7.1847 LRH opened to passenger traffic. Stations at HADDISCOE, SOMERLEYTON, MUTFORD and LOWESTOFT (Central). The railway was leased to the NORFOLK and became effectively part of that company.

1848 EC take over working of the NORFOLK without authority. This was ratified in 1849 but the NORFOLK retained its independance until it became part of the GREAT EASTERN some fifteen years later. About this time also a tramway (operated by the NORFOLK) was in operation to VAUXHALL FISH MARKET.

1851-1860

5.6.1851 HALESWORTH BECCLES + HADDISCOE (HBH) - Act - To build a line connecting the points of its title.

3.7.1854 HBH becomes EAST SUFFOLK (ES). Opened Goods 20.11, Passengers 4.12. Stations: BECCLES and ALDEBY.

23.6.1856 LOWESTOFT + BECCLES (LB) - Act   } Two local companies sponsored and built by Peto,
7.7.1856 YARMOUTH + HADDISCOE (YH) - Act   } the well-known railway contractor who lived locally.

23.7.1858 Peto sells LB and YH to ES on completion of lines.

1.6.1859 LB opened by ES. The line joined the NORFOLK at a junction just beyond MUTFORD. There was just the one intermediate station at CARLTON COLVILLE from where a goods line ran to South Harbour and a goods depot at KIRKLEY. Line worked by EC from its opening.

1.6.1859 YH opened by ES. Stations at ST OLAVES JUNCTION, ST OLAVES, BELTON and YARMOUTH SOUTH TOWN; there was short goods branch at YARMOUTH to SOUTH QUAY. Line worked by EC from opening. On this date also the ES was absorbed by the EC.

2.11.1860 WAVENEY VALLEY (WV). Had been authorised 3.7.1851 - Tivetshall to BUNGAY. Power to extend the line to BECCLES had been given 4.8.1853. It was opened progressively from Tivetshall and had reached as far as BUNGAY by this time. EARSHAM station was also opened on this date.

HADDISCOE STATIONS

The 1860 map shows the situation as described in the 'Regional History' series and confirmed by Clinker. Research indicates, however, that both these authorities are wrong. In particular the comment that at the time the line was opened a connecting spur from Fleet Junction to Haddiscoe was laid does not make any sense. It is clear that this so-called spur was part of the original EAST SUFFOLK line. RCH maps show

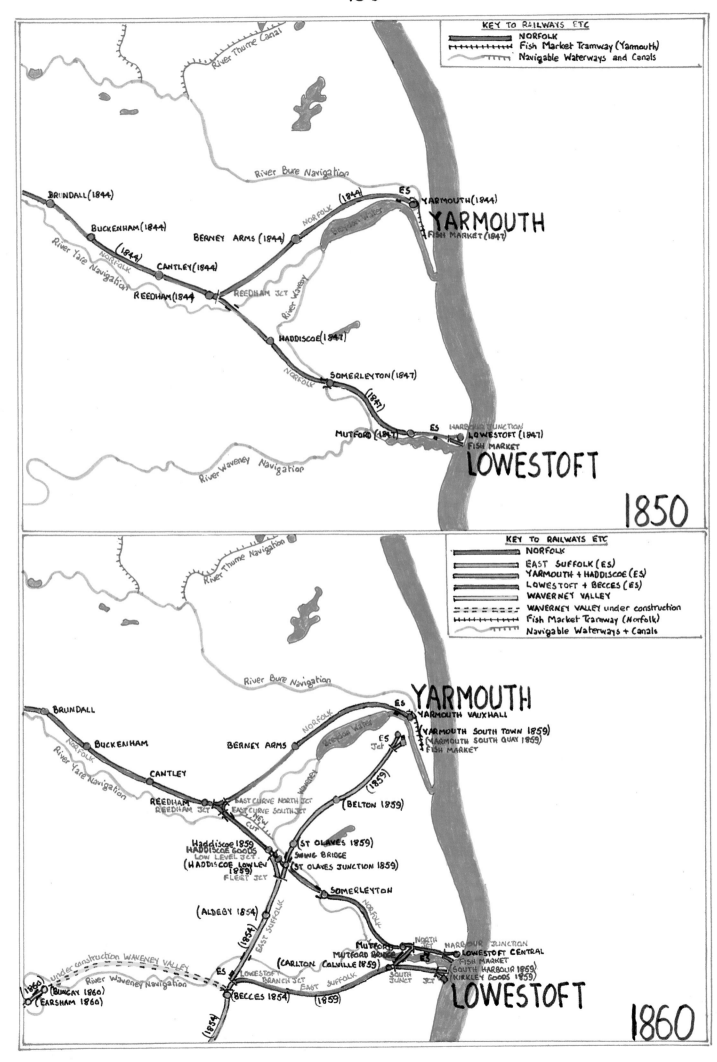

KEY TO RAILWAYS ETC
NORFOLK
Fish Market Tramway (Yarmouth)
Navigable Waterways and Canals

River Thurne Canal

River Bure Navigation

BRUNDALL (1844)

BUCKENHAM (1844)

(1844)

NORFOLK

River Yare Navigation

CANTLEY (1844)

REEDHAM (1844)

BERNEY ARMS (1844)

REEDHAM JCT

River Waveney

NORFOLK

(1844)

ES

YARMOUTH (1844)

YARMOUTH

FISH MARKET (1847)

Breydon Water

HADDISCOE (1847)

NORFOLK

SOMERLEYTON (1847)

(1847)

MUTFORD (1847)

River Waveney Navigation

ES

HARBOUR JUNCTION

LOWESTOFT (1847)

FISH MARKET

LOWESTOFT

1850

KEY TO RAILWAYS ETC
NORFOLK
EAST SUFFOLK (ES)
YARMOUTH + HADDISCOE (ES)
LOWESTOFT + BECCES (ES)
WAVERNEY VALLEY
WAVERNEY VALLEY under construction
Fish Market Tramway (Norfolk)
Navigable Waterways + Canals

River Thurne Navigation

River Bure Navigation

YARMOUTH

ES

YARMOUTH VAUXHALL

(YARMOUTH SOUTH TOWN 1859)

(YARMOUTH SOUTH QUAY 1859)

FISH MARKET

BRUNDALL

BUCKENHAM

NORFOLK

River Yare Navigation

CANTLEY

BERNEY ARMS

NORFOLK

Breydon Water

ES
Jct

(1859)

REEDHAM
REEDHAM JCT

EAST CURVE NORTH JCT
EAST CURVE SOUTH JCT
NEW
CUT

(BELTON 1859)

Haddiscoe 1859
HADDISCOE GOODS
LOW LEVEL JCT.
(HADDISCOE LOW LEVEL 1859)
FLEET JCT

(ST OLAVES 1859)
SWING BRIDGE
(ST OLAVES JUNCTION 1859)

SOMERLEYTON

NORFOLK

(ALDEBY 1854)

(1854)

East Suffolk

under construction WAVENEY VALLEY

River Waveney Navigation

ES

(1860)
(BUNGAY 1860)
(EARSHAM 1860)

LOWESTOFT
BRANCH JCT

(BECCES 1854)

(1854)

Mutford
MUTFORD BRIDGE

(CARLTON COLVILLE 1859)

East Suffolk

(1859)

NORTH
JCT

HARBOUR JUNCTION
LOWESTOFT CENTRAL
FISH MARKET

(SOUTH HARBOUR 1859)

SOUTH
JUNCT
JCT

(KIRKLEY GOODS 1859)

ES

LOWESTOFT

1860

151

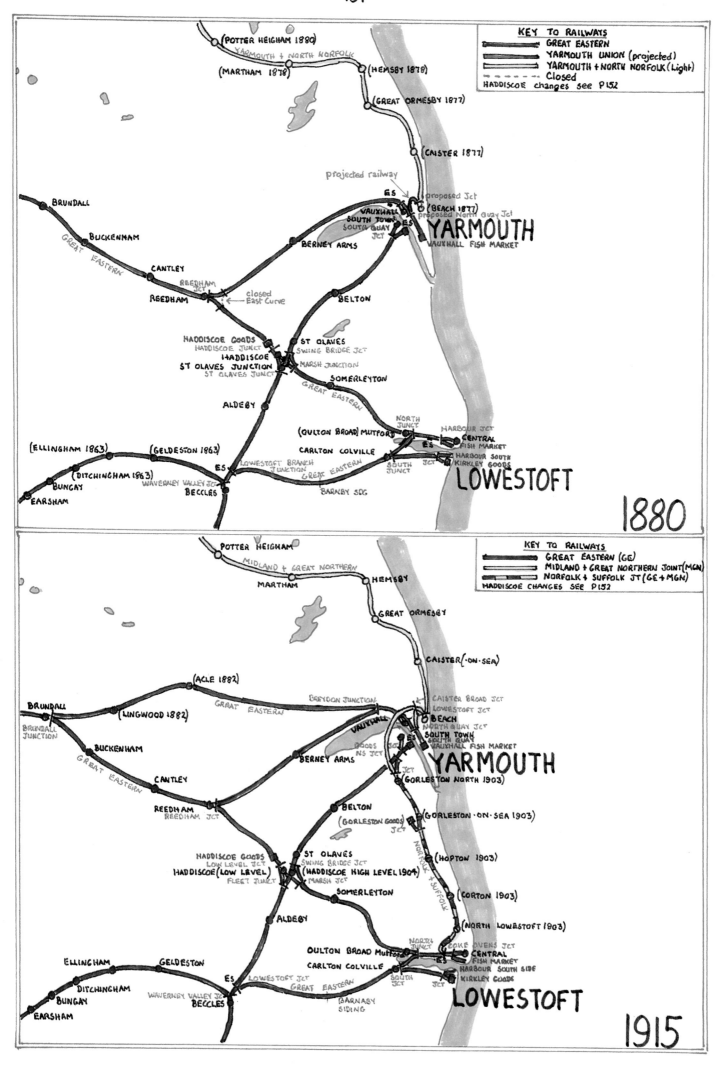

ST OLAVES JUNCTION station positioned at what is usually shown as Fleet Junction. The easiest way to show what appears to have happened is by a series of sketches - see below: (not to scale)

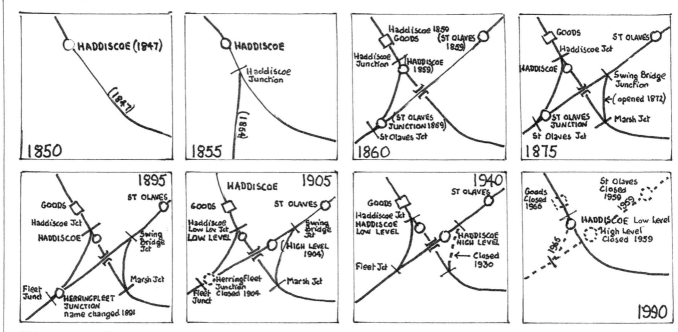

Notes: 1875 MAP   New junctions gave through running between Yarmouth and Lowestoft
1905 MAP   With the direct line YARMOUTH to LOWESTOFT the connecting junctions saw little use, but the HIGH LEVEL station served as a passenger exchange station
1940 MAP   Junctions redundant - taken out of use. Fleet to Low Level continued in use by some goods trains

1861-1880

7.8.1862 GREAT EASTERN(GE) formed by amalgamation of EASTERN COUNTIES, NORFOLK and others. All the lines within the map area were worked together - but see note relative to WAVERNEY VALLEY (WV) below.

2.3.1863 WV opened to BECCLES. Additional intermediate stations at DITCHINGHAM, ELLINGHAM and GELDESTON. The line was worked initially by the EASTERN COUNTIES (EC) but following disputes between EC and WV the WV worked its own line until absorbed by the GE.

21.7.1863 GE absorbs WV bringing all area lines under the same ownership.

20.7.1876 GREAT YARMOUTH + STALHAM (GYS) LIGHT RAILWAY authorised to construct a line between the points in its title.

7.8.1877 GYS opened between YARMOUTH and ORMESBY. Stations were YARMOUTH BEACH, CAISTER (later became CAISTER·ON·SEA) and GREAT ORMESBY.

27.5.1878 GYS extension authorised to North Walsham and name changed to YARMOUTH + NORTH NORFOLK LIGHT (YNNL).
In the meantime on 16·5·1878 line had opened from ORMESBY to a new station at HEMSBY.

15.7.1878 YNNL opened from HEMSBY to the next station on the line at MARTHAM.

17.1.1880 YNNL opened from MARTHAM to Catham with a station, within the map area, at POTTER HEIGHAM.

26.8.1880 YARMOUTH UNION (YU) - Authorised to build a line from BEACH to North Quay Junction on the Fish Market Tramway.

1881-1915

11.8.1881 YNNL becomes YARMOUTH + NORTH NORFOLK (YNN).

15.5.1882 YU opened (goods traffic). Direct BRUNDALL-YARMOUTH opened with intermediate stations LINGWOOD and ACLE.

1.7.1883 YNN, YU and Lynn + Fakenham merge to form EASTERN + MIDLANDS (EM) under control of the MIDLAND and GREAT NORTHERN.

1.7.1893 EM becomes MIDLAND + GREAT NORTHERN (MGN), the change of name reflecting the owning partners.

6.8.1897 LOWESTOFT JUNCTION (LJ) - Authorised to build a short line north from LOWESTOFT which would become part of the NORFOLK + SUFFOLK JOINT (NSJ).

25.7.1898 NSJ - Authorised to build several lines including one from YARMOUTH to link with the LJ which latter company became part of the NSJ. The lines were owned jointly by the GE and the MGN. Also at this time the MGN was authorised to build a connection from Caister Broad Junction to Gorleston to enable trains from the proposed NSJ to run into BEACH station in addition to SOUTH TOWN.

13.7.1903 NSJ and MGN connection authorised as above opened to all traffic. There were new stations opened

at GORLESTON NORTH, GORLESTON·ON·SEA, HOPTON (became HOPTON·ON·SEA), CORTON and NORTH LOWESTOFT. The railway was operated as part of the MIDLAND + GREAT NORTHERN system.

1904 Following the opening of the NORFOLK + SUFFOLK the GREAT EASTERN's Swing Bridge Junction to Marsh Junction became redundant. Most trains passing through HADDISCOE were travelling BECCLES to YARMOUTH or LOWESTOFT to Norwich. The station at St Olaves Junction which had become Herringfleet Junction in 1891 now closed and was replaced by a new exchange platform HADDISCOE HIGH LEVEL where the through lines crossed. This was a more convenient arrangement for any passengers needing to change trains. HADDISCOE HIGH LEVEL was later upgraded to full station status.

One name change during the period remains to be noted: OULTON BROAD (MUTFORD) dropped the Mutford portion of its title.

1916 -1935

Most railway centres suffered their first closures during the First World War and this area was no exception. In most cases also, although such closures were described as temporary, many became permanent. There were only two closures in this area and both really were temporary. These were both on the WAVERNEY VALLEY line. GELDESTON closed in May 1916 but re-opened, albeit as an unstaffed halt, in September; ELLINGHAM closed between May and Aug 1916.

Grouping had no obvious immediate effect as the three railway undertakings of the area remained as 3 undertakings. During the period following grouping most areas were subject to increasing road competition resulting in line and station closures. But the area saw not a single line or station closure; in fact, it produced the contrary result in that several halts were opened:

1922 GORLESTON GOLF LINKS HALT opened.

1923 Grouping: GREAT EASTERN becomes LONDON + NORTH EASTERN. BELTON becomes BELTON + BURGH. The area's two other railways retain their separate identities but become LNE and LMS owned.

1924 BRUNDALL GARDENS HALT opened.

1933 Halts opened at NEWTOWN (Yarmouth), CAISTER CAMP, CALIFORNIA, SCRATBY and POTTER HEIGHAM BRIDGE. The date of opening of this last halt is unclear but it appears likely it opened at the same time as the others. These halts were seasonal only and operated by a steam railcar, but some SATURDAYS-only, long-distance expresses called at CAISTER CAMP.

One final event during the period was yet a further name change for OULTON BROAD which became OULTON BROAD NORTH to distinguish it from Carlton Colville which had changed its name to OULTON BROAD SOUTH.

1936 -1963

1936 saw the MIDLAND + GREAT NORTHERN JOINT come entirely under the LONDON + NORTH EASTERN. which meant an identical fate befell the NORFOLK + SUFFOLK JOINT although the latter remained nominally independant until becoming part of BRITISH RAIL. The remainder of the period experienced loss of traffic and resulted in an accelerating rationalisation and closure programme.

1942 Gorleston North – closed.

1953 Withdrawal of passenger services on the Waverney Valley line and the consequent closure of passenger stations at: Earsham, Bungay, Ditchingham, Ellingham and Geldeston. The line remained open for goods.

1959 After a brief respite 1959 saw the loss of passenger services on two lines. First the MGN line to the north was closed completely including stations (halts) at Yarmouth Beach, Yarmouth Newtown, Caister·on·Sea, Caister Camp, California, Scratby, Great Ormesby, Hemsby, Martham, Potter Heigham Bridge and Potter Heigham. In fact, the seasonal halts saw their last use in 1958 although official closure was not until 1959. As if this was not enough, South Town to Beccles also lost its passenger service and the following passenger stations closed: Aldeby, Haddiscoe High Level, St Olaves and Belton + Burgh. Theoretically the goods service on the line remained but was little used; its official closure came five years later.

1960 From Bungay westwards on the Waverney Valley line closed completely.

1963 It might be thought, with the wholesale closures of the 'Fifties, the Beeching Report would have been able to leave the area untouched. But this was not the case. Two lines were scheduled for closure: Lowestoft to Beccles and Lowestoft to Yarmouth South Town (the connection to Beach station except for a short goods spur closed in 1959 with the rest of the MGN). Thus the proposed station closures were: BECCLES, OULTON BROAD SOUTH, NORTH LOWESTOFT, CORTON, HOPTON·ON·SEA and YARMOUTH SOUTH TOWN.

1964 - 1977

1964 There was no immediate implementation of the Beeching closure proposals, but lines already reduced to goods only were progressively closed. Fleet Junction to South Quay, having lost its traffic (including goods), was

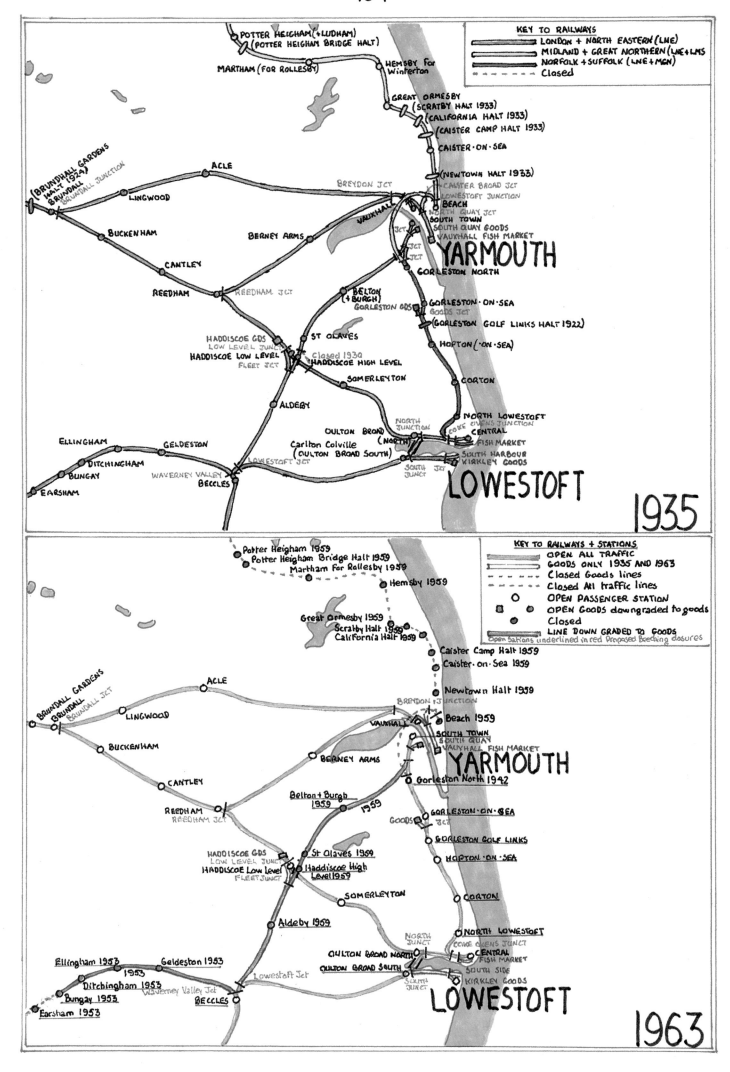

KEY TO RAILWAYS
LONDON + NORTH EASTERN (LNE)
MIDLAND + GREAT NORTHERN (LNE + LMS)
NORFOLK + SUFFOLK (LNE + MGN)
Closed

POTTER HEIGHAM (+LUDHAM)
(POTTER HEIGHAM BRIDGE HALT)
MARTHAM (FOR ROLLESBY)
HEMSBY For Winterton
GREAT ORMESBY
(SCRATBY HALT 1933)
(CALIFORNIA HALT 1933)
(CAISTER CAMP HALT 1933)
CAISTER·ON·SEA
(NEWTOWN HALT 1933)
CAISTER BROAD JCT
LOWESTOFT JUNCTION
BREYDON JCT
BEACH
NORTH QUAY JCT
SOUTH TOWN
SOUTH QUAY GOODS
VAUXHALL FISH MARKET
VAUXHALL
JCT
JCT
YARMOUTH
GORLESTON NORTH
GORLESTON·ON·SEA
GOODS JCT
(GORLESTON GOLF LINKS HALT 1922)
HOPTON (·ON·SEA)
CORTON
NORTH LOWESTOFT
COKE OVENS JUNCTION
CENTRAL
FISH MARKET
SOUTH HARBOUR
KIRKLEY GOODS
LOWESTOFT

(BRUNDALL GARDENS HALT 1924)
BRUNDALL
BRUNDALL JUNCTION
ACLE
LINGWOOD
BUCKENHAM
BERNEY ARMS
CANTLEY
REEDHAM
REEDHAM JCT
BELTON (+BURGH)
GORLESTON GDS
ST OLAVES
HADDISCOE GDS
LOW LEVEL JUNCT
HADDISCOE LOW LEVEL
FLEET JCT
Closed 1930
HADDISCOE HIGH LEVEL
SOMERLEYTON
ALDEBY
OULTON BROAD
(NORTH)
NORTH JUNCTION
ELLINGHAM
GELDESTON
Carlton Colville
(OULTON BROAD SOUTH)
DITCHINGHAM
BUNGAY
WAVERNEY VALLEY JCT
LOWESTOFT JCT
EARSHAM
BECCLES
SOUTH JUNCT

1935

KEY TO RAILWAYS + STATIONS
OPEN ALL TRAFFIC
GOODS ONLY 1935 AND 1963
Closed Goods lines
Closed All traffic lines
○ OPEN PASSENGER STATION
▣ OPEN GOODS downgraded to goods
● Closed
LINE DOWN GRADED TO GOODS
Open stations underlined in red Proposed Beeching closures

Potter Heigham 1959
Potter Heigham Bridge Halt 1959
Martham for Rollesby 1959
Hemsby 1959
Great Ormesby 1959
Scratby Halt 1959
California Halt 1959
Caister Camp Halt 1959
Caister·on·Sea 1959
Newtown Halt 1959
BREYDON JUNCTION
Beach 1959
VAUXHALL
SOUTH TOWN
SOUTH QUAY
VAUXHALL FISH MARKET
YARMOUTH
Gorleston North 1942
GORLESTON·ON·SEA
GOODS JCT
GORLESTON GOLF LINKS
HOPTON·ON·SEA
CORTON
NORTH LOWESTOFT
COKE OVENS JUNCT
CENTRAL
FISH MARKET
SOUTH SIDE
KIRKLEY GOODS
LOWESTOFT

BRUNDALL GARDENS
BRUNDALL
BRUNDALL JCT
ACLE
LINGWOOD
BUCKENHAM
BERNEY ARMS
CANTLEY
REEDHAM
REEDHAM JCT
Belton + Burgh 1959
1959
HADDISCOE GDS
LOW LEVEL JUNCT
St Olaves 1959
HADDISCOE Low Level
FLEET JUNCT
Haddiscoe High Level 1959
SOMERLEYTON
Aldeby 1959
OULTON BROAD NORTH
OULTON BROAD SOUTH
NORTH JUNCT
Ellingham 1953
Geldeston 1953
1953
Ditchingham 1953
Lowestoft Jct
Waverney Valley Jct
Bungay 1953
Earsham 1953
BECCLES
SOUTH JUNCT

1963

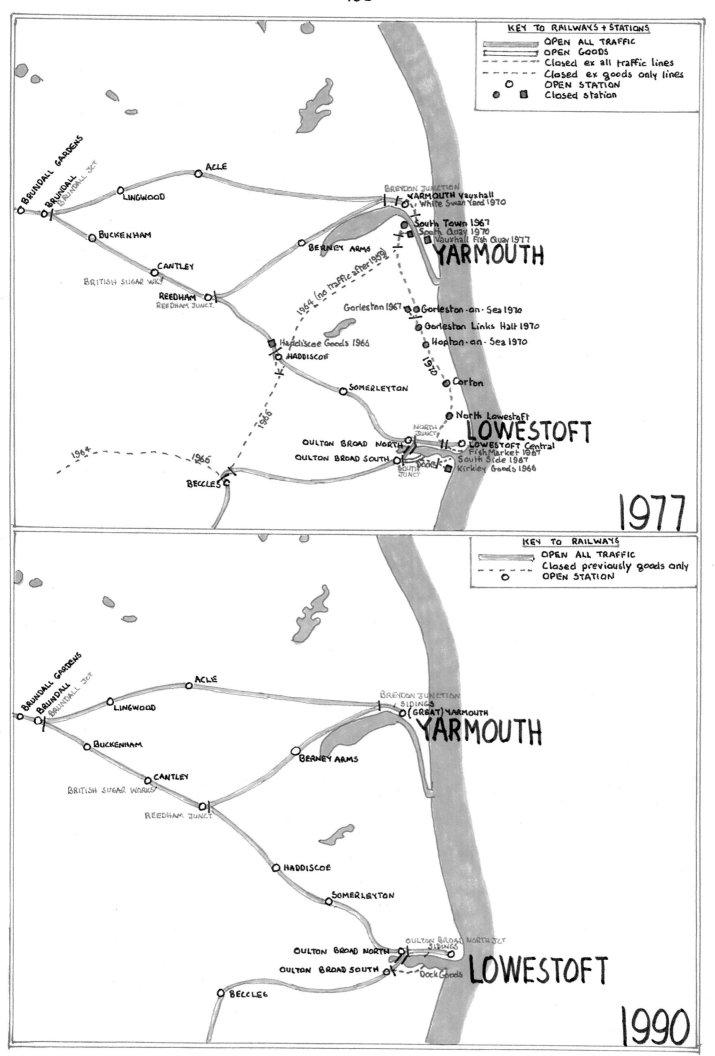

KEY TO RAILWAYS + STATIONS

OPEN ALL TRAFFIC
OPEN GOODS
Closed ex all traffic lines
Closed ex goods only lines
OPEN STATION
Closed station

BRUNDALL GARDENS
BRUNDALL
BRUNDALL JCT
LINGWOOD
ACLE
BUCKENHAM
CANTLEY
BRITISH SUGAR WKS
REEDHAM
REEDHAM JUNCT.
BERNEY ARMS
BREYDON JUNCTION
YARMOUTH Vauxhall
White Swan Yard 1970
South Town 1967
South Quay 1970
Vauxhall Fish Quay 1977
YARMOUTH
1964 (no traffic after 1969)
Gorleston 1967
Gorleston-on-Sea 1970
Gorleston Links Halt 1970
Hopton-on-Sea 1970
Corton
Haddiscoe Goods 1966
HADDISCOE
1966
SOMERLEYTON
North Lowestoft
NORTH JUNCT.
OULTON BROAD NORTH
OULTON BROAD SOUTH
SOUTH JUNCT
LOWESTOFT
LOWESTOFT Central
FishMarket 1967
South Side 1967
Kirkley Goods 1966
Dock
1964
1966
1966
BECCLES

1977

KEY TO RAILWAYS

OPEN ALL TRAFFIC
Closed previously goods only
OPEN STATION

BRUNDALL GARDENS
BRUNDALL
BRUNDALL JCT
LINGWOOD
ACLE
BUCKENHAM
CANTLEY
BRITISH SUGAR WORKS
REEDHAM JUNCT
BERNEY ARMS
BREYDON JUNCTION
SIDINGS
(GREAT) YARMOUTH
YARMOUTH
HADDISCOE
SOMERLEYTON
OULTON BROAD NORTH JCT
SIDINGS
OULTON BROAD NORTH
OULTON BROAD SOUTH
Dock Goods
LOWESTOFT
BECCLES

1990

closed. The Waveney Valley route was also cut back further during the year.

1965 The remaining goods-only lines closed during the year. These were remainder of the Waveney Valley line and Beccles to Haddiscoe.

1966 Goods stations closed: Haddiscoe, Kirkley and Gorleston.

1967 Goods stations closed: Lowestoft South Side, Lowestoft Fish Market.

1970 After a two year respite on closures, White Swan Yard and South Quay Goods were both closed. At last a start was made on the Beeching proposals with closure of the NORFOLK + SUFFOLK line to all traffic. This resulted in the following station closures: Yarmouth South Town, Gorleston-on-Sea, Gorleston Golf Links Halt, Hopton-on-Sea, North Lowestoft and Corton. The other line proposed for closure under Beeching, LOWESTOFT to the South, has survived and in fact still remains open into the 1990's.

1977 Final closure was Vauxhall Fish Quay after 130 years service.

1978 - 1990

The story of this final period is soon told in that nothing happened. Two proposals of the period are, however, worth recording. First in the mid-eighties it was proposed to close the line between Reedham Junction and Breydon Junction, but this has been resisted. The other proposal, not yet implemented, is additional platforms at OULTON BROAD NORTH to enable trains from the south to call at the station, which station has to date only served passengers on the Norwich line.

To conclude this chapter a family tree chart of the area railways is shown below:

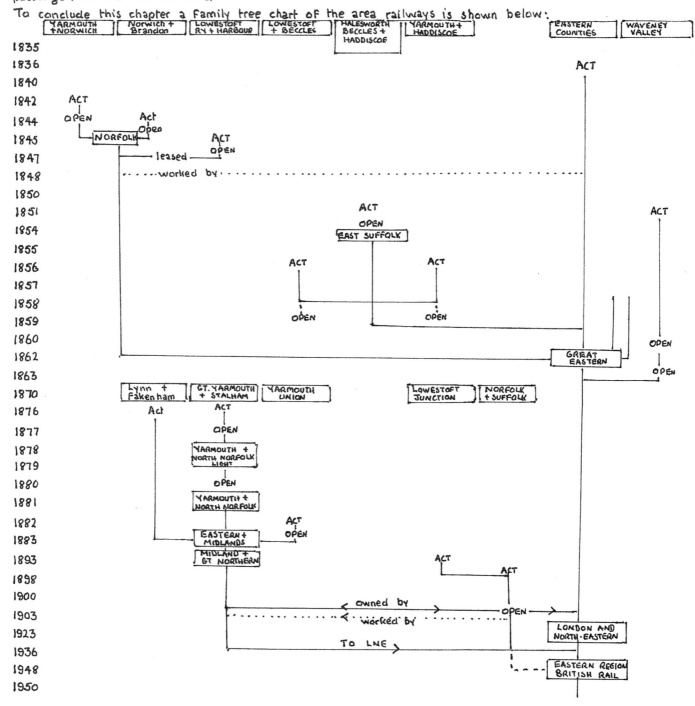

NORTHAMPTON

Although ultimately NORTHAMPTON became a railway centre with lines radiating in all directions it has remained something of a backwater. This appears strange in view of its established importance both as a county town and administrative centre and the centre of the boot manufacturing industry before the start of the nineteenth century. In addition NORTHAMPTON had become an important staging point on road routes to the north; indeed, at this time the inn-keeping industry had grown to be the town's largest employer. In many ways it formed a natural half-way house on the proposed LONDON + BIRMINGHAM. But in the event the LONDON + BIRMINGHAM passed the town by, the popular explanation for this action being the townspeople's objections. Although some contemporary reports appear to confirm this, an objective examination of the situation makes it an unlikely explanation. As others have deduced, a more likely explanation is the local topography as the contour maps of the area show. As was said at the time it was easy enough to reach NORTHAMPTON - the problems arose in trying to leave it. An identical difficulty had faced the canal engineers that any fall to the Nene valley would need to be balanced by a corresponding climb on the route northwards. The canal solution was a tunnel near Rugby and a branch canal to NORTHAMPTON which when constructed had seventeen locks in its short length. The LONDON + BIRMINGHAM railway had the identical problems to the canal and logically it dealt with them in the same way with a tunnel south of Rugby and a short branch line to NORTHAMPTON. Although the line continued beyond Northampton, this latter portion was only single track. Despite strenuous later efforts this poor start was never really overcome and is reflected in the 1990's railway network at Northampton with its branch-line service, which although now a loop line, gives a slower time for journeys to London than was available some sixty or seventy years earlier.

The first two maps show relief and navigable water, thereby illustrating these early difficulties, and show why NORTHAMPTON has always been a railway backwater.

1800-1840

The year 1800 saw opening of the Grand Junction Canal, a late arrival in the canal field. In the main this late date of opening was due to the difficult terrain in the vicinity of NORTHAMPTON. Near the town there were no less than three substantial canal tunnels and even then NORTHAMPTON was by-passed and the contour map shows the reason. Pressure from the town, however, ensured the building of a branch canal, but this short branch, falling by 17 locks to the Nene Valley to join the Nene Navigation, did not open until 1815.

Railway development, as mentioned above, followed the same pattern. The LONDON + BIRMINGHAM was authorised in 1833 and was eventually opened to traffic throughout in 1838. In the map area there were stations at WEEDON, BLISWORTH (sited where the road to NORTHAMPTON crossed the railway) and ROADE. As with the canal this part of the railway was the last to be completed due to the difficulties with Kilsby tunnel. This cost over three times the original estimated cost and it is possible the line engineers, the Stephensons, spread the story about the town's opposition to the railway to divert possible flak about the costs. The difficulties were in part due to trial bores not being made, relying on the railway tunnel being close to the canal tunnel. There is no doubt that the Stephensons were excellent locomotive engineers but as line engineers they were really not very good. Apart from their errors with Kilsby Tunnel there was the strange proposal with the Leeds + Hull as mentioned in the Hull chapter. Also the collapse of the Dee Bridge within a year of opening for traffic was held by the Board of Trade to be their responsibility. With other structures too they need help in practicalities of design.

1841-1855

The only event of note during this period was the BLISWORTH to Peterborough line. This was authorised in 1842, to be constructed by the LONDON + BIRMINGHAM, and opened three years later in 1845. There were stations within the map area at: NORTHAMPTON and BILLING ROAD. The following year the LONDON + BIRMINGHAM became part of the LONDON + NORTH WESTERN.

In the meantime from as early as the mid-1830's Northampton tried to encourage a through line from the north which it hoped would give NORTHAMPTON a direct link to LONDON. But these early schemes all came to nothing. Eventually in 1853 the LONDON + NORTH WESTERN obtained powers to build a line to the north as the 1855 map shows, but this was only to be of local branch status as will be seen.

The only other event to record was also in 1853. The original BLISWORTH station, sited to afford the best road communication with NORTHAMPTON, was closed and replaced by a more conveniently sited station from a railway operating point of view; it was close to the junction of the branch line to NORTHAMPTON.

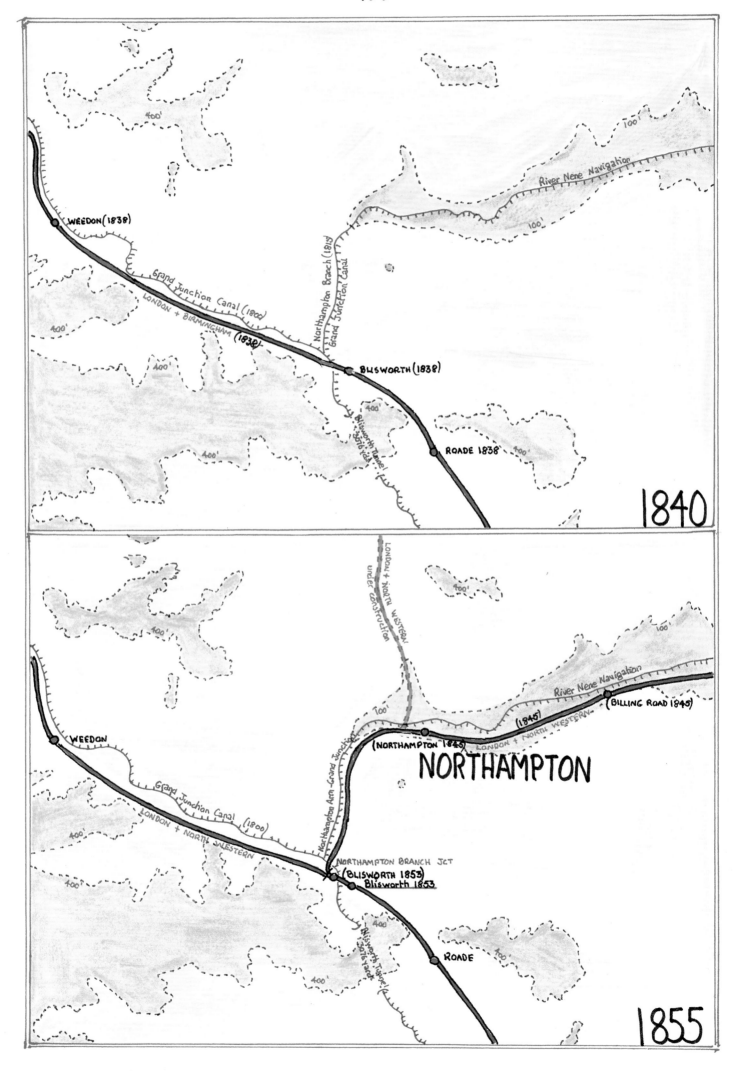

1840

1855

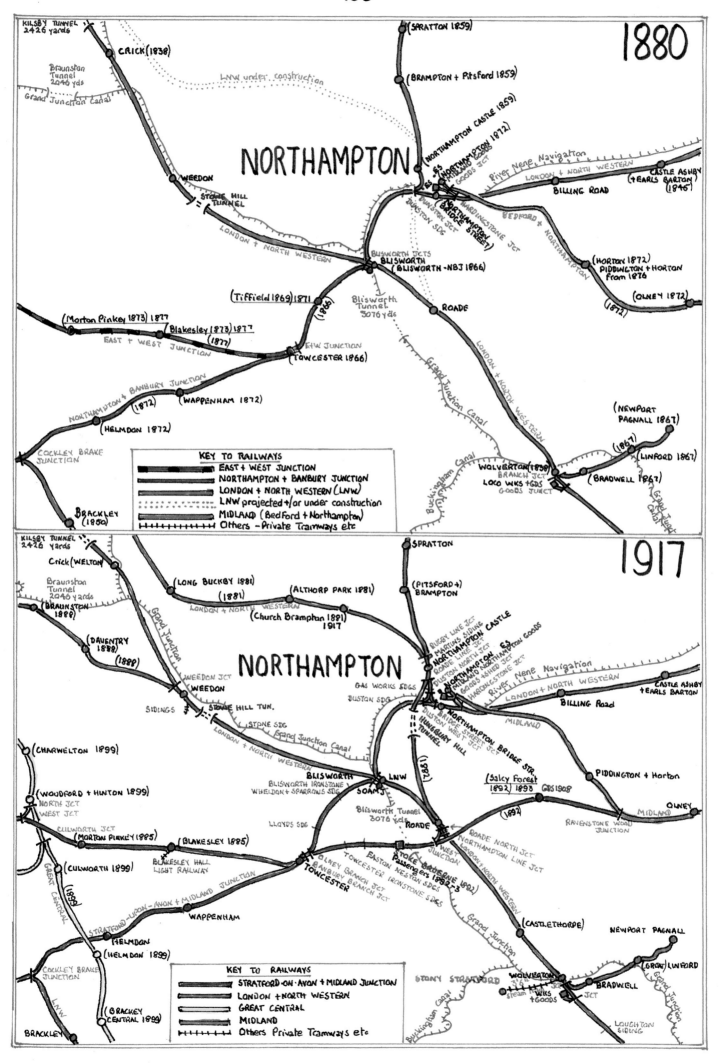

The remaining maps covering the development of NORTHAMPTON are on a somewhat smaller scale, thus enabling a somewhat larger area to be covered. The canal network is shown on the next two of these, up to 1917. After this date the area's canal network had ceased to have any significance on the railways, although it is of interest to note that the canal network has, in the long term, fared better than that of the railways. Rationalisation has decimated the railways whilst, apart from the derelict Buckingham Canal, the canal network remains intact although now devoted purely to pleasure activities.

1856-1880

16. 2. 1859 LONDON + NORTH WESTERN (LNW) open a line from NORTHAMPTON (Duston Junction) to Market Harborough. There were stations, within the map area, at NORTHAMPTON CASTLE, BRAMPTON + PITSFORD (which after a period when it was known as BRAMPTON became PITSFORD + BRAMPTON), and SPRATTON. The town had hoped that this would be a main line through the town but it was only ever accorded branch status.

28. 7. 1863 NORTHAMPTON + BANBURY JUNCTION (NBJ) - Authorised.

23. 6. 1864 EAST + WEST JUNCTION (EWJ) - Authorised.

1. 5. 1866 NBJ opened to all traffic, from a station (adjoining the LNW station) at BLISWORTH to TOWCESTER. The main traffic appears to have been iron ore. An intermediate station at TIFFIELD was opened in 1869 but closed in 1871 just before the remainder of the line opened (1872).

2. 9. 1867 LNW opened branch from WOLVERTON to NEWPORT PAGNALL. There were intermediate stations at BRADWELL and LINFORD (later became GREAT LINFORD). WOLVERTON had been an original LONDON + BIRMINGHAM station opened in 1838 and being the line's mid-point was selected as the site of an engine shed and locomotive works.

1. 6. 1872 NBJ opened from TOWCESTER to COCKLEY BRAKE JUNCTION with the LNW and access to the latter's Merton Str. terminus at Banbury (had opened for goods to Helmdon in August 1871). Intermediate stations at: WAPPENHAM and HELMDON. Until it became part of the STRATFORD-UPON-AVON + MIDLAND JUNCTION in 1910, the line was worked by the LNW during most of its independant existence.

10. 6. 1872 BEDFORD + NORTHAMPTON opened to a temporary station at NORTHAMPTON which became a goods station when the permanent station was opened. The line had been authorised 5.7.1865, was worked by the MIDLAND from the outset although not absorbed by that company until 1895. There were two intermediate stations within the map area at: OLNEY and HORTON (later became PIDDINGTON and HORTON and finally PIDDINGTON).

1. 7. 1873 EWJ opened TOWCESTER to Fenny Compton. Map area stations: BLAKESLEY and MORTON PINKEY. The passenger service was withdrawn 1.8.1877 due to the financial difficulties of the company.

15. 8. 1879 EASTON, NESTON MINERAL + TOWCESTER, ROADE + OLNEY JUNCTION (ENMTROJ) - Authorised.

1880 LNW - work progressing on the line from ROADE to Rugby via NORTHAMPTON.

1881-1917

1. 12. 1881 LNW opened NORTHAMPTON to RUGBY. CASTLE station rebuilt. Intermediate map area stations at LONG BUCKBY, ALTHORP PARK and CHURCH BRAMPTON.

3. 4. 1882 LNW opened NORTHAMPTON to ROADE at last putting NORTHAMPTON on a through north-south route.

10. 8. 1882 ENMTROJ name changed to STRATFORD-UPON-AVON, TOWCESTER + MIDLAND JUNCTION (SUATMJ).

1. 11. 1882 WOLVERTON + STONY STRATFORD TRAMWAY (WSS) - Authorised.

22. 2. 1885 EWJ re-opened to passengers, together with the stations at BLAKESLEY and MORTON PINKEY.

27. 5. 1887 WSS opened - gauge 3'6". The company had already changed its name and route twice. It was, and would continue to be, in financial difficulties. It also continued to change its name and to keep closing and re-opening. Eventually purchased by LNW after its third period in Receivership. It was used to carry LNW employees to Wolverton Works once it came into LNW hands.

1. 3. 1888 LNW opened DAVENTRY branch from a junction at WEEDON. Map area stations: DAVENTRY and BRAUNSTON. Proposals for the line started as early as 1845 but authorisation took forty years being eventually obtained in 1885!

1. 12. 1892 SUATMJ opened from TOWCESTER to Ravenstone Wood Junction. Stations SALCY (or SALCEY) FOREST and STOKE BRUERNE. It closed to passengers after only four months on 31.3.1893, but continued in use for goods and some through passenger trains.

15. 3. 1899 GREAT CENTRAL (GC) opened for passenger traffic. Map area stations: CHARWELTON, WOODFORD + HINTON, CULWORTH, HELMDON and BRACKLEY CENTRAL. Connection to EWJ at WOODFORD where goods depot and engine shed were opened making it an important railway community. There was a further connection from CULWORTH JUNCTION to the GREAT WESTERN at Banbury. The area line network was now complete although the merger of the EWJ, NBJ, and SUATMJ remains to be recorded.

1.1.1909 STRATFORD·UPON·AVON + MIDLAND JUNCTION (SMJ) - Formed. Act 1·8·1908. Merger of: EAST + WEST JUNCTION, STRATFORD·UPON·AVON, TOWCESTER + MIDLAND JUNCTION and Evesham, Redditch + Stratford·upon·Avon.

1.7.1910 SMJ absorb the NORTHAMPTON + BANBURY JUNCTION.

1.1.1917 LONDON + NORTH WESTERN (LNW) close CHURCH BRAMPTON to passenger traffic as a wartime economy.

Before looking at the next period it is appropriate take a brief look at engine sheds in the area. The first shed opened was that at WOLVERTON thought to have opened in 1838. It was the LONDON + BIRMINGHAM's No.1 shed due to its position at the mid-point on the line. A locomotive and carriage works was established at the same time. This latter continued to expand, and in spite of the concentration of locomotive production at Crewe in the 1860s it continued as wagon carriage works and remains in use for this purpose up to the present time. The later growth led to closure of the engine shed about 1874 when locomotives were concentrated at NORTHAMPTON, shed facilities having grown up in the triangular junction area between Bridge Street and Castle. The MIDLAND also had a small shed at NORTHAMPTON dating from the opening of the Bedford to NORTHAMPTON line. The other shed opened in the area was the GREAT CENTRAL shed at WOODFORD opened in 1898. This was an half·way staging post on the GREAT CENTRAL's London Extension. This was also one of the few locations where the GREAT CENTRAL had some connections with other railways. The resulting goods and shed facilities made WOODFORD into a rail community.

1918-1940

This period saw railways under serious pressure from road competition, but there is little evidence on the map of any changes. In the early 1930's NORTHAMPTON at last got a good express service to London with timings down to 70 minutes for the 66·mile journey.

1919 LNW re·opened CHURCH BRAMPTON.

1923 GROUPING. The LNW, SMJ and MIDLAND became part of the LONDON MIDLAND + SCOTTISH (LMS) whilst only the GREAT CENTRAL joined the LONDON + NORTH EASTERN (LNE).

1926 LMS close STONY STRATFORD - WOLVERTON Tramway - brought about as a result of the General Strike.

1931 LMS close CHURCH BRAMPTON - Reason - Inconvenient location and road competition. Other similar stations were planned for closure - and new halts were planned. In the event neither closures nor openings were implemented.

1933 LMS open new Goods Depot at NORTHAMPTON. The central situation away from the main line made it a useful freight sorting centre. But this did nothing for the express service to London and it became increasingly hard to find express paths to NORTHAMPTON with lines to the town becoming increasingly cluttered with goods.

1940 It will be noted that the whole period has seen no change in the passenger station situation, the only opening in 1919 being balanced by closure of the same station in 1931, although Northampton (Mid) closed.

1941-1963

In spite of growing road competition NORTHAMPTON's railway network remained totally intact until nationalisation. But from 1949 a steady programme of station closures set in.

1949 Spratton closed to passengers.

1950 Pitsford + Brampton closed to passengers.

1951 Helmdon (ex SMJ) and Wappenham closed to passengers. The line continued in use for freight but that too was lost the following year.

1952 Stoke Bruern Goods closed. Crockley Brake Junction to Ravenstone Wood Junction closed to all traffic. Morton Pinkey, Blakesley and Towcester closed to passengers, but this portion of the ex SMJ to Blisworth was retained for goods traffic. Billing (on the Peterborough line) closed. Following this, a brief closure respite followed. But the decimisation process started again in 1958.

1958 DAVENTRY Branch closed to passengers together with stations at Braunston and Daventry. All traffic closure was five years later in 1963. Welton and Weedon, intermediate stations on the main line, were also closed. On the ex-GC main line Culworth closed to all traffic.

1960 Althorp Park - closed. Blisworth closed.

1962 NORTHAMPTON to Bedford line closed to passengers with stations Piddington and Olney but this line did retains its goods traffic

1963 Charwelton closed to all traffic; Helmdon (ex GC) lost its passenger service but continued to handle goods. Then, of course, the BEECHING REPORT was unveiled. At this stage, with only 12 area stations remaining, it was proposed to close 75% of them. The casualties were to be: NORTHAMPTON - BRIDGE STREET, CASTLE ASHBY + EARLS BARTON (closing the Peterborough line), BRADWELL, GREAT LINFORD, NEWPORT PAGNALL (closing the branch), WOODFORD HALSE, BRACKLEY CENTRAL (closing the ex-GC main line), ROADE and CASTLETHORPE (two intermediate stations on the main line).

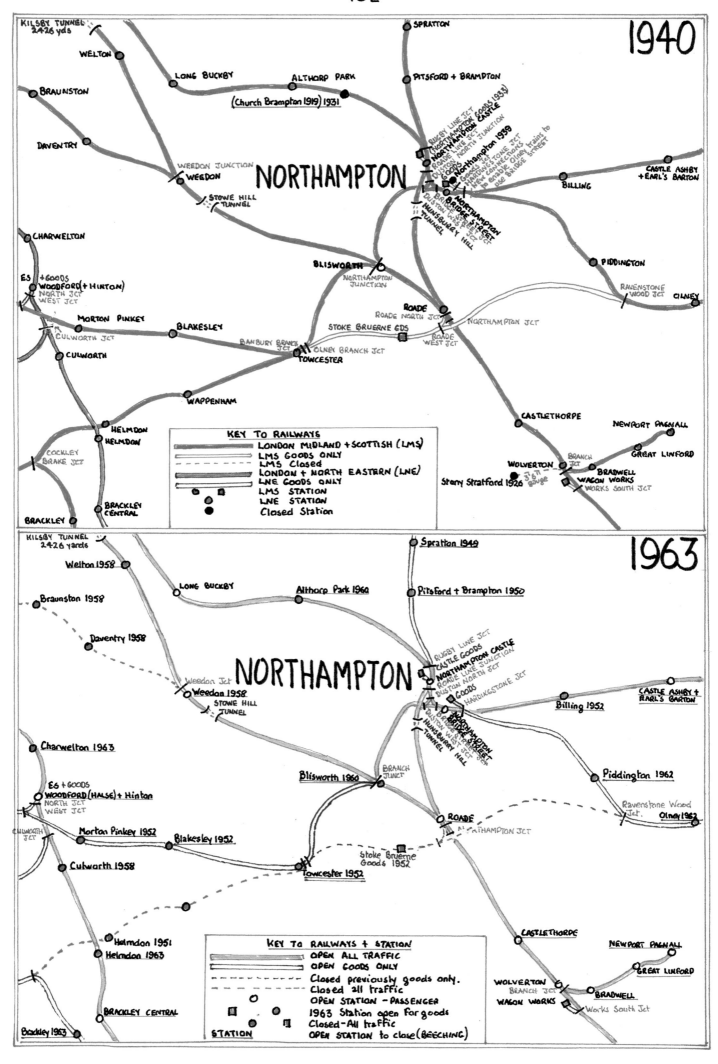

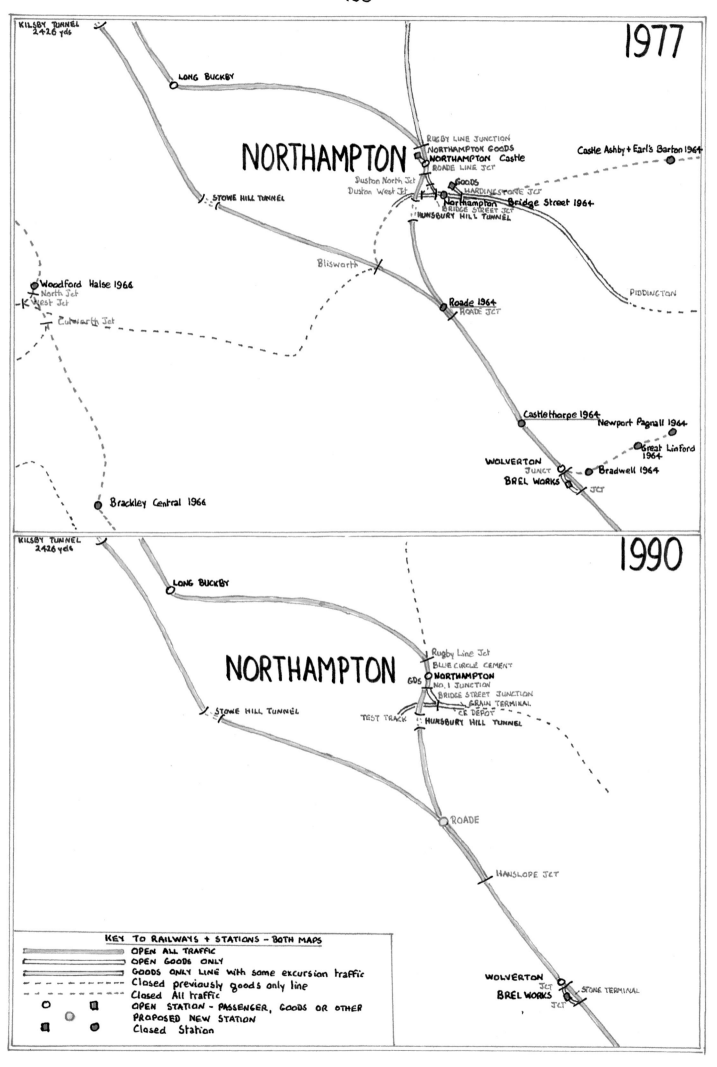

1977

KILSBY TUNNEL
2426 yds

LONG BUCKBY

NORTHAMPTON

RUGBY LINE JUNCTION
NORTHAMPTON GOODS
NORTHAMPTON Castle
ROADE LINE JCT

Castle Ashby + Earl's Barton 1964

Duston North Jct
Duston West Jct

STOWE HILL TUNNEL

GOODS
HARDINGSTONE JCT
Northampton Bridge Street 1964
BRIDGE STREET JCT
HUNSBURY HILL TUNNEL

Blisworth

PIDDINGTON

Woodford Halse 1966
North Jct
West Jct

Roade 1964
ROADE JCT

Culworth Jct

Castlethorpe 1964
Newport Pagnall 1964

Great Linford 1964

WOLVERTON
JUNCT
BREL WORKS
Bradwell 1964
JCT

Brackley Central 1966

KILSBY TUNNEL
2426 yds

1990

LONG BUCKBY

NORTHAMPTON

Rugby Line Jct
BLUE CIRCLE CEMENT
NORTHAMPTON
GDS
No.1 JUNCTION
BRIDGE STREET JUNCTION
GRAIN TERMINAL
CE DEPOT
TEST TRACK
HUNSBURY HILL TUNNEL

STOWE HILL TUNNEL

ROADE

HANSLOPE JCT

KEY TO RAILWAYS + STATIONS — BOTH MAPS
OPEN ALL TRAFFIC
OPEN GOODS ONLY
GOODS ONLY LINE with some excursion traffic
Closed previously goods only line
Closed All traffic
OPEN STATION — PASSENGER, GOODS OR OTHER
PROPOSED NEW STATION
Closed Station

WOLVERTON
BREL WORKS
JCT
STONE TERMINAL
JCT

1964-1977

The effects of the Beeching Report on various centres have already been noted. In most cases the bulk of the report's recommendations were carried out, sometimes with substitute closures for some of those published. In a few places, the proposals were almost totally ignored - Chester being a good example of this tactic. In yet other places it could take ten years or more to complete the programme or five or six years might pass before a start was made, as noted in the case of Yarmouth + Lowestoft. NORTHAMPTON came in none of these categories, but in the one which implemented all the proposals with neither additions or subtractions within a short time. In fact, but for the special pleading noted below it appears that all would have been closed by the end of 1964.

During 1964 the NEWPORT PAGNALL BRANCH passenger service was withdrawn resulting in closure of Bradwell, Great Linford and Newport Pagnall. Goods service persisted for a further period but the branch closed entirely in 1967. The line to Peterborough also closed to passengers during the year leading to the closure of Northampton (Bridge Street) and Castle Ashby + Earl's Barton. Goods traffic finished shortly afterwards but a few short spurs in Northampton itself remained until the close of the period. Also during the year the main line intermediate stations at Roade and Castlethorpe closed, leaving only WOLVERTON (on the main line) still open. Also during the year the last remnants of the SMJ were closed except for a possible GC connection.

The only Beeching proposed closures not implemented in 1964 were those on the old Great Central main line, and in this case there was a special reason since there was an appeal, which postponed the intended 1964 closure, presented by the railway unions on the grounds of hardship to the railway community of WOODFORD HALSE. However, closure of the line had been inevitable from as early as 1948 when progressive run-down had started. At the time of the 'Good Doctor's' report BR actually regarded the main line as terminating at Banbury with a branch to London! This may appear strange but the entire line has often been compared to an umbilical cord and its failure to generate traffic had resulted from the lack of connections with the rest of the network. To really appreciate its isolation an interesting exercise would be to take a pre-war Bradshaw and work out the shortest time it would take to travel by rail from RUGBY to RUGBY CENTRAL, or LEICESTER CENTRAL to LEICESTER LONDON ROAD. Even looking at the shortest rail distance is quite an eye-opener. The appeal was reluctantly turned down and line and stations closed in 1966.

Also during the period the Olney goods line was cut back to Piddington, and in fact was until closure in 1981 operated by the army. It served an ordanance depot. The only goods-only line remaining was that to the north used to bring freight into the NORTHAMPTON FREIGHT SORTING CENTRE. This line did however continue to carry some excursion passenger trains.

However, the town's freight traffic did little for NORTHAMPTON's passenger services. Electrification brought a dramatic reduction in most journey times but at NORTHAMPTON it had the reverse effect. This was due to the fact that trains from London calling there had to use the freight lines and secure a path between goods trains. 80 minutes became the shortest journey time comparing unfavourably with 70 minutes in the early 1930's.

1978-1990

In many places this period has shown modest revivals, but not at NORTHAMPTON, and further rationalisation has taken place; all the goods-only lines have gone with the exception of industrial spurs in the town centre. Freight has declined although NORTHAMPTON still undertakes some remarshalling and the loop lines through the town used for diversion purposes enable main-line expresses to maintain 100mph schedules. But this has not helped the people of NORTHAMPTON to reach LONDON in a decent time. As mentioned above the best 1990 time is 80 minutes, 10 minutes slower than 60 years ago, whilst RUGBY, 16 miles further from London, is reached a full 30 minutes quicker!

1991 - FUTURE

The future of NORTHAMPTON's railways is tinged with hope, at least on the passenger train timings to London. This is on two counts: The reduction of freight could lead to some acceleration of London trains, and not before time. The other hopeful factor is a proposed new station at ROADE. If this is to be served by main-line expresses with parking available it should enable NORTHAMPTON to be reached from London in an hour, including the car journey from ROADE. However, if it is to be an additional stop on the existing service it will just mean an additional stop and could make present timings worse.

It is to be hoped that BR will have got it right for once, but I don't think we can bank on it at this stage. It would be nice to think, however, that at last the 70-minute barrier of the 1930's might well be broken even if it will have taken over 60 years to do it.

PONTYPRIDD

Most railway centres have unique sets of circumstances influencing their development even though some or all of these might be found elsewhere. At Pontypridd two main factors influenced development; both have been noted at other centres. These factors were: First, coal and iron and associated industries; and secondly, relief, since the area is cut into by deep, steepsided valleys which dictated transport routes from the earliest times. However, if the reasons for development were commonplace and mundane Pontypridd had three unusual features associated with its railways, including both a world first, and a Welsh first, and though these did not influence the area development they are worth recording. First, it was in this area that the world's first steam locomotive to run on rails made its first journey, Richard Trevethick's locomotive being used to carry iron from Penydarren along a tramway to the Glamorganshire Canal at Navigation House. It is recorded that this journey was undertaken for a wager of five hundred guineas. The use of steam, though satisfactory for traction, was not pursued since the locomotive distorted the cast iron rails due to its weight. The second unique event and a Welsh first is that Pontypridd became the earliest railway centre in the principality. My earliest map showing railways in Wales either opened or under construction is dated 1839. Only five railways are shown and all effectively radiate from PONTYPRIDD. The third unusual feature of this railway centre was its non-existance as a name until the mid-1860's when it became Pontypridd solely on the initiative of the local postmaster. In the early days of the nineteenth century there was on the west bank of the Taff a substantial colliery known as PONTYPRYDD, whilst on the opposite bank there was an ironworks known as NEWBRIDGE. The TAFF VALE railway sited its station close to the ironworks and was known as NEWBRIDGE. The name change may have been prompted to avoid confusion between other local settlements with the same name and particularly that near CRUMLIN.

The intricacies of the local network have led to a different format being used for this centre. The first two maps are at standard scale but include relief accentuating the confinement of the early lines to the valleys. The four following maps cover a smaller area but are at 1" to the mile, the last of these being dated 1926 but including subsequent openings. The final four maps revert to the smaller scale and exclude details except those related to line and station closures.

1790-1835

9.6.1790 GLAMORGANSHIRE CANAL - Act. Authorised building of a canal from Merthyr Tidvile to The Bank near Cardiff. A later Act authorised extension to the Cardiff Docks area. The canal on completion was 25½ miles long, with 51 locks, one short tunnel (115 yards), and it rose 543 feet following the river Taff which it crossed by a viaduct at ABERCYNON. The main canal opened in 1794 and the extension four years later. The owners of iron works and collieries were encouraged to build tramroads linking with it. Some of the longer of these are sketched in on the first map.

28.3.1793 ABERDARE CANAL - Act. This was a simple route with a rise of only 26'. It was also authorised to be fed by tramways. In spite of this easy route almost twenty years passed before construction began. But once a start had been made, completion was rapid and it opened for traffic in August 1812.

21.2.1804 PENYDARREN PLATEWAY (which opened about 1802 to avoid the congested heavily locked section of GLAMORGAN-SHIRE Canal) witnessed the first steam locomotive to run on rails. By this time the canal was proving to be inadequate and there were frequent disputes amongst the directors regarding shortcomings of facilities provided to them as iron-masters, whilst complaining of the canal's use of their water. In addition to this, colliery workings frequently led to subsidence and the bursting of canal banks.

20.5.1825 RUMNEY - Act. Although its Act described it as a railway it was in fact a tramway to 4'2" gauge to run from Lower Rhymney to what later became Bassaleg Junction near Newport feeding traffic to the MONMOUTHSHIRE Canal at that point. It was not opened throughout until 1836. It was later reformed to be converted into a railway proper and absorbed by the BRECON & MERTHYR in the early 1860's.

31.8.1835 GREAT WESTERN - Act.

As noted above, the area's canals were becoming increasingly inadequate and tramroads were already more important since they were able to penetrate areas unreachable by canal and connect directly to their industrial users. At about this time a group of the directors of the GLAMORGANSHIRE resigned and set about the promotion of the TAFF VALE Railway.

1836-1854

21.6.1836 TAFF VALE (TV) - Act.

8.10.1840 TV opened from Cardiff (or Caerdiff as the 1839 map spells it) to NAVIGATION HOUSE. There appear to have

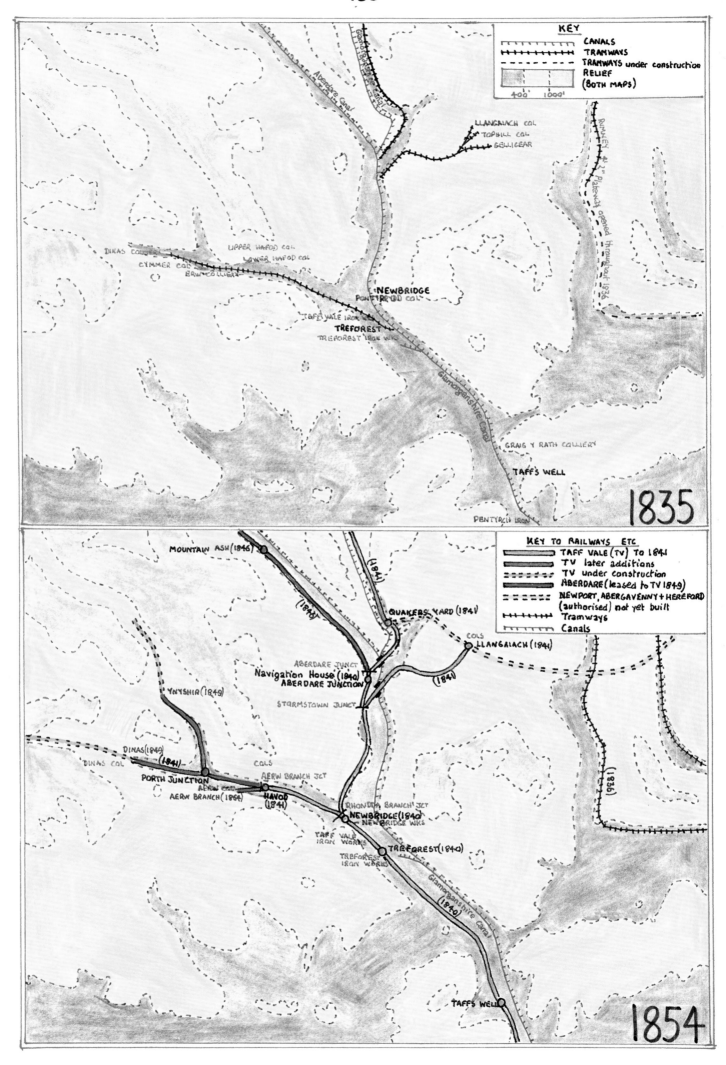

166

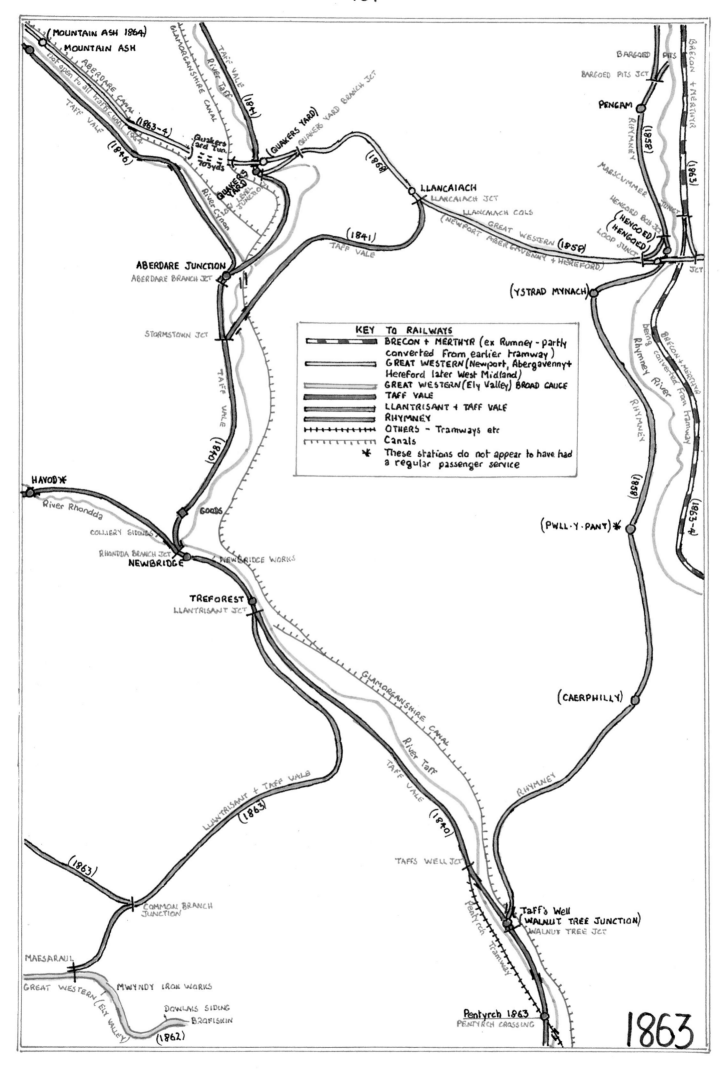

1863

been intermediate stations within the map area at TREFOREST and TAFF'S WELL.

28.4.1841 TAFF VALE(TV) opened the remainder of its main line between NAVIGATION HOUSE and Merthyr. It appears that a further intermediate station was opened at QUAKERS YARD but the initial use at this site might well have been restricted to goods traffic only.

6.1841 TV opened from Rhondda Branch Junction at NEWBRIDGE (Pontypridd) to Havod (later Trehafod) and Dinas.

12.1841 TV opened branch to Llangaiach (spelling is from contemporary railway sources). This branch would appear to have been limited to coal traffic to begin with.

It can be seen therefore that by the end of 1841 the railway had virtually duplicated the earlier canal system and its feeder tramways. The canal company which had hitherto had more traffic than it could cope with and had reduced tolls and given free periods, due to a clause in its constitution limiting dividends to 8% was not too concerned and re-acted by increasing charges for traffic where works etc were close to the canal but maintaining cheap rates for competitive traffic. In 1844 an agreement between canal, railway and Lord Bute, owner of Cardiff Docks, appeared likely. The canal company withdrew, even with the signs of writing on the wall. This action led to the railway duplicating the few remaining feeder lines of their remaining monopoly accelerating the steady decline of canal traffic and revenues.

31.7.1845 ABERDARE - Act for a line closely following the canal. Sponsored by the TV.

4.1846 ABERDARE opened. With its comparatively level route and no major engineering problems this was quickly completed. Aberdare canal traffic fell to a trickle which in turn further starved GLAMORGANSHIRE Canal of further traffic and revenues which had hitherto been a useful feeder connection.

3.8.1846 NEWPORT, ABERGAVENNY + HEREFORD - Act. Strange that a railway with this title should penetrate the area but authorisation included a line through Crumlin to QUAKERS YARD and to continue to give access to Aberdare and its coal.

1.1.1849 ABERDARE leased to TV for 999 years; effectively becomes part of TV.

During the year TV extended its line up the Rhondda Valley (both main valley and Rhondda Fach). In fact authority for both these lines had been obtained some years earlier but the TV were not anxious to go ahead until they were sure that from coal traffic alone the line would be remunerative enough. This cautious policy of remunerative expansion made the TV throughout its existence one of the best dividend payers of all time, in the railway sector.

27.7.1854 RHYMNEY - ACT

During the year TV opened the Aerw Colliery Branch (one mile long).

1855 - 1863

The main network of the area could be said to be in place by the end of the 1840's, but there was still a great deal of development to follow. So far as the TV were concerned this consisted of a series of branch lines into the subsidiary valleys. The other company lines that became established in the area served parallel valleys (as with the RHYMNEY) or sought to divert traffic to other ports (BARRY to Barry; NEWPORT, ABERGAVENNY + HEREFORD to Newport with lines also to Swansea and a competitive outlet to Cardiff).

13.7.1857 ELY VALLEY - Act. This was the first (and last) broad gauge line to penetrate the area.

9.1.1858 NEWPORT ABERGAVENNY + HEREFORD (NAH) opened from Tredegar Junction to QUAKERS YARD (later to become HIGH LEVEL) with a branch to QUAKERS YARD (TV station); stations at HENGOED and LLAN CAIACH (this latter station was also used by the TV branch and was a different site to the original station.

31.1.1858 RHYMNEY opened for goods between Rhymney and a junction with NAH (see above). Exact date unclear but was open by the end of the month.

25.2.1858 RHYMNEY opened for goods between Hengoed Branch Junction and TAFF'S WELL (which was renamed WALNUT TREE JUNCTION in 1863). Opened for passengers 31·3. Stations: PENGAM, HENGOED, YSTRAD MYNACH and CAERPHILLY.

1.8.1859 BRECON + MERTHYR TYDFIL JUNCTION - Act. Usually known simply as BRECON + MERTHYR (BM).

14.6.1860 WEST MIDLAND (WM) formed. So far as this area is concerned the effect was that the NAH as one of the constituents of the WM became a part of that concern. Shortly afterwards WM concluded an agreement to become part of the GREAT WESTERN (GW) but the legal merger did not take place until 1863.

1.1.1861 ELY VALLEY (EV) leased to GW.

7.6.1861 LLANTRISANT + TAFF VALE JUNCTION (LTVJ) - Authorisation.

1.8.1861 RUMNEY Reincorporated as a railway - to convert existing tramway (Act 1825 - opened throughout in 1836).

8.6.1862 GW open EV Mwyndy Branch - for goods only - BROAD GAUGE line - the only one in the area. Rather strange that this should be so, particularly as the TAFF VALE engineer was none other than the famous I.K. Brunel, but he was influenced by the nature of the terrain.

1863 LTVJ opened to goods from Llantrisant Branch Jct (Treforest) to Maesaraul Jct and Common Branch Junction.

28. 7.1863 RUMNEY vested in BRECON+MERTHYR (BM) since the former had not the financial resoures available to convert tramway to railway having delayed the decision to do this for too long. It would appear, however, that some work on this project had been undertaken as the Maesewmmer connection with the GREAT WESTERN (GW) was made within months.

1. 8.1863 WEST MIDLAND merged with GW. About this time TAFFS WELL became WALNUT TREE JUNCTION as noted earlier.

28.12.1863 GW opened Maesewmmer connection with BM ex Rumney as mentioned above.

STATION NAMES + OPENING DATES

Station names and opening dates can at times present great difficulty to obtain strict accuracy. Looking first at names, different authorities can quote the same station by different titles. For example, Bradshaw will often add a suffix to distinguish between two stations with the same name but in separate ownership. But the railway companies themselves did not need such distinction, which only became necessary after grouping if one company took over identically named stations close together or in different parts of the country. In the Pontypridd area all these changes were made 1.7.1924 but in practice some must have been used from 1922 as all the smaller companies had become part of the GW by this date. Also, changes in the name of a place do not always co-incide with the station change of name, and Bradshaw may be misleading in not always picking up changes until later. With Welsh stations the position is even more difficult, since stations can change from English to Welsh spelling and even from Welsh to English; these changes too rarely co-incided with the place name change. An early map, for example, shows Cardiff as CAERDIFF. PONTYPRIOD itself presents a problem: the name itself was altered on a precise date in the mid-1860's but when the station changed its name is unclear; it appears for a short time on RCH maps as PONTYPRIDD JUNCTION. All one can do, therefore, is take the version shown on a map of the period. If changes are frequent sometimes the same later version is used on all maps (e.g HENGOED). Turning to opening dates, some of the difficulties have already been noted. But in an area such as SOUTH WALES there are two further difficulties. The first difficulty is this: In an area where prime use of railways is coal and goods traffic, the carriage of passengers has also been linked to mining, and industry stations were often opened as unadvertised halts and used only by work-people. These halts often did not appear in Bradshaw or on RCH maps. The second difficulty is that in a congested area such as Pontypridd as the network expanded it was difficult to find space to show all station names on national maps. The stations on the first four maps in this chapter are restricted to those on RCH maps unless strong evidence exists for inclusion of others. Some doubtful stations have, however, been included, but these inclusions on the maps are usually distinguished by ✳ against the name on the map.

1864-1884

1. 1.1864 PENTYRCH possiby closed by this time. It had at any rate disappeared from Bradshaw.

5.10.1864 GW open NAH line from QUAKERS YARD to Middle Duffryn to passenger traffic. It appears a good service over most of the line had commenced the previous year and that full opening had only been delayed due to problems with Quakers Yard Tunnel.

3.12.1864 GW convert ELY VALLEY line, within the map area, to mixed gauge so that traffic exchange with the LLANTRISANT + TAFF VALE (LTV) at Maesaraul could be improved.

6. 7.1865 ALEXANDRA NEWPORT DOCK – Act.

31.12.1865 BM opened throughout Bassaleg to PENGAM.

1. 5.1866 BM – all ex-RUMNEY now open.

15. 7.1867 TAFF BARGOED JOINT – GW obtain Act – to be jointly owned by GW and RHYMNEY (RH).

1. 4.1871 RH open Penallta Loop (from Penallta Junction to Ystrad Junction).

13. 5.1872 GW convert EV to standard gauge (previously mixed – see 3.12.1864 above).

21. 1.1875 LTV (opened to goods in 1863) now opened for passenger traffic. Leased to TV for 999 years.

20.12.1875 TAFF BARGOED JOINT (GW and RH) opened goods. Opened passengers 1.2.1876.

21. 7.1879 TREFERIG VALLEY (TrV) – Act.

8. 8.1878 PONTYPRIDD, CAERPHILLY + NEWPORT (PCN) – Act.

18. 8.1882 ALEXANDRA NEWPORT DOCK becomes ALEXANDRA (NEWPORT + SOUTH WALES) DOCK + RAILWAY.

18. 8.1882 QUAKERS YARD + MERTHYR JOINT – Act obtained by RH to be GW and RH joint.

30. 4.1883 TrV opened by this date.

30. 6.1883 TrV leased to TV (effective date); date of Act was 14.7.1884.

7. 7.1884 PCN opened between PONTYPRIDD (and junction with TV to be known as PC+N Junction) to Penrhos (and a junction with the RHYMNEY).

14. 8.1884 BARRY DOCK + RAILWAY – Act.

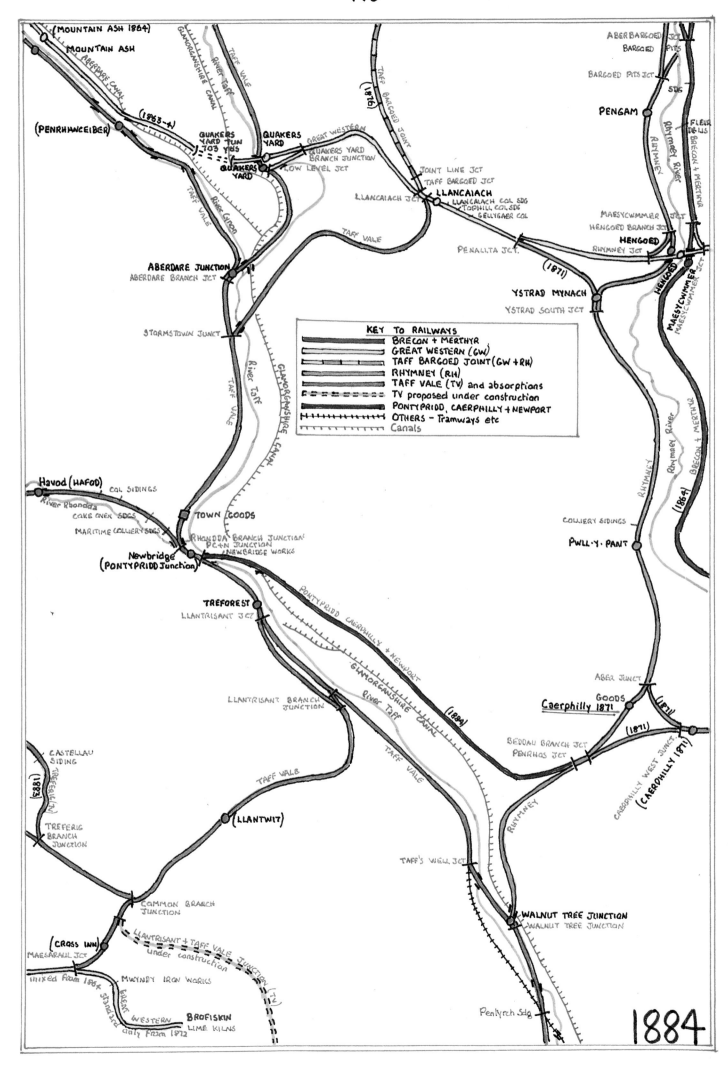

1884

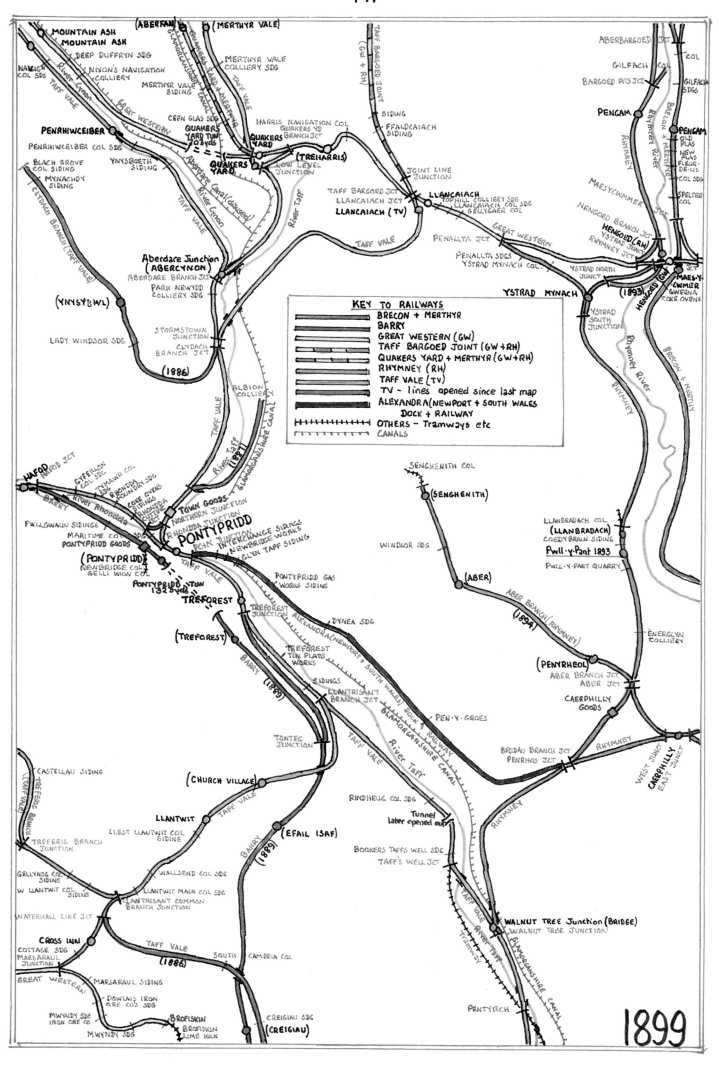

1899

1885-1899

25.6.1886 BUTE DOCKS TRANSFER ACT - would become CARDIFF RAILWAY in 1897.

11.9.1886 TAFF VALE (TV) open further portion of LTVJ from Common Branch Junction to Waterhall Junction via CREIGIAU.

4.4.1886 QUAKERS YARD + MERTHYR JOINT (GW + Rhymney) opened.

31.12.1886 TV opened YNYSYBWL BRANCH to goods traffic by this date (precise date is not recorded).

1887 TV opened from PONT-SHON NORTON JUNCTION to ALBION COLLIERY (Goods only).

28.12.1887 PONTYPRIDD, CAERPHILLY + NEWPORT (PCN) passenger service commenced. Run by ALEXANDRA but by GW from 1899. No doubt some of the halts shown on the 1926 map came into use at this time but no halts shown on RCH 1899 map.

1.1.1889 LTVJ fully absorbed by TV; TREFERIG VALLEY fully absorbed by TV 1.7.1889.

13.5.1889 BARRY DOCKS + RAILWAY open line to HAFOD. By 1899 stations at: CREIGIAU, EFAIL ISAF, TREFOREST and PONTYPRIDD.

1.3.1890 TV initiate passenger service on YNYSYBWL BRANCH.

5.8.1891 BARRY DOCKS + RAILWAY becomes BARRY.

30.11.1893 RHYMNEY opened loop from Ystrad North Junction to GW (quoted by GW as NAH but appears in error per RCH maps).

1.2.1894 RHYMNEY opened branch to SENGHENITH (Aber branch).

6.8.1897 PCN vested in ALEXANDRA (NEWPORT + SOUTH WALES) DOCK + RAILWAY.

6.8.1897 BUTE DOCKS COMPANY becomes CARDIFF.

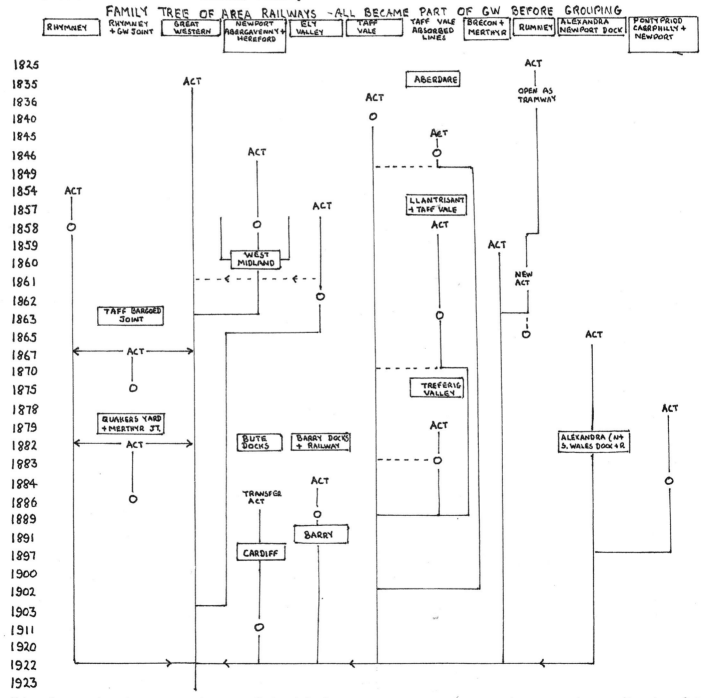

FAMILY TREE OF AREA RAILWAYS - ALL BECAME PART OF GW BEFORE GROUPING

Notes: ACT - parliamentary authorisation; O first substantial opening; - - - - - shows leased; continuous line shows full absorption where it joins another company line.

1900-1940

This period covers two maps. But since the 1926 map is a composite map, showing both pre-grouping ownership and post-map-date additions, the period has been divided into two, by showing, first openings and then closures.

OPENINGS:

1900 TAFF VALE opened Ynysybwl South Curve.

1900 TAFF VALE (TV) opened extension of Branch to Albion Colliery continuing this to YNYSYDWR JUNCTION.

1.8.1901 BARRY opened from Tyn·y·Cae to PENRHOS UPPER (later became Penrhos South).

31.7.1902 ABERDARE fully absorbed by TV.

1.7.1903 ELY VALLEY fully absorbed by GREAT WESTERN (GW).

2.1.1905 BARRY opened PENRHOS LOWER to BARRY JUNCTION with BRECON + MERTHYR (BM); also goods branch at ENERGLYN.

1.8.1906 RHYMNEY opened CYLLA BRANCH. This was goods only and never carried passenger traffic.

1.3.1911 CARDIFF opened throughout to all traffic. A dispute with the TV led to the junction with the latter company being in fact only used once by the ceremonial opening train. This factor led to the progressive closure of the line from the PONTYPRIDD end.

1.1.1922 Pregrouping mergers ensured that all railways in the area became vested in the GW from this date. These were: RHYMNEY (including joint lines with GW), BARRY, CARDIFF, BRECON + MERTHYR, TAFF VALE and the ALEXANDRA (NEWPORT + SOUTH WALES) DOCK + RAILWAY.

Following grouping, as might be expected, with all area railways coming under a united management, the main trend was rationalisation of duplicate routes. But within this policy some new lines were built to create new through routes and reduce track maintenance. Two such events affected the area: A triangular junction layout at COMMON BRANCH and a remodelling at TONTEG, where resiting of the station and a new connection reduced track and allowed the resited halt to serve both BARRY and TAFF VALE lines, rather than the TAFF VALE alone as hitherto. Apart from new stations shown in red on the map (1926) it is possible that some of the others shown also opened post-grouping.

STATION, PLATFORM OR HALT

Undoubtedly there is some confusion about the difference between a station, a platform and a halt, and this difficulty is compounded by the difference in treatment by the different railway companies plus frequent inconsistency of treatment within a single company. What follows gives some indication of the system on the GREAT WESTERN who probably had more platforms and halts than the other three post-grouping railways put together: STATION usually handled both passengers and goods; sometimes goods were at a nearby goods-only station, and they would be controlled by one or more signal boxes. PLATFORM would be a small passenger-only station with a small staff, no station master and often without a signal box. A HALT was similar to PLATFORM but usually without any staff. This classification was usually applied on opening and tended to not reflect any subsequent changes. It also appears to have only applied in the 20th century since before this time all passenger stopping places, however small, were stations with all the facilities of the definition.

Other companies had different systems: In this area, for example, the TAFF VALE had several PLATFORMS, but on control passing to the GREAT WESTERN they were renamed as HALTS even though RCH maps continue to show them as PLATFORMS. Research applied to a limited cross-section of HALTS and PLATFORMS on RCH maps does suggest that, however named on the maps, a distinctive style is applied to those that were unstaffed.

Following nationalisation there has been an increasing tendency for unstaffed stations and this is the reason why no distinction between stations and halts is made on the later maps in this book.

CLOSURES:

CANALS: Complete closure of the ABEDARE and upper reaches of the GLAMORGANSHIRE took place at the turn of the century. Following further cut-backs of the upper portion the system was virtually disused by grouping. Some traffic on the lower reaches continued, however, until official closure in 1942.

PASSENGER: Some duplicate passenger services were closed during the period, although in most cases goods traffic was retained. Pre-grouping closures: Coedpemaen (1915) was described at the time as temporary, but it was finally closed 1932; GYFEILON HALT (1918) and TRAM ROAD HALT (1922). The remaining passenger station closures were all in the period 1930 to 1932. The 1930 closures were: GLYN TAFF, PONTYPRIDD CRAIG, TONTEG (replaced) and TREFOREST HL. In 1931: NANTGARW LL, RHYDYFELIN LL, TONYGWYNLAIS and UPPER BOAT. In 1932: BERW ROAD, CILFYNND, LLANFABON ROAD, NELSON and TRAVELLERS REST. In addition the unadvertised LLANBRADACH COLLIERY HALT closed at some time during the period.

COMPLETE: CARDIFF: line TREFOREST to RHYDYFELIN (1925), RHYDYFELIN (1931) to south of UPPER BOAT (1940).

TAFF VALE: Llancaiach Branch (1932). Tonteg (1930 when new connection opened). Common Branch Junction to Llantrisant Common and Treferig Branch (1935).

BARRY: Penrhos Lower to Barry Junction including Energlyn Goods Branch (1926).

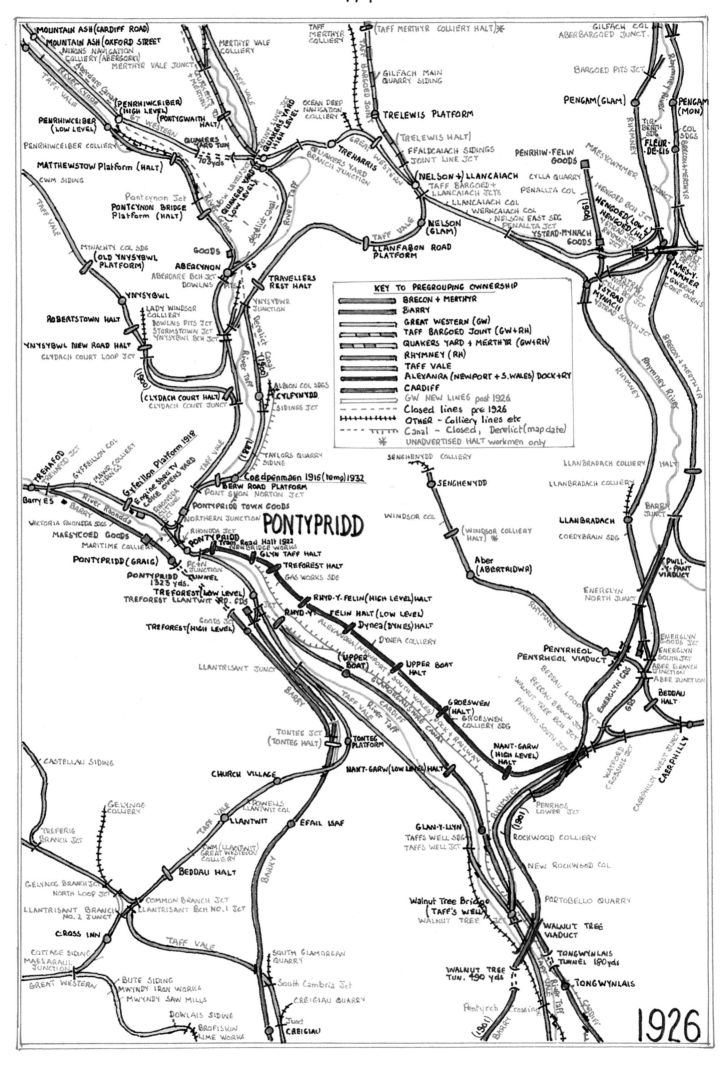

PONTYPRIDD

KEY TO PREGROUPING OWNERSHIP

BRECON + MERTHYR
BARRY
GREAT WESTERN (GW)
TAFF BARGOED JOINT (GW+RH)
QUAKERS YARD + MERTHYR (GW+RH)
RHYMNEY (RH)
TAFF VALE
ALEXANRA (NEWPORT + S.WALES) DOCK+RY
CARDIFF
GW NEW LINES post 1926
Closed lines pre 1926
OTHER - Colliery lines etc
Canal - Closed, Derelict (map date)
UNADVERTISED HALT workmen only

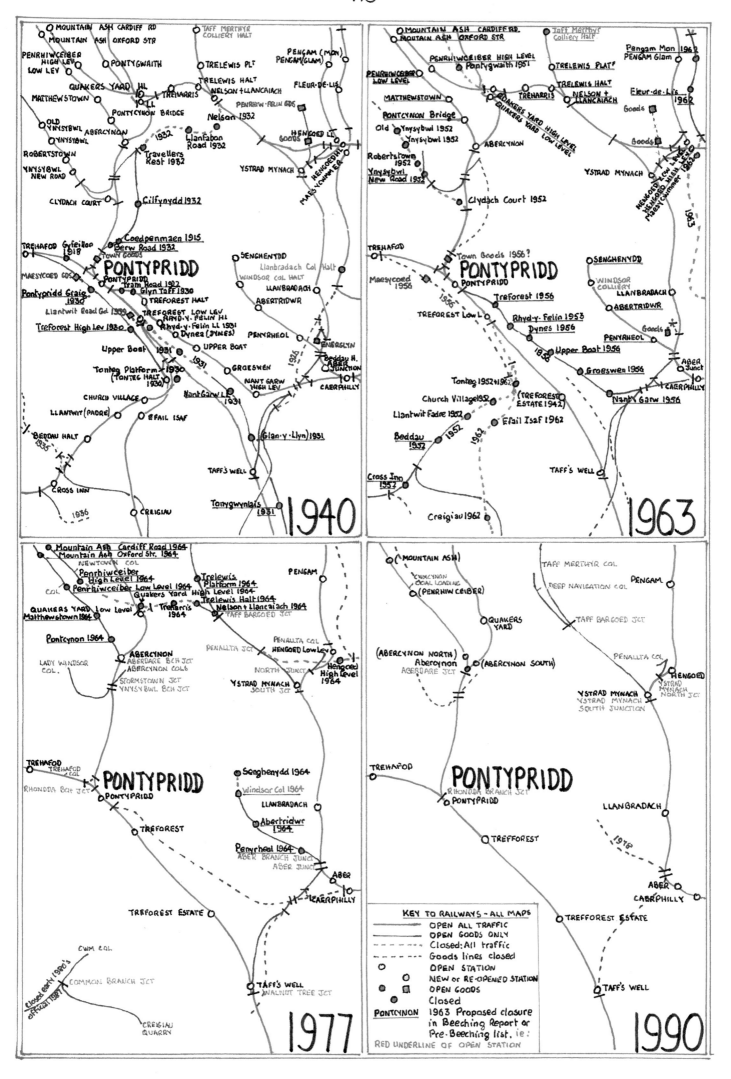

1941-1963

During the early part of this period suprisingly little of the network was lost. The main reason for this was that lines fanning out to the north served different collieries, whilst lines south went to different ports.

The first to go really belongs to the previous period, the bulk of the ex Cardiff line closing to all traffic in 1931. But just a little goods traffic did use the portion shown as open for goods on the 1940 map and it was re-opened in early 1950's on a regular basis for 12 months before complete closure, when a short new spur took its surviving mineral traffic into the ex Taff Vale. There was also a wartime opening, TREFOREST ESTATE (1942).

1951 Quakers Yard High Level to Merthyr closed. PONTYGWAITH was the only map area station affected.

1952 Ynysybwl Branch closed to passengers. Goods to Lady Windsor Colliery persisted for another 25 years. Also closed during the year, Treforest to Llantrisant and stations: CROSS INN, BEDDAU, LLANTWIT FADRE, CHURCH VILLAGE and TONTEG. Goods retained on the lines from Common Junction to service colliery traffic.

1956 Following a short respite the ex PCN lost its passenger service but remained open for goods. Closure of halts at: Treforest, Rhyd·y·Felin (this halt actually closed 1953), Dynes, Upper Boat, Groeswen and Nant Garw.

Following these comparatively few closures in an area with many duplicate routes there was a period of six years with no closures to be followed by a very extensive number of closures compressed into the three year period 1962 to 1964 inclusive.

1962 The ex Brecon + Merthyr line closed to passengers, with most of the goods traffic the following year. This only involved the loss of three stations: PENGAM(MON), FLEUR DE LIS and MAES·Y·CWMMER. In this connection there is a rare error in Clinker who regards FLEUR·DE·LIS and PENGAM as the same station! Also closed was ex·Barry line from Treforest with the loss of 2½ stations: EFAIL ISAF, CREIGIAU and TONTEG (the half – the other platforms having closed in 1952 with the Llantrisant line).

1963 No closures, but before Beeching the following listed for closure: HENGOED HIGH LEVEL, MOUNTAIN ASH-CARDIFF ROAD, NELSON + LLANCAIACH, PENRHIWCEIBER HIGH LEVEL, QUAKERS YARD HIGH LEVEL, TREHARRIS, TRELEWIS PLATFORM, TRELEWIS HALT. As a result of these proposals the 'Good Doctor' just failed to equal this list but did recommend the closure of: ABERTRIDWR, MATTHEWSTOWN, MOUNTAIN ASH - OXFORD STREET, PENYRHEOL, PENRHIWCEIBER LOW LEVEL, PONTCYNON BRIDGE and SENGHENYDD.

1964-1977

1964 During the year fifteen stations were closed and this was every station on the two lists noted above. Rarely have the Beeching recommendations for any area been so completely and quickly implemented. Half the closures were made in March and the rest were gone before the end of June. Having so swiftly taken action it is perhaps not suprising that the remainder of the period saw not a single passenger station closed. The only other events were loss of some lines previously reduced to goods only.

1978-1990

In this final period further goods-only lines have been lost but there have been no passenger station losses, since although Abercynon did close it was only a rebuilding and has in fact been replaced by two stations, one on each line from the junction – ABERCYNON NORTH and ABERCYNON SOUTH.

A sign of revival has been re-opening of the Aberdare Branch to passenger traffic resulting in the reopening of the stations at MOUNTAIN ASH and PENRHIWCEIBER.

The similarities of the 1990 network to that of the mid-1840's are quite remarkable. There are in fact but two minor differences. The Rhymney line to Cardiff has been retained in prefence to the Rumney but this follows an identical route at the other side of the valley. Llancaiach is served by a goods feeder line but from the ex Rhymney line instead of the 1841 goods line from just north of Pontypridd.

1991 - FUTURE

There are no known plans for either expansion or contraction of the area network although there may be some goods-only closures if further contraction of the coal industry takes place.

The network is of course only a shadow of its former self and as late as 1947 there were places on the Taff just south of Pontypridd where there were fourteen parallel tracks carrying traffic, with a round dozen of these carrying through traffic, mainly coal.

One final curiosity worth noting is that in spite of its undoubted importance as a strategic focal point of routes, PONTYPRIDD never had a major marshalling yard or engine shed. But with fourteen tracks, not to mention river and canal crammed into a narrow valley, there simply was no room available.

SWANSEA

The hinterland of SWANSEA had been important as an industrial centre for over a hundred years before the advent of railways. Coal was in fact exploited from early in the eighteenth century, whilst copper, tin plate, iron furnaces and associated industries were all well established before the dawn of the nineteenth century. Swansea, too, was growing as a port for both imports and exports, tin from Cornwall being the main early import. In spite of these needs Swansea Docks were a late development, since NORTH DOCK, the first to open, was not in use until 1852. But the navigable Tawe with numerous wharves linking to the canal system proved adequate in early days. It is in this respect interesting to note that dock development at Swansea co-incided with the arrival of the first railway in 1850.

The canals in this area were amongst the most profitable in Wales. The Swansea Canal was paying an 18% dividend as late as 1860. It was sold to the GREAT WESTERN in 1871/2 and continued profitable until 1894. After this date further loss of traffic led to closure in 1931. The Tennant Canal also carried good volumes and traffic reached its peak of 200,000 tons in 1866. But this had halved by 1895 and continued decline resulted in closure in the early 1930's. Only the Smith did not prosper; it carried little traffic after the 1850's — closure date not known.

TO 1844

29.6.1804 OYSTERMOUTH - Act.

25.3.1807 OYSTERMOUTH opened to passengers. Although at this stage it was a horse-drawn tramway, it is usually referred to as the world's first passenger-carrying line. There was also a branch to quarries as the 1844 map shows. At Swansea the line terminated close to what would later become the HIGH STREET terminus of the SOUTH WALES RAILWAY. It was a unique line in many ways; constructed originally to a gauge of approximately 4'0", it was authorised in its Act to utilise horse, man or other means of propulsion. In actual fact it has used no less than seven different ways of propelling its rolling stock — Horses, Human, Sails, Steam, Petrol, Diesel, Electricity - on occasion using three different methods at the same time. It ran into financial difficulties from the start and many costly litigation battles were fought over it. It was also the earliest railway put out of business by road competition, being forced to close in 1825. But it later resumed operation between legal battles. It was altered to standard gauge in the mid-1850's and there were several changes of both name and ownership. SWANSEA IMPROVEMENTS + TRAMWAYS obtained running powers in the 1870's. The SWANSEA + MUMBLES was formed in 1879, by a former owner, and also worked the line, but legal wrangles continued. The service was finally withdrawn in 1960. Full details see The Swansea + Mumbles Railway by C.E. Lee (Oakwood Press).

31.8.1835 GREAT WESTERN (GW) - Act.

10.5.1844 MIDLAND - Act. It would be some time before the company reached SWANSEA by running powers and absorption of local concerns.

1845-1854

4.8.1845 SOUTH WALES - Act. A broad gauge line to link with the GREAT WESTERN. The line, initially, was authorised to run from Chepstow to both Fishguard and Pembroke, but five years would pass before the first portion was open for traffic (Chepstow to Swansea).

16.7.1846 LONDON + NORTH WESTERN (LNW) formed.

3.8.1846 VALE OF NEATH - Authorised. This company opened no lines within the map area but would absorb the SWANSEA + NEATH.

2.7.1847 SWANSEA VALLEY (SV) - Act.

19.6.1850 SOUTH WALES (SW) opened from Chepstow to SWANSEA (HIGH STREET). RCH map of 1854 shows intermediate stations at LANDORE and LLANSAMLET. Some authorities quote opening as one day earlier.

1852 SWANSEA NORTH DOCK opened.

6.1852 SW opened HIGH STREET JUNCTION to NORTH DOCK SIDINGS for goods traffic. HIGH STREET GOODS was also in use by this time giving further connections to wharves on the River Tawe.

12.1852 SV opened for goods from SWANSEA to Glais.

11.10.1852 SW opened from LANDORE to Carmarthen Junction. Initially there were no passenger stations within the map area on this section of line.

3.7.1854 SWANSEA HARBOUR TRUST - Act. There had been previous Harbour Trustees but this new Act gave power to the Trustees to "lay down rails and turnplates" and these powers were extended as further docks were built. Part of the railway was leased to VALE OF NEATH and thus became part of the GW. The rest of the dock railways, together with docks themselves, were vested in the GW from 1.7.1923.

Docks were opened as follows: NORTH (1852), SOUTH (1859), PRINCE OF WALES (1882), KINGS (23.11.1909) and QUEENS (1920). Swansea would ultimately become the busiest port in Wales.

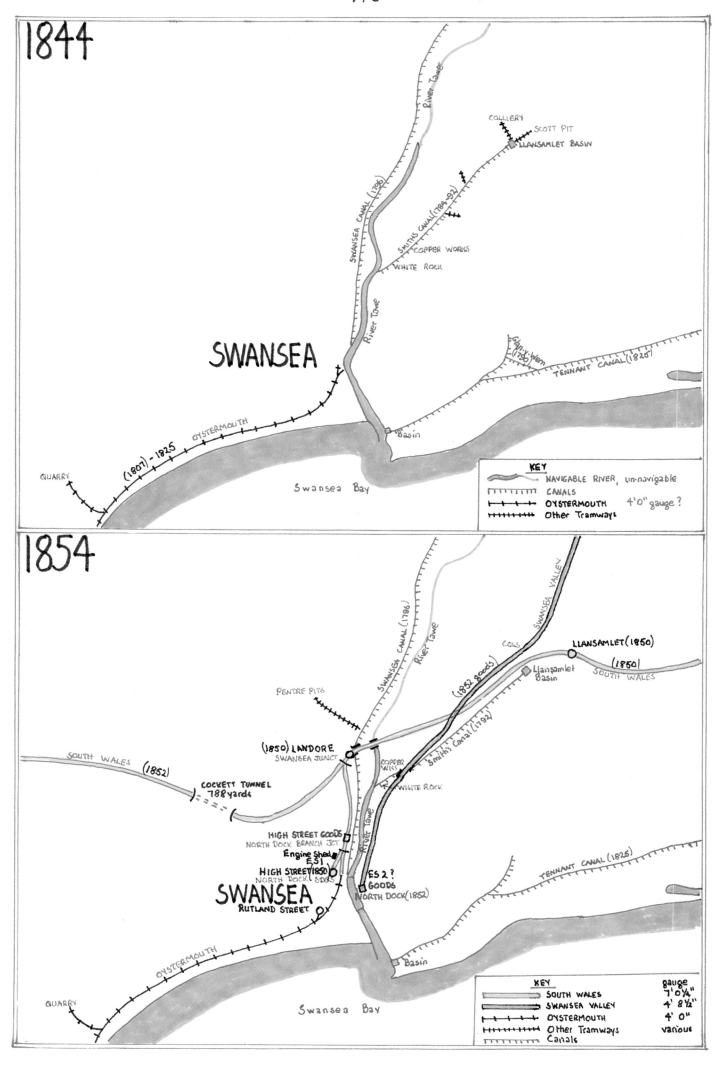

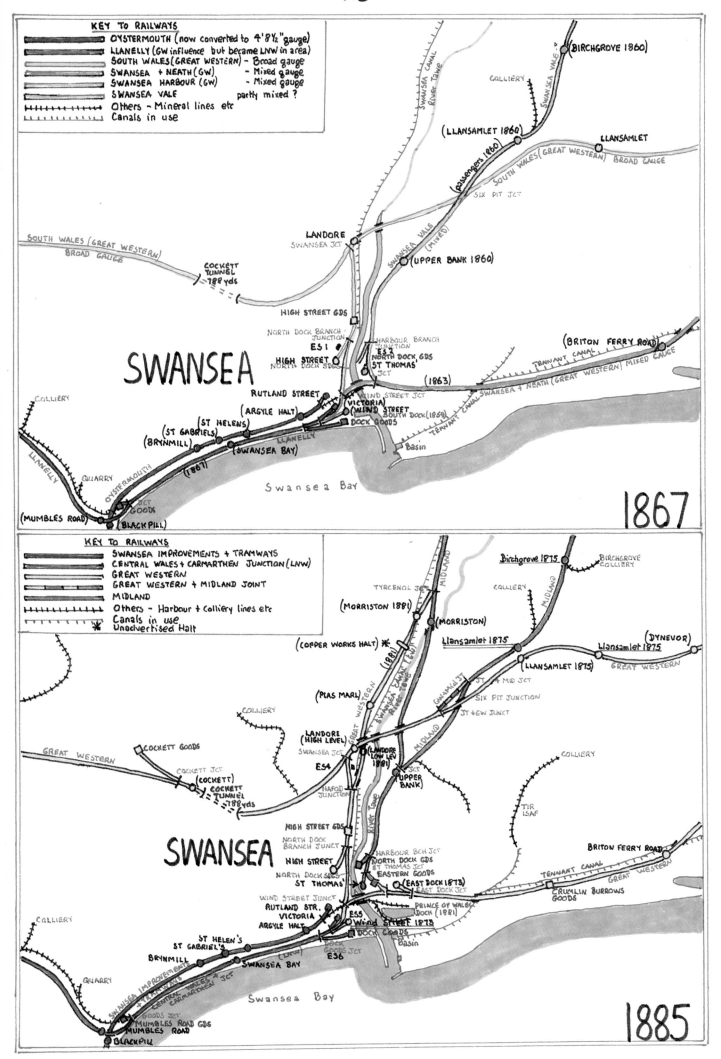

1867

KEY TO RAILWAYS

OYSTERMOUTH (now converted to 4'8½" gauge)
LLANELLY (GW influence but became LNW in area)
SOUTH WALES (GREAT WESTERN) - Broad gauge
SWANSEA + NEATH (GW) - Mixed gauge
SWANSEA HARBOUR (GW) - Mixed gauge
SWANSEA VALE - partly mixed?
Others - Mineral lines etc
Canals in use

SWANSEA

Swansea Bay

1885

KEY TO RAILWAYS

SWANSEA IMPROVEMENTS + TRAMWAYS
CENTRAL WALES + CARMARTHEN JUNCTION (LNW)
GREAT WESTERN
GREAT WESTERN + MIDLAND JOINT
MIDLAND
Others - Harbour + Colliery lines etc
Canals in use
Unadvertised Halt

SWANSEA

Swansea Bay

1855-1867

15. 6. 1855 SWANSEA VALE - Act. This company had a complex history. SWANSEA VALLEY had been incorporated in 1845 and was to become part of SOUTH WALES (SW) but the latter company lacked the powers to do this. It was therefore reformed as SWANSEA VALE (SV) and was ultimately absorbed by the MIDLAND.

10. 8. 1857 SWANSEA HARBOUR - Act. Covered line from SW NORTH DOCK to SOUTH DOCK (under construction) and WIND STREET.

1859 SWANSEA SOUTH DOCK - opened.

9. 1859 SWANSEA HARBOUR. Line authorised two years earlier now opened for goods traffic possibly at same time as Dock opened.

21. 2. 1860 SV having taken over SWANSEA VALLEY opened from SWANSEA to Pontadawre for passenger traffic. Stations within map area: UPPER BANK, LLANSAMLET and BIRCHGROVE. It is not clear if these stations all opened with the start of the passenger service from ST THOMAS' but Llansamlet and Birchgrove both closed in 1875 when passengers were diverted via Morriston.

6. 8. 1861 SWANSEA + NEATH (SN) - Act.

4. 6. 1862 SWANSEA HARBOUR line (see above 1857 and 1859) leased for 1000 years to VALE OF NEATH (VN) - Broad gauge.

7. 1863 SN opened from WIND STREET to Neath, where it joined VN. Station BRITON FERRY (mixed gauge).

1. 8. 1863 SW absorbed by GREAT WESTERN (GW).

5. 8. 1863 SN leased to VN.

1. 2. 1865 VN absorbed by GW. Briton Ferry appears to have become BRITON FERRY ROAD about this time but date is unclear; it could well be an error on earlier maps.

14. 12. 1867 LLANELLY RAILWAY + DOCK (original line authorised 19·6·1928) - reached SWANSEA VICTORIA from Pontardulais. There were intermediate stations at: SWANSEA BAY and MUMBLES ROAD (this portion, authorised 1861, became part of LNW).

SECTION OF LINE	ORIGINAL GAUGE	ORIGINATING COMPANY	NOTES	DATE TO MIXED	DATE TO STANDARD
RUTLAND STREET - OYSTERMOUTH + Branch to Quarry	4'0"	OYSTERMOUTH	Original gauge may have been 4'2". Exact conv. date unclear		1855 - 1859
SWANSEA HARBOUR RAILWAY	BG	SWANSEA HARBOUR		15.7.1863	11.5.1872
SOUTH WALES MAIN LINE	BG	SOUTH WALES			12.5.1872
SWANSEA VALE JUNCTION BRANCH	BG	SWANSEA VALE			13.5.1872
SIX PIT JUNCTION	Std	SWANSEA VALE	a standard line that became mixed	2.1857	not known
LANDORE - SWANSEA HIGH STREET	BG	SOUTH WALES			13.5.1872
NORTH DOCK BRANCH	BG	SOUTH WALES			13.5.1872
WIND STREET to Middle Duffryn	MG	SWANSEA + NEATH	map area section opened mixed		11.5.1872

CHANGE OF GAUGE OF SWANSEA LINES 1855 TO 1875

1868-1885

LLANELLY mentioned above originally looked as though it would become part of the GW and was in fact merged with them by an ACT of 24·6·1889. But the line to SWANSEA after a change of name ultimately became part of the LONDON + NORTH WESTERN (LNW). Details of name changes, see ✱ below.

1871 - 73 SV progressively opened its loop line from UPPER BANK via MORRISTON and Clydach to Glais.

1. 3. 1873 WIND STREET closed to passengers, to save crossing harbour bridges. Continued in use for goods traffic. A new passenger station, EAST DOCK, brought into use.

Around this time, exact date unclear, GW carried SOUTH WALES main line over SV at SIX PIT JUNCTION. It is thought little use had been made of broad gauge connection to SWANSEA (see note in table above).

1. 7. 1874 SV leased to MIDLAND, effective from this date. Date of ACT - 30.7.1874.

1. 3. 1875 MIDLAND withdraw passenger service on SV line via Llansamlet; line retained for goods and line previously referred to as loop line (via MORRISTON) became main line.

11. 8. 1876 SV vested in MIDLAND.

1881 PRINCE OF WALES DOCK opened, sometimes referred to as EAST DOCK.

9. 5. 1881 GW opened from HAFOD JUNCTION (Landore) to MORRISTON and to Tyrcenal Junction with MIDLAND.

10. 8. 1882 RHONDDA + SWANSEA BAY (RSB) - ACT. This was the first Act. There were subsequent acts in 1890, 1891, 1892 and 1895 authorising variations and extensions.

1. 1. 1885 LLANSAMLET (GW) replaced by a new station, with the same name, adjoining MIDLAND station which had been downgraded to goods only in 1875.

✱

16. 6. 1871 SWANSEA + CARMARTHEN (S+C) formed after a legal battle to take over part of LLANELLY (see 14·12·1867 above).

21. 7. 1873 S+C becomes CENTRAL WALES + CARMARTHEN JUNCTION (CWCJ) and under LNW control.

21. 7. 1891 CWCJ completely absorbed by LNW.

1886-1899

21. 7. 1891 CENTRAL WALES + CARMARTHEN JUNCTION fully absorbed by LONDON + NORTH WESTERN.

30. 12. 1893 RHONDDA + SWANSEA BAY (RSB) opened Aberavon to Briton Ferry and Briton Ferry Dock Branch. Work commences on continuation of line to SWANSEA.

14. 12. 1894 RSB opened for freight to SWANSEA.

14. 3. 1895 RSB opened for passenger services to SWANSEA - RIVERSIDE, used Harbour Trustees lines until 7.5.1899. The company established workshops at DANYGRAIG. Passenger stations: DANYGRAIG and JERSEY MARINE.

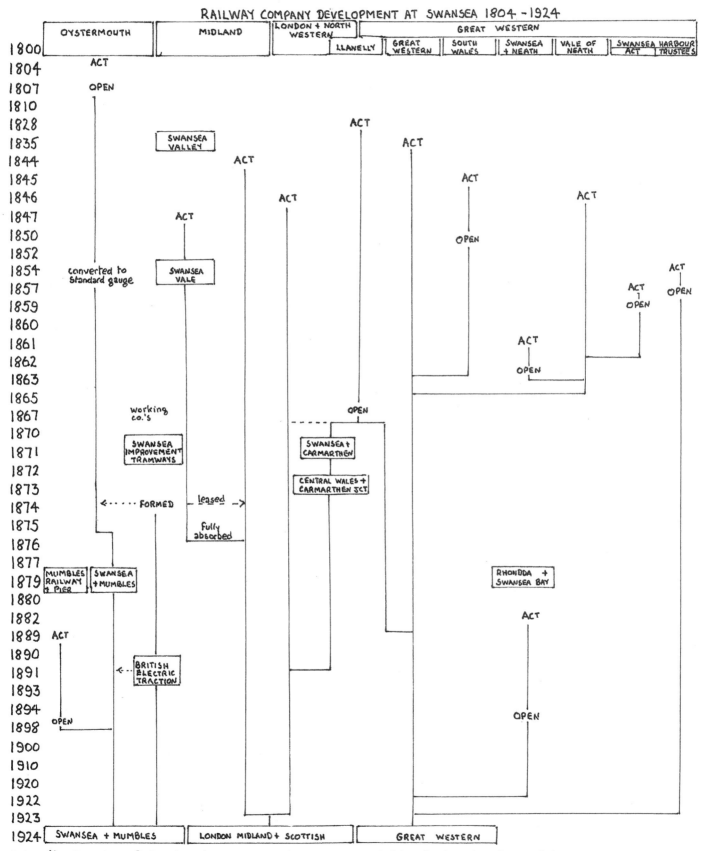

RAILWAY COMPANY DEVELOPMENT AT SWANSEA 1804 - 1924

Notes: (1) OPEN shows first substantial opening. Opening dates of later Great Western lines not shown.

(2) The chart does not show the full intricacies of SWANSEA + MUMBLES legal battles and agreements

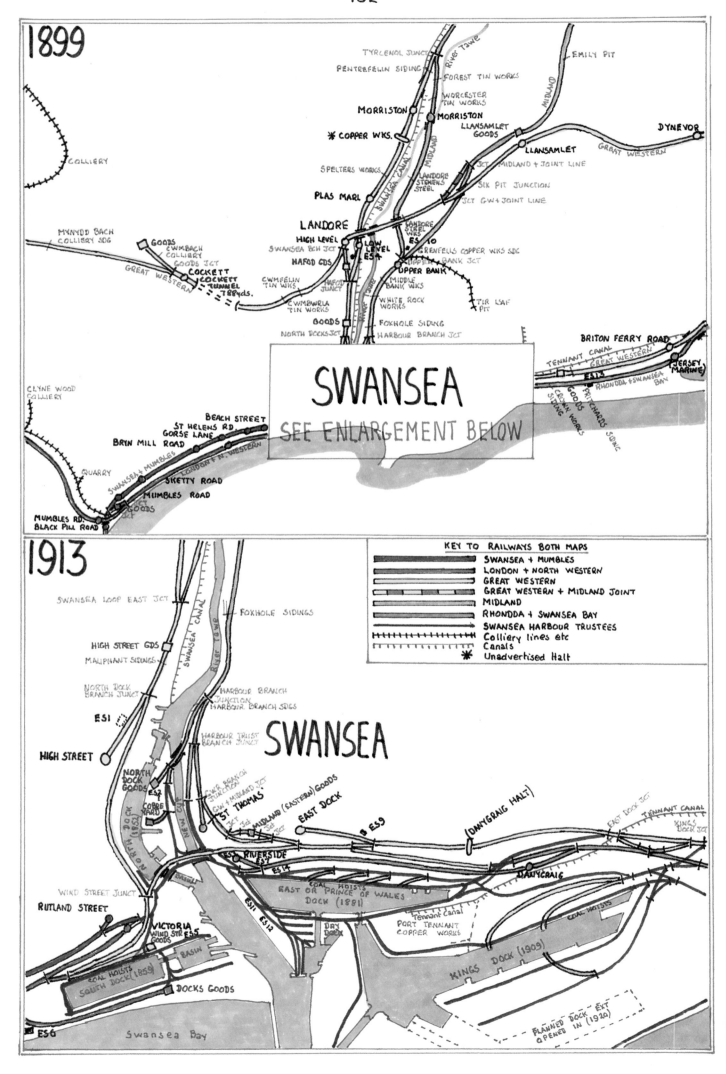

1899

COLLIERY

TYRCENOL JUNCT.
PENTREFELIN SIDING
FOREST TIN WORKS
EMILY PIT
RIVER TAWE
WORCESTER TIN WORKS
MORRISTON
MORRISTON
LLANSAMLET GOODS
DYNEVOR
✱ COPPER WKS.
MIDLAND
GREAT WESTERN
LLANSAMLET
SPELTERS WORKS
JCT. MIDLAND + JOINT LINE
SIX PIT JUNCTION
PLAS MARL
LANDORE SIEMENS STEEL
JCT. GW + JOINT LINE
SWANSEA CANAL
MIDLAND
MYNYDD BACH COLLIERY SDG.
LANDORE
HIGH LEVEL
LOW LEVEL ES 4
LANDORE STEEL WKS. ES 10
GRENFELLS COPPER WKS. SDG
GOODS
CWMBACH COLLIERY
GOODS JCT.
SWANSEA BCH JCT.
HAFOD GDS.
UPPER BANK JCT.
GREAT WESTERN
COCKETT
COCKETT TUNNEL 788 YDS.
CWMFELIN TIN WKS.
HAFOD JUNCT.
UPPER BANK
MIDDLE BANK WKS.
CWMBWRLA TIN WORKS
WHITE ROCK WORKS
TIR LLAF PIT
GOODS
FOXHOLE SIDING
NORTH DOCKS JCT.
HARBOUR BRANCH JCT.
BRITON FERRY ROAD
TENNANT CANAL
GREAT WESTERN
CLYNE WOOD COLLIERY
JERSEY MARINE
GOODS
ES 15
RHONDDA + SWANSEA BAY
CROWN WORKS
PRITCHARDS SIDING

BEACH STREET
ST HELENS RD.
GORSE LANE
BRYN MILL ROAD
SWANSEA + MUMBLES
QUARRY
LONDON + N. WESTERN
SKETTY ROAD
MUMBLES ROAD
GOODS
MUMBLES RD.
BLACK PILL ROAD

SWANSEA
SEE ENLARGEMENT BELOW

1913

SWANSEA LOOP EAST JCT.
FOXHOLE SIDINGS
SWANSEA CANAL
RIVER TAWE
HIGH STREET GDS.
MAULIPHANT SIDINGS
NORTH DOCK BRANCH JUNCT.
HARBOUR BRANCH JUNCTION
HARBOUR BRANCH SDGS.
ES1
SWANSEA
HIGH STREET
HARBOUR TRUST BRANCH JUNCT.
NORTH DOCK GOODS
ES2
SKR BRANCH JUNCTION
GW + MIDLAND JCT.
COPPER YARD
ST THOMAS
MIDLAND (EASTERN) GOODS
EAST DOCK
DANYGRAIG HALT)
EAST DOCK JCT.
TENNANT CANAL
KINGS DOCK JCT.
ES9
NEW CUT
MIDLAND JCT.
RIVERSIDE ES14
NORTH DOCK (1852)
DANYGRAIG
WIND STREET JUNCT.
BASIN
ES11 ES12
COAL HOISTS
EAST OR PRINCE OF WALES DOCK (1881)
TENNANT CANAL
RUTLAND STREET
PORT TENNANT COPPER WORKS
DRY DOCK
COAL HOISTS
VICTORIA
WIND ST. ESS
GOODS
BASIN
COAL HOISTS
SOUTH DOCK (1859)
KINGS DOCK (1909)
DOCKS GOODS
ES6
PLANNED DOCK EXT. OPENED IN (1920)
Swansea Bay

KEY TO RAILWAYS BOTH MAPS
SWANSEA + MUMBLES
LONDON + NORTH WESTERN
GREAT WESTERN
GREAT WESTERN + MIDLAND JOINT
MIDLAND
RHONDDA + SWANSEA BAY
SWANSEA HARBOUR TRUSTEES
Colliery lines etc
Canals
✱ Unadvertised Halt

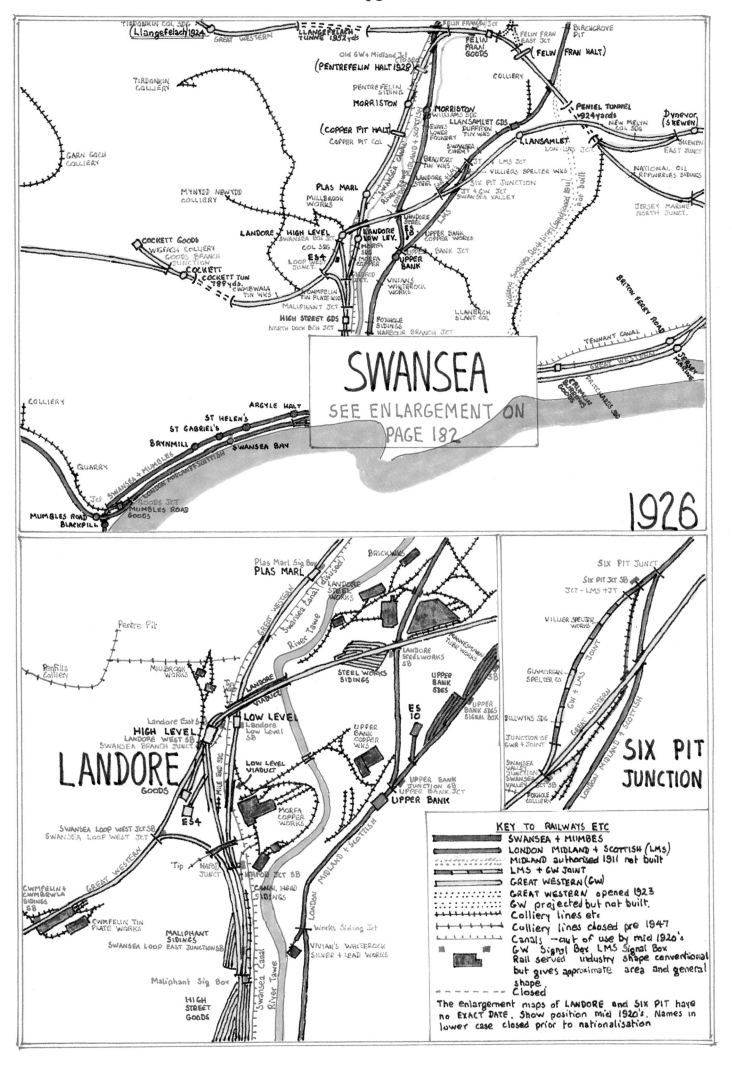

SWANSEA
SEE ENLARGEMENT ON
PAGE 182

1926

LANDORE

SIX PIT JUNCTION

KEY TO RAILWAYS ETC

SWANSEA + MUMBLES
LONDON MIDLAND + SCOTTISH (LMS)
MIDLAND authorised 1911 not built
LMS + GW Joint
GREAT WESTERN (GW)
GREAT WESTERN opened 1923
GW projected but not built.
Colliery lines etc
Colliery lines closed pre 1947
Canals — out of use by mid 1920's
GW Signal Box LMS Signal Box
Rail served industry shape conventional
but gives approximate area and general
shape
Closed

The enlargement maps of LANDORE and SIX PIT have
no EXACT DATE. Show position mid 1920's. Names in
lower case closed prior to nationalisation

1900-1926

15. 8. 1904 GREAT WESTERN (GW) - Authorisation for SWANSEA DISTRICT LINES (Neath Loop was authorised five years later).

5. 3. 1906 GW opened LANDORE WESTERN LOOP to goods traffic

4. 6. 1906 GW opened LANDORE WESTERN LOOP to passenger traffic. At last through trains calling at SWANSEA only had one reversal.

1909 KINGS DOCK opened.

14. 7. 1913 GW opened SWANSEA DISTRICT LINE from Skewen East Junction via FELIN FRAN and LLANGEFELACH to Morlais South and Hendy Junctions. Also from Lonlas Junction via (what became) JERSEY MARINE NORTH JUNCTION to Jersey Marine South Junction.

8. 5. 1914 GW opened from MORRISTON to Felin Fran (joining SWANSEA DISTRICT LINE mentioned above).

19. 5. 1915 GW - SWANSEA DISTRICT LINE (Neath Loop) opened. Only the start of this line is shown on the map. It ran in an easterly direction from a new junction, JERSEY MARINE NORTH.

1920 QUEENS DOCK opened.

1. 1. 1922 GW absorbed RHONDDA + SWANSEA BAY as a prelude to grouping.

1. 1. 1923 Grouping - LONDON + NORTH WESTERN and MIDLAND both became part of LONDON MIDLAND + SCOTTISH (LMS).

1. 7. 1923 SWANSEA HARBOUR TRUSTEES docks and railways vested in GW.

3. 8. 1923 GW open line north from a junction at FELIN FRAN. The line had been authorised in 1911 but was never fully completed. The planned triangular junction layout at Felin Fran was also not completed but the projected site is indicated on the 1926 map.

22. 9. 1924 GW closed LLANGEFELACH to passengers but the station remained open for goods. Some authorities show spelling as LLANGYFELACH and both spellings appear on maps. The one first quoted appears to have been in use whilst it was a passenger station.

SWANSEA ENGINE SHEDS

Details are shown below in tabular form. Some early information is unclear and dates in doubt have ? to show the position is unclear. The number allocated to each shed in the table is used on the maps to identify the various sheds:

No.	Name	Originating Company	Date Opened	Notes	Date Closed
1	SWANSEA HIGH STREET	SOUTH WALES	6.1850	Situated just to the north of the station, it was replaced by Landore (see 4).	? 1874
2	SWANSEA	SWANSEA VALLEY	? 1852	One authority quotes 1860 when line opened to passengers. But goods traffic commenced in 1852. Was replaced by UPPER BANK (see 10).	? 1893
3	SWANSEA VNR RIVERSIDE	VALE OF NEATH	1863	Closed by GW. Replaced by 5 below.	1881
4	LANDORE	GREAT WESTERN	1874	Replacing High Street (see 1 above), enlarged 1932. After closure to steam became BR LOCO DEPOT on the same site. Still in use.	12.6.1961 to steam
5	BURROWS LODGE	SWANSEA HARBOUR TRUSTEES Powlesland + Mason ✳	1881	Adjoining GW Goods Depot of same name at South Dock (shown as Wind Street on maps) purchased by GW 1.1.1924. Official closure:	20.4.1924
6	SWANSEA VICTORIA also known as: Paxton Street	LONDON + NORTH WESTERN	6.1.1882	Prior to opening LNW had rented accommodation from GW.	31.8.1959
7	RIVERSIDE WESTLAKE	SWANSEA HARBOUR TRUSTEES William Westlake ✳	1886	Replaced by new shed on nearby site - March 1894 when RSB station built.	22.2.1900
8	RIVERSIDE RSB	RHONDDA + SWANSEA BAY	12.1894	Closed when passenger lines relaid.	1898
9	EAST DOCK	GREAT WESTERN	26.9.1893	Still used for some stabling.	11.7.1964
10	UPPER BANK	MIDLAND	1893	Replaced 2 above. Other replacement sites were considered. Took 20 years before MIDLAND came to grips with problem of 2's cramped central site.	4.2.1963
11	PRINCE OF WALES	HARBOUR TRUSTEES Rowland ✳	1. 8.1891	Taken over by Trustees 29.5.1905, replaced by 12.	1912
12	PRINCE OF WALES	SWANSEA HARBOUR TRUSTEES	1912	Replaced 11 above. To GW 1.7.1923. Site is still used for stabling.	2.6.1930
13	DANYGRAIG	RHONDDA + SWANSEA BAY	1896	Workshop adjoining still in use.	16.3.1964
14	RIVERSIDE	SWANSEA HARBOUR TRUSTEES Rowland ✳	5.1905	Land leased from RSB. To Powlesland + Mason ✳ in 1910. To GW 1.1.1924.	20.4.1924

✳ Contractors who built sheds and worked engines on SWANSEA HARBOUR TRUSTEES lines.

ENLARGEMENT MAPS:
(A) THE CENTRAL AREA:

In the original planning of this SWANSEA Chapter there were to be two maps of the central area dated 1899 and 1926 to co-incide with the dates of the general maps. However, there was so little difference between the two dates that one map dated 1913 has been used instead. This has enabled two other interesting enlargements to be included. The only changes affecting the central area between 1899 and 1926 were:

1922 Cobre Yard closed.

1923 Grouping had only one significant effect: Swansea Docks and Dock Railways came under GREAT WESTERN control.

1924 Queens Dock had been brought into major use in 1920; work on other facilities now fully complete.

Finally it is worthy of note that the impressive maze of Dock lines does not include the Midland marshalling yard located beyond the eastern margin of the map.

(B) LANDORE

This is a composite map of pre and post-grouping era showing a full selection of rail-served industries. It serves to emphasise the importance attained in the SWANSEA hinterland of freight movement also influenced by the importance of SWANSEA as a port providing export outlets.

(C) SIX PIT JUNCTION

This locality is of interest containing the only joint line in the area. Its early history too is interesting but somewhat obscure. The SWANSEA VALLEY line was built making a flat crossing with the SOUTH WALES main line. At this stage it appeared certain that the two railways would merge and broad gauge rails were laid into SWANSEA. However, it was discovered that the SOUTH WALES could not legally absorb the smaller company. As a result of this the SWANSEA VALLEY became the SWANSEA VALE and fell into the clutches of the MIDLAND. Once this happened it appears unlikely that any great use would be made of the broad gauge rails and connection, but when the rails were removed is not known. When the SOUTH WALES, now part of the GREAT WESTERN, was narrowed the flat crossing was replaced by the flyover and the connections shown on the map, although no definite confirmation is in either GREAT WESTERN or MIDLAND records.

1927-1940

There were some new developments during this period. The GREAT WESTERN policy of opening unstaffed halts, as noted elsewhere, was followed in the area. COPPER PIT, used as an unadvertised stopping place, became an advertised halt. PENTREFELIN opened in 1928 and LLANDARCY PLATFORM about the same time. This latter opening co-incided with new goods lines in the vicinity to serve the Anglo-Iranian oil refinery which in turn was the result of the latest dock, Queens, being dedicated to oil traffic.

The planned MIDLAND line from FELIN FRAN was abandoned after grouping, no doubt due to all SWANSEA DOCKS coming into the hands of the GREAT WESTERN.

The two canals were virtually disused by this time and in 1928 the GW were authorised to close the shallow NORTH DOCK.

Turning to rail closures, the first victim was the ex RHONDDA & SWANSEA BAY line which lost its passenger service in 1933 and resulted in closure of passenger stations at RIVERSIDE, DANYGRAIG, BALDWINS HALT and JERSEY MARINE. Goods traffic continued but the line was closed entirely between Riverside and Danygraig and traffic diverted onto the parallel line. The remainder was progressively re-aligned so that it became part of the remaining lines or could be so worked. The next withdrawal of passenger services was the suprising one of the parallel ex SWANSEA & NEATH line only three years later in 1936. This resulted in further passenger station closures of EAST DOCK, DANYGRAIG HALT and BRITON FERRY ROAD. But the line continued to carry heavy freight traffic to SWANSEA's newer and deep water docks to the east of the Tawe. These lines remain open up to the present day (early 1990's).

1941-1963

This period saw the closure or proposed closure of every remaining passenger station in the area, with the exception of SWANSEA HIGH STREET, as the chronology which follows shows. This was possibly partly a result of nationalisation bringing all area railways under a united management within the WESTERN REGION.

1947 LLANDARCY PLATFORM closed. The only pre-nationalisation closure.

1950 ST THOMAS', UPPER BANK, MORRISTON (EAST) closed. Line continued in use for freight.

1954 LANDORE LOW LEVEL - Closed.

1956 PLAS MARL, COPPER PIT PLATFORM, MORRISTON (WEST), PENTREFELIN and FELIN FRAN all closed. The line between

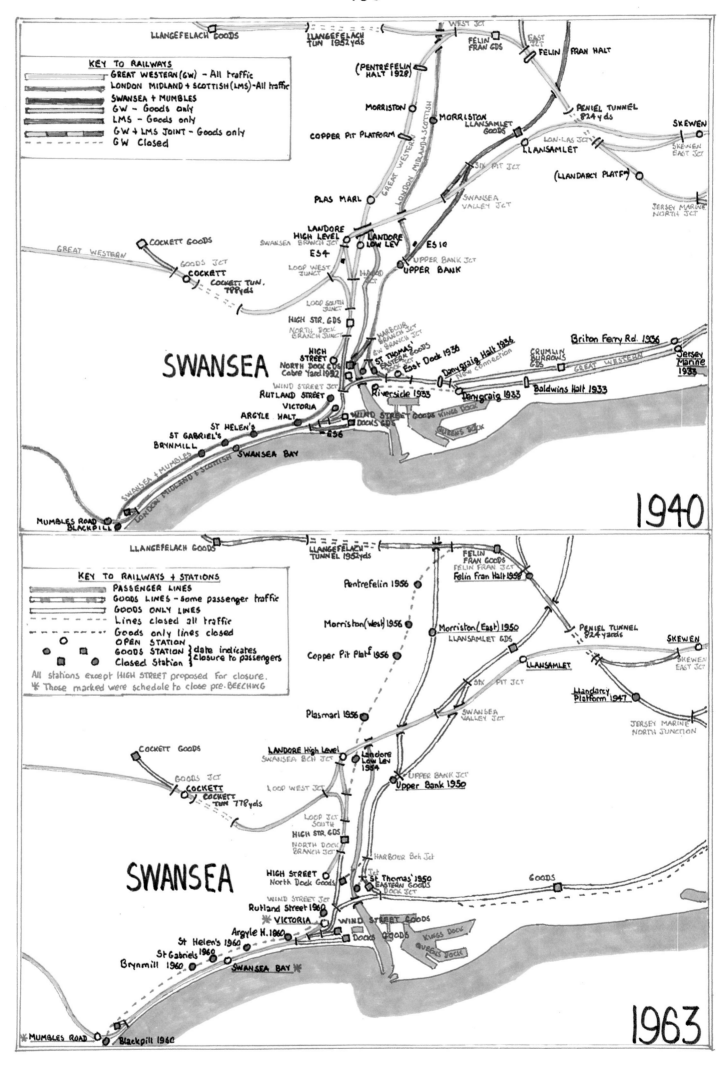

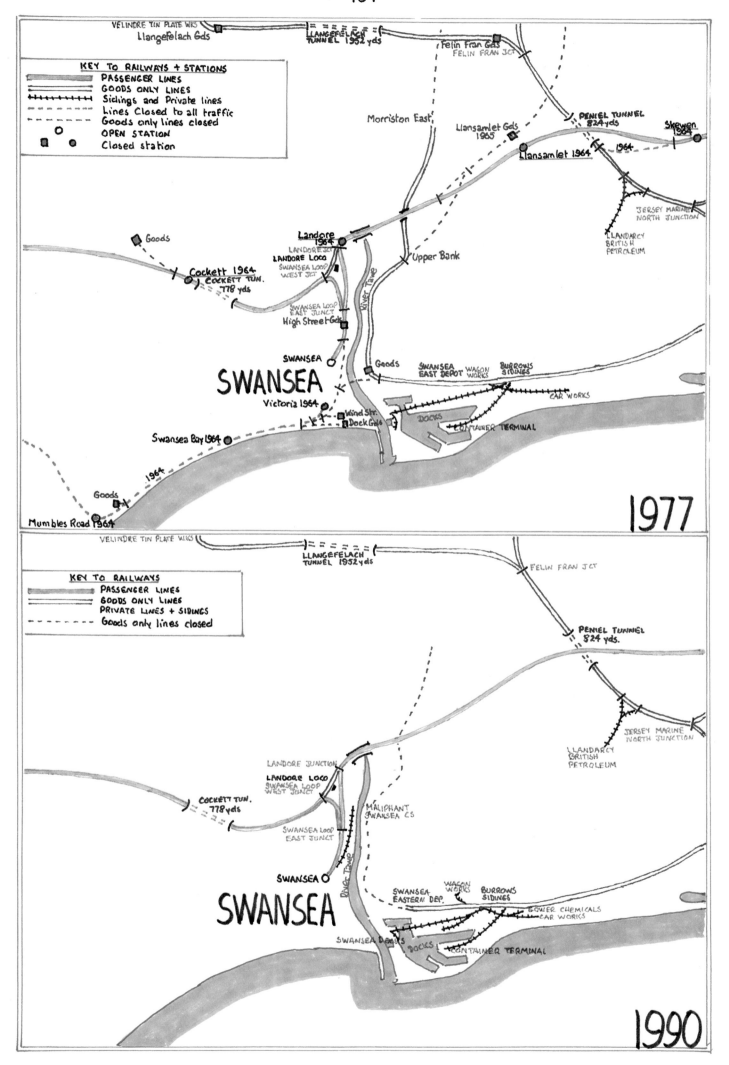

KEY TO RAILWAYS + STATIONS
PASSENGER LINES
GOODS ONLY LINES
Sidings and Private lines
Lines Closed to all traffic
Goods only lines closed
○ OPEN STATION
■ ● Closed station

VELINDRE TIN PLATE WKS
Llangefelach Gds
LLANGEFELACH TUNNEL 1952 yds
Felin Fran Gds
FELIN FRAN JCT

Morriston East
Llansamlet Gds 1965
Llansamlet 1964
PENIEL TUNNEL 824 yds
Skewen 1964
1964

Goods
Cockett 1964
COCKETT TUN. 778 yds.
Landore 1964
LANDORE JCT
LANDORE LOCO
SWANSEA LOOP WEST JCT
Upper Bank
JERSEY MARINE NORTH JUNCTION
LLANDARCY BRITISH PETROLEUM

River Tawe
SWANSEA LOOP EAST JUNCT
High Street Gds
SWANSEA
Goods
SWANSEA EAST DEPOT
WAGON WORKS
BURROWS SIDINGS
CAR WORKS

Victoria 1964
Wind Str.
Dock Gds
DOCKS
CONTAINER TERMINAL
Swansea Bay 1964
1964
Goods
Mumbles Road 1964

1977

KEY TO RAILWAYS
PASSENGER LINES
GOODS ONLY LINES
PRIVATE LINES + SIDINGS
Goods only lines closed

VELINDRE TIN PLATE WKS
LLANGEFELACH TUNNEL 1952 yds
FELIN FRAN JCT

PENIEL TUNNEL 824 yds.

COCKETT TUN. 778 yds.
LANDORE JUNCTION
LANDORE LOCO
SWANSEA LOOP WEST JUNCT
MALIPHANT SWANSEA CS
JERSEY MARINE NORTH JUNCTION
LLANDARCY BRITISH PETROLEUM

SWANSEA LOOP EAST JUNCT
River Tawe
SWANSEA
SWANSEA EASTERN DEP.
WAGON WORKS
BURROWS SIDINGS
GOWER CHEMICALS CAR WORKS

SWANSEA DOCKS
DOCKS
CONTAINER TERMINAL

1990

Hafod Junction and Felin Fran West Junction was closed to all traffic.

1960 SWANSEA + MUMBLES completely closed. This had not been nationalised, being regarded as a passenger tramway. But some goods traffic was carried up to the date of closure; it has therefore been classified as a railway. Stations closed: ARGYLE, ST HELEN'S, ST GABRIEL'S, BRYNMILL, BLACKPILL and the terminus RUTLAND STREET.

1963 The closure programme would have continued without publication of the BEECHING REPORT and the undermentioned had been proposed for closure before the report was issued:

VICTORIA, SWANSEA BAY and MUMBLES ROAD. All the ex LNW lines and dock connections were to close entirely since by this time all docks freight was concentrated on the newer deeper docks east of the Tawe. South Dock was to close.

The BEECHING REPORT recommended the following closures:

COCKETT, LANDORE, LLANSAMLET and SKEWEN.

In the meantime, as the map shows, the SWANSEA DISTRICT LINE had been reduced to goods only, although it did continue to be used by some passenger expresses not calling at SWANSEA.

1964 - 1977

1964 The development story of this period is quickly and simply told. The year saw implementation of all the closure proposals contained in the two groups shown above. This left HIGH STREET as the only station open in the entire area. With closure of other stations this was now known simply as SWANSEA.

1965 Following the closure of South Dock, this led to the closure of all goods lines to the west of the River Tawe. Other goods traffic closures were Midland lines except for a spur truncated at Morriston. The other short spurs shown on the map also closed in the early part of the period.

DOCK TRAFFIC continued to be important, however, and SWANSEA had become the premier Welsh port. The 1977 map (and that of 1990) show rail-served industry, including the expanding oil refinery, and indicate the continued freight importance of the area, albeit on a much reduced scale.

1978 - 1990

With the previous rationalisation having decimated the area network there were but minor changes during this period, the only loss being the ex Midland spur to Morriston. However, the line from Felin Fran northwards has also been cut back, but outside the map area.

However, in contrast with situations elsewhere no new developments have taken place.

1991 - FUTURE

No new future developments are in the pipe-line and the only likely events appear to be further rationalisation of the goods-only network. The line north from Felin Fran could close completely and VELINDRE TIN PLATE is threatened with closure. After completing this chapter, news of the impossible actually happening appears possible. The leaked report on the privatisation of the Inter-City services recommends termination of the service at SWANSEA. No doubt if this does go ahead it could be the thin end of the wedge so far as the westward passenger line is concerned, followed at a later date by SWANSEA itself. The government policy with regard to railways continues to defy any rational explanation, since every time a line has its remotest section amputated it makes the new terminal just as vulnerable to suffer an identical fate in the future.

TIVERTON JUNCTION

TIVERTON JUNCTION, in marked contrast to the other centres described in this atlas, is a small place with never more than four lines radiating from it. Nevertheless it is interesting from a development point of view in the way it both contrasts and reflects the pattern of the larger centres besides having its own unique features.

1800-1850

1814 First portion of the GRAND WESTERN CANAL opened from Tiverton to Loudwell Lock. This was part of an ambitious scheme to link Bristol and Exeter but only the Taunton to Tiverton section was ever completed and only this first portion opened saw much use.

1835 GREAT WESTERN (GW) - Authorised 31st August. All area lines would eventually be absorbed by them.

1836 BRISTOL + EXETER (BE) - Authorised 13th May to connect the points of its title. There was local support for the line between Taunton and Exeter to pass through Tiverton, but geographical considerations dictated that the direct route using the Culm Valley was selected. This avoided the tight curves of the Exe valley. However, the Act did authorise a branch to Tiverton.

1838 GRAND WESTERN CANAL opened to Taunton. However, this final portion with its boat hoists was never profitable due to heavy maintenance and operating costs, not to mention the sparse traffic carried.

1843 BE opened on 1st May to a temporary terminus at BEAMBRIDGE and an intermediate station at WELLINGTON. The line was broad gauge (7'0¼") and due to BE shortage of funds was worked by GW.

1844 BE extended to reach Exeter exactly one year later. Beambridge temporary station and engine shed were closed and new stations opened at TIVERTON ROAD, COLLUMPTON and HELE. With funds still in short supply the authorised branch to Tiverton was not built and the powers lapsed. TIVERTON ROAD was sited where the Tiverton Road crossed the railway to enable travellers to Tiverton to continue their journey by road. When the station opened it was in open country with only one building near the station — Park Farm.

1848 After a struggle with the GRAND WESTERN CANAL the branch was reauthorised and opened on 12th June. There was just one station, a terminal one at TIVERTON. Tiverton Road becomes TIVERTON JUNCTION. Works on branch to accommodate double track – but built single and never doubled.

1849 BE takes over working of its own system from GW.

1851-1880

1852 BE lease GRAND WESTERN canal. Fully purchased 1863 and Taunton section abandoned in 1865.

1860 STOKE CANON station opened. 1867 Stations opened at: SILVERTON and BURLESCOMBE.

1873 CULM VALLEY (Light) - Authorised on 15th May to build a standard gauge line from TIVERTON JUNCTION to Hemyock.

1874 EXE VALLEY - Act (30th June). Line from junction near STOKE CANON to north of TIVERTON.

1875 TIVERTON + NORTH DEVON - Act (19th July) From end-on junction with the EXE VALLEY to Morebath Jct (Barnstaple line). On same day BE obtained powers to build EXE VALLEY line.

1876 GW (on 1st January) absorb BE and thus take over powers to build the EXE VALLEY line.
GW (on 1st March) convert line between Taunton and Exeter to mixed gauge.
On 29th May CULM VALLEY line opened. Stations: UFFCULME, CULMSTOCK and HEMYOCK. Worked GW.

During the year new main line intermediate stations at: SILVERTON and BURLESCOMBE. Also about this time name changes: Collumpton became CULLOMPTON whilst HELE became HELE + BRADNINCH. GW now had three different types of gauge at TIVERTON JUNCTION: mixed on the main line, standard to HEMYOCK and broad to TIVERTON.

1880 GW absorbed the CULM VALLEY by purchase.

1881-1890

1884 GW (on 28th June) convert TIVERTON branch to standard gauge.

1884 TIVERTON + NORTH DEVON opened, station at BAMPTON. Worked by GW.

1885 GW opened EXE VALLEY line. Stations at: BRAMFORD SPEKE, THORVERTON, UP EXE + SILVERTON, CADELEIGH + BICKLEIGH and TIVERTON. This last station replaced the original Tiverton Branch station which then became the goods station for Tiverton.

The network was now complete and remained in place for 75 years. All that happend was opening of new stations or replacing stations on various lines.

A note about engine sheds: Tiverton Junction shed appears to have opened in 1848 with the opening of the branch but there could have been an early shed at TIVERTON. What is certain is a replacement shed was built in 1876 coinciding with opening of a shed at HEMYOCK.

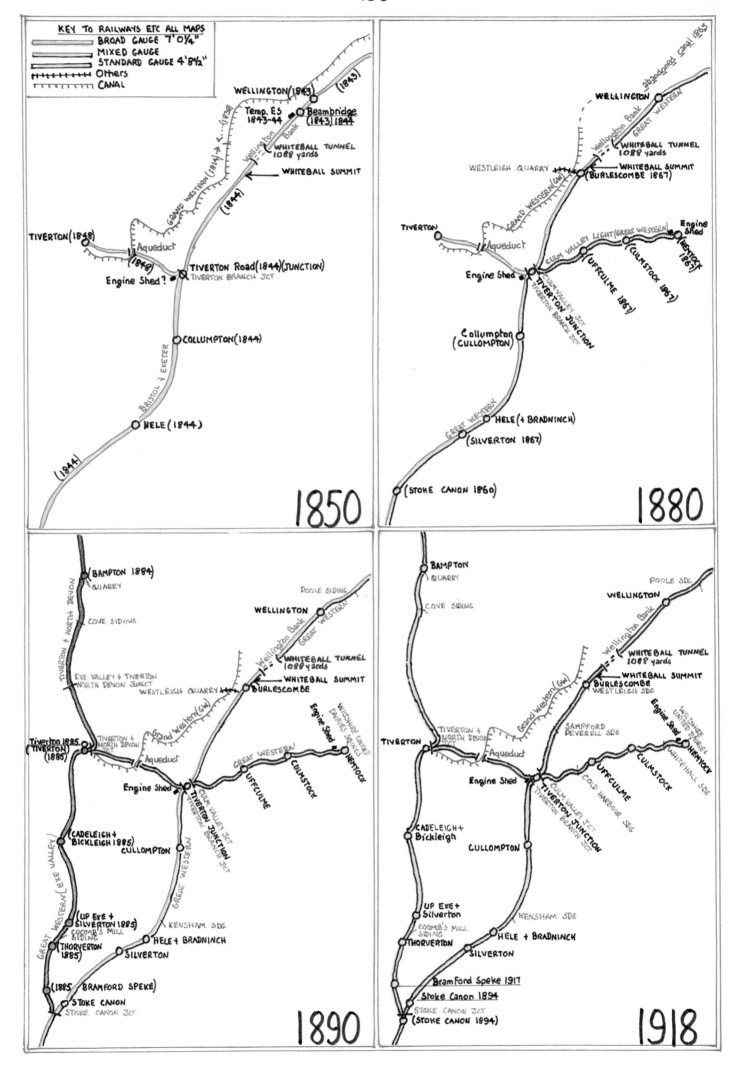

KEY TO RAILWAYS ETC ALL MAPS
BROAD GAUGE 7'0¼"
MIXED GAUGE
STANDARD GAUGE 4'8½"
Others
CANAL

1850

WELLINGTON (1843) (1843)
Temp. E.S. 1843-44 ● Beambridge (1843) 1844
WHITEBALL TUNNEL 1088 yards
WHITEBALL SUMMIT
GRAND WESTERN (1814) C.... (1838)
Wellington Bank
(1844)
TIVERTON (1848)
Aqueduct (1848)
Engine Shed?
Tiverton Road (1844)(Junction)
TIVERTON BRANCH JCT
COLLUMPTON (1844)
BRISTOL & EXETER
HELE (1844)
(1844)

1880

WELLINGTON
abandoned Canal 1865
Wellington Bank   GREAT WESTERN
WHITEBALL TUNNEL 1088 yards
WHITEBALL SUMMIT (BURLESCOMBE 1867)
WESTLEIGH QUARRY
GRAND WESTERN (GW)
TIVERTON
Aqueduct
Engine Shed
CULM VALLEY LIGHT (GREAT WESTERN)
CULM VALLEY JCT
UFFCULME 1867
CULMSTOCK 1867
Engine Shed HEMYOCK 1867
TIVERTON JUNCTION
TIVERTON BRANCH JCT
Collumpton (CULLOMPTON)
GREAT WESTERN
HELE (& BRADNINCH)
(SILVERTON 1867)
(STOKE CANON 1860)

1890

BAMPTON 1884)
QUARRY
COVE SIDING
TIVERTON & NORTH DEVON
EXE VALLEY & TIVERTON NORTH DEVON JUNCT
Tiverton 1885 (TIVERTON) (1885)
TIVERTON & NORTH DEVON JCT
Aqueduct
Engine Shed
CULM VALLEY JCT
TIVERTON JUNCTION
TIVERTON BRANCH JCT
GREAT WESTERN (EXE VALLEY)
(CADELEIGH & BICKLEIGH 1885)
CULLOMPTON
GREAT WESTERN
(UP EXE & SILVERTON 1885)
COOMB'S MILL SIDING
KENSHAM SDG
THORVERTON (1885)
SILVERTON
HELE & BRADNINCH
(1885) BRAMFORD SPEKE)
STOKE CANON
STOKE CANON JCT
POOLE SIDING
WELLINGTON
Wellington Bank   GREAT WESTERN
WHITEBALL TUNNEL 1088 yards
WHITEBALL SUMMIT
WESTLEIGH QUARRY   BURLESCOMBE
GRAND WESTERN (GW)
Engine Shed
WILTSHIRE DAIRIES SPRINGS
HEMYOCK
UFFCULME
CULMSTOCK

1918

BAMPTON
QUARRY
COVE SIDING
TIVERTON & NORTH DEVON
TIVERTON
Aqueduct
Engine Shed
CULM VALLEY JCT
TIVERTON JUNCTION
TIVERTON BRANCH JCT
CADELEIGH & Bickleigh
CULLOMPTON
UP EXE & Silverton
COOMB'S MILL SIDING
KENSHAM SDG
THORVERTON
SILVERTON
HELE & BRADNINCH
Bramford Speke 1917
Stoke Canon 1894
STOKE CANON JCT
(STOKE CANON 1894)
POOLE SDG
WELLINGTON
Wellington Bank
WHITEBALL TUNNEL 1088 yards
WHITEBALL SUMMIT
BURLESCOMBE
WESTLEIGH SDG
Grand Western (GW)
SAMPFORD PEVERELL SDG
Engine Shed
WILTSHIRE UNITED DAIRIES
HEMYOCK
WHITEHALL SDG
UFFCULME
COLD HARBOUR SDG
CULMSTOCK

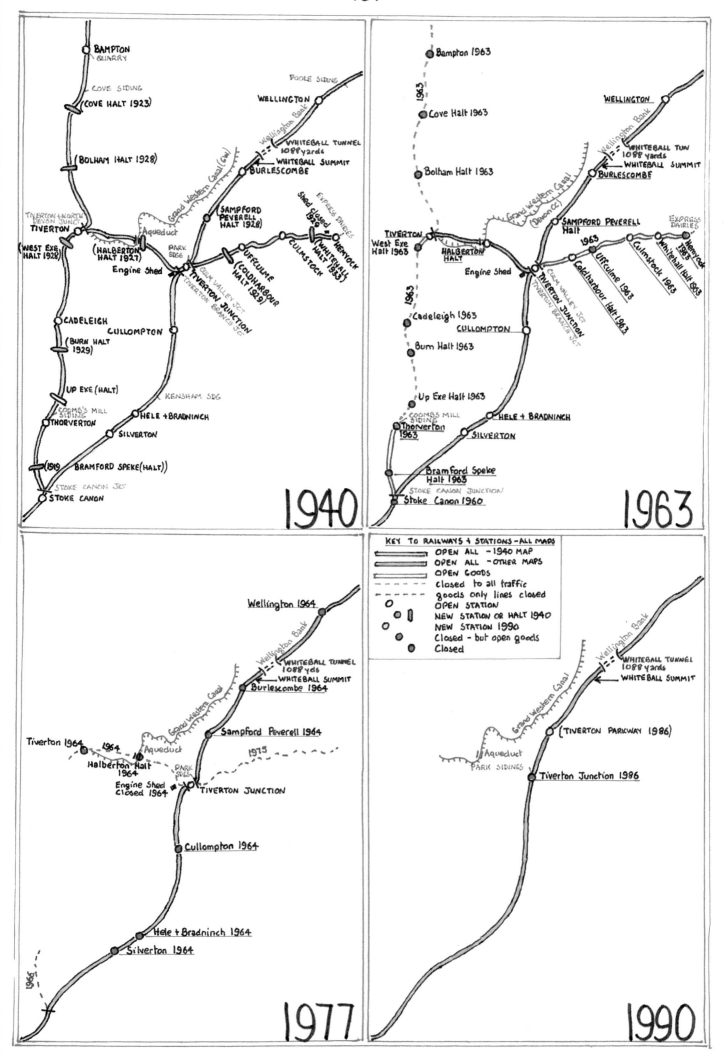

1891-1918

As noted already there were no network changes during this period although it was a time during which importance of TIVERTON JUNCTION increased albeit to serve purely local needs. A small railway community was built up over the years and industries that would be railway served were attracted to the vicinity. Wiltshire United Dairies (later part of Express Dairies) built a milk factory at Hemyock and traffic off the Culm Valley branch was collected by a daily milk express at the junction. Pig-pen sidings and meat sidings served a slaughterhouse (Lloyd Maunders) and there was even a Tiverton Junction Auction market owing its existance to this developing meat and cattle traffic. There was also a butter platform at the station serving a nearby factory and later a sheepskin factory.

Turning to other wider developments there are still some events for the period to record:

1892 On 20th May the mixed gauge main line was converted to standard gauge. Broad gauge abandoned.

1894 TIVERTON + NORTH DEVON was fully absorbed by the GREAT WESTERN (GW) on 1st July.

    Also during the year STOKE CANON was rebuilt to the south so that it served both the main line and the EXE VALLEY line.

1905 UP EXE + SILVERTON becomes UP EXE. The following year CADELEIGH + BICKLEIGH became CADELEIGH.

1917 The final event to record is the area's first station closure (excepting rebuildings and closure of the temporary terminus at Beambridge): this was the closure of BRAMFORD SPEKE. But this was only a war-time economy measure and it would re-open in 1919.

1919-1940

At most centres this was a period when rationalisation commenced. However, as seen elsewhere the GW by its use of unstaffed halts attempted to retain revenue whilst curtailing expenses. That pattern is reflected in this area where, although some stations were down-graded to halts, there were no closures but many new halts were opened:

1919 BRAMFORD SPEKE re-opened as a full station. But it had been downgraded to halt status by 1923.

1923 COVE HALT opened. UP EXE downgraded to halt status.

1927 HALBERTON HALT opened.

1928 Halts opened at: WEST EXE, BOLHAM and SAMPFORD PEVERELL (this latter was later staffed and is shown as a station).

1929 Halts opened at: BURN, COLDHARBOUR (previous siding location). Hemyock Engine Shed closed.

1932 During this year most main-line stations had platform loops added to ease express traffic flows. At TIVERTON JCT considerable extra siding accomodation was added. There was also a scheme for laying continuous quadruple track between TIVERTON JUNCTION and SAMPFORD PEVERELL but this was not implemented.

1933 WHITEHALL HALT opened.

1940 PARK SIDINGS opened at TIVERTON JUNCTION.

1941-1963

1960 STOKE CANON station closed — The area's first real closure.

1963 The BEECHING REPORT divides passenger station closures into two categories, those recommended and those already under consideration before the report. This latter category has stations already closed before the report specially marked (but none of the area's many 1963 closures are shown as already closed). It is therefore quite unique to find that an area with only one station closure in 120 years now had every area station included on one or other of the two lists. Those under consideration before the report include every station closed in 1963 whilst the remainder were included as recommendations for closure.

1964-1977

1964 All the Beeching closure proposals were implemented with the exception of TIVERTON JUNCTION, which reverted to its original function as a railhead for Tiverton. The Hemyock branch remained open for milk traffic and a goods spur to Thorverton on the EXE VALLEY line was retained to serve Coomb's Mill.

1966 The remaining goods spur to Thorverton closed.

1975 Hemyock branch closed completely following loss of milk traffic to road competition.

1978-1990

Although the Junction Goods had closed in 1967, private siding traffic to the slaughterhouse had continued but this was ultimately lost until only Park Sidings remained in use. Then in 1984 it was decided to replace the station by TIVERTON PARKWAY on the site of Sampford Peverell with motorway connections. It is very difficult to see the logic of this since if one needs to use a motorway to reach a station, why use the station? However, this decision was implemented in 1986. The main line remains open of course and strangely enough so too does the canal remnant - although now devoted solely to pleasure.

BRISTOL

BRISTOL was the place where the seeds of the GREAT WESTERN germinated with its unique broad gauge of 7'0¼". It is therefore strange to note that from a very early date their monopoly in the area was broken when in 1845 the MIDLAND were allowed to snatch the broad gauge BRISTOL + GLOUCESTER with powers to run into TEMPLE MEADS. Then at a later stage the MIDLAND were again involved in a somewhat questionable deal in connection with the SOMERSET + DORSET although the villains in this case were the LONDON + SOUTH WESTERN. The GREAT WESTERN, having been approached by the S+D about take-over, put plans before the LSW for sharing the line which penetrated LSW territory and could have been in breach of a parliamentary agreement about lines in each other's territories. The LSW seized the chance to get into GW territory without any reciprocal agreement and took over the S+D with the MIDLAND.

1820-1842

31.12.1820 By this date the Kennet + Avon canal gave connection via the Avon and the Thames between BRISTOL and London.

19.6.1828 AVON + GLOUCESTERSHIRE (AGS) incorporated. This standard gauge tramway promoted by the Kennet + Avon Canal was intended to carry coal from Westerleigh Pits to the Avon near Keynsham.

19.6.1828 BRISTOL + GLOUCESTERSHIRE (BGS) incorporated. A similar enterprise authorised on the same day. The same coal resources were to be tapped but transportation was to be to the Floating harbour at BRISTOL; at a later date it was to be extended north and make junction with AGS at Keynsham Jct. near Mangotsfield.

17.7.1832 AGS opened throughout. Horse drawn and gravity tramway.

6.8.1835 BGS opened throughout. This too was a horse-drawn and gravity tramway.

31.8.1835 GREAT WESTERN (GW) - Act.

19.5.1836 BRISTOL + EXETER (BE) - Act.

1.7.1839 BRISTOL + GLOUCESTER (BG) - Act to convert BGS to a full railway. It was to be standard gauge and would continue north to Gloucester.

31.8.1840 GW opened between BRISTOL and BATH. There was but one intermediate station — at KEYNSHAM — but additional stations were opened before the end of the year at SALTFORD and TWERTON. None of the planned stations were in fact completed when the line opened. There were no less than eight tunnels on this short stretch of line and there would be a further two at the other side of BATH.

14.6.1841 GW commence passenger services on BE - BRISTOL to Bridgwater. Intermediate stations at NAILSEA and CLEVEDON ROAD. BE Bristol terminal station not brought fully into use until 1844 or 1845. Trains, meanwhile, had to reverse into the unfinished GW station. Later through trains used the Express Platform.

30.6.1841 GW opened BATH to Chippenham. Through services between London and BRISTOL commenced.

1842 BG conversion of tramway in progress — still planned as standard gauge.

1843-1852

13.4.1843 BG lease to GW agreed. Line now to be Broad gauge.

10.5.1844 MIDLAND formed.

8.7.1844 BG opened from BRISTOL (Junction with GW near Marsh Lane) to Gloucester. Only one map area intermediate station — at YATE — but MANGOTSFIELD was thought to have opened shortly afterwards and certainly before the end of 1846. Some mixed gauge track was provided at Mangotsfield for the AGS. This first station at MANGOTSFIELD was to the north of what later became North Junction. Goods traffic started 2.9.1844.

1.1.1845 BG and Birmingham + Gloucester worked as one pending merger (defeated in parliament on technical and minor details) and pending expected absorption by GW.

7.5.1845 MIDLAND take possession of BG by virtue of lease dated 1.5.1845 !! Fully absorbed 3.8.1846.

30.6.1846 WILTS SOMERSET + WEYMOUTH - Act. This railway was vested in the GW before its authorised lines in the map area were opened.

28.7.1847 BE - CLEVEDON ROAD became YATTON. Branch to CLEVEDON opened (worked by GW who had worked all BE lines since its opening under a leasing agreement).

1.5.1849 BE disagreement with GW. Lease terminated and BE commences to work its own railway.

1.7.1851 KENNET + AVON CANAL (including AGS tramway) absorbed by GW. Tramway virtually disused by this time. We now have the situation with the two initial tramways: the broad gauge BG owned by standard gauge MIDLAND, whilst the broad gauge GW had acquired the standard gauge AGS.

1.1852 BE open Loco Works and Engine Shed at Bath Road. GW shed was north-east of TEMPLE MEADS.

The end of this period marks the end of the area broad gauge monopoly since commencing the following year the MIDLAND would be actively engaged in converting their line to mixed gauge.

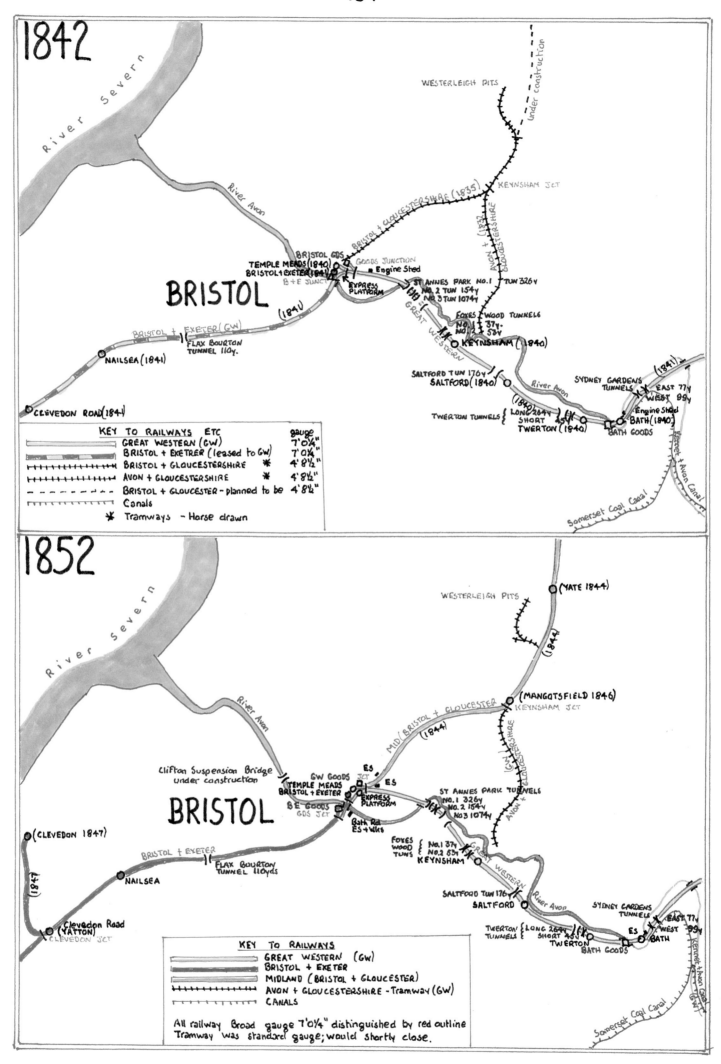

1842

River Severn

River Avon

WESTERLEIGH PITS

Under construction

KEYNSHAM JCT

BRISTOL & GLOUCESTERSHIRE (1835)

AVON + (1832)

GLOUCESTERSHIRE

BRISTOL GDS

TEMPLE MEADS (1840)
BRISTOL + EXETER (1841)
B + E JUNCT

GOODS JUNCTION

Engine Shed

EXPRESS PLATFORM

BRISTOL

St ANNES PARK No.1
No.2 TUN 154y
No.3 TUN 1074y

TUN 326y

(1841)

BRISTOL + EXETER (GW)

GREAT WESTERN

FOXES WOOD TUNNELS
No.1 37y
No.2 52y

KEYNSHAM (1840)

FLAX BOURTON
TUNNEL 110y.

NAILSEA (1841)

SALTFORD TUN 170y
SALTFORD (1840)

River Avon

SYDNEY GARDENS
TUNNELS

(1841)

EAST 77y
WEST 99y

Engine Shed

CLEVEDON ROAD (1841)

TWERTON TUNNELS {
LONG 264y
SHORT   45y
TWERTON (1840)

BATH (1840)

BATH GOODS

Somerset Coal Canal

Kennet + Avon Canal

KEY TO RAILWAYS ETC	gauge
GREAT WESTERN (GW)	7'0¼"
BRISTOL + EXETRER (leased to GW)	7'0¼"
BRISTOL + GLOUCESTERSHIRE	4'8½"
AVON + GLOUCESTERSHIRE	4'8½"
BRISTOL + GLOUCESTER - planned to be	4'8½"
Canals	
✳ Tramways - Horse drawn	

1852

River Severn

River Avon

WESTERLEIGH PITS

(YATE 1844)

(1844)

(MANGOTSFIELD 1846)

KEYNSHAM JCT

MID/ BRISTOL + GLOUCESTER

(1844)

Clifton Suspension Bridge
under construction

ES JCT

ES

GW GOODS

TEMPLE MEADS
BRISTOL + EXETER

B E GOODS
GDS JCT

EXPRESS PLATFORM

Bath Rd
ES + Wks

(GW) AVON + GLOUCESTERSHIRE

St ANNES PARK TUNNELS
No.1 326y
No.2 154y
No.3 1074y

BRISTOL

(CLEVEDON 1847)

BRISTOL + EXETER

FLAX BOURTON
TUNNEL 110yds

NAILSEA

FOXES
WOOD
TUNS {
No.1 37y
No.2 52y

KEYNSHAM

GREAT WESTERN

(1847)

Clevedon Road
(YATTON)
CLEVEDON JCT

SALTFORD TUN 176y
SALTFORD

River Avon

SYDNEY GARDENS
TUNNELS

EAST 77y
WEST 99y

TWERTON
TUNNELS {
LONG 264y
SHORT   45y
TWERTON

ES

BATH

BATH GOODS

Somerset Coal Canal

Kennet + Avon Canal (GW)

KEY TO RAILWAYS	
GREAT WESTERN (GW)	
BRISTOL + EXETER	
MIDLAND (BRISTOL + GLOUCESTER)	
AVON + GLOUCESTERSHIRE - Tramway (GW)	
CANALS	

All railway Broad gauge 7'0¼" distinguished by red outline
Tramway was standard gauge; would shortly close.

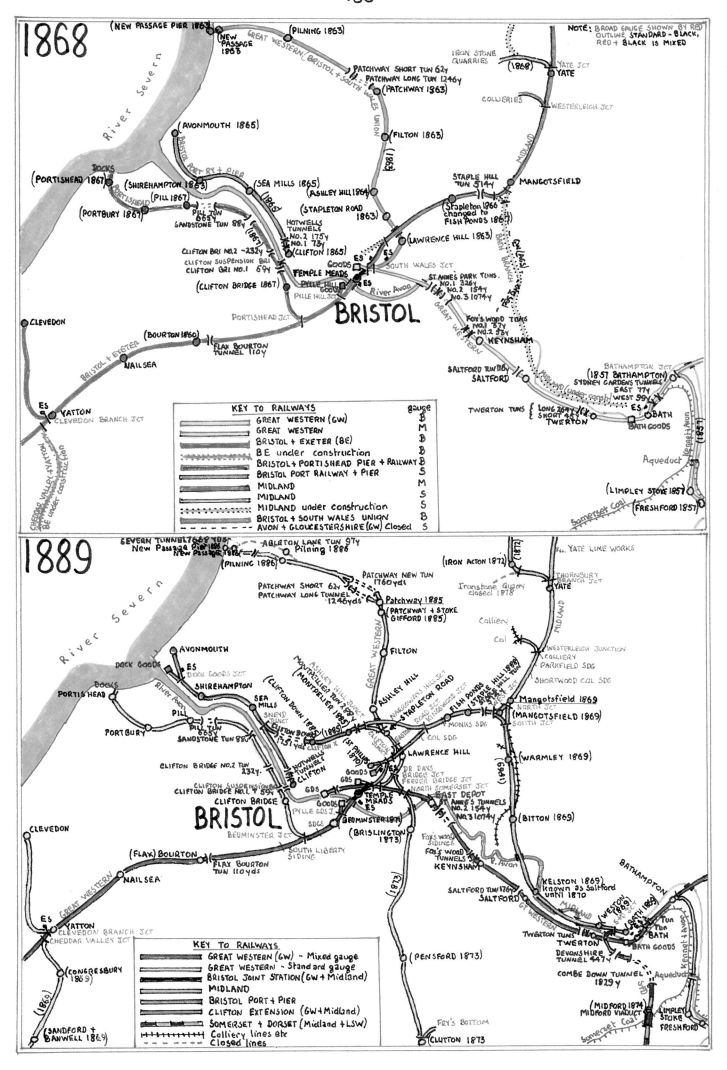

1953-1868

22.7.1854. MIDLAND introduce standard gauge trains into TEMPLE MEADS but the broad gauge rails were retained under the terms of the BRISTOL + GLOUCESTER and the GREAT WESTERN(GW) lease agreement, although in practice the 7'0¼" rails were not used by the GW. However, the BRISTOL + EXETER (BE) did make use of the broad gauge access for coal trains from Westerleigh.

2.2.1857 GW opened from Bradford Junction to Bathampton Junction. The line had been authorised by the WILTS, SOMERSET + WEYMOUTH which had been absorbed by the GW in 1851 before work on this portion commenced. The line required two diversions of the Kennet and Avon Canal, which had also been absorbed by the GW in 1851. A station was opened at BATHAMPTON, on the main line. Within the map area stations were opened at: LIMPLEY STOKE and FRESHFORD. The line, of course, was broad gauge.

27.7.1857 BRISTOL + SOUTH WALES UNION (BSWU) - Act.

17.7.1862 BRISTOL PORT RAILWAY + PIER (BPRP) - Incorporated.

7.8.1862 SOMERSET + DORSET (SD) formed by a merger of Somerset Central and Dorset Central. It had no railways in the map area at the time of the merger, but the new company's BATH EXTENSION would play an important part in the future.

29.6.1863 BRISTOL + PORTISHEAD PIER + RAILWAY (B+P) - Incorporated.

2.7.1863 BRISTOL + NORTH SOMERSET (BNS) - Act.

8.9.1863 BSWU opened broad gauge line between BRISTOL (SWU Jct) and NEW PASSAGE. Intermediate stations: LAWRENCE HILL, STAPLETON ROAD, FILTON, PATCHWAY and PILNING. There was a ferry link across the Severn to SOUTH WALES line.

1864 MIDLAND - BATH branch authorised.   BSWU opened additional station at ASHLEY HILL.

14.7.1864 CHEDDAR VALLEY + YATTON (CVY) - Act.

6.3.1865 BPRP opened from BRISTOL (HOTWELLS) to AVONMOUTH. Intermediate stations at: SEA MILLS and SHIREHAMPTON. Railway worked by GW and MIDLAND and was standard gauge.

19.6.1865 BE take over powers of CVY.

5.7.1865 AVON + GLOUCESTERSHIRE (AGS) Tramway abandoned by GW. It would, however, re-open later.

1.4.1866 MIDLAND opened STAPLETON station. Name changed to FISH PONDS the following year (1.7.1867).

28.6.1866 BRISTOL HARBOUR RAILWAY - Incorporated. Joint venture BE, GW and Bristol Corporation.

18.4.1867 B+P opened its broad gauge line worked by the BE. Stations: CLIFTON BRIDGE, PILL, PORTBURY and PORTISHEAD.

15.8.1867 BPRP authorised to build CLIFTON EXTENSION (to be worked jointly by GW and MIDLAND).

1.8.1868 BSWU absorbed by GW (Act 13/7/1868).

1869-1889

3.8.1869 BE opened CVY - YATTON to Cheddar. Intermediate stations (map area): CONGRESBURY and SANDFORD + BANWELL.

4.8.1869 MIDLAND opened Bath branch to passengers. New station at MANGOTSFIELD where a triangular junction gave access to BATH from both BRISTOL and the north. Stations: WARMLEY, BITTON, KELSTON, WESTON and BATH. The line opened for goods traffic on 1st September.

2.5.1870 MIDLAND open ST PHILIPS independant terminal station at BRISTOL.

25.5.1871 CLIFTON EXTENSION of BPRP to GW and MIDLAND. BPRP retained independance but working by GW + MIDLAND continued.

2.8.1871 SD Bath Extension authorised.

11.3.1872 BRISTOL HARBOUR RAILWAY opened from TEMPLE MEADS to WAPPING WHARF. A mixed gauge goods line.

26.5.1872 MIDLAND - BRISTOL to Gloucester has broad gauge rails removed.

2.9.1872 MIDLAND opened THORNBURY branch. Map area station: IRON ACTON.

1.8.1873 GW Midland Junction at BRISTOL to North Somerset Junction converted to mixed gauge.

9.8.1873 GW by this date had converted BSWU line to narrow gauge.

3.9.1873 BNS opened from North Somerset Jct to Radstock. Map area stations: BRISLINGTON and PENSFORD - standard gauge.

20.7.1874 SD BATH EXTENSION opened to MIDLAND station at BATH. Intermediate map area station: MIDFORD.

1.10.1874 On this day three separate lines opened meeting at Ashley Hill Junction. CE from CLIFTON DOWN (GW and MIDLAND), GW - Ashley Hill Loop, and MIDLAND from Kingswood Junction. Earlier in the year the GW main line from North Somerset Junction to Bathampton junction had been converted to mixed gauge as a prelude to the narrowing of the branch through LIMPLEY STOKE to Bradford-on-Avon a few days later.

16.3.1875 GW Thingley Junction to BATHAMPTON converted to mixed gauge.

1.6.1875 BE BRISTOL to Highbridge converted to mixed gauge. 15.11.1875 BE YATTON to Wells narrowed.

1.11.1875 S+D vested jointly in MIDLAND and LONDON + SOUTH WESTERN (See comment in opening remarks).

1.1.1876 BE absorbed by GW.   1.8.1876 BRISTOL HARBOUR RAILWAY absorbed by GW.

22.2.1877 BPRP open AVONMOUTH DOCK. 24.2.1877 CE opened from Sneyd Park to CLIFTON DOWN (goods only).

1.1.1878 TEMPLE MEADS reconstruction completed (authorised 19.6.1865 and worked started soon after).

7. 1879 Dock at PORTISHEAD opened.   29.9.1879 YATTON to CLEVEDON narrowed by GREAT WESTERN (GW).

24.1.1880 GW narrowed PORTISHEAD line (still independant at this date but worked by GW).

Before continuing this chronology it is appropriate to mention some additional information regarding the MIDLAND Thornbury and Bath branches. When the MIDLAND had fully absorbed the BRISTOL + GLOUCESTER in 1846 it sought to open a branch to Bath but this was rejected by parliament and it was 1864 before authorisation was obtained for both Bath and Thornbury branches. At this time finance was tight and what funds were available were allocated to the Bath branch. However, as the map shows it was the Thornbury branch which was first partly opened with a spur to a local iron mine although ironically this went out of business and was unused by 1878, although still appearing on an RCH map of 1889. The track of this goods stub was lifted in 1892. This, apart from an 1888 station opening, was the area's final MIDLAND DEVELOPMENT.

1881 AVON + GLOUCESTERSHIRE Tramroad, now in GREAT WESTERN (GW) ownership, re-opened, the gauge difference no longer being a problem.

1. 7.1884 BRISTOL + NORTH SOMERSET absorbed by GW.

1. 7.1884 BRISTOL + PORTISHEAD PIER + RAILWAY absorbed by GW, but Portishead Dock was excluded from the transfer.

6. 8.1885 WESTON, CLEVEDON + PORTISHEAD STEAM TRAMWAY (WCPST) - authorised. As title indicates this was a tramway, but it would ultimately become a light railway (see 1898 below). It would be many years, however, before its line reached the map area.

1. 9.1885 CLIFTON EXTENSION (CE) passenger service from both TEMPLE MEADS and ST PHILIPS to AVONMOUTH commenced by GW and MIDLAND. The MIDLAND service only lasted a year was then continued by GW alone (stations - see map).

1. 6.1886 GW BRISTOL LOOP - FEEDER BRIDGE JCT to DR DAYS BRIDGE JUNCTION opened.

1. 9.1886 GW opened SEVERN TUNNEL for goods. Passenger traffic commenced 1/12/1866. New PILNING station opened adjacent to the old but on the tunnel connecting line. At the same time the old line through Pilning (original station) to New Passage and New Passage Pier was closed completely together with its stations.

1.11.1888 MIDLAND opened new station at STAPLE HILL. The final MIDLAND development.

1890 -1918

25. 7.1890 BRISTOL PORT RAILWAY + PIER vested jointly in GW and MIDLAND who had worked the line since its opening and had already absorbed this railway's CLIFTON EXTENSION.

10. 4.1892 GW opened BRISTOL AVOIDING LINE - Marsh South Junction to Pylle Hill Junction and Marsh North Junction to a junction near St Annes Park. This enabled main-line expresses to avoid TEMPLE MEADS station.

20. 5.1892 GW abolished the broad gauge which by this time had been reduced to mixed gauge on the main line and the harbour branch and only therefore required removal of the broad gauge rails.

1.12.1897 WCPST opened from Weston to a station at CLEVEDON adjoining the GW station; a siding exchange connection was established with the GW. Still classified as a steam tramway although some goods traffic carried.

1898 GW obtain authorisation for WRINGTON VALE LIGHT RAILWAY (WVL).

9. 8.1898 WCPST becomes a light railway and changes its name to WESTON, CLEVEDON + PORTISHEAD (WCP). It was also re-authorised to extend to Portishead, earlier powers having lapsed.

5. 2.1900 GW open line from AVONMOUTH to Pilning Junction, the last 1¾ miles using the Pilning to New Passage line which had been closed when the SEVERN TUNNEL opened. Line was goods only.

4.12.1901 GW opened WVL from a junction at CONGRESBURY to BLAGDON with intermediate stations at: WRINGTON, LANGFORD and BURRINGTON. A small engine shed was opened, but this may have been during the following year and it was closed in 1924.

1. 5.1903 GW opened SOUTH WALES DIRECT line from Badminton to Stoke Gifford Junction where the line split to make junctions at both FILTON and PATCHWAY. From London this provided not only a direct line to South Wales via the Severn Tunnel but an additional route to BRISTOL which would assume increasing importance. Stations in the map area: BADMINTON, CHIPPING SODBURY, COALPIT HEATH and WINTERBOURNE. Two months later loop connections at Westerleigh were opened giving access to YATE and the north from the GW in both up and down directions.

22.11.1903 GW deviation at AVONMOUTH - Gloucester Road to Holesmouth Junction. Avonmouth terminus closed to make way for new docks. AVONMOUTH DOCKS became new passenger terminus. By this time also the MIDLAND connection at Easton Road Junction had been removed. It had become redundant when the ST PHILIPS AVONMOUTH service was withdrawn in 1886 with all trains running into TEMPLE MEADS. Some authorities indicate the connection was removed in 1899. The line was retained as a siding and would in due course be re-instated by British Rail.

4.10.1906 GW opened BRISTOL HARBOUR EXTENSION RAILWAY - Wapping Wharf Junction to Ashton Junction and a branch to CANON'S MARSH. All goods only lines. Also opened at this time was Bedminster West Loop. ASHTON GATE opened as a football platform (15/9), whilst AVONCLIFF near FRESHFORD (shown on some later maps) also opened.

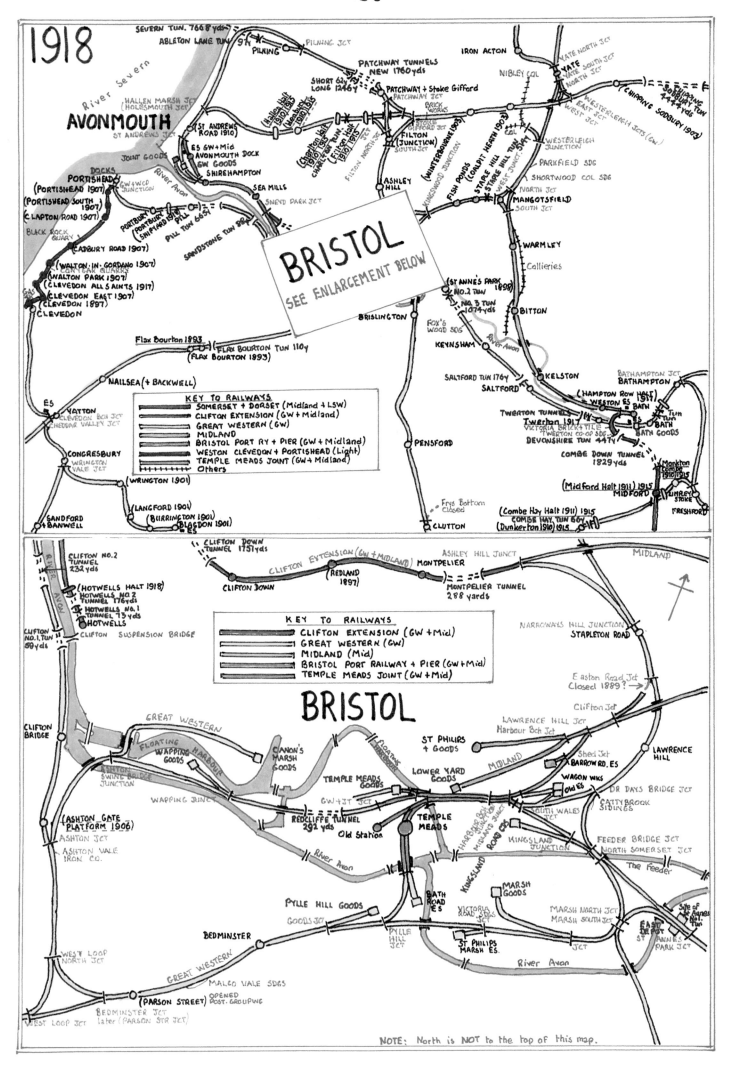

1918

SEVERN TUN. 7668 yds
ABLETON LANE TUN
River Severn

AVONMOUTH

HALLEN MARSH JCT
(HOLESMOUTH JCT)
ST ANDREWS JCT

ST ANDREWS
ROAD 1910
ES GW+Mid
AVONMOUTH DOCK
GW GOODS
SHIREHAMPTON

JOINT GOODS

DOCKS
PORTISHEAD
(PORTISHEAD 1907)
(PORTISHEAD SOUTH 1907)
(CLAPTON ROAD 1907)

BLACK ROCK QUARY

(CADBURY ROAD 1907)

(WALTON-IN-GORDANO 1907)
(WALTON PARK 1907)
(CLEVEDON ALL SAINTS 1917)
(CLEVEDON EAST 1907)
(CLEVEDON 1897)
CLEVEDON

GW+WCO JUNCTION
River Avon
PORTBURY
(PORTBURY SHIPYARD 1918)
PILL
PILL TUN 66Y
SANDSTONE TUN 88Y

PORTBURY
SNEYD PARK JCT
SEA MILLS

PILNING JCT
PILNING

SHORT 62Y
LONG 1246Y

PATCHWAY TUNNELS
NEW 1760 yds

PATCHWAY + STOKE GIFFORD
PATCHWAY JCT
BRICK WORKS
STOKE
GIFFORD

(Hallen Halt 1910)1916
Henbury 1910/1916
(Charlton Halt 1910/1916)
CHARLTON TUN. 1910/1915
FILTON TUN. 1910/1915
FILTON NORTH JCT
FILTON
JUNCTION
SOUTH JCT

ASHLEY HILL

(WINTERBOURNE 1903)
KINGSWOOD JUNCTION
FISH PONDS
(COALPIT HEATH 1903)
STAPLE HILL TUN
STAPLE HILL 5041
WEST JUNCT

IRON ACTON
NIBLEY COL

YATE NORTH JCT
YATE
YATE SOUTH JCT
NORTH JCT
WESTERLEIGH EAST JCT
WEST JCT
WESTERLEIGH JCTS (GW)

SODBURY TUN
4444 yds
(CHIPPING SODBURY 1903)

WESTERLEIGH
JUNCTION
PARKFIELD SDG
SHORTWOOD COL SDG

NORTH JCT
MANGOTSFIELD
SOUTH JCT

WARMLEY
Collieries

(ST ANNES PARK 1898)
NO. 2 TUN
NO. 3 TUN
1074 yds

BITTON

FOX'S WOOD SDG
River Avon

KEYNSHAM

SALTFORD TUN 176Y
SALTFORD

KELSTON

BATHAMPTON JCT
BATHAMPTON

(HAMPTON ROW HALT 1917)
WESTON ES
BATH

TWERTON TUNNELS
TWERTON 1917
VICTORIA BRICK+TILE
TWERTON CO-OP SDG
DEVONSHIRE TUN 447Y

TUN TUN
BATH
BATH GOODS

COMBE DOWN TUNNEL
1829 yds

MONKTON
COMBE 1910/1915

LIMPLEY
STOKE

FRESHFORD

BRISLINGTON

Flax Bourton 1893
FLAX BOURTON TUN 110Y
(FLAX BOURTON 1893)

NAILSEA (+ BACKWELL)

ES
YATTON
CLEVEDON BCH JCT
CHEDDAR VALLEY JCT

CONGRESBURY
WRINGTON
VALE JCT

(WRINGTON 1901)

(LANGFORD 1901)

SANDFORD
+ BANWELL

(BURRINGTON 1901)
BLAGDON 1901)
ES

KEY TO RAILWAYS
SOMERSET + DORSET (Midland + LSW)
CLIFTON EXTENSION (GW + Midland)
GREAT WESTERN (GW)
MIDLAND
BRISTOL PORT RY + PIER (GW + Midland)
WESTON CLEVEDON + PORTISHEAD (Light)
TEMPLE MEADS JOINT (GW + Midland)
Others

BRISTOL
SEE ENLARGEMENT BELOW

PENSFORD

Frys Bottom
Closed

CLUTTON

(COMBE HAY HALT 1911) 1915
COMBE HAY TUN 66Y
(DUNKERTON 1910) 1915

(Midford Halt 1911) 1915
MIDFORD

CLIFTON NO. 2
TUNNEL
232 yds
River Avon

(HOTWELLS HALT 1918)
HOTWELLS NO. 2
TUNNEL 176 yds
HOTWELLS NO. 1
TUNNEL 75 yds
HOTWELLS

CLIFTON
NO. 1 TUN
59 yds
CLIFTON SUSPENSION BRIDGE

CLIFTON
BRIDGE

CLIFTON DOWN
TUNNEL 1751 yds

CLIFTON DOWN

(REDLAND
1897)

CLIFTON EXTENSION (GW + MIDLAND)
MONTPELIER

MONTPELIER TUNNEL
288 yards

ASHLEY HILL JUNCT

MIDLAND

NARROWAYS HILL JUNCTION
STAPLETON ROAD

KEY TO RAILWAYS
CLIFTON EXTENSION (GW + Mid)
GREAT WESTERN (GW)
MIDLAND (Mid)
BRISTOL PORT RAILWAY + PIER (GW + Mid)
TEMPLE MEADS JOINT (GW + Mid)

BRISTOL

GREAT WESTERN
FLOATING HARBOUR
WAPPING
GOODS

ASHTON
SWING BRIDGE
JUNCTION

WAPPING JUNCT

CANON'S
MARSH
GOODS

ST PHILIPS
+ GOODS

LOWER YARD
GOODS

TEMPLE MEADS
GOODS

GW + JT JCT

REDCLIFFE TUNNEL
292 yds
Old Station

TEMPLE
MEADS

MIDLAND

Easton Road Jct
Closed 1889? →
Clifton Jct

LAWRENCE HILL JCT
Harbour Bch Jct

Shed Jct
BARROW RD. ES

WAGON WKS
OWES

LAWRENCE
HILL

DR DAYS BRIDGE JCT
CATTYBROOK
SIDINGS

SOUTH WALES JCT

(ASHTON GATE
PLATFORM 1906)
ASHTON JCT
ASHTON VALE
IRON CO.

PYLLE HILL GOODS

GOODS JCT

River Avon

PYLLE
HILL
JCT

BATH
ROAD
ES

VICTORIA
ROAD SDG

MARSH
GOODS

HARBOUR BCH
SUBURBAN
MIDLAND JUNCT
KINGSLAND
ROAD CPG

KINGSLAND
JUNCTION
NORTH SOMERSET JCT
FEEDER BRIDGE JCT
The Feeder

MARSH NORTH JCT
MARSH SOUTH JCT

Site of
St Annes
No.1 Tun
EAST
DEPOT
ST ANNES
PARK JCT

BEDMINSTER

WEST LOOP
NORTH JCT

GREAT WESTERN

MALCO VALE SDGS
OPENED
POST-GROUPING

(PARSON STREET)

BEDMINSTER JCT
later (PARSON STR JCT)

WEST LOOP JCT

ST PHILIPS
MARSH ES.

JCT

River Avon

NOTE: North is NOT to the top of this map.

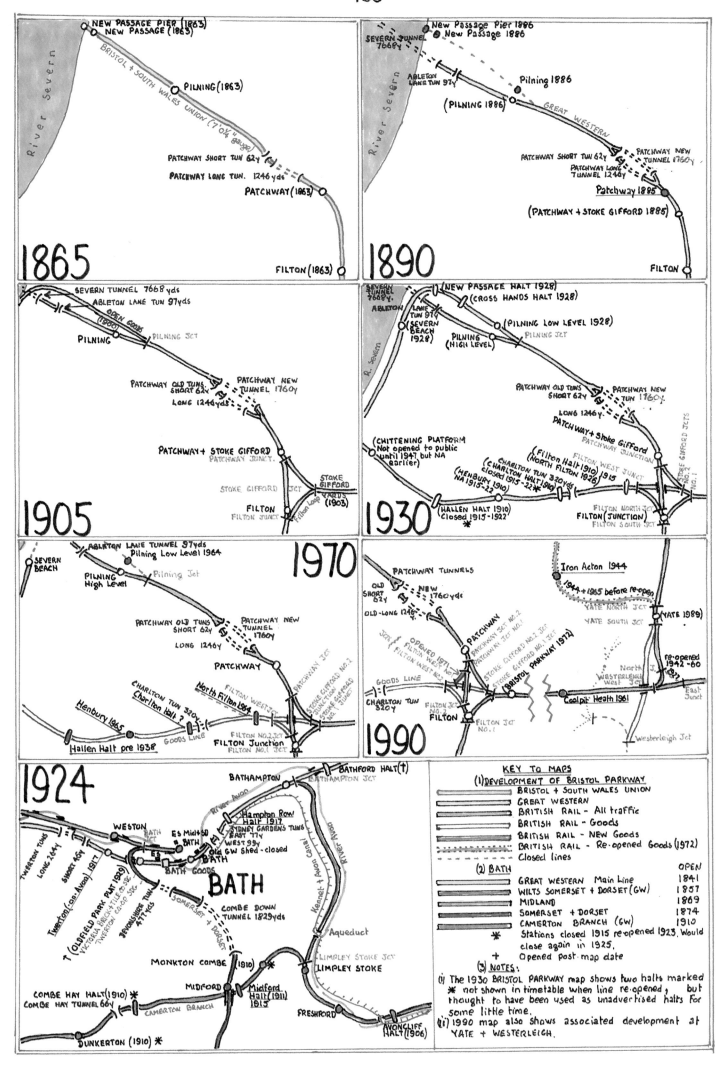

1865

NEW PASSAGE PIER (1863)
NEW PASSAGE (1863)
River Severn
BRISTOL + SOUTH WALES UNION (7.0¼ gauge)
PILNING (1863)
PATCHWAY SHORT TUN 62y
PATCHWAY LONG TUN. 1246yds
PATCHWAY (1863)
FILTON (1863)

1890

New Passage Pier 1886
New Passage 1886
SEVERN TUNNEL 7668y
River Severn
ABLETON LANE TUN 97y
Pilning 1886
(PILNING 1886)
GREAT WESTERN
PATCHWAY SHORT TUN 62y
PATCHWAY NEW TUNNEL 1760y
PATCHWAY LONG TUNNEL 1246y
Patchway 1885
(PATCHWAY + STOKE GIFFORD 1885)
FILTON

1905

SEVERN TUNNEL 7668yds
ABLETON LANE TUN 97yds
OPEN GOODS (1900)
PILNING
PILNING JCT
PATCHWAY OLD TUNS. SHORT 62y
PATCHWAY NEW TUNNEL 1760y
LONG 1246yds
PATCHWAY + STOKE GIFFORD
PATCHWAY JUNCT.
STOKE GIFFORD JCT
STOKE GIFFORD YARDS (1903)
FILTON
FILTON JUNCT.
Filton Loop

1930

SEVERN TUNNEL 7668y
ABLETON LANE TUN 97y
NEW PASSAGE HALT 1928)
(CROSS HANDS HALT 1928)
SEVERN BEACH 1928
(PILNING LOW LEVEL 1928)
PILNING (HIGH LEVEL)
PILNING JCT
PATCHWAY OLD TUNS SHORT 62y
PATCHWAY NEW TUN 1760y
LONG 1246y.
PATCHWAY + STOKE GIFFORD
PATCHWAY JUNCTION
(CHITTENING PLATFORM Not opened to public until 1947 but NA earlier)
(Filton Halt 1910 (NORTH FILTON 1926) 1915
(CHARLTON HALT 1916) CHARLTON TUN 320yds closed (1915-22*
(HENBURY 1910 NA 1915-22)
STOKE GIFFORD JCTS NO.2 NO.1
FILTON WEST JUNCT.
HALLEN HALT 1910 Closed 1915-1922 *
FILTON (JUNCTION)
FILTON NORTH JCT.
FILTON SOUTH JCT.

1970

SEVERN BEACH
ABLETON LANE TUNNEL 97yds
Pilning Low Level 1964
PILNING High Level
Pilning Jct.
PATCHWAY OLD TUNS SHORT 62y
PATCHWAY NEW TUNNEL 1760y
LONG 1246y
PATCHWAY
CHARLTON TUN 320y Charlton Halt ?
North Filton 1964
PATCHWAY JCT
FILTON WEST JCT
STOKE GIFFORD NO.2 JCT
STOKE GIFFORD JUNCTION NO.1 JUNCT.
Henbury 1865
GOODS LINE
Hallen Halt pre 1938
FILTON Junction
FILTON NO.1 JCT

1990

PATCHWAY TUNNELS
OLD SHORT 62y
NEW 1760yds
OLD-LONG 1246y
Iron Acton 1944
1944 + 1865 before re-open
YATE NORTH JCT
YATE (1989)
YATE SOUTH JCT
OPENED 1971
FILTON WEST No.1 JCT
PATCHWAY No.2
PATCHWAY JCT No.1
STOKE GIFFORD No.2 JCT
STOKE GIFFORD No.1 JCT
(BRISTOL PARKWAY 1972)
re-opened 1942-60
North J.
WESTERLEIGH West Jct
East Junct
GOODS LINE
CHARLTON TUN 320y
FILTON JCT. No.2
FILTON
FILTON JCT No.1
Coalpit Heath 1961
Westerleigh Jct

1924

BATHFORD HALT (†)
BATHAMPTON
BATHAMPTON JCT
River Avon
Hampton Row Halt 1917
SYDNEY GARDENS TUNS EAST 77y WEST 99y
WESTON
E5 Mid+50
BATH
Old GW Shed - closed
TWERTON TUNS LONG 264y SHORT 45y
BATH JCT.
BATH GOODS
BATH
SOMERSET + DORSET
T (OLDFIELD PARK PLAT 1929)
VICTORIA BRICK + TILE CO SDG
TWERTON CO-OP SDG
DEVONSHIRE TUN 447yds
Kennet + Avon Canal
River Avon
COMBE DOWN TUNNEL 1829yds
Aqueduct
MONKTON COMBE (1910)
LIMPLEY STOKE JCT
LIMPLEY STOKE
COMBE HAY HALT (1910) *
COMBE HAY TUNNEL 66y
MIDFORD
Midford Halt (1911) 1915
CAMERTON BRANCH
FRESHFORD
AVONCLIFF HALT (1906)
DUNKERTON (1910) *

KEY TO MAPS

(1) DEVELOPMENT OF BRISTOL PARKWAY

BRISTOL + SOUTH WALES UNION
GREAT WESTERN
BRITISH RAIL - All traffic
BRITISH RAIL - Goods
BRITISH RAIL - NEW Goods
BRITISH RAIL - Re-opened Goods (1972)
Closed lines

(2) BATH   OPEN
GREAT WESTERN Main Line   1841
WILTS SOMERSET + DORSET (GW) 1857
MIDLAND   1869
SOMERSET + DORSET   1874
CAMERTON BRANCH (GW)   1910
* Stations closed 1915 re-opened 1923. Would close again in 1925.
† Opened post-map date

(3) NOTES:
(i) The 1930 BRISTOL PARKWAY map shows two halts marked * not shown in timetable when line re-opened, but thought to have been used as unadvertised halts for some little time.
(ii) 1990 map also shows associated development at YATE + WESTERLEIGH.

7. 8 .1907 WESTON CLEVEDON + PORTISHEAD (WCP) opened from CLEVEDON to PORTISHEAD. Intermediate stations at: CLEVEDON EAST, CLEVEDON ALL SAINTS (opened 1917), WALTON PARK, WALTON·IN·GORDANO, CADBURY ROAD (WESTON·IN·GORDANO), CLAPTON ROAD and PORTISHEAD SOUTH.

2. 7.1908 ROYAL EDWARD DOCK opened at AVONMOUTH. New dock lines brought into use.

2. 11. 1908 GW Westerleigh Loops in use for all traffic following resolution of disputes between GW and MIDLAND, which had resulted in periods of dis·use for most of the time since initial opening.

9. 5.1910 GW opened new route Hallen Marsh Junction to Stoke Gifford Junction together with Filton West Curve. New stations and halts: HENBURY (station); HALLEN, CHARLTON and FILTON (halts).

9. 5.1910 GW opened extension of the CAMERTON Branch from Camerton to LIMPLEY STOKE. The prime purpose was movement of coal and for most of its route the railway followed the course of the abandoned Somerset Coal Canal. It however opened for passengers and within the map area there were stations/halts as follows: DUNKERTON COL. HALT*, DUNKERTON, COMBE HAY HALT, MIDFORD HALT* and MONKTON COMBE (* these two halts were opened 9/10/1911, and 27/2/1911 respectively). The network had now reached its maximum development and although further station openings would follow in the interwar period the only further new lines were under BRITISH RAIL.

22. 3.1915 Saw wartime economy closures to passengers only on two . lines:

    (1) Holesmouth Junction to FILTON JUNCTION — Closure of halts : FILTON, HALLEN and CHARLTON. The station at HENBURY also closed but continued in use for workmen's trains and an unadvertised public service — it is not known if any of these services in fact used the halts.

    (2) CAMERTON branch including all stations listed above under 9·5·1910.

1917 GW closed TWERTON — war-time economy? Never re-opened but was later replaced by a re-sited station.

1918 AVONMOUTH LIGHT opened its first ¾ mile. This had been authorised in 1893 and after revivals in 1903, and 1912 construction of its two-mile length started in 1908. It was a short dock line absorbed into the CLIFTON EXTENSION dock lines in 1927; the remainder was abandoned, PORTBURY SHIPYARD HALT opened during the year.

BRISTOL'S NEW RAILWAY CENTRE AND ITS DEVELOPMENT - BRISTOL PARKWAY

1851 As noted elsewhere, by this date the national main-line network was in place but in the area to become Bristol's present-day railway centre there was not a single line within its confines and a further twelve years would pass before the first railway line penetrated the vicinity.

1865 The BRISTOL + SOUTH WALES UNION was the first line opened in 1863 to give BRISTOL a more direct route into Wales. But it was of little real strategic importance being a single broad gauge line to a difficult ferry crossing over the River Severn.

1890 Another twenty-five years have passed to the next map and now at last the route has achieved importance, a result of the opening of the SEVERN TUNNEL. It is now a doubled track main line from BRISTOL to South Wales. The line to the ferry at NEW PASSAGE has been closed.

1905 This map shows the first development to the area's establishment as a route centre, junction status having been achieved as the result of the SOUTH WALES DIRECT line opening, giving London a direct link to South Wales in addition to an alternative route to BRISTOL. Also at this time part of the old route to the ferry was re·opened and extended to AVONMOUTH giving a freight route from the new deep·water docks to London whilst avoiding BRISTOL.

1930 The next development in 1910 was to complete the cross·roads between PATCHWAY and FILTON with a line from AVONMOUTH to Stoke Gifford Junction where new extensive sidings were laid out. A passenger service was introduced but was of little importance. It was withdrawn in 1915 as a war·time economy but was re·instated in 1922. The AVONMOUTH - Pilning passenger service started in 1928.

1970 BEECHING resulted in loss of passenger services between AVONMOUTH and NORTH FILTON and the AVONMOUTH to Pilning Junction service was cut back to SEVERN BEACH.

1990 Further development took place in this period. 1971 saw a new goods curve to enable docks freight traffic to take one of three routes. 1972 BRISTOL PARKWAY opened at the focal point of four trunk passenger lines, destinations BRISTOL, South Wales, London and, by using the Westerleigh Junctions, Birmingham and the north. With its excellent services it has become firmly established as BRISTOL's new passenger route centre at the expense of TEMPLE MEADS. It has, however, achieved importance as a freight route centre although this is without any freight sorting in the vicinity, but again the line from Avonmouth gives access to all parts of the country.

The position is similar in a way to that noted under NOTTINGHAM but with this important advantage, that BRISTOL has its PARKWAY station besides PATCHWAY and FILTON whereas NOTTINGHAM's route centre, TRENT, has no station.

BATH(DEVELOPMENT)

On this map, showing the position just after grouping, lines are coloured to show their opening dates. In contrast to the late development of BRISTOL PARKWAY, Bath conforms to the normal pattern in that all the lines except the first two to open are now closed and have been so from the mid 1960's at the latest.

1919-1940

During this period BRISTOL's railway development continued to reflect the national pattern. There was, first of all, reopening of passenger stations which had been closed as a wartime economy measure, although not all of these were reopened. Then there was withdrawal of some unremunerative passenger services, most of these being amongst the latest openings. Also, as noted elsewhere in areas of GREAT WESTERN(GW) influence, a policy of opening unstaffed halts was pursued in an effort to increase revenues without incurring associated expenses.

16. 8. 1920 BRISTOL CORPORATION take over Sneyd Park Junction to HOTWELLS from GW and MIDLAND. This line had originally been planned to run to a central station in BRISTOL but was blocked by the Bristol Harbour authorities. The link was established later by the CLIFTON EXTENSION. The portion transferred had become a little-used branch and was now due to become a road.

19. 9. 1921 HOTWELLS closed. Passenger service now terminated at the workmen's halt which had opened in 1918.

3. 7. 1922 Sneyd Junction to Hotwells Halt closed completely.

1. 1. 1923 GROUPING - This had no effect on the railways and joint undertakings in the area. Numbers remained unchanged.

26. 3. 1923 GW close PORTBURY SHIPYARD HALT.

1922 - 23 GW reopened lines to passengers closed as a wartime economy measure: AVONMOUTH to FILTON JUNCTION (10.7.1922). An unadvertised passenger service had operated in the interim period and there is some evidence that the 3 halts were in use as unadvertised stopping places although not appearing in Bradshaw. Almost a year later to the day CAMERTON BRANCH line and stations re-opened, with the exception of Midford Halt.

21. 9. 1925 GW CAMERTON BRANCH closed to passengers. Goods traffic continued.

10. 7. 1927 GW closed Westerleigh North to East Junction curve.

23. 6. 1928 GW commenced passenger service over AVONMOUTH to Pilning Junction line. New stations were opened at: PILNING (LOW LEVEL), on site of original station, CROSS HANDS HALT, NEW PASSAGE HALT and SEVERN BEACH.

14. 9. 1931 GW close WRINGTON branch to passengers. Stations closed: WRINGTON, LANGFORD, BURRINGTON and BLAGDON. Goods continued.

20. 5. 1940 WESTON CLEVEDON + PORTISHEAD closed to all traffic but part of track use by GW for storage. Stations closed were: CLEVEDON, CLEVEDON EAST, CLEVEDON ALL SAINTS, WALTON PARK, WALTON-IN-GORDANO, CADBURY ROAD, CLAPTON ROAD, PORTISHEAD SOUTH and PORTISHEAD.

Apart from the above branches and lines it remains to record GW halts and stations opened. Dates are indicated where known. These were: ASHTON GATE PLATFORM (after opening, closing, then re-opening as a football halt, opened as a full station 23.5.1926), HAM GREEN HALT (23.12.1926) HORFIELD (14.5.1927), LONG ASHTON (12.7.1926), NORTH FILTON (site of earlier Filton Halt 12.7.1926) OLDFIELD PARK (May 1929), NIGHTINGALE VALLEY HALT (June 1928 and closed 12.9.1932), PARSON STREET (1926?). LMS closed KELSTON in 1940, the only LMS action of the period.

ENGINE SHED DETAILS

No.	NAME	ORIGINATING COMPANY	OPEN	CLOSED	NOTES
1	AVONMOUTH	GW + Mid	1905	1924	possibly replaced earlier BPRP shed closed 1901 (site of new Dock).
2	BATH	GW	1840	1880	replaced by new shed near Goods Yard. See 3 below.
3	BATH	GW	1880	1961	replaced 2 above.
4	BATH	Mid	1869	1966	see 5 below.
5	BATH (GREEN PARK)	S+D	1878		built adjoining 4 above. Became one shed.
6	BLAGDON	WVL (GW)	1901	1924	no actual shed - just a stabling point.
7	BRISTOL (BARROW ROAD)	B+G	1846	1965	rebuilt by Midland in 1873.
8	BRISTOL	GW	1840	1877	original GW shed - closed when BE absorbed - stock to their shed, see 9.
9	BRISTOL (TEMPLE MEADS)	BE	1850	1934	absorbed 8 stock when BE absorbed by GW. Rebuilt, see 10 below.
10	BRISTOL (BATH ROAD)	GW	1934	1960	rebuild of 9 above. BR use site for modern loco depot.
11	BRISTOL (SPM)	GW	1910	1964	site now used by BR DMU depot. Modern SPM depot of BR is on the site of Marsh Goods - used for HST's.
12	CLEVEDON	WCP	1897	1940	
13	YATTON	GW	1879	1960	replaced probable BE shed on the same site.

Note: For 1990 BR depots see notes to No's 10 and 11 above.

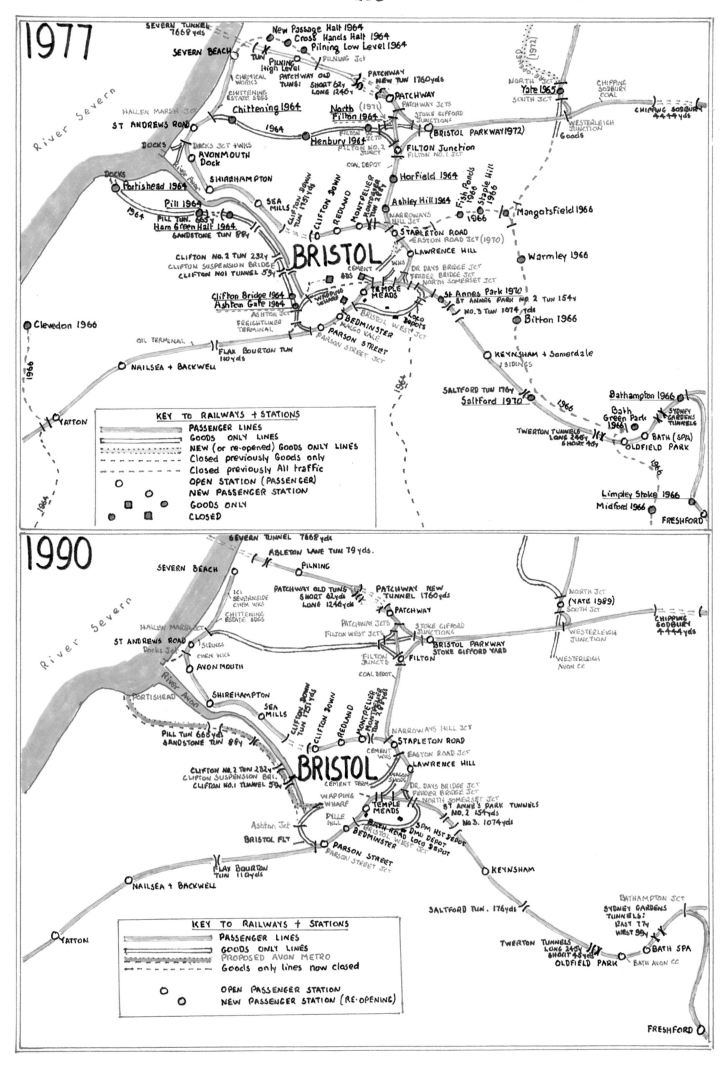

1941-1963

After the active development and/or rationalisation noted in all the previous periods, this period was comparatively quiet. This was perhaps partly due to the fact that following nationalisation the area embraced, to begin with, parts of three regions before common sense prevailed and all came within the WESTERN region.

1941 CHITTENING PLATFORM in unadvertised use. May have opened earlier. In timetables from 1947. LMS CLIFTON DOWNS to FISH PONDS passenger traffic withdrawn. GW closed LONG ASHTON.

1942 GW re-opened Westerleigh East Curve for wartime goods traffic. Final closure of this curve was in 1960.

1944 LMS withdraw Thornbury branch passenger service. IRON ACTON station closed. Line retained for goods traffic.

1950 Camerton branch closed completely. Wrington to Blagdon closed completely.

1953 BRISTOL ST PHILIPS closed to passengers. Train service used TEMPLE MEADS. St Philips goods retained. Weston Bath closed.

1959 North Somerset Line closed to passengers. Stations closed at: BRISLINGTON, WHITCHURCH HALT, PENSFORD and CLUTTON. The line remained open for goods traffic.

1961 Wayside stations on the SOUTH WALES DIRECT main line closed at: WINTERBOURNE, COALPIT HEATH and CHIPPING SODBURY

1962 PORTBURY closed.

1963 The BEECHING REPORT proposed closure of about three-quarters of the area's remaining stations and these are indicated on the 1963 map in the usual way. Mentioned in the report as under consideration for closure prior to the publication of the report was the Cheddar Valley line and this was closed to passengers during the year together with the short remaining goods spur on the Wrington Valley line. Full closure followed in 1964. It remains to note one final closure in 1963, namely FLAX BOURTON; this was unusual in that it was a Beeching recommendation actually implemented during the year of the report's publication.

1964 -1977

This was a period of rationalisation following Beeching, although not all the report's proposals for the area were put into effect. There were, however, some important positive developments including three new stretches of line, albeit that two of these were re-instatements of lines previously closed, but all involved laying new track. In addition, a new station - BRISTOL PARKWAY - was opened. A chronology of the main events follows:

1964 SEVERN BEACH to PILNING passenger service withdrawn. Stations closed: NEW PASSAGE, CROSS HANDS and PILNING LOW LEVEL.
TEMPLE MEADS to AVONMOUTH passenger service via Henbury withdrawn. Stations closed: CHITTENING, HENBURY and NORTH FILTON (but they continued to be served by regular workmen's trains until 1966 and by some occasional trains until the end of the period). The line continued to be used for goods traffic from the docks at AVONMOUTH.
PORTISHEAD branch passenger service withdrawn. Stations closed: PILL, HAM GREEN, CLIFTON BRIDGE, PORTISHEAD and ASHTON GATE (although this latter station continued in use as a football halt and it is believed some workpeople's trains were run after official closure). The branch remained open for goods. HORFIELD and ASHLEY HILL closed.
ST PHILIPS to Lawrence Hill becomes a siding (to Wagon Works). TEMPLE MEADS to WAPPING closed.

1965 BRISTOL - Gloucester local service via MANGOTSFIELD withdrawn. YATE closed. Westerleigh Goods closed.
Kingswood Junction to Ashley Hill Junction closed completely. CANONS MARSH and branch closed.
All traffic withdrawn from both CHEDDAR VALLEY and NORTH SOMERSET lines.

1966 CLEVEDON Branch closed to all traffic. Station closure: CLEVEDON
BRISTOL - BATH (ex LMS) and BATH to Templecombe passenger services withdrawn. Closure of stations at: FISH PONDS, STAPLE HILL, MANGOTSFIELD, WARMLEY, BITTON, BATH GREEN PARK and MIDFORD. S+D closed completely by early 1967.
Other intermediate station closures were: LIMPLEY STOKE and BATHAMPTON.

1967 No stations closed! But now goods-only lines centred on Mangotsfield closed. Thornbury branch closed completely. Bristol East Yards closed.

1968 Severn Beach to Pilning closed completely.

1969 Bristol-Yate passenger services withdrawn. Gloucester trains routed via Filton, Stoke Gifford and Westerleigh Junctions.

1970 Intermediate station closures: ST ANNE'S PARK and SALTFORD — the final station closures.
New connection - EASTON ROAD JCT - to give access to industrial users of St Philips site to the rest of the rail network

1971 NEW West Filton curve (goods only).

1972 NEW: Portion of Thornbury branch re-opened to serve stone quarries. BRISTOL PARKWAY opened.

1978-1990

This was an uneventful period so far as BRISTOL'S railway network was concerned. During the period rail dock traffic declined and by the end of the period the PORTISHEAD branch had become disused as also had the connections to docks at AVONMOUTH. However, the AVONMOUTH to Filton West Junction line has retained importance serving quite substantial rail-linked industries on the Severn coast. One positive event remains to be noted: The re-opening of the station at YATE in 1989.

1991 - FUTURE

There is one interesting development proposal for the future, that is the AVON METRO. This is planned to run from WAPPING WHARF, using disused goods lines still in situ; then, after crossing the Avon it will link into the disused branch to PORTISHEAD. The proposed route is indicated on the final map.

BRISTOL, with its excellent main-line services to London and all parts of the UK, will continue to retain its strategic importance as a railway centre although, as related earlier, this appears to have shifted to PARKWAY from TEMPLE MEADS.

LONDON - CENTRAL

As mentioned in the PREFACE, LONDON presents problems in presentation as a railway centre due to the complex pattern of development which could almost justify a complete volume in itself. In this volume the central area is covered, and this will be followed by further chapters in future volumes as shown on the map at the end of this chapter (page 224).

The central area itself will also be covered again in greater depth so far as individual railway companies are concerned, and each of the other areas has one or more 'centres', such as CLAPHAM JUNCTION, FINSBURY PARK etc, which will merit detailed development maps.

In defining the central area for purposes of this chapter, an area has been selected to include every terminal station past and present and its approaches, together with the whole of the CIRCLE line. The chapter is divided into two main parts. The first part treats CENTRAL LONDON in the same format as other centres in the atlas, the only difference being the larger scales used. Thus, there are two pages of maps, with two maps to the page, with a facing chronology but at a scale of 1" to a mile. There then follows a further four maps at a scale of 2" to a mile covering a marginally smaller area but comprising double page spreads to show the increasing complexities in a clear and uncluttered format. There is a large date gap between the final two maps since LONDON saw only modest alterations to its main-line network during the period. The first section concludes with a specially drawn diagramatic map showing 1991 routes from the terminal stations together with BRITISH RAIL regions and distinguishing between main and secondary routes.

The second part of the chapter is devoted to London's unique UNDERGROUND. First there is a family tree of all the companies which ultimately became part of the LONDON PASSENGER TRANSPORT BOARD in 1933 and in addition there is an indication of the modern line names which each company or group of companies became; subsequent changes of name of the entire undertaking and the addition of new lines have also been included. Following this are two specially drawn maps of the system. The first map shows the LPTB as at formation in 1933 together with the originating company and a clear indication of modern line name. The map shows every station including some closed just before formation of LTPB. Line changes are indicated and station closures with dates are indicated. Proposed extensions, not completed, are shown and all new extensions opened are shown in a distinctive style, up to the end of 1947 and nationalisation when the LTPB became LONDON TRANSPORT. A second map completes the story from 1948 to 1991, again distinguishing extensions, closures and showing extensions not yet completed or proposed. The WATERLOO + CITY has never been part of the underground by ownership but it clearly forms part of the system and has been included on the maps. Finally in this section there is a brief note on some complex changes in the system which though shown on the maps are difficult to follow exactly what happened, and a table showing works, depots and other stock stabling points completes the story. The aim of this section has been to give a comprehensive but concise account of the development of the system. Details of company rivalries and policies, manipulation and difficulties will be covered to a limited extent in the further LONDON chapters in future volumes.

In the chronology which follows, accompanying the first four maps, the date is the opening date. Following the date is the name of the railway opening the section of line. The first time a railway appears in the chronology it is followed by an abbreviation – used in subsequent entries – and a date which is that of parliamentary sanction; these two items are bracketed. Next, after details of section opened, will be a brief note about changes of name

and name of any other company which would absorb the company. Other information included in the entry is selective. One final significant point relative to maps is of interest, in that the first map is dated 1840 and contains quite a lot of development; an earlier map dated 1835 would be a blank sheet of paper!

1836-1840

12. 2.1836 LONDON + GREENWICH (LG 17.5.1833) opened BERMONDSEY to DEPTFORD. The railway retained its independent existence until grouping but was leased to the SOUTH EASTERN in 1845 from which date it became effectively a part of that company and is so shown on all maps after that date.

14.12.1836 LG now opened between LONDON BRIDGE (London's first terminus) and Deptford. Bermondsey station closed.

20. 7.1837 LONDON + BIRMINGHAM (LB 6.5.1833) opened from CAMDEN to Boxmore. Railway became one of the constituents of the LONDON + NORTH WESTERN (LNW 16.7.1846).

16.10.1837 LB opened to EUSTON. Cable traction was introduced up Camden Bank and lasted until 1844.

19. 5.1838 LONDON + SOUTHAMPTON (LS 25.7.1834) opened from NINE ELMS to Woking Common. Some authorities quote 21.5 as the opening date (probably the difference between ceremonial and public opening). The company changed its name to LONDON + SOUTH WESTERN (LSW 4.6.1839).

4. 6.1838 GREAT WESTERN (GW 31.8.1835) opened from PADDINGTON to Maidenhead. Broad gauge. It is worthy of note, however, that at this time not all railways were standard gauge, and minor variations apart from those shown on the first map existed at that time. At a later date the SOUTH EASTERN engineered a part of its line to facilitate conversion to broad gauge if necessary.

24.12.1838 LG now opened throughout (LONDON BRIDGE to Greenwich).

1. 6.1839 LONDON + CROYDON (LC 12.6.1835) opened from Corbett's Lane Junction (with LG) to Norwood Junction. This company amalgamated with the LONDON + BRIGHTON (15.7.1837) to form the LONDON BRIGHTON + SOUTH COAST (LBSC 27.7.1846).

18. 6.1839 EASTERN COUNTIES (EC 4.7.1836) opened from DOG ROW (Mile End Road) to Romford. Amalgamated with other companies to become the GREAT EASTERN (GE 7.8.1862).

1. 7.1839 EC extended from its temporary terminus to Webb Square SHOREDITCH.

6. 7.1840 LONDON + BLACKWALL (incorporated as COMMERCIAL 28.7.1836, reformed with new title 17.8.1839) opened from Blackwall to MINORIES. Initially cable hauled. Stations (map area): LEMAN STREET and SHADWELL. Company retained nominal independence until grouping but was leased in perpetuity to the GREAT EASTERN on 1.1.1866 and effectively became part of that company from that date.

15. 9.1840 NORTHERN + EASTERN (N+E 4.7.1836) opened between Stratford and Broxbourne (outside the map area) but with running powers over EC to SHOREDITCH. Company absorbed by EC 1.1.1844.

1841-1850

2. 8.1841 LONDON + BLACKWALL opened from MINORIES to a new terminus at FENCHURCH STREET.

20. 5.1842 SOUTH EASTERN (SE 21.6.1836) opened Redhill to Tonbridge. At a later date the company obtained running powers over the LG, the LC and the LONDON + BRIGHTON to run into LONDON BRIDGE. These lines were widened and became dedicated to the SE and part of the SE system. The company amalgamated with the LONDON CHATHAM + DOVER in 1899 to run as one railway known as the SOUTH EASTERN + CHATHAM.

27. 5.1844 WEST LONDON (WL - authorised 21.6.1836 as BIRMINGHAM, BRISTOL + THAMES JUNCTION but name changed to WL 23.7.1840) opened from Willesden, and a junction with LB and a turnplate connection and flat crossing with GW, to KENSINGTON. It was mixed gauge and had a passenger service for a few months only, becoming a goods-only line before the end of the year. Leased to LB and GW in 3.1846. By a later Act of 1854 leased jointly to LNW and GW.

1. 5.1844 LC and SE opened new terminal station at BRICKLAYERS ARMS to avoid the need to pay the heavy tolls LG were charging. This resulted in LG coming to terms with the two larger companies and LONDON BRIDGE soon became in practical terms a joint station of the SE and the LBSC (the successor of the LC from 1846). The Croydon passenger trains were withdrawn in 1845 but the SE continued to use the station for passengers until 1852. They took over the branch entirely which, with lack of space at LONDON BRIDGE, became important for goods and as a loco works and engine shed. The SE also built Willow Walk goods branch for the LBSC opened in 1849.

11. 7.1848 LSW extended their line from NINE ELMS (now reduced to goods only) to a new terminal at WATERLOO. An intermediate station was opened at VAUXHALL.

26. 9.1850 EAST + WEST INDIA DOCKS + BIRMINGHAM JUNCTION (EWIDBJ 26.8.1846) opened between Bow Jct and ISLINGTON for goods. Controlled by LNW it changed its name to NORTH LONDON (NL in 1853).

8. 8.1850 GREAT NORTHERN (GN 26.8.1846) opened to public from the north to a temporary station at MAIDEN LANE.

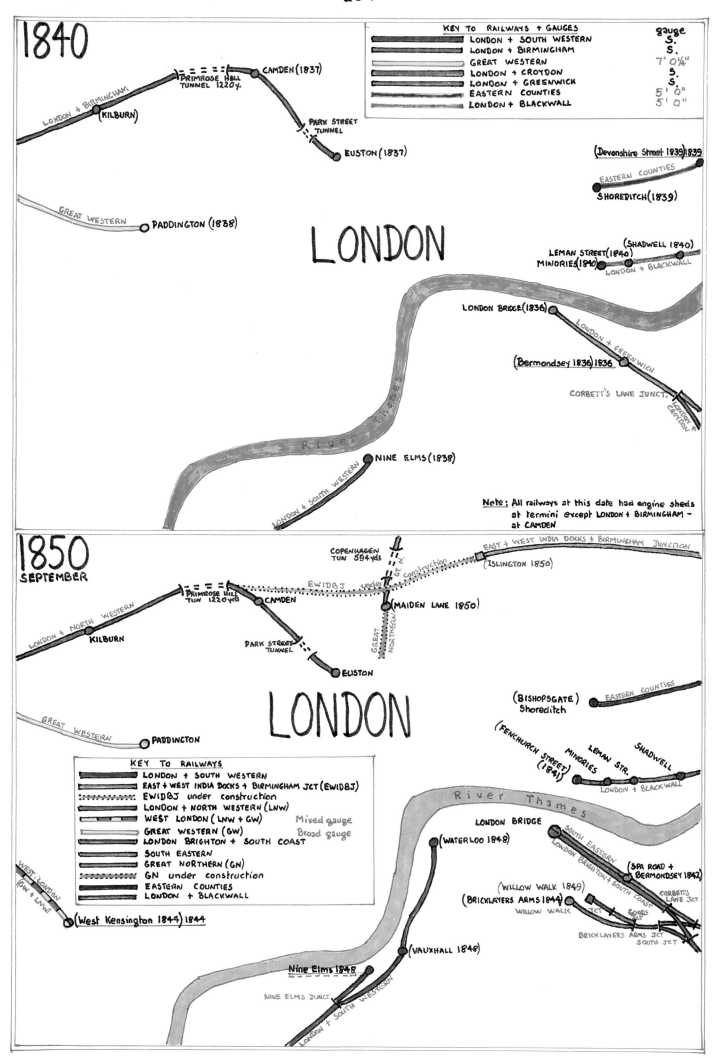

1840

KEY TO RAILWAYS + GAUGES
LONDON + SOUTH WESTERN — gauge S.
LONDON + BIRMINGHAM — S.
GREAT WESTERN — 7' 0¼"
LONDON + CROYDON — S.
LONDON + GREENWICH — S.
EASTERN COUNTIES — 5' 0"
LONDON + BLACKWALL — 5' 0"

LONDON + BIRMINGHAM
(KILBURN)
PRIMROSE HILL TUNNEL 1220y.
CAMDEN (1837)
PARK STREET TUNNEL
EUSTON (1837)

GREAT WESTERN
PADDINGTON (1838)

LONDON

(Devonshire Street 1839) 1839
EASTERN COUNTIES
SHOREDITCH (1839)

(SHADWELL 1840)
LEMAN STREET (1840)
MINORIES (1840)
LONDON + BLACKWALL

LONDON BRIDGE (1836)
LONDON + GREENWICH
(Bermondsey 1836) 1836
CORBETT'S LANE JUNCT.
LONDON + CROYDON

River Thames

NINE ELMS (1838)
LONDON + SOUTH WESTERN

Note: All railways at this date had engine sheds at termini except LONDON + BIRMINGHAM — at CAMDEN

1850
SEPTEMBER

COPENHAGEN TUN 594yds
EAST + WEST INDIA DOCKS + BIRMINGHAM JUNCTION
GT. N.
EWIDBJ under construction
(ISLINGTON 1850)
PRIMROSE HILL TUN 1220yds
CAMDEN
(MAIDEN LANE 1850)
LONDON + NORTH WESTERN
KILBURN
PARK STREET TUNNEL
GREAT NORTHERN
EUSTON

GREAT WESTERN
PADDINGTON

LONDON

(BISHOPSGATE) Shoreditch
EASTERN COUNTIES

(FENCHURCH STREET (1841)
MINORIES
LEMAN STR.
SHADWELL
LONDON + BLACKWALL

KEY TO RAILWAYS
LONDON + SOUTH WESTERN
EAST + WEST INDIA DOCKS + BIRMINGHAM JCT (EWIDBJ)
EWIDBJ under construction
LONDON + NORTH WESTERN (LNW)
WEST LONDON (LNW + GW) — Mixed gauge
GREAT WESTERN (GW) — Broad gauge
LONDON BRIGHTON + SOUTH COAST
SOUTH EASTERN
GREAT NORTHERN (GN)
GN under construction
EASTERN COUNTIES
LONDON + BLACKWALL

River Thames

LONDON BRIDGE
(WATERLOO 1848)
SOUTH EASTERN
LONDON BRIGHTON + SOUTH COAST
SPA ROAD + BERMONDSEY 1842
(WILLOW WALK 1849)
(BRICKLAYERS ARMS 1844)
WILLOW WALK
CORBETTS LANE JCT
JCT
EGORS JCT
BRICKLAYERS ARMS JCT SOUTH JCT

WEST LONDON (GW + LNW)
(West Kensington 1844) 1844

(VAUXHALL 1848)
Nine Elms 1848
NINE ELMS JUNCT
LONDON + SOUTH WESTERN

1850 - 1860

The previous map was dated part way through the year so that chronology faces the maps to which it relates.

7.12.1850 EAST + WEST INDIA DOCKS + BIRMINGHAM JUNCTION (EWIDBJ) opened from ISLINGTON to CAMDEN TOWN. This line had been constructed with goods traffic as its main objective. But since the main goods connections were not in place, a passenger service started to earn revenue until these were in place. Stations within the map area were opened at: HACKNEY, NEWINGTON ROAD + BALLS POND, HIGHBURY + ISLINGTON, CALEDONIAN RD., MAIDEN LANE and CAMDEN TOWN (name soon changed to CAMDEN ROAD).

9.6.1851 EWIDBJ completed from CAMDEN TOWN to a junction with LONDON + NORTH WESTERN (LNW). Additional station opened HAMPSTEAD ROAD (later became CHALK FARM). EWIDBJ changed its name to NORTH LONDON (NL 1·1·1853).

14.10.1852 GREAT NORTHERN (GN) opened from Maiden Lane (temporary terminus now closed) to KINGS CROSS.

16.1.1854 GREAT WESTERN (GW) opened departure platforms at new terminus. Arrival side opened 29·5·1854. The old station became a goods station.

13..4.1854 LONDON TILBURY + SOUTHEND (LTS 17·6·1852) opened between Forest Gate and Tilbury (outside the map area). This company was sponsored by the EASTERN COUNTIES (EC) and LONDON + BLACKWALL and used FENCHURCH STREET. It should therefore logically have become part of the GREAT EASTERN (GE). However, shortage of funds caused it to be leased to the contractor. It then ran itself until absorbed by the MIDLAND in 1912.

29.3.1858 WEST END OF LONDON + CRYSTAL PALACE (WELCP 4·8·1853) opened to PIMLICO (sometimes referred to as BATTERSEA PIER). Worked by LONDON BRIGHTON + SOUTH COAST (LBSC) and absorbed by that company 23·7·1860.

2.1.1860 HAMPSTEAD JUNCTION (HJ 20·8·1853) opened from CAMDEN TOWN, on the NORTH LONDON, to Willesden Junction. It was promoted by LNW and absorbed by that company 15·7·1867.

1.10.1860 VICTORIA STATION + PIMLICO (23·7·1858) opened from a junction with WELCP (by this date part of LBSC) to VICTORIA. Half the capital was subscribed by the LBSC and it was this half of lines and station which opened. In the interim the LONDON CHATHAM + DOVER (LCD 1·8·1859) had obtained running powers over this line, and would in due course be authorised to build its own line to VICTORIA and share the station, its own separate station, with the GW. Thus the line was mixed gauge track.

1861 - 1870

25.8.1862 LCD opened from Herne Hill to VICTORIA, which as mentioned above was in fact two adjoining stations. The LCD was originally authorised as the EAST KENT (EK 4·8·1853) and changed its name 1·8·1859. Extra tracks were laid across the bridge and opened 1·8·1866. Additional fly-over connection opened 1·5·1867.

10.1.1863 METROPOLITAN (MET 7·8·1854) opened from PADDINGTON to FARRINGDON STREET. This railway was originally the NORTH METROPOLITAN (15·8·1853) but was reformed and NORTH dropped from the title. Connection made with the GN at KINGS CROSS and later with the MIDLAND on 17·2·1868.

2.3.1863 WEST LONDON EXTENSION (WLE 13·8·1859) opened from KENSINGTON (Addison Road) to Clapham Junction. The joint owners of the line were GW and LNW (⅓ each) and LONDON + SOUTH WESTERN (LSW) and LBSC (⅙ each).

1.6.1864 LCD opened from Herne Hill to BLACKFRIARS (later became BLACKFRIARS BRIDGE and was downgraded to a goods-only station).

13.6.1864 MET opened from PADDINGTON (BISHOP'S ROAD) to HAMMERSMITH.

1.11.1864 SOUTH EASTERN (SE) opened between LONDON BRIDGE and CHARING CROSS. An intermediate station, BLACKFRIARS, opened at the same time, but closed 31·12·1868 and was replaced by WATERLOO JUNCTION opened 1·1·1869. A connection with the LSW was established but was little used.

21.12.1864 LCD opened to LUDGATE HILL (temporary station). Permanent station opened 1·6·1865.

1.11.1865 NL opened from a triangular junction at Dalston to a joint station with the LNW at BROAD STREET. There was, in addition to the station at DALSTON JUNCTION, an intermediate station at SHOREDITCH, and further station was opened in 1867 at HAGGERSTON.

23.12.1865 MET opened FARRINGDON STREET to MOORGATE STREET and to West Street where a junction would be made with LCD.

1.1.1866 LCD line continued from LUDGATE HILL to an end-on junction with MET at West Street.

13.8.1866 LBSC opened from LONDON BRIDGE to Brixton. Map area station: SOUTH BERMONDSEY.

1.9.1866 SE opened to CANNON STREET. Most SE trains for CHARING CROSS now ran via CANNON STREET.

17.2.1868 MIDLAND (10·5·1844) made KINGSCROSS connection with MET (Goods traffic used MIDLAND line from 1867).

13.4.1868 METROPOLITAN + ST JOHN'S WOOD (MSJW 29·7·1864) opened BAKER STREET to SWISS COTTAGE. Absorbed by MET 3·7·1882.

1.10.1868 MIDLAND opened to ST PANCRAS.

1.10.1868 MET opened PADDINGTON to GLOUCESTER RD. Extended to SOUTH KENSINGTON on 24·12·1868.

1.10.1868 METROPOLITAN DISTRICT (DIST 29·7·1864) opened KENSINGTON to GLOUCESTER RD and to WESTMINSTER BRIDGE by 24·12.

12.4.1869 DIST opened from GLOUCESTER ROAD to WEST BROMPTON.

30.5.1870 DIST opened from WESTMINSTER BRIDGE to BLACKFRIARS.

1871-1880

After the continuous development of previous periods, this decade was comparatively quiet.

With the Circle virtually complete in 1870 it might have been expected that the early 1870's would have seen this vital link completed. However, difficulties arose because the powers that be insisted that this should be a joint project, and quite apart from the engineering difficulties the METROPOLITAN DISTRICT (DIST) in its impoverished state found difficulty in providing even a modest capital input into the project.

In spite of this failure some interesting connections were made during the decade. The METROPOLITAN (MET) made connection with the GREAT EASTERN (GE) at LIVERPOOL STREET, part of a grand plan to link Manchester and Paris. It was little used because if trains from the MET wished to reach the SOUTH EASTERN they had to cross all the very busy lines of the GE. Early use was therefore restricted to local traffic but this lasted only a few months and this traffic was lost when MET opened its BISHOPSGATE station.

Another MET connection was at WEST STREET and junction with the LONDON CHATHAM + DOVER (LCD) and although used for passengers its main importance was to facilitate goods exchange.

The MET opened to ALDGATE in 1876 whilst DIST had reached MANSION HOUSE in 1871. DIST also extended to the west and south reaching Richmond, Ealing and Putney Bridge during the decade.

Turning to main-line developments, these too were restricted to connections to facilitate traffic exchange, with one notable exception. Some of these have already been noted and the SOUTH EASTERN made a further two. The first was via the EAST LONDON where a connection was made with the GE at SHOREDITCH; this particular route would later be run by the MET but remained outside the Underground until nationalisation. The other link, opened in 1878, enabled SE trains from LONDON BRIDGE to run to BLACKFRIARS and thence onto the MET.

The period saw two new terminal stations opened, both in 1874. HOLBORN VIADUCT opened to deal with the terminating traffic of the LCD due to the difficulties and congestion experienced at Ludgate Hill by terminating passenger trains conflicting in their movements with through goods traffic. A through station was also opened at SNOW HILL, sometimes referred to as HOLBORN VIADUCT LOW LEVEL.

The major event of the decade was, however, the opening of LIVERPOOL STREET. The GE had been experiencing considerable difficulties at its cramped remote BISHOPSGATE station and an earlier attempt to share BROAD STREET had failed. When the station finally opened the old terminus was down-graded to goods only. In the meantime a temporary Low Level station on the new line had opened in 1872 and this continued in use for many years well patronised by homeward commuters who used to board up trains so they obtained a seat on the subsequent down working.

LONDON's main-line network in the central area was now just about complete, with just the GREAT CENTRAL to come, and would remain unchanged for over 100 years. The further development of the central area would be growth of its underground system. This is highlighted in the subsequent maps.

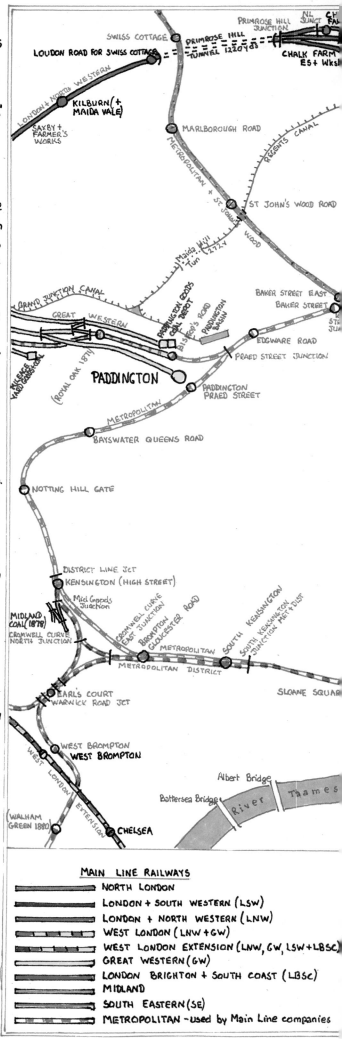

MAIN LINE RAILWAYS

NORTH LONDON
LONDON + SOUTH WESTERN (LSW)
LONDON + NORTH WESTERN (LNW)
WEST LONDON (LNW + GW)
WEST LONDON EXTENSION (LNW, GW, LSW + LBSC)
GREAT WESTERN (GW)
LONDON BRIGHTON + SOUTH COAST (LBSC)
MIDLAND
SOUTH EASTERN (SE)
METROPOLITAN - used by Main Line companies

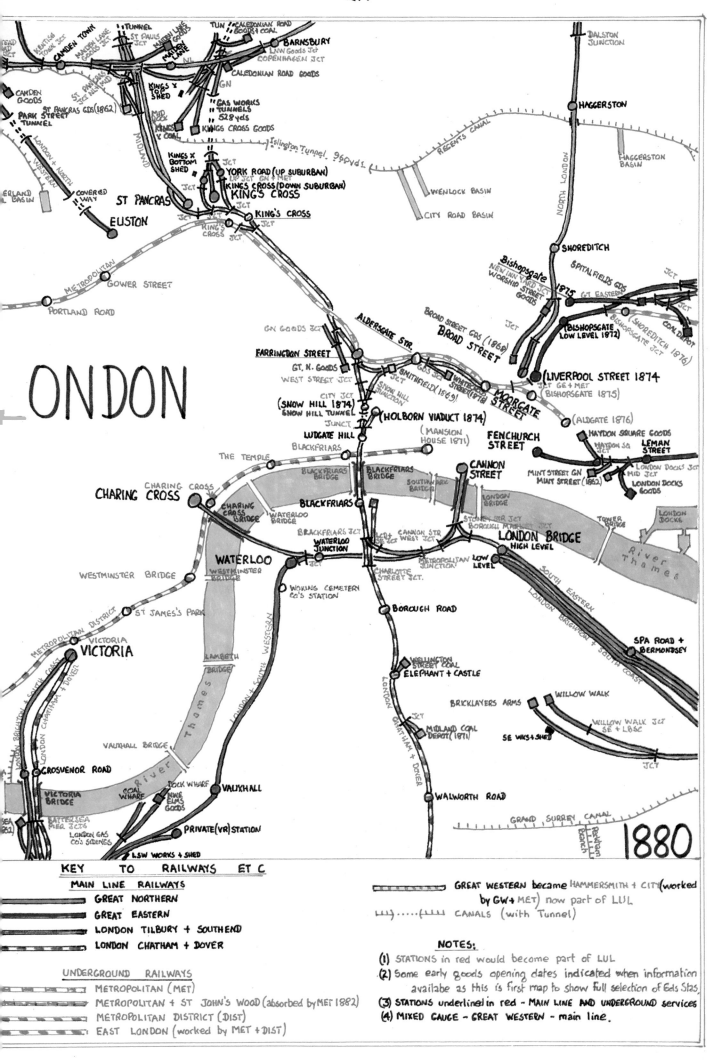

LONDON

1880

KEY TO RAILWAYS ETC

MAIN LINE RAILWAYS
- GREAT NORTHERN
- GREAT EASTERN
- LONDON TILBURY + SOUTHEND
- LONDON CHATHAM + DOVER

UNDERGROUND RAILWAYS
- METROPOLITAN (MET)
- METROPOLITAN + ST JOHN'S WOOD (absorbed by MET 1882)
- METROPOLITAN DISTRICT (DIST)
- EAST LONDON (worked by MET + DIST)

GREAT WESTERN became HAMMERSMITH + CITY (worked by GW + MET) now part of LUL

CANALS (with Tunnel)

NOTES:
(1) STATIONS in red would become part of LUL
(2) Some early goods opening dates indicated when information available as this is first map to show full selection of Gds Stns
(3) STATIONS underlined in red – MAIN LINE AND UNDERGROUND services
(4) MIXED GAUGE – GREAT WESTERN – main line.

1881-1890

There was no development of the main-line network during this period, but some adjustment of stations on the LCD lines through LUDGATE HILL took place. Blackfriars (Bridge) was reduced to a goods-only station in 1885 and was effectively replaced by a new station - ST PAULS - opened the following year. This new station, besides handling through trains, also acted as a terminus for some trains that could not be adequately dealt with by HOLBORN VIADUCT's short platforms.

The only other main-line events were the opening of some new goods depots.

However, the decrease in main-line development during this decade was balanced by further development of the underground including the first tube line. Events are looked at relative to each underground line in turn:

METROPOLITAN:

25. 9.1882 ALDGATE to TOWER HILL (later MARK LANE) opened.

6. 10.1884 BISHOPSGATE to WHITECHAPEL and CIRCLE completed, both in conjunction with METROPOLITAN DISTRICT. There were other lines opened also outside central area including extension of SWISS COTTAGE line.

METROPOLITAN DISTRICT:

6.10.1884 Completion of CIRCLE with MET. Junction with EAST LONDON at WHITECHAPEL.

3. 6.1889 Putney Bridge to Wimbledon opened.

EAST LONDON:

1. 10.1884 Underground service WHITECHAPEL to NEW CROSS started.

CITY + SOUTH LONDON

18.12.1890 KING WILLIAM STREET to Stockwell opened. This had been authorised 28.7.1884 as CITY OF LONDON + SOUTHWARK SUBWAY but changed name 25.7.1890.

One final matter of interest shown on the map was a new railway, THE REGENTS CANAL, CITY + DOCKS. This was to run from a junction with the GREAT WESTERN near ROYAL OAK and follow the course of the REGENT'S CANAL to the Docks. It had been authorised in 1882 and kept alive by subsequent Acts until 1903. It was never started, however. Its proposed route is shown on the map together with its proposed City branch and connection with the GREAT NORTHERN.

The map also identifies engine sheds open as at the map date and these, together with some sheds just outside the area, are shown below (early sheds at terminal stations are not always included):

No	SHED	CO.	OPENED	CLOSED	NOTES
1	NINE ELMS	LSW	1838	1967	also works
2	CAMDEN	LNW	1838	1962	steam ✱A
3	BRICKLAYERS ARMS	SE	1844	1962	also works
4	KINGS CROSS TOP	GN	1851	1963	
5	KINGS CROSS BOTTOM	GN	1862	1965	steam ✱B
6	PADDINGTON	GW	1838	1855	to 7
7	WESTBOURNE PARK	GW	1855	1906	to Old Oak
8	CHARING CROSS	SE	stabling only		sub to 3
9	CANNON STREET	SE	1866	1926	

Notes: ✱ A closed diesels 1960 ; ✱ B closed Diesels 1980.

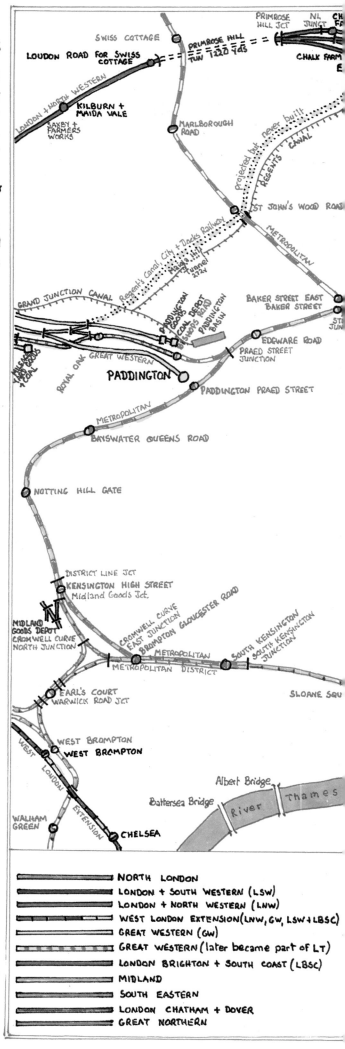

LONDON

1890

KEY TO RAILWAYS

GREAT EASTERN

LONDON TILBURY + SOUTHEND

REGENTS CANAL, CITY + DOCKS (projected)

METROPOLITAN (MET) used by main line traffic

UNDERGROUND LINES

METROPOLITAN (MET)

METROPOLITAN + METROPOLITAN DISTRICT

METROPOLITAN DISTRICT (DIST)

CIRCLE + MET

CIRCLE + DIST

CIRCLE, MET + DIST

EAST LONDON (worked by MET + DIST)

CITY + SOUTH LONDON

CANAL, Canal Basin, Canal Tunnel

NOTES:

(1) STATIONS underlined in red - both main line and underground services

(2) GREAT WESTERN Main line was mixed gauge until MAY 1892

(3) STATIONS IN RED ARE THOSE WHICH WOULD ULTIMATELY BECOME PART OF THE LONDON UNDERGROUND.

(4) ENGINE SHEDS - Coded as per table bottom of page 212.

1891-1910

During this period the final main-line development occured, with the opening of the GREAT CENTRAL's London Extension to MARYLEBONE in 1899.

The Underground network, however, continued to expand within the central area covered by the map, and in the outer suburban area. Development is recorded under the headings of the individual companies (but formation, authorisation and mergers are not shown — see family tree on page 213 for these details):

METROPOLITAN:

Openings were confined to outer area. Electrification of lines commenced in 1905. The connection with the GREAT EASTERN at LIVERPOOL STREET was closed.

METROPOLITAN DISTRICT:

Expansion here was also confined to the outer area. UPMINSTER was opened to DISTRICT services in 1902.

EAST LONDON:

Electric traction was used from 1913 and from this date it was worked by the METROPOLITAN but would become part of the SOUTHERN at grouping before becoming part of LT after nationalisation.

GREAT NORTHERN + CITY

14. 2. 1904 Opened FINSBURY PARK to MOORGATE STREET.

1. 7. 1913 Taken over by METROPOLITAN.

CITY + SOUTH LONDON

25. 2. 1900 BOROUGH to MOORGATE STREET opened. King William Str. was closed.

3. 6. 1900 Southward extension to Clapham Common opened.

17. 11. 1901 MOORGATE STREET to ANGEL opened.

12. 5. 1907 ANGEL to EUSTON opened.

WATERLOO + CITY (LSW)

8. 8. 1898 Opened — see note 3 on map.

CENTRAL LONDON

30. 7. 1900 Shepherd's Bush to BANK opened.

28. 7. 1912 BANK to LIVERPOOL STREET opened. Shown as under construction on the map.

BAKER STREET + WATERLOO

10. 3. 1906 BAKER STREET to WESTMINSTER BRIDGE ROAD opened.

5. 8. 1906 WESTMINSTER BRIDGE ROAD to ELEPHANT + CASTLE opened.

27. 3. 1907 BAKER STREET to GREAT CENTRAL (later became MARYLEBONE) opened.

15. 6. 1907 MARYLEBONE to EDGWARE ROAD opened.

1. 12. 1913 EDGWARE ROAD to PADDINGTON opened. Shown as a projected line on the map. When built followed a different course as the 1990 map shows.

GREAT NORTHERN PICCADILLY + BROMPTON:

15. 12. 1906 Hammersmith to Finsbury Park via KINGS CROSS opened.

30. 11. 1907 HOLBORN to STRAND (name later changed to ALDWYCH) opened.

CHARING CROSS EUSTON + HAMPSTEAD

22. 6. 1907 CHARING CROSS to Golders Green and beyond opened.

Separate specially drawn diagramatic maps cover the development of the underground from 1933. On the next main map there-fore only details of openings before that date will be included.

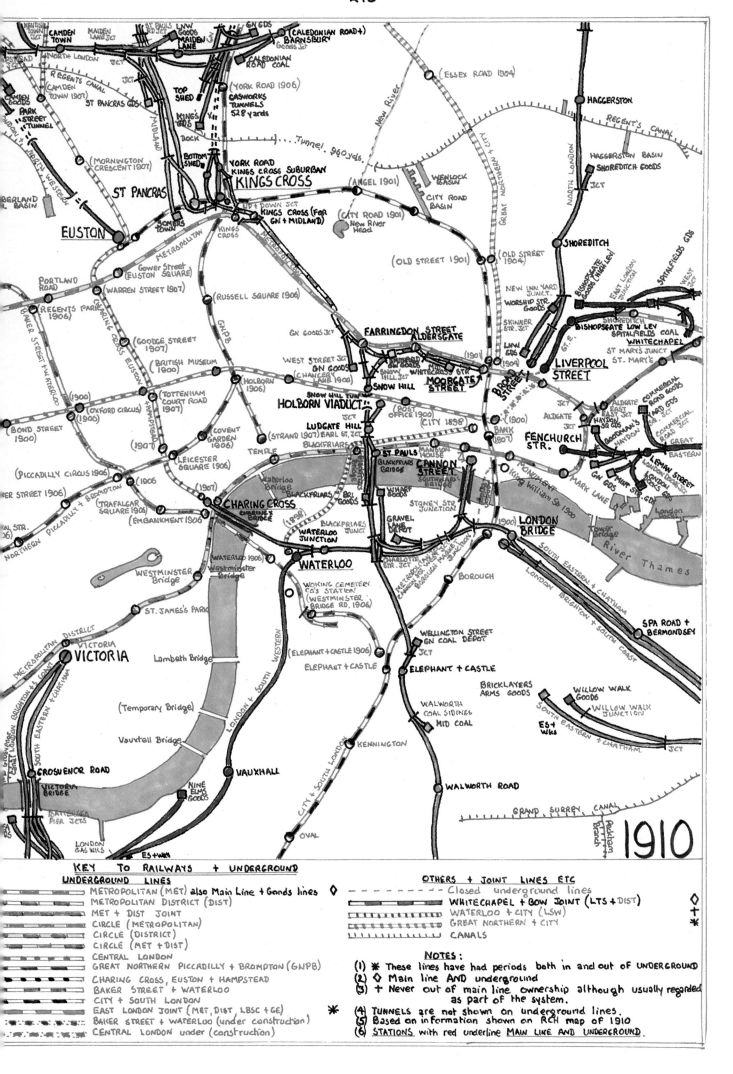

KEY TO RAILWAYS + UNDERGROUND

UNDERGROUND LINES

▭▭▭▭▭	METROPOLITAN (MET) also Main Line + Goods lines ◇
▭▭▭▭▭	METROPOLITAN DISTRICT (DIST)
▭▭▭▭▭	MET + DIST JOINT
▭▭▭▭▭	CIRCLE (METROPOLITAN)
▭▭▭▭▭	CIRCLE (DISTRICT)
▭▭▭▭▭	CIRCLE (MET + DIST)
▭▭▭▭▭	CENTRAL LONDON
▭▭▭▭▭	GREAT NORTHERN PICCADILLY + BROMPTON (GNPB)
▭▭▭▭▭	CHARING CROSS, EUSTON + HAMPSTEAD
▭▭▭▭▭	BAKER STREET + WATERLOO
▭▭▭▭▭	CITY + SOUTH LONDON
▭▭▭▭▭	EAST LONDON JOINT (MET, DIST, LBSC + GE)
▭▭▭▭▭	BAKER STREET + WATERLOO (under construction)
▭▭▭▭▭	CENTRAL LONDON under (construction)

OTHERS + JOINT LINES ETC

– – – – – –	Closed underground lines ◇
▭▭▭▭▭	WHITECHAPEL + BOW JOINT (LTS + DIST) +
▭▭▭▭▭	WATERLOO + CITY (LSW) *
▭▭▭▭▭	GREAT NORTHERN + CITY
⊥⊥⊥⊥⊥	CANALS

NOTES:

(1) * These lines have had periods both in and out of UNDERGROUND
(2) ◇ Main line AND underground
(3) + Never out of main line ownership although usually regarded as part of the system.
(4) TUNNELS are not shown on underground lines.
(5) Based on information shown on RCH map of 1910
(6) STATIONS with red underline MAIN LINE AND UNDERGROUND.

1910

1911-1990

This is a long period to be covered by just one map, but apart from underground developments, which are dealt with separately, this period saw few changes in the mainline network. It was in fact 1987 before a line closure took place and even in this case the service continued via a new connection to enable trains to use LIVERPOOL STREET. (see map - line to Broad Street).

Some other lines have seen downgrading for a period, for example the cross-city link has recently, after being goods for a period, been upgraded to give CHANNEL TUNNEL links with the North. In the Beeching Report only one line in the central area was scheduled for closure - this was the West London Line. In the event, although its traffic was reduced, it has always retained some passenger services and is likely to become of increasing importance as a cross-city alternative route once the Channel Tunnel is opened.

One small inexplicable closure remains to be noted: the lines to the City from KINGS CROSS. In view of the proposed use of this station as an international station this appears strange unless there are plans to improve these old links, but at the time of writing no firm proposals have been formulated.

Other closures have been the loss of some intermediate stations and the closure of every goods depot in the area; dates these closed are shown in most cases.

It remains to record briefly the pre-1933 events on the Underground:

GREAT NORTHERN + CITY became part of METROPOLITAN 1913.
NORTHERN LINE: re-opened 1924 after reconstruction
CENTRAL: BANK to LIVERPOOL STREET opened 1912.
BAKERLOO: EDGWARE ROAD to PADDINGTON opened 1913.
        PADDINGTON to Queens Park opened 1915.

FUTURE DEVELOPMENTS

Projected developments within the central area shown on the map are: A new terminal at BATTERSEA, but what its purpose will be is difficult to visualise. There is also a proposal to extend the JUBILEE LINE; the full details of this will be found within the UNDERGROUND SECTION. As mentioned above, the CHANNEL TUNNEL will have important further repercussions on the network whilst the proposed privatisation of railways will also have some effect. This could possibly result in the closure of MARYLEBONE with such services as are retained being with LONDON UNDERGROUND LIMITED.

1991 ROUTE NETWORK

The next map, and final map so far as this section of the Chapter is concerned, is on page 218 and shows the main routes radiating from the various terminal stations; the main routes and secondary routes are distinguished on the map which also shows how most terminals are linked to LUL Circle line. The map, although diagramatic, is approx. to scale so far as individual stations are concerned.

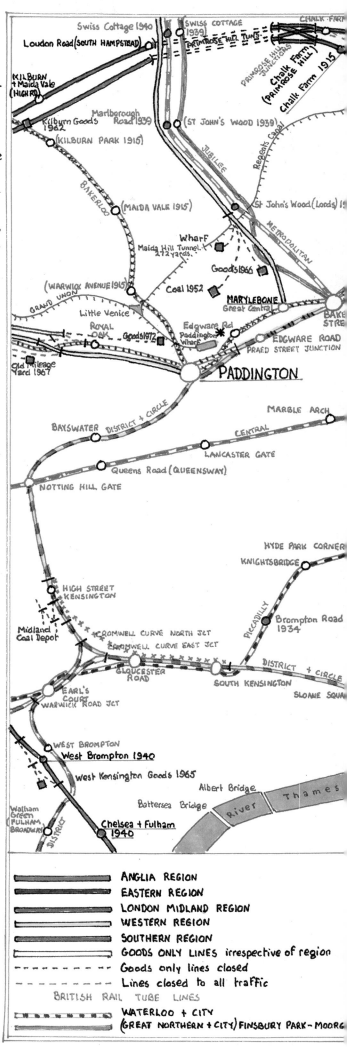

	ANGLIA REGION
	EASTERN REGION
	LONDON MIDLAND REGION
	WESTERN REGION
	SOUTHERN REGION
	GOODS ONLY LINES irrespective of region
	Goods only lines closed
	Lines closed to all traffic

BRITISH RAIL TUBE LINES

	WATERLOO + CITY
	(GREAT NORTHERN + CITY) FINSBURY PARK - MOORG

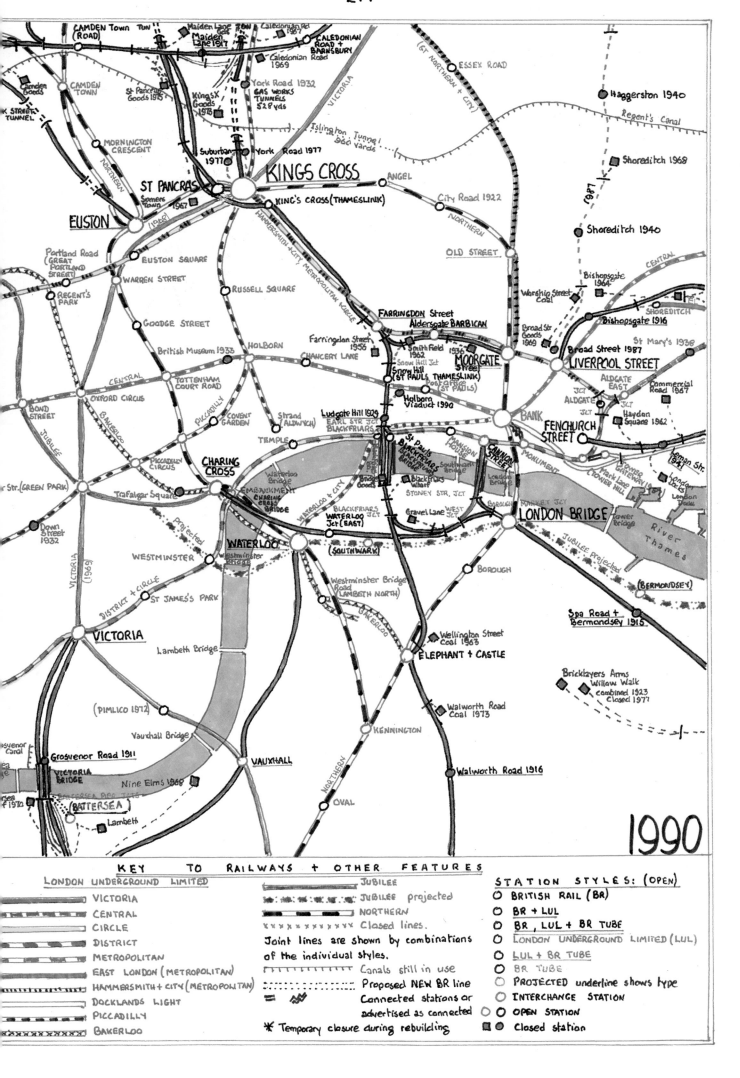

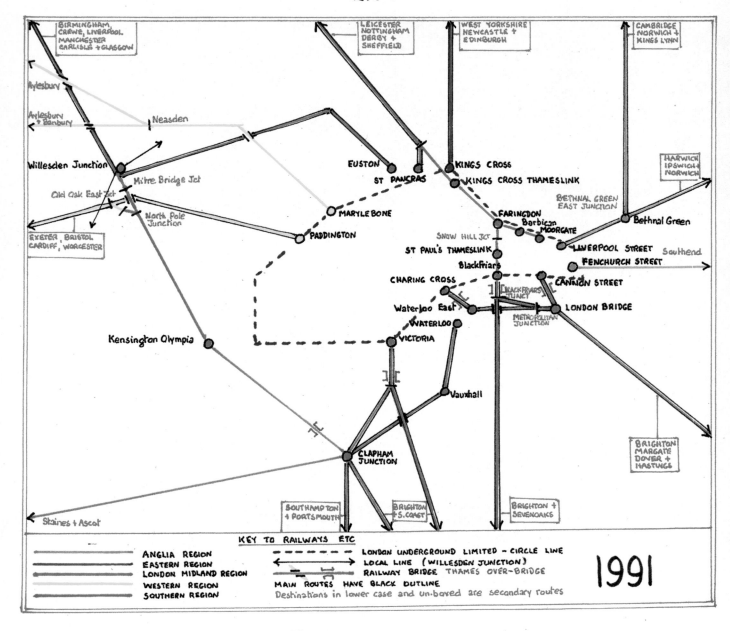

BIRMINGHAM, CREWE, LIVERPOOL MANCHESTER CARLISLE + GLASGOW

LEICESTER NOTTINGHAM DERBY + SHEFFIELD

WEST YORKSHIRE NEWCASTLE + EDINBURGH

CAMBRIDGE NORWICH + KINGS LYNN

Aylesbury

Aylesbury + Banbury

Neasden

Willesden Junction

Mitre Bridge Jct

Old Oak East Jct

North Pole Junction

EXETER, BRISTOL CARDIFF, WORCESTER

EUSTON

ST PANCRAS

KINGS CROSS

KINGS CROSS THAMESLINK

HARWICH IPSWICH + NORWICH

BETHNAL GREEN EAST JUNCTION

MARYLEBONE

PADDINGTON

FARINGDON

Barbican

MOORGATE

Bethnal Green

SNOW HILL JCT

ST PAUL'S THAMESLINK

LIVERPOOL STREET

Southend

FENCHURCH STREET

BlackFriars

CHARING CROSS

Waterloo East

WATERLOO

Kensington Olympia

VICTORIA

BLACKFRIARS JUNCT

METROPOLITAN JUNCTION

CANNON STREET

LONDON BRIDGE

Vauxhall

CLAPHAM JUNCTION

BRIGHTON MARGATE DOVER + HASTINGS

Staines + Ascot

SOUTHAMPTON + PORTSMOUTH

BRIGHTON + S.COAST

BRIGHTON + SEVENOAKS

KEY TO RAILWAYS ETC

ANGLIA REGION
EASTERN REGION
LONDON MIDLAND REGION
WESTERN REGION
SOUTHERN REGION

LONDON UNDERGROUND LIMITED - CIRCLE LINE
LOCAL LINE (WILLESDEN JUNCTION)
RAILWAY BRIDGE THAMES OVER-BRIDGE
MAIN ROUTES HAVE BLACK OUTLINE
Destinations in lower case and un-boxed are secondary routes

1991

THE UNDERGROUND

This section commences with a family tree showing company origins of the system. This is followed by two special maps showing; origins in 1933 and development up to 1947 under the LPTB, and development in the post·nationalisation era. Finally on page 224 is a chart showing LUL works, depots and stabling points. The maps etc intend to give both a concise and comprehensive cover of all main events. However there are three instances where complex developments cannot be fully shown on the maps and these are commented upon below:

(1) GREAT NORTHERN + CITY:

Sponsored by GREAT NORTHERN to carry main line and suburban passengers to the City. Purchased by METROPOLITAN in 1913. After 1933 worked as part of NORTHERN LINE. Following crash at MOORGATE terminal station it was closed by LONDON TRANSPORT. Re·opened by BRITISH RAIL and now linked to suburban services of BR.

(2) BAKER STREET + STANMORE:

Opened as independant concern but became part of METROPOLITAN before absorption into LPTB. Transferred to BAKERLOO line in 1939 which included new lines as far as FINCHLEY ROAD. As far as WEMBLEY PARK LPTB lines were quadruple track. Middle lines were BAKERLOO with station platforms; Outer lines were METROPOLITAN and did not have METROPOLITAN platforms except at FINCHLEY ROAD and WEST HAMPSTEAD. The final change made the BAKERLOO tracks part of the JUBILEE line, easing traffic flows through BAKER STREET which was given yet another complex rebuild of lines, levels and junctions.

(3) WATFORD JUNCTION

In 1982 the BAKERLOO service was terminated at STONEBRIDGE PARK and for a long time before this very few trains ran through to WATFORD JUNCTION most services terminating at HARROW + WEALDSTONE. But services were restored in 1984 but only as far as HARROW + WEALDSTONE. This is the reason why, on the 1948-1991 map, the stations between WEMBLEY CENTRAL and HARROW + WEALDSTONE inclusive have a red underline.

FAMILY TREE OF LONDON'S UNDERGROUND LINES 1850-1990

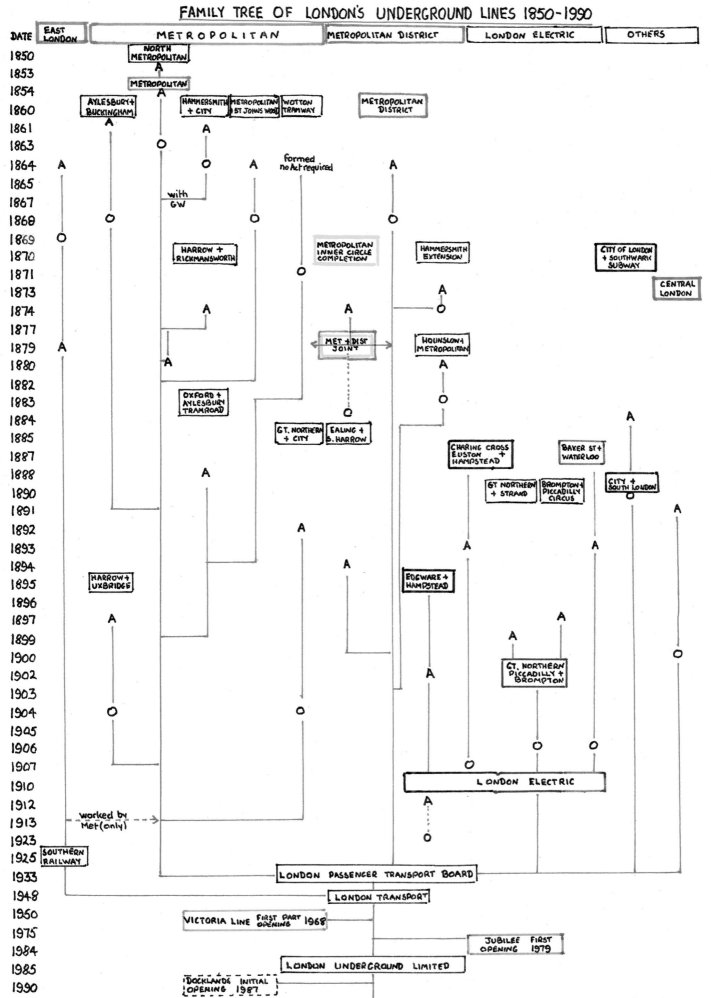

Notes: A is ACT of Parliament. O is date of FIRST section opened; if no O shown, indicates no opening until absorbed. Absorptions may be lease or long-term working agreement. Outline colours where used identify modern line names - see maps p.222 et seq.

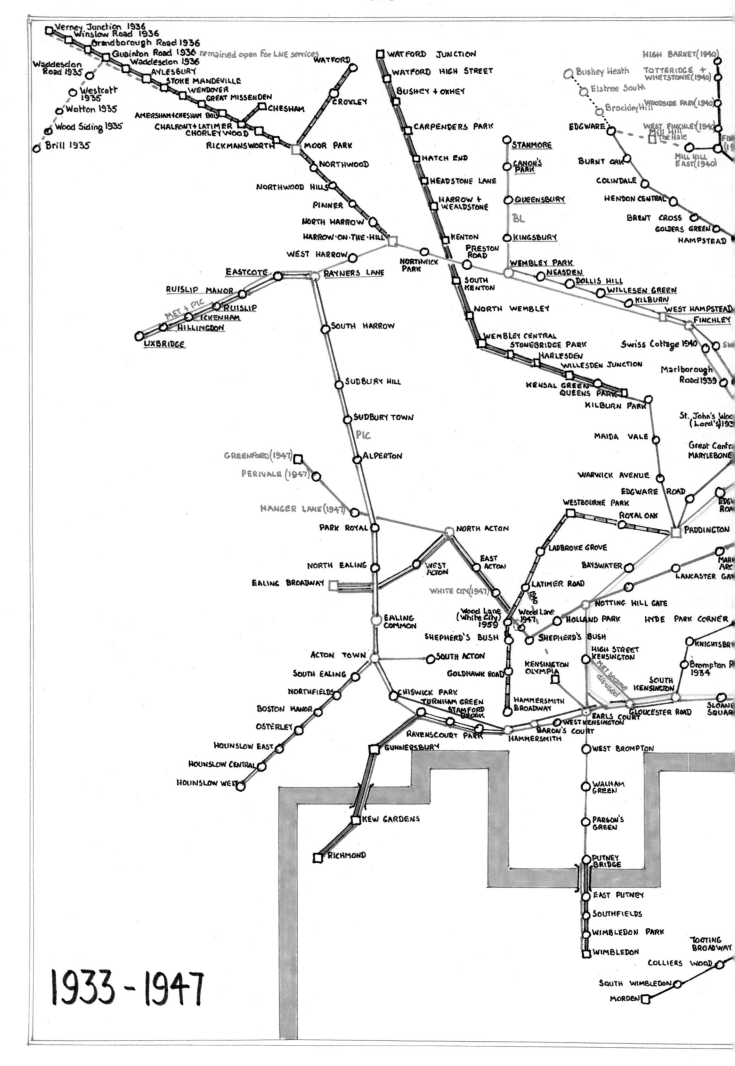

1933-1947

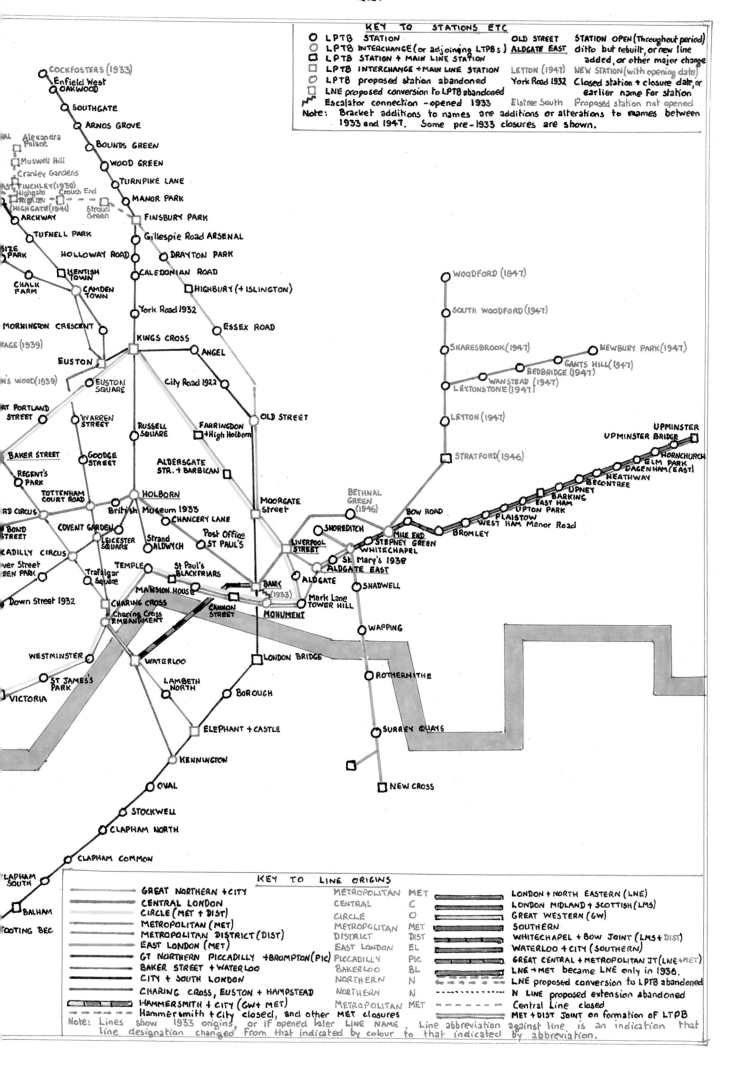

KEY TO STATIONS ETC

O	LPTB STATION	OLD STREET	STATION OPEN (throughout period)
O	LPTB INTERCHANGE (or adjoining LTPBs)	ALDGATE EAST	ditto but rebuilt, or new line added, or other major change
□	LPTB STATION + MAIN LINE STATION	Leyton (1947)	NEW STATION (with opening date)
□	LPTB INTERCHANGE + MAIN LINE STATION	York Road 1932	Closed station + closure date, or earlier name for station
O	LPTB proposed station abandoned		
□	LNE proposed conversion to LPTB abandoned	Elstree South	Proposed station not opened

Escalator connection - opened 1933

Note: Bracket additions to names are additions or alterations to names between 1933 and 1947. Some pre-1933 closures are shown.

KEY TO LINE ORIGINS

	GREAT NORTHERN + CITY	METROPOLITAN MET	LONDON + NORTH EASTERN (LNE)
	CENTRAL LONDON	CENTRAL C	LONDON MIDLAND + SCOTTISH (LMS)
	CIRCLE (MET + DIST)	CIRCLE O	GREAT WESTERN (GW)
	METROPOLITAN (MET)	METROPOLITAN MET	SOUTHERN
	METROPOLITAN DISTRICT (DIST)	DISTRICT DIST	WHITECHAPEL + BOW JOINT (LMS + DIST)
	EAST LONDON (MET)	EAST LONDON EL	WATERLOO + CITY (SOUTHERN)
	GT NORTHERN PICCADILLY + BROMPTON (PIC)	PICCADILLY PIC	GREAT CENTRAL + METROPOLITAN JT (LNE + MET)
	BAKER STREET + WATERLOO	BAKERLOO BL	LNE + MET became LNE only in 1936.
	CITY + SOUTH LONDON	NORTHERN N	LNE proposed conversion to LPTB abandoned
	CHARING CROSS, EUSTON + HAMPSTEAD	NORTHERN N	N LINE proposed extension abandoned
	HAMMERSMITH + CITY (GW + MET)	METROPOLITAN MET	Central Line closed
	Hammersmith + City closed, and other MET closures		MET + DIST JOINT on formation of LTPB

Note: Lines show 1933 origins, or if opened later LINE NAME Line abbreviation against line is an indication that
line designation changed from that indicated by colour to that indicated by abbreviation.

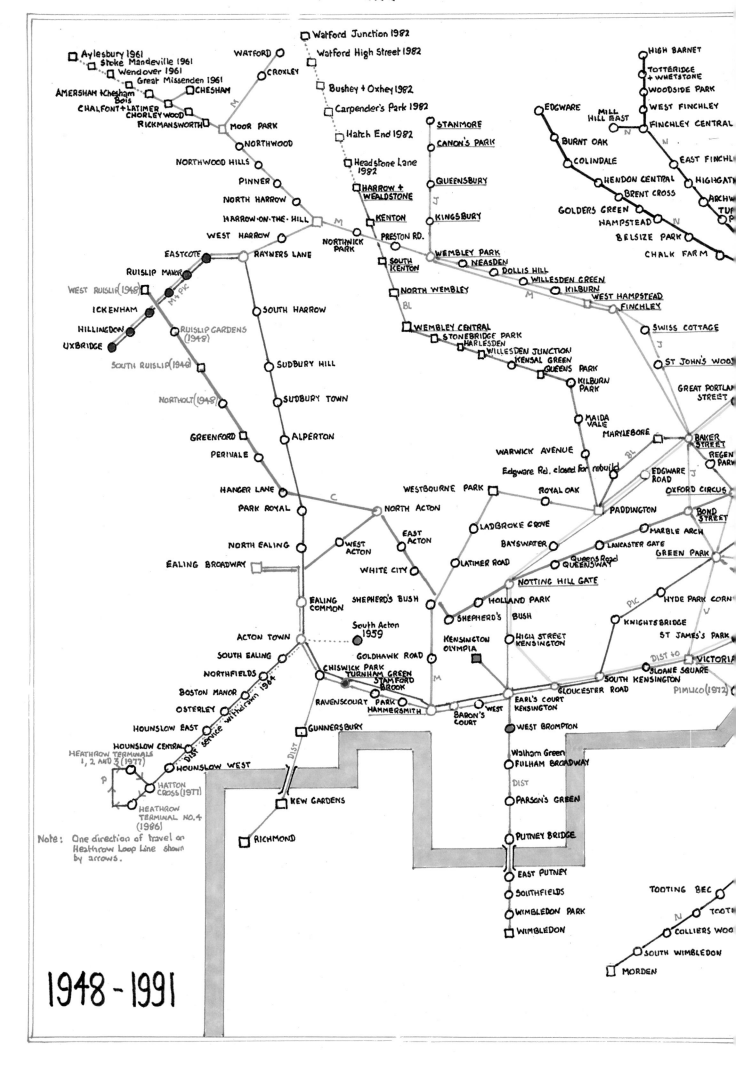

1948 - 1991

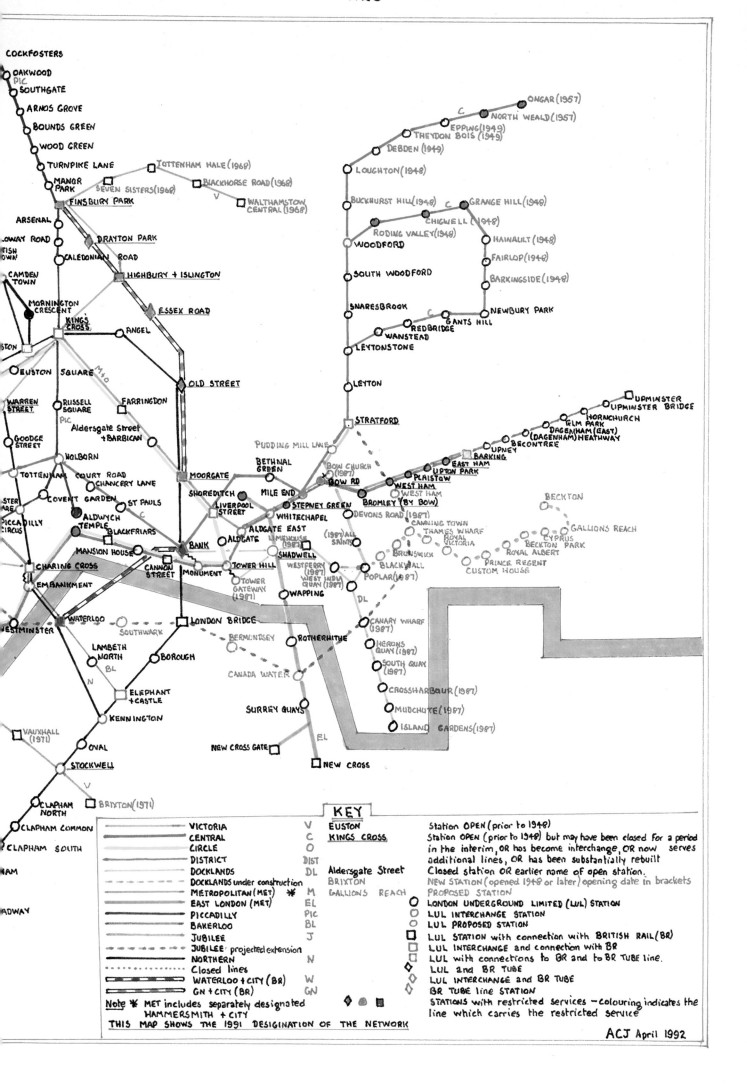

KEY

—— VICTORIA	V
—— CENTRAL	C
—— CIRCLE	O
—— DISTRICT	DIST
—— DOCKLANDS	DL
—— DOCKLANDS under construction	
—— METROPOLITAN (MET) ✳	M
—— EAST LONDON (MET)	EL
—— PICCADILLY	PIC
—— BAKERLOO	BL
—— JUBILEE	J
- - - JUBILEE projected extension	
—— NORTHERN	N
- - - Closed lines	
▭▭ WATERLOO + CITY (BR)	W
▭▭ GN + CITY (BR)	GN

Note ✳ MET includes separately designated
HAMMERSMITH + CITY
THIS MAP SHOWS THE 1991 DESIGNATION OF THE NETWORK

EUSTON — Station OPEN (prior to 1948)
KINGS CROSS — Station OPEN (prior to 1948) but may have been closed for a period in the interim, OR has become interchange, OR now serves additional lines, OR has been substantially rebuilt
Aldersgate Street — Closed station OR earlier name of open station.
BRIXTON — NEW STATION (opened 1948 or later) opening date in brackets
GALLIONS REACH — PROPOSED STATION
○ LONDON UNDERGROUND LIMITED (LUL) STATION
◎ LUL INTERCHANGE STATION
○ LUL PROPOSED STATION
▢ LUL STATION with connection with BRITISH RAIL (BR)
▢ LUL INTERCHANGE and connection with BR
▢ LUL with connections to BR and to BR TUBE line.
◆ LUL and BR TUBE
◇ LUL INTERCHANGE and BR TUBE
◇ BR TUBE line STATION
STATIONS with restricted services — colouring indicates the line which carries the restricted service

ACJ April 1992

LONDON UNDERGROUND LIMITED - WORKS, DEPOTS + STABLING

No.	Name OR Location	Location details	line(s) served	Notes
1	ACTON WORKS	Spur lines south of Acton Town	ALL	Official opening 1923
2	STONEBRIDGE PARK	Spur line from station	BAKERLOO	
3	UPMINSTER	beyond station	DISTRICT	
4	WHITE CITY	spur south of station between running lines	CENTRAL	Original Central Terminus
5	NORTHFIELDS	loop Northfields - Boston Manor	PICCADILLY	
6	EALING COMMON	loop Acton Town + Ealing Common	PICCADILLY + DISTRICT	
7	HAMMERSMITH	spur trailing into terminus	HAMMERSMITH + CITY	
8	WEMBLEY PARK	spur to north of station	METROPOLITAN + JUBILEE	
9	NEASDEN	loop between Neasden + Wembley Park	METROPOLITAN + JUBILEE	Opened 1882 to replace Edgware Road. Can also serve: METROPOLITAN + PICCADILLY
10	RUISLIP	loop between Ruislip Gardens + Ruislip West	CENTRAL PICCADILLY	
11	Uxbridge	facing connection approaching station	METROPOLITAN	Stabling sidings only
12	High Barnet	spur trailing into terminus	NORTHERN	Stabling sidings only
13	COCKFOSTERS	loop between Oakwood + Cockfosters	PICCADILLY	
14	NORTHUMBERLAND PARK	spur from Tottenham Hale	VICTORIA	Served by staff Halt
15	HAINAULT	loop between Hainault + Grange Hill	CENTRAL	
16	LONDON ROAD	spur from Lambeth North	BAKERLOO	
17	Stanmore	facing spur approaching station	JUBILEE	
18	EDGWARE	trailing spur approaching station	NORTHERN	Small depot
19	GOLDERS GREEN	facing spur down approach to station	NORTHERN	
20	BECKTON	not known	DOCKLANDS	proposed depot
21	POPLAR	Facing spur from All Saints to Poplar	DOCKLANDS	maintenance depot
22	NEW CROSS	Facing spur on station approach	EAST LONDON	
23	HIGHGATE	spur between running lines (south)	NORTHERN	
24	MORDEN	on southward continuation of line	NORTHERN	situated at South Morden

Reversal sidings sometimes used for stabling at WOODFORD, LOUGHTON (Central) and ARNOS GROVE (Piccadilly).

MAP SHOWING APPROXIMATE AREAS TO BE COVERED IN FUTURE VOLUMES ON LONDON.

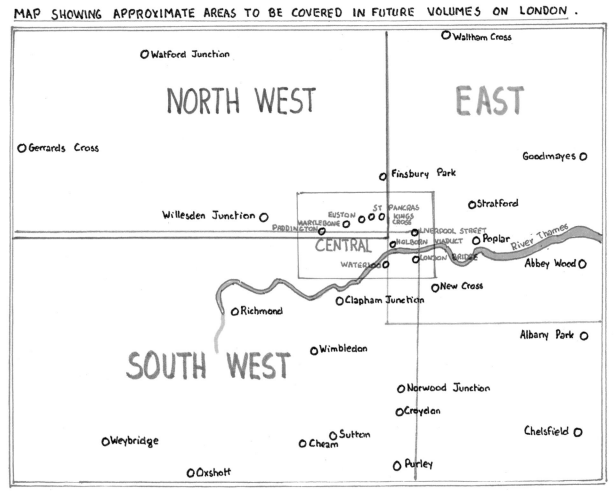

GUILDFORD

GUILDFORD enjoys a unique position as a railway centre within the Southern Railway area, being the only place in that area, except London, to have lines reaching it from all three pre-grouping companies. These pre-grouping companies all tended to develop within specific areas with clearly defined boundaries, with the boundary often being a joint line: Kent and the east was the monopoly of the SOUTH EASTERN + CHATHAM, the west being the preserve of the LONDON + SOUTH WESTERN whilst the central portion was almost exclusively in the hands of the LONDON BRIGHTON + SOUTH COAST. This factor led to GUILDFORD becoming a natural first choice in the area for inclusion in this first volume.

GUILDFORD was the most important town in West Surrey and although it was by-passed by the LONDON + SOUTH WESTERN main line to Southampton it quickly developed into a railway centre with lines radiating to all points of the compass as the following chronology shows:

1830-1845

25. 7.1834 LONDON + SOUTHAMPTON (LS) - Act.

21. 6.1836 SOUTH EASTERN (SE) - Act.

19. 5.1838 LS opened from London (Nine Elms) to Woking Common. Map area station opened at WOKING.

24. 9.1838 LS opened from Woking Common to Shapley Heath. Intermediate station opened at FARNBOROUGH.

4. 6.1839 LS changes its name to LONDON + SOUTH WESTERN (LSW).

10. 5.1844 GUILDFORD JUNCTION (GJ) - Act.

5. 5.1845 GJ opened from a junction at WOKING to GUILDFORD. Worked by LSW.

27. 7.1845 GJ absorbed by LSW.

1846-1855

16. 7.1846 READING GUILDFORD + REIGATE (RGR) - Act.

27. 7.1846 LONDON BRIGHTON + SOUTH COAST (LBSC) formed. A merger of London + Brighton with London + Croydon.

4. 7.1849 RGR opened between Reading and FARNBOROUGH. There was, in addition to Farnborough, an intermediate station at BLACKWATER. This latter station was one of several local stations which kept changing its name: + SANDHURST was added to the title in 1851 but this was dropped the following year.

20. 8.1849 RGR opened from FARNBOROUGH to ASH JUNCTION (with LSW - see below). There were two intermediate stations, both having frequent name changes: ASH, which became ASH + ALDERSHOT in 1855, and NORTH CAMP ALDERSHOT (but this latter station did not open for public use until 1858).

20. 8.1849 LSW opened two sections of line from GUILDFORD: First GUILDFORD to ASH JUNCTION, and the other line was to SHALFORD JUNCTION. There were no intermediate stations on either line. The RGR had obtained running powers over both lines to enable a through service to run by linking its two sections of line.

20. 8.1849 RGR opened between Dorking and SHALFORD (with planned connection with the second LSW line mentioned above). Intermediate stations, within the map area, were opened at: SHALFORD (for Godalming), CHILWORTH + ALBURY.

8. 10.1849 LSW opened between ASH JUNCTION and FARNHAM; besides FARNHAM, a station was opened close to the junction, also called ASH. This was another station subject to frequent name changes.

15. 10.1849 RGR opened between SHALFORD and SHALFORD JUNCTION to allow the through running mentioned above.

15. 10.1849 LSW SHALFORD JUNCTION to GODALMING opened. (This first station later became a goods depot.)

15. 3.1850 RGR leased to SE.

17. 6.1852 RGR fully absorbed by SE.

30. 6.1852 LONDON NECROPOLIS incorporated to establish a large cemetery at Brookwood. Had powers to construct a 3/4 mile railway from a junction with LSW. LSW agreed to work line. (See also under LONDON for this company private station near Waterloo).

28. 7.1852 LSW opened from FARNHAM to Alton.

1. 12.1854 LONDON NECROPOLIS line opened.

7.1855 ASH station (SE) changed its name, becoming ASH + ALDERSHOT for the next three years.

Following these two periods of quite intense activity, further development was spread over a longer period of time and except for minor events would be concluded by the end of 1885, the date of the next map. The subsequent 105 years is also relatively inactive both from development and rationalisation aspects contrasting sharply with the situation with centres elsewhere but shared to some extent by other centres in the area.

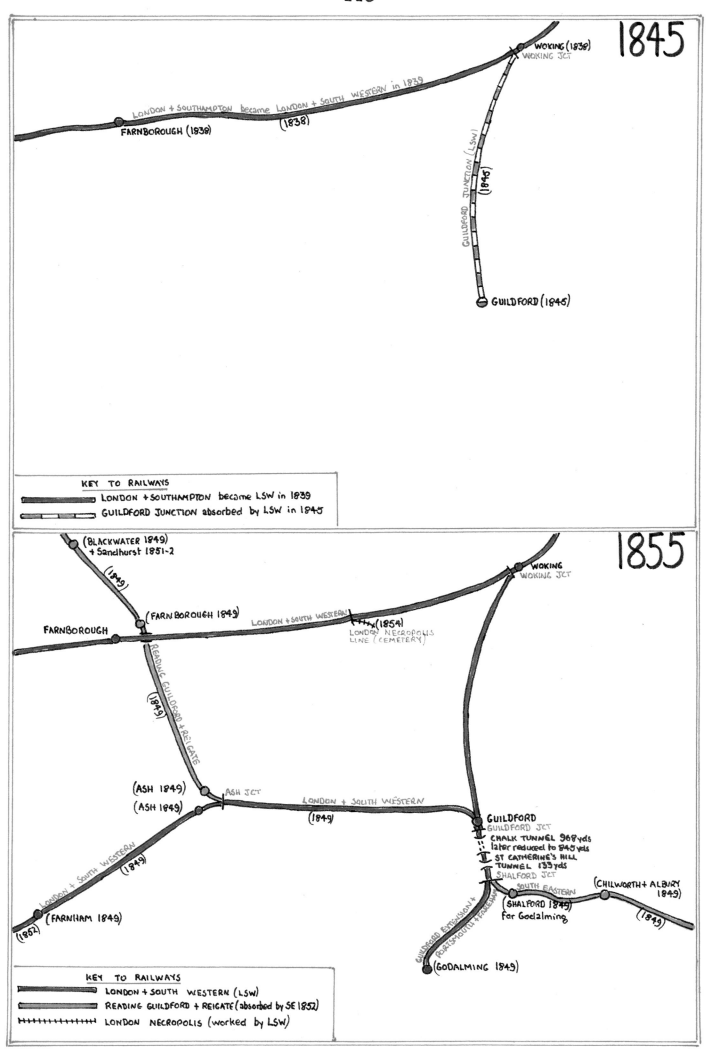

1845

WOKING (1838)
WOKING JCT

LONDON + SOUTHAMPTON became LONDON + SOUTH WESTERN in 1839

FARNBOROUGH (1838)   (1838)

GUILDFORD JUNCTION (LSW)   (1845)

GUILDFORD (1845)

KEY TO RAILWAYS

LONDON + SOUTHAMPTON became LSW in 1839

GUILDFORD JUNCTION absorbed by LSW in 1845

1855

(BLACKWATER 1849)
+ Sandhurst 1851-2

WOKING
WOKING JCT

(1849)

(FARNBOROUGH 1849)

FARNBOROUGH

LONDON + SOUTH WESTERN   X (1854)
LONDON NECROPOLIS
LINE (CEMETERY)

READING GUILDFORD + REIGATE (1849)

(ASH 1849)   ASH JCT

(ASH 1849)

LONDON + SOUTH WESTERN   (1849)

GUILDFORD
GUILDFORD JCT
CHALK TUNNEL 968 yds
later reduced to 845 yds
ST CATHERINE'S HILL
TUNNEL 133 yds
SHALFORD JCT

LONDON + SOUTH WESTERN   (1849)

SOUTH EASTERN   (CHILWORTH + ALBURY 1849)

GUILDFORD EXTENSION +
PORTSMOUTH + FAREHAM

SHALFORD 1849
for Godalming   (1849)

(FARNHAM 1849)

(1852)

GODALMING 1849

KEY TO RAILWAYS

LONDON + SOUTH WESTERN (LSW)

READING GUILDFORD + REIGATE (absorbed by SE 1852)

LONDON NECROPOLIS (worked by LSW)

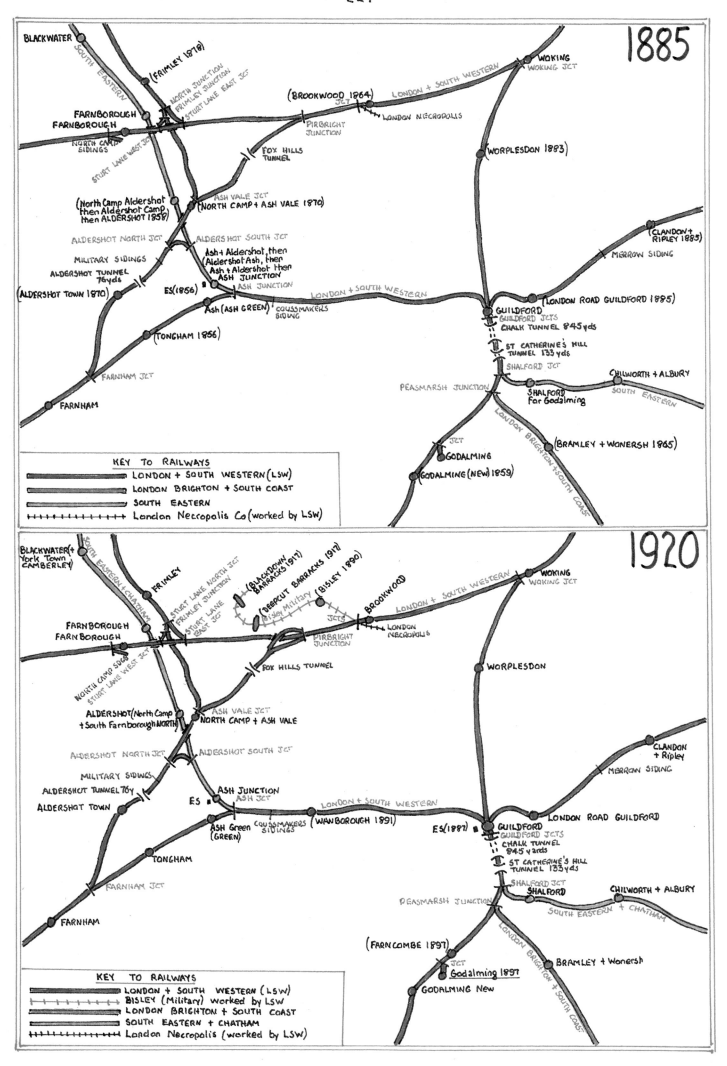

1856-1885

1. 1.1859 LONDON + SOUTH WESTERN (LSW) opened from GODALMING to Havant. A new station was opened at GODALMING, but the original station continued in use for terminating trains. There was an intermediate station, just outside the map area, at MILFORD.

1. 8.1859 LONDON CHATHAM + DOVER (LCD) formed. This railway would have no influence over the railways in the GUILDFORD area, but would, eventually, in 1899 combine with the SOUTH EASTERN (SE) to form the SOUTH EASTERN + CHATHAM (SEC).

6. 8.1860 HORSHAM + GUILDFORD DIRECT (HGD) - Act.

29. 7.1864 HGD absorbed by LONDON BRIGHTON + SOUTH COAST (LBSC). Construction of the railway was well advanced by this time and it would be opened shortly by the LBSC.

2.10.1865 LBSC opened from West Horsham to PEASMARSH JUNCTION at GUILDFORD. There was one intermediate map area station at BRAMLEY which became BRAMLEY + WONERSH in 1888.

2. 5.1870 LSW opened from PIRBRIGHT JUNCTION, on the main line, to FARNHAM JUNCTION. Intermediate stations were opened at ALDERSHOT (also known at various times as ALDERSHOT TOWN + CAMP and ALDERSHOT TOWN) and at NORTH CAMP + ASH VALE (also had some name changes).

18. 3.1878 LSW opened from Ascot to STURT LANE JUNCTIONS. There was an intermediate station at FRIMLEY.

2. 6.1879 LSW opened from FRIMLEY JUNCTION (just to the north of Sturt Lane Junctions) to join the Pirbright to Farnham line just to the north of NORTH CAMP + ASH VALE. Before the end of the year the LSW had also opened a spur linking ASH with ALDERSHOT.

20. 5.1885 LSW opened from Hampton Court Junction via Effingham Junction to GUILDFORD. There were intermediate stations on this line at GUILDFORD LONDON ROAD and CLANDON + RIPLEY. It would appear in fact from the opening dates of stations that the line into GUILDFORD was opened from Leatherhead 2.2.1885 and the Hampton Court line linked in three months later. This certainly appears a more logical sequence of events.

RAILWAY CENTRES IN THE SOUTH EAST

When planning was undertaken for this atlas, it was decided that the number of pre-grouping maps for any centre would not be fixed but would vary dependent upon the pattern of events at individual centres. But early in the project it was decided that all centres would have the same four maps in the post-grouping period to give comparison of the similarities in rationalisation and revival. A grouping map of 1940 is convenient to show the events of grouping, since by this date control had passed to the goverment. 1963 shows early rationalisation together with the BEECHING proposals. 1977 saw, in the main, the end of closures, and the final map shows in many cases a modest revival, together with future proposals. When a start was made on research for this GUILDFORD chapter it soon became clear that this pattern was not appropriate for centres in the South-east in much the same way as it had been unsuitable for LONDON. However, this general pattern has been retained for GUILDFORD to give comparison with centres elsewhere. But future South Eastern Centres will be planned with a lesser number of postgrouping maps although selected from the four dates used elsewhere.

1886-1920

14. 7.1890 BISLEY (Military) opened from a junction near BROOKWOOD to BISLEY, run by the LSW. At this stage trains ran only in connection with the National Rifle Association meetings.

1. 8.1899 SE and LCD, after years of infighting due to the antagonism of the two chairmen, agree to merge. From this date run by a joint management committee, known as SOUTH EASTERN + CHATHAM (SEC).

30. 6.1901 LSW convert PIRBRIGHT JUNCTION into a fly-over junction to improve through running and timings.

25. 7.1917 BISLEY extended to DEEPCUT BARRACKS for wartime goods traffic. Passenger traffic was also carried from 1.8.1917.

1.12.1917 BISLEY further extended to BLACKDOWN BARRACKS for passengers and goods.

This was the point in time of maximum development of the system, although there is, as mentioned above, no real development after 1885.

To complete the picture it just remains to record the openings (and one closure) of additional intermediate stations from 1856 to 1920, together with some name changes.

OPENINGS: BROOKWOOD (1864 - built at the expense of the London Necropolis Co), FARNCOMBE (1897 to replace GODALMING terminal station which became a goods-only station), TONGHAM (1856), WAN BOROUGH (1891) and WORPLESDON (1883).

NAME CHAGES: These are shown on the maps in the order the main changes took place. The latest name, if station is still open, is always shown in CAPITALS.

ENGINE SHEDS: The area was poorly provided with engine sheds and details of only two have been found; these are shown below in the usual tabular format:

No.	NAME	COMPANY	OPENED	CLOSED	NOTES
1	ASH	SOUTH EASTERN	1856	1946	exact closure date is unclear
2	GUILDFORD	LONDON + SOUTH WESTERN	1887	1967	may have replaced earlier shed

1921 - 1940

1. 1. 1923 Formation of the SOUTHERN RAILWAY which included all the railways in the GUILDFORD area. In the chart of the origins of each railway shown below, all local companies are shown, together with absorption details. ACT shows year of parliamentary sanction; O shows date of first area opening; subsidiary companies that opened after being absorbed are shown thus: ·········· ; leasing – – – – ; fully absorbed ————.

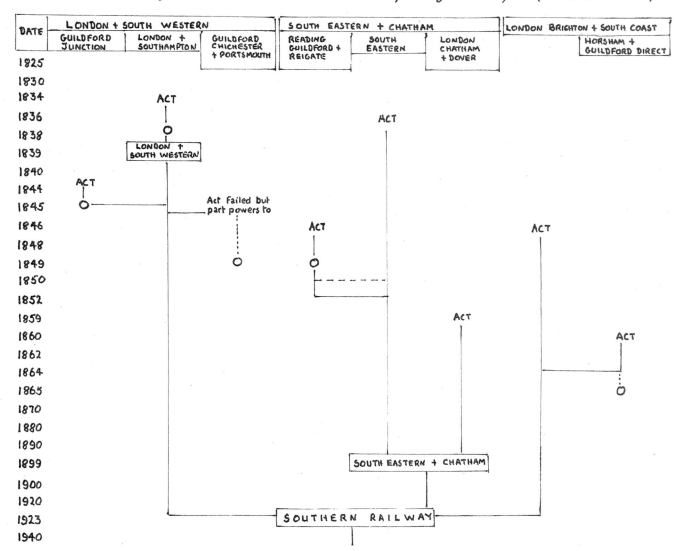

12. 7. 1925 First electrified line reaches GUILDFORD. News is broadcast by Town Crier. Electrification programme continued and by end of the period most lines through GUILDFORD had been dealt with or early conversion was planned.

4. 7. 1937 Ash Junction to Farnham Junction closed and stations at ASH GREEN and TONGHAM. Through traffic was diverted via the Aldershot curve.

1941 - 1963

This period did not show a single change in the area network or in opening or closing of stations, although the two special tramways closed as will be noted. It is only publication of the BEECHING REPORT in the final year of the period which calls for comment. Even the report proposals can be quickly told. Three stations were

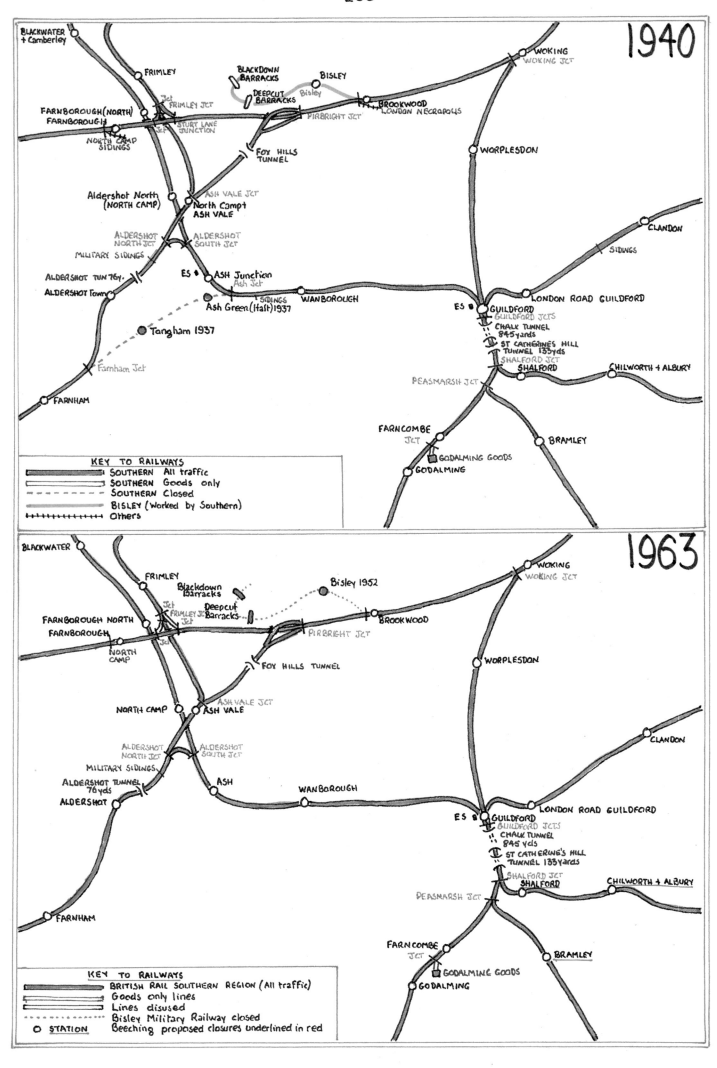

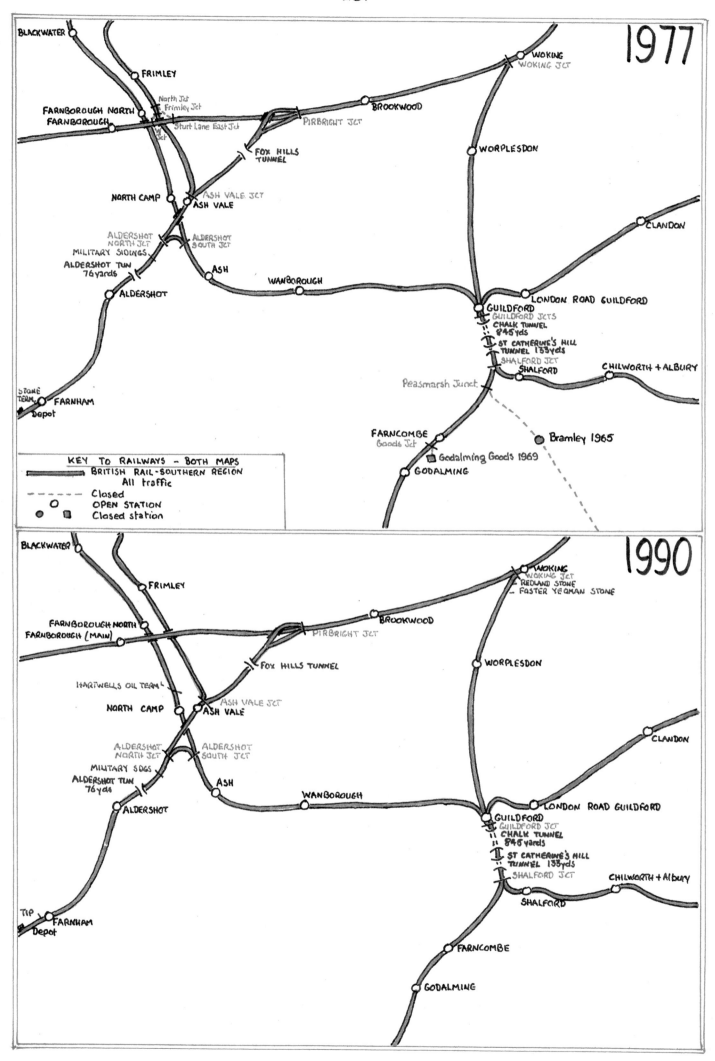

1977

KEY TO RAILWAYS - BOTH MAPS
— BRITISH RAIL-SOUTHERN REGION
All traffic
--- Closed
○ OPEN STATION
● ■ Closed station

1990

proposed for closure: BRAMLEY, CHILWORTH + ALBURY and SHALFORD. The two lines on which these stations were located were also scheduled for total closure to passengers — these were GUILDFORD to Horsham and GUILDFORD to Dorking.

As mentioned above, however, the two specialist lines radiating from BROOKWOOD closed during this period. The BISLEY railway saw its final train in 1952 although it appears that the portion of line beyond Bisley station may have lost most of its traffic at the end of the war. The cemetery line also lost its traffic but for different reasons, though also associated with the war. The London station, together with a train, were severely damaged by enemy action and although the line was used subsequently it led to its early demise. Actual closing date is not recorded, but probably before the end of the war.

1964 - 1977

This is a further period in which little happened so far as the area's railway network was concerned:
First the Beeching proposals. The Horsham line had traffic withdrawn on 14·6·1965 with the consequent closure of BRAMLEY on the same date. But the Dorking line had closure averted and still remains in use at the time of writing (1991).

The area's only goods-only station — GODALMING (first station) — closed in 1969. Sturt Lane Junctions were taken out of use at about this time, but they had never seen much traffic throughout their life after the first few months.

1978 - 1990

There is nothing to record during this period. The final map does show some current lineside rail users, but the area has never been particularly important for freight, except for a time from military sources. Carriage of passengers has always been the area priority.

1991 - FUTURE

No plans for future openings or closures are known and the area and its network, having shown little change in the last 105 years, seems unlikely to change in the future.

In fact, the main area changes in the last 105 years have been station name changes, particularly in the Aldershot area where even the 1990 map shows two such changes!

CANTERBURY

CANTERBURY as a railway centre does have quite a few strange and unusual features and it is of interest to note these before looking at the chronology of events.

CANTERBURY did have a 'First' in that it witnessed the first fare paying passenger service which was also steam hauled, Stephenson's Invicta performing this feat on the 3rd of May 1830 on the opening of the CANTERBURY + WHITSTABLE, although it only did this on the central level section of line. The line was engineered by Joseph Locke and included a 1012-yard tunnel. The line was leased to the contractor who went bankrupt. Traction was changed to working by stationary engines. This line also had another 'First', being the first to issue season tickets which were introduced in 1834. One final unusual feature of the line was its early closure in 1931. As seen elsewhere, the first railway to close in an area was usually the last to open, but this railway was the first both to open and close (for passenger traffic).

Another unusual feature of CANTERBURY was the lack of connections between the lines. The earliest lines soon became part of the SOUTH EASTERN. The lines promoted by the EAST KENT looked as though they too would be absorbed. But differences arose and the EAST KENT which changed its name to the LONDON CHATHAM + DOVER made no connection with CANTERBURY's other lines. However, the two companies settled their differences in 1899 and merged to form the SOUTH EASTERN + CHATHAM, but over 90 years later they remain unconnected!

1825-1850

10. 6. 1825 CANTERBURY + WHITSTABLE (CW) Act.

3. 5. 1830 CW ceremonial opening. Public traffic started the following day between terminal stations at CANTERBURY and WHITSTABLE.

19. 3. 1832 CW extension opened to WHITSTABLE HARBOUR. It is interesting to note the BRADSHAWS RAILWAY MAP of 1839 does not show the CW and it could be that a service was not running at that time, perhaps due to the financially constrained circumstances of the operator.

21. 6. 1836 SOUTH EASTERN (SE) Act.

29. 9. 1844 CW leased to and worked by SE. It was from this date operated by steam traction throughout.

6. 2. 1846 SE opened from Ashford to CANTERBURY (later to become CANTERBURY WEST). There was one intermediate station within the map area at CHILHAM, but an additional station at CHARTHAM was added in 1859.

13. 4. 1846 SE opened from CANTERBURY to Ramsgate. There was a flat crossing with CW but a connection was soon laid with that railway and CW trains then began to use the SE station and the CW station closed to passengers. There was only one intermediate station on this extension within the map area and this was at GROVE FERRY. However, an additional station was opened at STURRY two years later.

1851-1865

4. 8. 1853 EAST KENT (EK) authorised. Supported by the SE who expected to absorb it, but things didn't work out in that way as will be seen.

4. 8. 1853 CW fully absorbed by SE.

17. 8. 1857 HERNE BAY + FAVERSHAM (HBF) authorised to link the points of its title.

25. 1. 1858 EK opened from Chatham to FAVERSHAM with an intermediate map area station at TEYNHAM.

1. 8. 1859 EK becomes LONDON CHATHAM + DOVER (LCD).

13. 8. 1859 HBF changes its name to MARGATE with additional powers to extend its line to that point.

12. 4. 1860 LCD opened goods-only branch from FAVERSHAM to CREEK with an additional short spur to a Coal Wharf.

9. 7. 1860 LCD opened from FAVERSHAM to CANTERBURY (would later become CANTERBURY EAST). There were no intermediate stations opened at that time but SELLING was opened in December.

1. 8. 1860 MARGATE opened from FAVERSHAM, and a junction with the LCD, to WHITSTABLE. No intermediate stations.

13. 7. 1861 MARGATE opened from WHITSTABLE to HERNE BAY. No intermediate stations.

22. 7. 1861 LCD opened from CANTERBURY to Dover. Intermediate stations were opened within the map area at ADISHAM and BEKESBOURNE.

6. 8. 1861 MARGATE again changes its name, this time to KENT COAST (KC).

7. 8. 1862 KC leased to LCD with effect from 1·9·1863.

1. 9. 1863 KC lease to LCD - effective date. In the meantime had been worked by LCD.

1. 10. 1863 KC opened from HERNE BAY to MARGATE. No map area intermediate stations opened at this time.

CANTERBURY's railway development was now virtually complete. There was only the ELHAM VALLEY line to open, which would give CANTERBURY its second junction; and the EAST KENT (Light) on the fringe of the area.

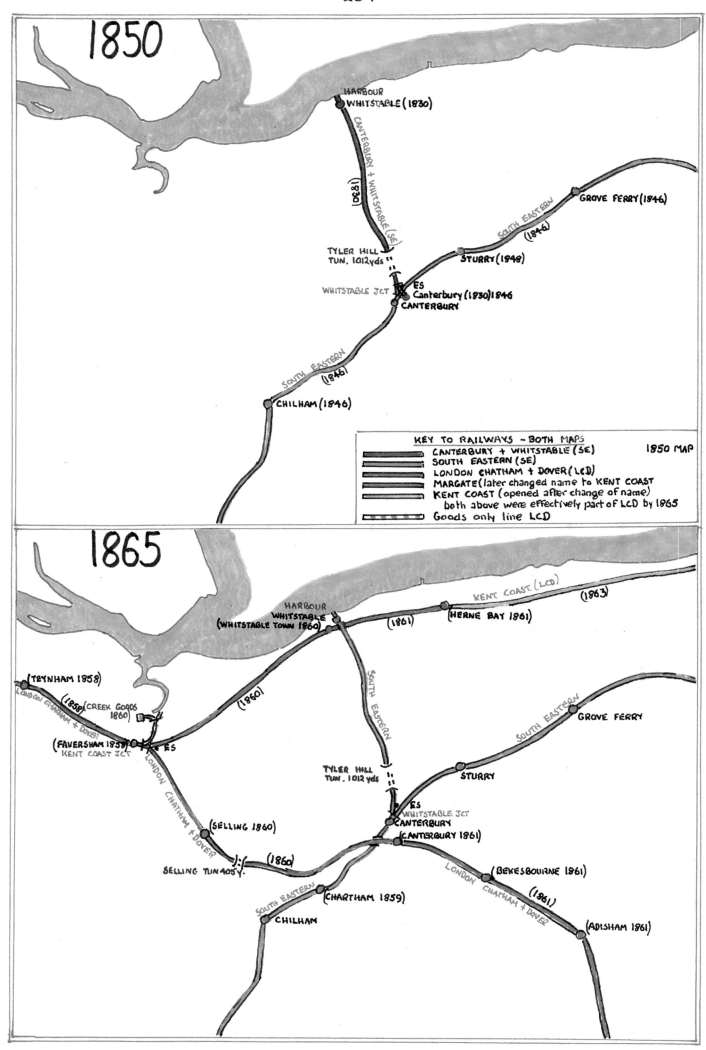

1850

HARBOUR
WHITSTABLE (1830)

CANTERBURY + WHITSTABLE (SE)

(1830)

GROVE FERRY (1846)

SOUTH EASTERN

(1846)

TYLER HILL
TUN. 1012 yds

STURRY (1848)

WHITSTABLE JCT

ES
Canterbury (1830)1846
CANTERBURY

SOUTH EASTERN

(1846)

CHILHAM (1846)

KEY TO RAILWAYS - BOTH MAPS

CANTERBURY + WHITSTABLE (SE)
SOUTH EASTERN (SE)
LONDON CHATHAM + DOVER (LCD)
MARGATE (later changed name to KENT COAST)
KENT COAST (opened after change of name)
    both above were effectively part of LCD by 1865
Goods only line LCD

1850 MAP

1865

HARBOUR
WHITSTABLE
(WHITSTABLE TOWN 1860)

KENT COAST (LCD)

(1863)

(1861)

HERNE BAY 1861)

(TEYNHAM 1858)

LONDON CHATHAM + DOVER

(1858)

(CREEK GOODS 1860)

(1860)

SOUTH EASTERN

(FAVERSHAM 1858)

ES

KENT COAST JCT

LONDON CHATHAM + DOVER

TYLER HILL
TUN. 1012 yds

GROVE FERRY

SOUTH EASTERN

(SELLING 1860)

STURRY

ES
WHITSTABLE JCT
CANTERBURY

(CANTERBURY 1861)

SELLING TUN 405 y.

(1860)

(BEKESBOURNE 1861)

LONDON CHATHAM + DOVER

(1861)

SOUTH EASTERN

(CHARTHAM 1859)

CHILHAM

(ADISHAM 1861)

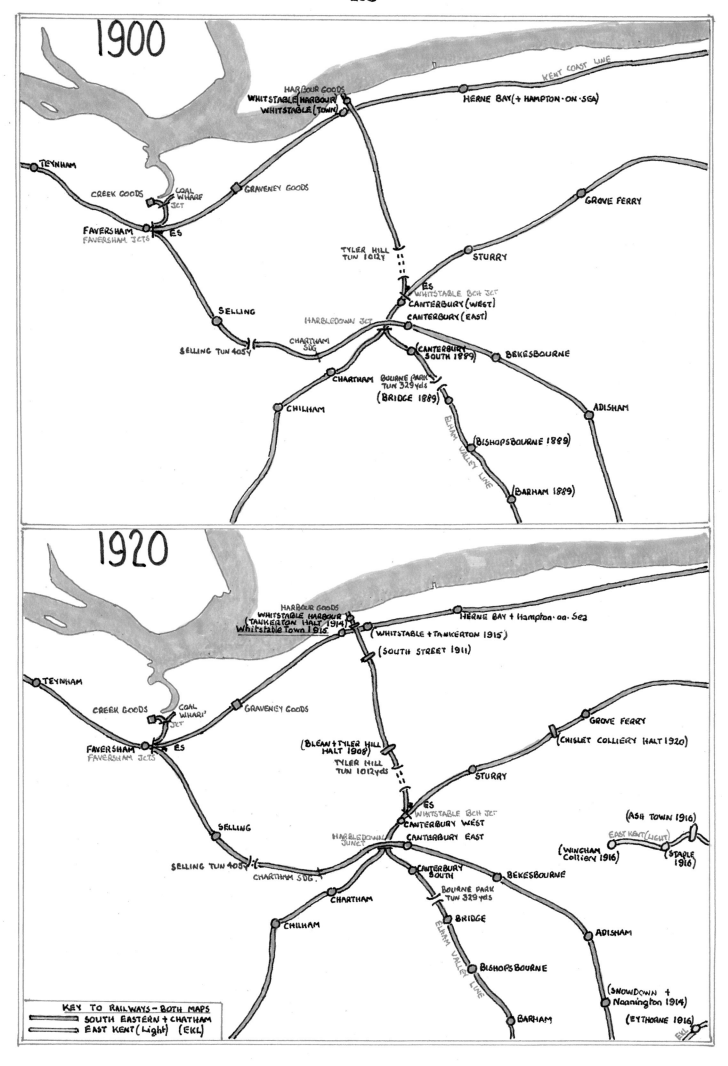

1900

TEYNHAM

CREEK GOODS
COAL WHARF JCT
GRAVENEY GOODS

KENT COAST LINE

HARBOUR GOODS
WHITSTABLE HARBOUR
WHITSTABLE (TOWN)

HERNE BAY (+ HAMPTON·ON·SEA)

GROVE FERRY

FAVERSHAM
FAVERSHAM JCTS
ES

TYLER HILL
TUN 1012Y

STURRY

SELLING

ES
WHITSTABLE BCH JCT
CANTERBURY (WEST)
CANTERBURY (EAST)

HARBLEDOWN JCT

SELLING TUN 405Y

CHARTHAM SDG

(CANTERBURY SOUTH 1889)

BEKESBOURNE

CHARTHAM
BOURNE PARK
TUN 329yds

CHILHAM

(BRIDGE 1889)

ADISHAM

(BISHOPSBOURNE 1889)

ELHAM VALLEY LINE

(BARHAM 1889)

1920

TEYNHAM

CREEK GOODS
COAL WHARF JCT
GRAVENEY GOODS

HARBOUR GOODS
WHITSTABLE HARBOUR
(TANKERTON HALT 1914)
Whitstable Town 1915

HERNE BAY + Hampton·on·Sea

(WHITSTABLE + TANKERTON 1915)
(SOUTH STREET 1911)

GROVE FERRY
(CHISLET COLLIERY HALT 1920)

FAVERSHAM
FAVERSHAM JCTS
ES

(BLEAN + TYLER HILL HALT 1908)
TYLER HILL
TUN 1012yds

SELLING

STURRY

(ASH TOWN 1916)

ES
WHITSTABLE BCH JCT
CANTERBURY WEST
CANTERBURY EAST

HARBLEDOWN JUNCT

EAST KENT (LIGHT)

SELLING TUN 405Y

CHARTHAM SDG.

(WINGHAM COLLIERY 1916)

(STAPLE 1916)

CANTERBURY SOUTH

BEKESBOURNE

CHARTHAM
BOURNE PARK
TUN 329yds

CHILHAM

BRIDGE

ADISHAM

BISHOPSBOURNE

ELHAM VALLEY LINE

(SNOWDOWN + Nonnington 1914)

BARHAM

(EYTHORNE 1916)

EKL

KEY TO RAILWAYS — BOTH MAPS
SOUTH EASTERN + CHATHAM
EAST KENT (Light) (EKL)

1866-1900

31. 7. 1871 KENT COAST fully absorbed by the LONDON CHATHAM + DOVER (LCD).

18. 7. 1881 ELHAM VALLEY (LIGHT) (EVL) - Authorised. Originally, rival schemes for linking Folkestone with CANTERBURY were proposed by the SOUTH EASTERN (SE) and the LCD. Both failed, but the nominally independant EVL was authorised, with SE support. Having obtained authorisation, there matters rested as the SE's principal concern was not to build the connection but to ensure that the LCD did not build it. However, further threats by the LCD caused the SE to progress in the undertaking and the initial delay resulted in the line now having to be built to main-line standards rather than the earlier conceived branch-line standards.

28. 7. 1884 SE obtain EVL powers to construct the line.

4. 7. 1887 SE opened southern portion of EVL from Cheriton Junction to BARHAM. Local rumours circulating at the time said the northern portion would be built by the LCD. There was probably no truth in this, but proposals for an LCD connection at CANTERBURY were certainly explored. They came to nothing due to the antagonism of the two company chairmen. This was a pity since an LCD link at CANTERBURY would have ensured main-line status, which in effect was lost when the SE+LCD merged in 1899 reducing the line to rural branch status.

1. 7. 1889 SE opened remainder of EVL between BARHAM and HARBLEDOWN JUNCTION at CANTERBURY. Intermediate stations were opened at: BISHOPSBOURNE, BRIDGE and CANTERBURY SOUTH (opened as SOUTH CANTERBURY).

25. 6. 1891 EVL Fully absorbed by SE.

1. 8. 1899 SE + LCD combine to form the SOUTH EASTERN + CHATHAM (SEC). The merger resulted in the two stations at CANTERBURY needing to be distinguished, EAST being added to the LCD station, and WEST to the SE station. Below is a family tree of the area railway development showing authorisations (A, usually ACT), changes of name, mergers, absorptions and first openings in the area (O):

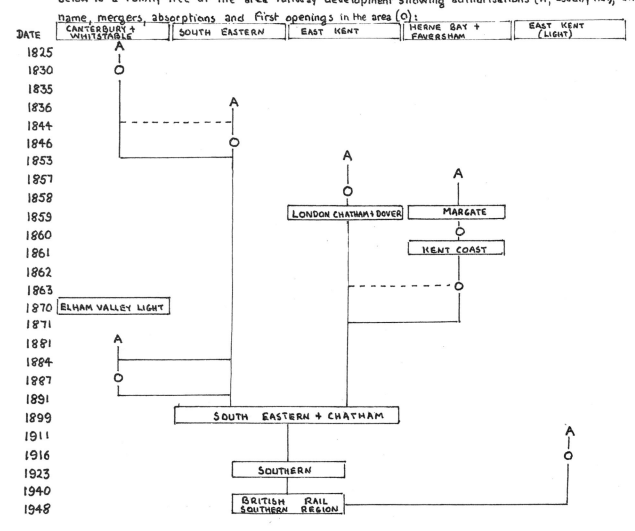

1901-1920

19. 6. 1911 EAST KENT LIGHT (EKL) - Light Railway Order. The main purpose of this undertaking was transportation of coal from the Kent Coalfield. First portion was opened towards the end of 1912. Only a small portion of its lines were within the map area.

16. 10. 1916 EKL passenger services commenced. Within the map area there were stations at: WINGHAM COLLIERY, STAPLE

16.10.1916 ASH TOWN (said to have been a halt and presumably unstaffed) and EYTHORNE.

It remains to record intermediate new stations opened during the period. These were: BLEAN + TYLER HILL HALT (1908 but known as TYLER HILL HALT from 1912 to 1915), CHISLET COLLIERY HALT (1920), SNOWDOWN HALT (1914), SOUTH STREET HALT (1911) and TANKERTON (1914).

There were only two engine shed locations in the area and these are detailed below in the usual tabular format (there may also have been a small shed at Canterbury East):

No.	Name / Location		Company	Opened	Closed	Notes
1	CANTERBURY WEST		SE	1846	1955	sub shed to Ashford. Originally known as Canterbury; West added on merger with LCD
2	FAVERSHAM	1st shed	LCD	1858	1890	small shed opened shortly after line. Then second and larger shed added. After closure to steam was used by diesels. But used as a stabling point for a time thereafter.
		2nd shed		1860	1959	
		diesels		1959	1964	

1921-1940

1923 The Grouping, the first event of the period had no effect upon the area. The SOUTH EASTERN + CHATHAM became part of the SOUTHERN (SR) but the area's other railway, the EAST KENT LIGHT (EKL), remained independant and outside the grouping.

1924 SR undertook survey of ELHAM VALLEY LINE with a view to singling or possible closure to passengers. However, the recommendations of the report were not implemented until 1931.

1925 EKL extended to CANTERBURY ROAD with an intermediate station at WINGHAM TOWN.

1928 SR opened AYLESHAM station, between ADISHAM and SNOWDOWN.

1930 CHESTFIELD + SWALECLIFFE opened. With this final station opening, development reached a zenith. But this would be short-lived as rationalisation commenced the following year.

1931 Saw the start of rationalisation. The ELHAM VALLEY line plan of 1924 was discovered gathering dust at WATERLOO, it was examined and implemented, the line being singled throughout most of its length and station staff drastically reduced.

Also during the year the CANTERBURY to WHITSTABLE HARBOUR passenger service was withdrawn. This meant closure of: BLEAN + TYLER HILL HALT, SOUTH STREET HALT, TANKERTON HALT and WHITSTABLE HARBOUR. The line, however, remained open for goods traffic until the early 1950's.

1940 ELHAM VALLEY line closed to public traffic and used for military purposes; used for housing a large gun, the BOCHE BUSTER.

1941-1963

1947 With the end of hostilities the ELHAM VALLEY line was handed back to the SOUTHERN and passenger services were introduced but only, it appears, on the southern portion of the line, outside the map area. But the northern portion was used for goods traffic. It was obvious that potential passengers had long found alternative means of travel and were unlikely to be lured back. It is recorded that some-one making a return journey on the line at this time found only one other passenger on the outward journey, whilst on the return journey the train was not quite as well patronised.

1948 ELHAM VALLEY LINE closed completely. Stations CANTERBURY SOUTH, BRIDGE, BISHOPBOURNE and BARHAM were officially closed, having been out of use since 1940 when line handed over to the military. EKL had escaped grouping, but it did not escape nationalisation and became part of BRITISH RAIL SOUTHERN REGION on 1st January, and its passenger service was withdrawn at the end of October. This resulted in closure of map area stations at: CANTERBURY ROAD, WINGHAM TOWN, WINGHAM, STAPLE, ASH TOWN and EYTHORNE. Goods traffic on the northern portion continued until 1951, and on the short southern portion within the map area goods traffic persisted until 1964.

1952 Canterbury to Whitstable Harbour closed completely, although the line re-opened briefly the following year to help with damage caused by flooding.

1963 BEECHING report dealt suprisingly with the area in that there was not even a single recommendation for closure.

During what would normally be the final two periods virtually nothing happened in this area and the final map could well have been that for 1963. However, a 1991 map has been included for rounding-off purposes and

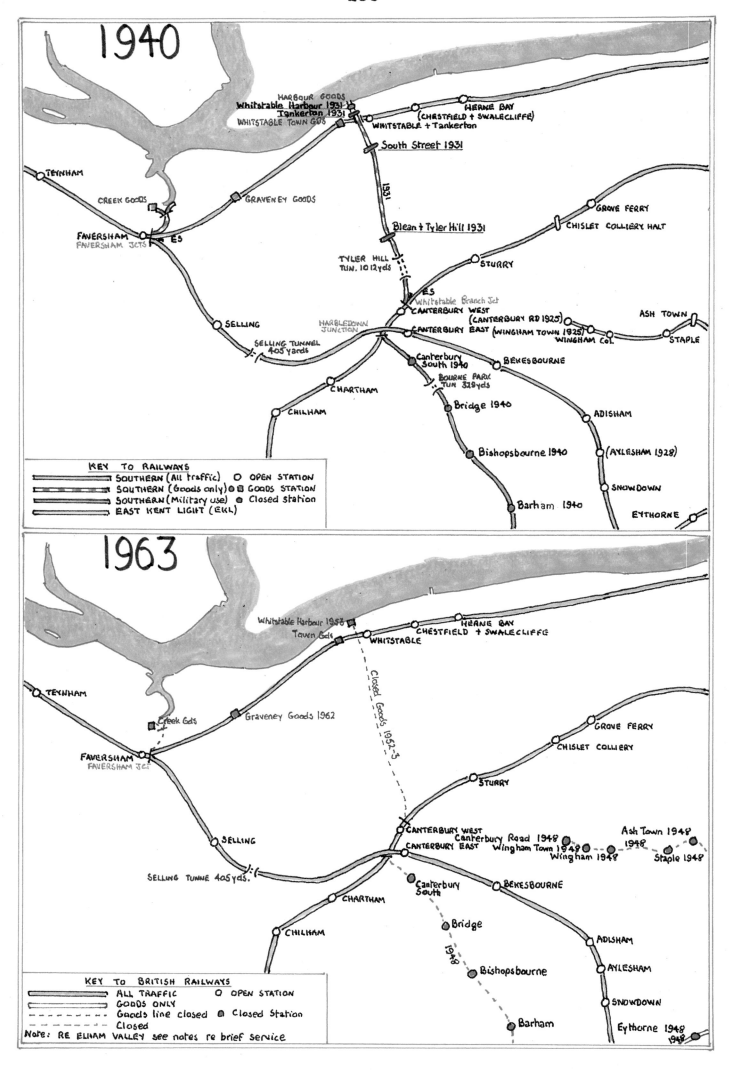

the break made at 1963 to highlight that such closures as were made in the area were implemented in the period prior to publication of the Beeching Report.

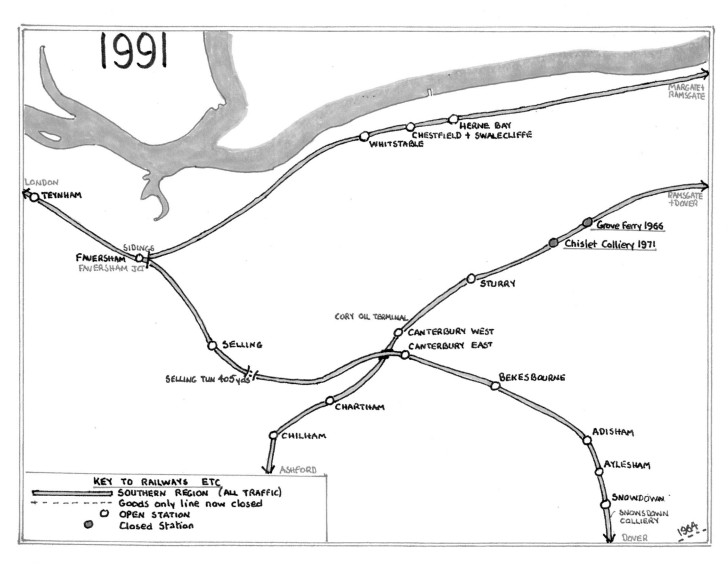

1964 - 1977

1964 As already mentioned this year saw the closure of the remaining portion of the EAST KENT LIGHT within the map area. A further portion, outside the map area, in fact remained open until the miner's strike of 1984.

1966 GROVE FERRY closed.

1971 CHISLET COLLIERY closed (the Halt had been dropped from the title in 1969).

1978 - 1991

There were no developments or closures during this period.

1992 - FUTURE

There are no known future developments or closures planned within the area.

POSTSCRIPT

It was intended on this final page to do a brief update for each centre mentioning the events of the years since compilation. In the event only one year has passed since the date of the final maps, and in many cases events of 1991 have been included. A few maps have in fact included all 1991 events and have been so dated, whilst in yet other cases nothing has happened. However, a selection of updated maps, if appropriate may be included in the final volume of the series.

However, there is one major (Major) event worth mentioning in connection with a leaked document regarding the privatisation of the railways and the major (Major) reductions in the Inter-City network. This will affect many centres and has been referred to where chapters have been completed subsequent to publication of this report in the national press. Below are listed the centres whose Inter-City routes would be affected:

EDINBURGH will lose all Inter-City routes to the north serving Perth, Inverness, Dundee and Aberdeen

BRADFORD will lose its Inter-City status

HULL will lose Inter-City status.

CHESTER will lose Inter-City status if the proposed downgrading of the Holyhead line is implemented.

LINCOLN will lose its through status on an Inter-City route apart from losing its own service.

SHREWSBURY and TELFORD both lose their Inter-City services.

SWANSEA retains INTER-CITY status but the continuation to the west is scheduled for the axe. At a later date this could ultimately put a question mark against its own service.

BRISTOL whilst retaining Inter-City status, it is proposed that Inter-City links with Hereford and Worcester will be cut.

It has been argued that peripheral services are not making a profit and should be withdrawn. As usual this ignores the effect on the core system because part of that immediately becomes peripheral and in turn becomes vulnerable to future economy cuts.

April 1992